NO
SEA

OF THE

OF THE

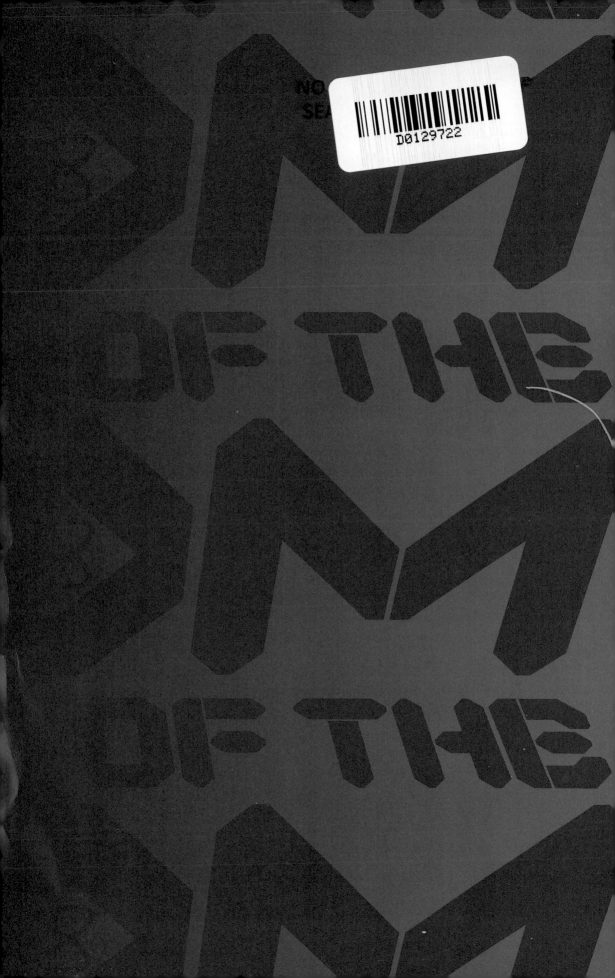

[chil__X]
[dren__X]

CHILDREN OF THE ATOM BY VITA AYALA VOL. 1. Contains material originally published in magazine form as CHILDREN OF THE ATOM (2021) #1-6 and MARVE'S VOICES (2020) #1. First printing 2021. ISBN 978-1-302-92173-6. Published by MARVEL WORLDWIDE, INC., a subsidiary of MARVEL ENTERTAINMENT, LLC. OFFICE OF PUBLICATION: 1290 Avenue of the Americas, New York, NY 10104. © 2021 MARVEL No similarity between any of the names, characters, persons, and/or institutions in this magazine with those of any living or dead person or institution is intended, and any such similarity which may exist is purely coincidental. **Printed in Canada.** KEVIN FEIGE, Chief Creative Officer; DAN BUCKLEY, President, Marvel Entertainment; JOE QUESADA, EVP & Creative Director; DAVID BOGART, Associate Publisher & SVP of Talent Affairs; TOM BREVOORT, VP, Executive Editor; NICK LOWE, Executive Editor, VP of Content, Digital Publishing; DAVID GABRIEL, VP of Print & Digital Publishing; JEFF YOUNGQUIST, VP of Production & Special Projects; ALEX MORALES, Director of Publishing Operations; DAN EDINGTON, Managing Editor; RICKEY PURDIN, Director of Talent Relations; JENNIFER GRÜNWALD, Senior Editor, Special Projects; SUSAN CRESPI, Production Manager; STAN LEE, Chairman Emeritus. For information regarding advertising in Marvel Comics or on Marvel.com, please contact Vit DeBellis, Custom Solutions & Integrated Advertising Manager, at vdebellis@marvel.com. For Marvel subscription inquiries, please call 888-511-5480. **Manufactured between 8/13/2021 and 9/14/2021 by SOLISCO PRINTERS, SCOTT, QC, CANADA.**

10 9 8 7 6 5 4 3 2 1

CHILDREN OF THE ATOM

Writer:	Vita Ayala
Artists:	Bernard Chang (#1-2) &
	Paco Medina (#3-6)
	with Walden Wong (Inks, #6)
Color Artists:	Marcelo Maiolo (#1-2) &
	David Curiel (#3-6)
Letterer:	VC's Travis Lanham
Cover Art:	R.B. Silva with
	Jesus Aburtov (#1, #3-4) &
	David Curiel (#2, #5-6)

Head of X:	Jonathan Hickman
Design:	Tom Muller
Editors:	Chris Robinson &
	Shannon Andrews
	Ballesteros
Senior Editor:	Jordan D. White

Collection Editor:	Jennifer Grünwald
Assistant Editor:	Daniel Kirchhoffer
Assistant Managing Editor:	Maia Loy
Assistant Managing Editor:	Lisa Montalbano
VP Production & Special Projects:	Jeff Youngquist
SVP Print, Sales & Marketing:	David Gabriel
Editor in Chief:	C.B. Cebulski

CHILDRE

CHILDRE

OF THE

OF THE

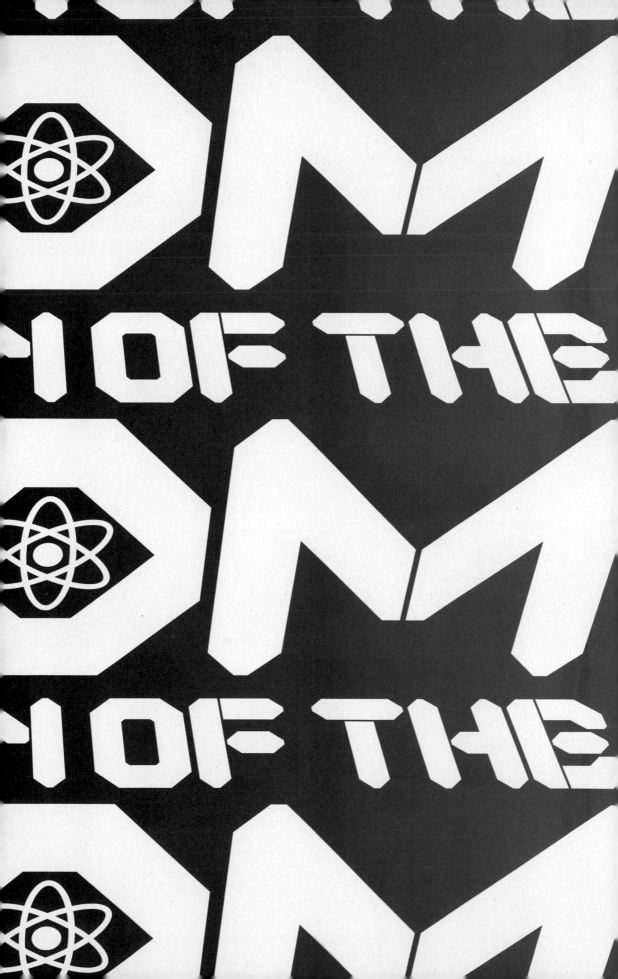

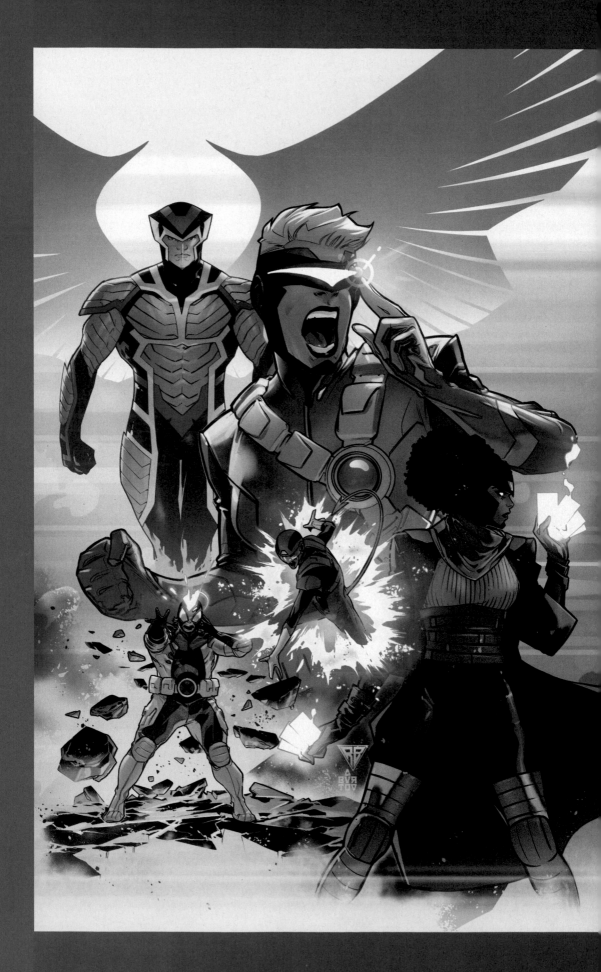

Uncanny

1

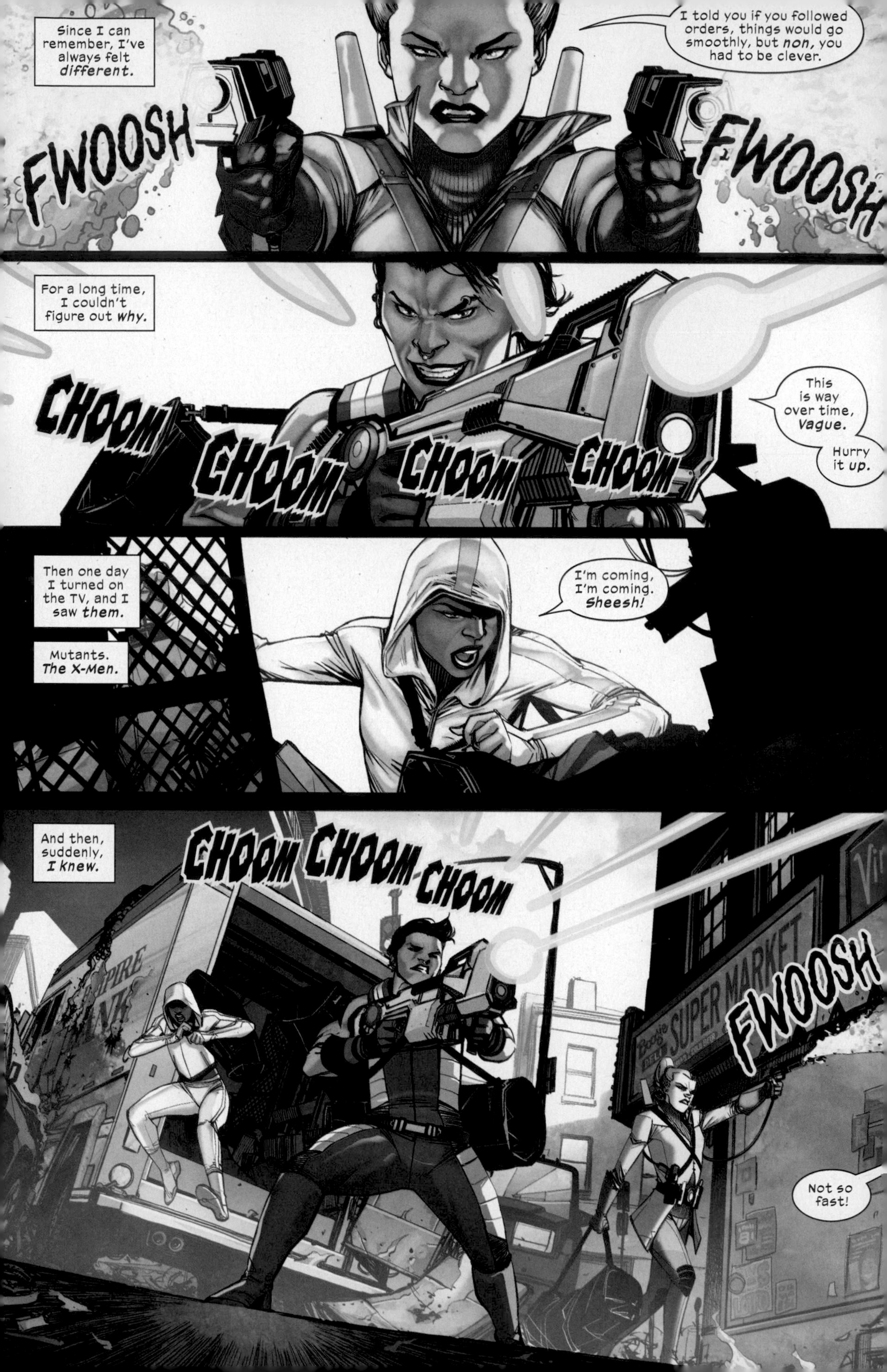
Since I can remember, I've always felt *different.*
I told you if you followed orders, things would go smoothly, but *non,* you had to be clever.
FWOOSH
FWOOSH
For a long time, I couldn't figure out *why.*
CHOOM
CHOOM
CHOOM
CHOOM
This is way over time, *Vague.*
Hurry it *up.*
Then one day I turned on the TV, and I saw *them.*
Mutants. *The X-Men.*
I'm coming, I'm coming. *Sheesh!*
And then, suddenly, *I knew.*
CHOOM CHOOM CHOOM
FWOOSH
SUPER MARKET
Not so fast!

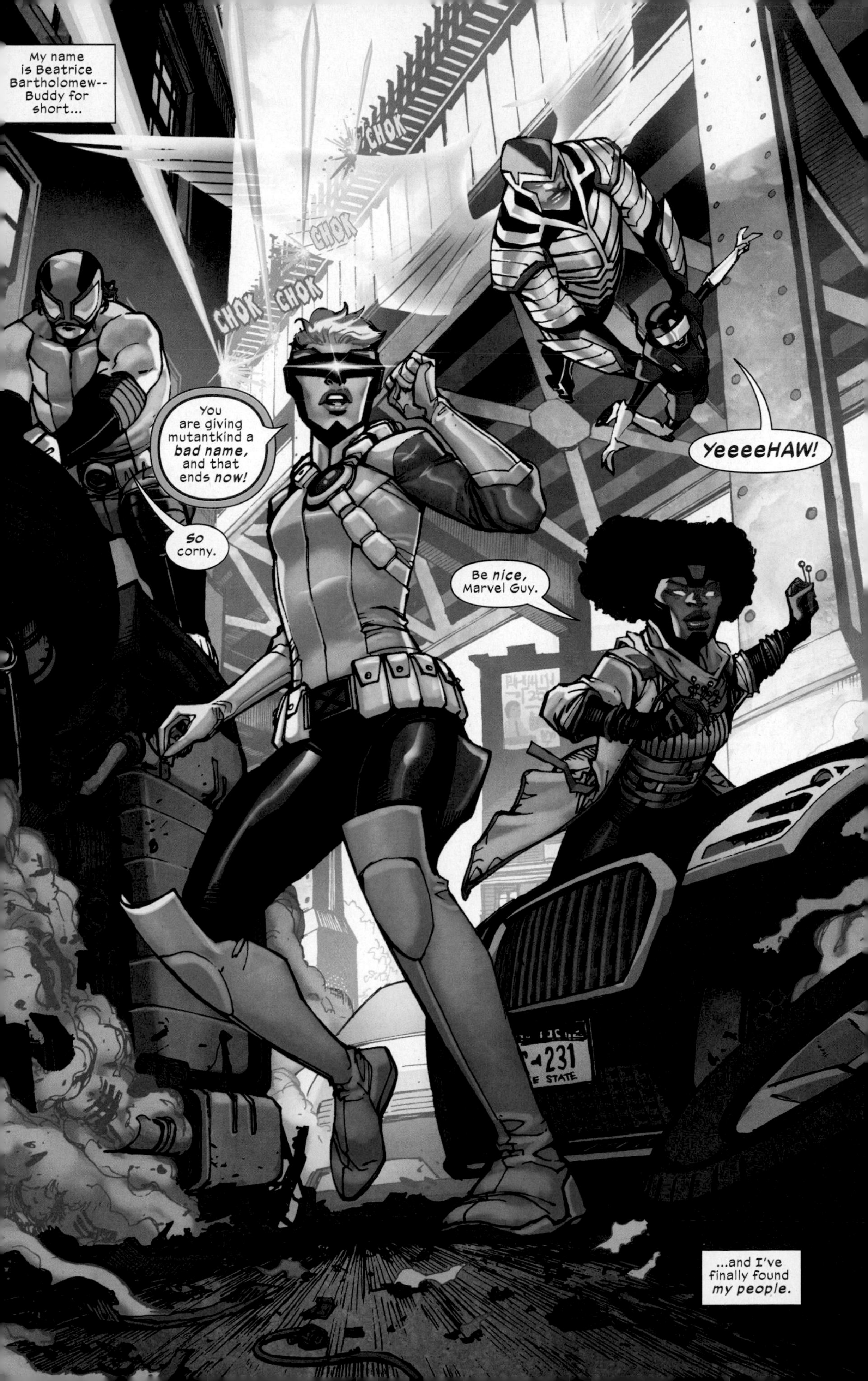
My name is Beatrice Bartholomew-- Buddy for short...
CHOK
CHOK
CHOK
CHOK
You are giving mutantkind a *bad name,* and that ends *now!*
So corny.
YeeeeHAW!
Be *nice,* Marvel Guy.
...and I've finally found *my people.*

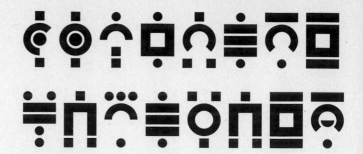

OLD ENOUGH TO KNOW BETTER

Mutants around the world have flocked to the island-nation of Krakoa for safety, security and to be part of the first mutant society.

But not all mutants have made that journey...

Cherub    Marvel Guy    Cyclops-Lass

Gimmick    Daycrawler

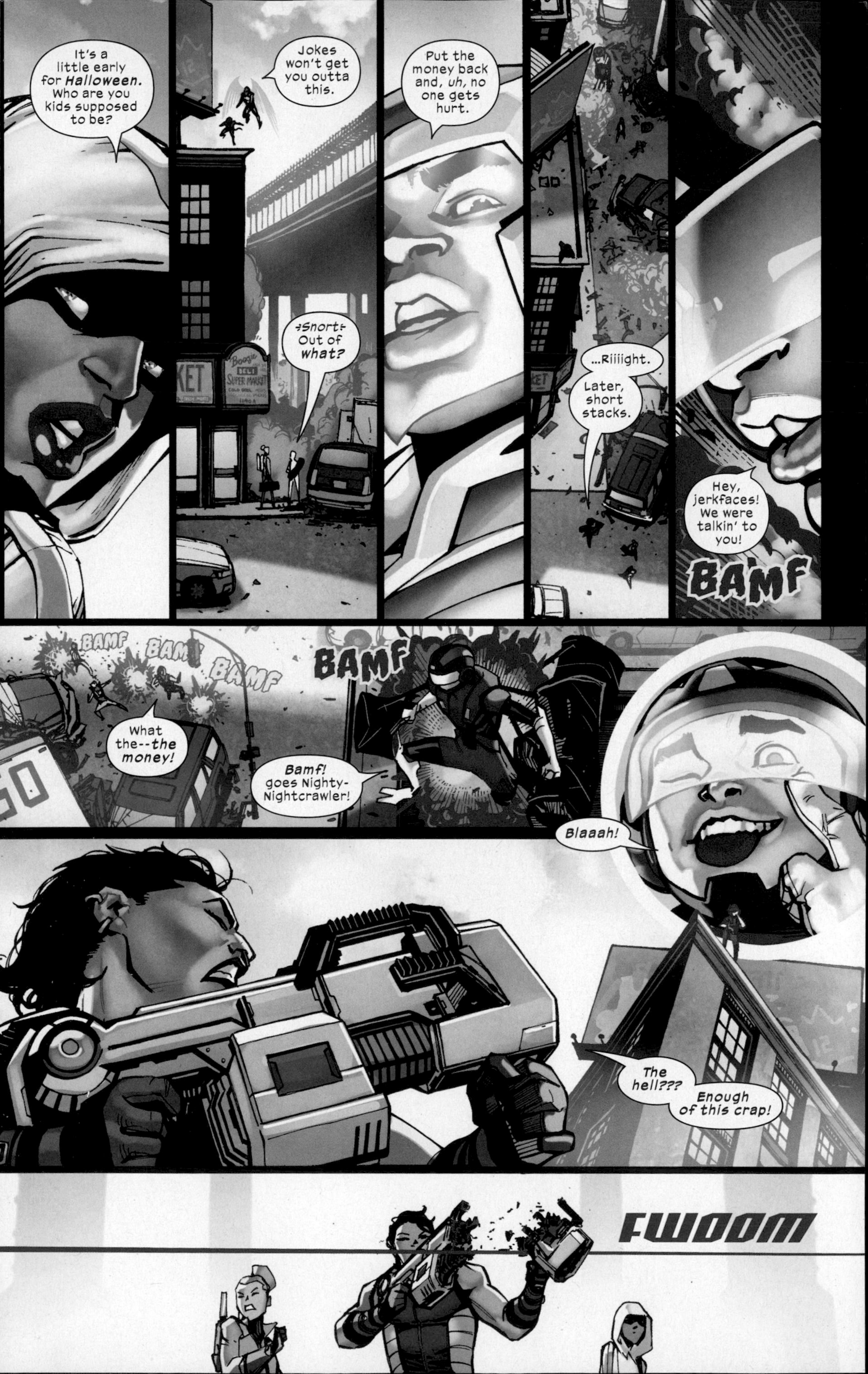

It's a little early for Halloween. Who are you kids supposed to be?
Jokes won't get you outta this.
=Snort= Out of what?
Put the money back and, uh, no one gets hurt.
...Riiiight.
Later, short stacks.
Hey, jerkfaces! We were talkin' to you!
BAMF
BAMF
BAMF
BAMF
What the--the money!
BAMF
Bamf! goes Nighty-Nightcrawler!
Blaaah!
The hell???
Enough of this crap!
FWOOM

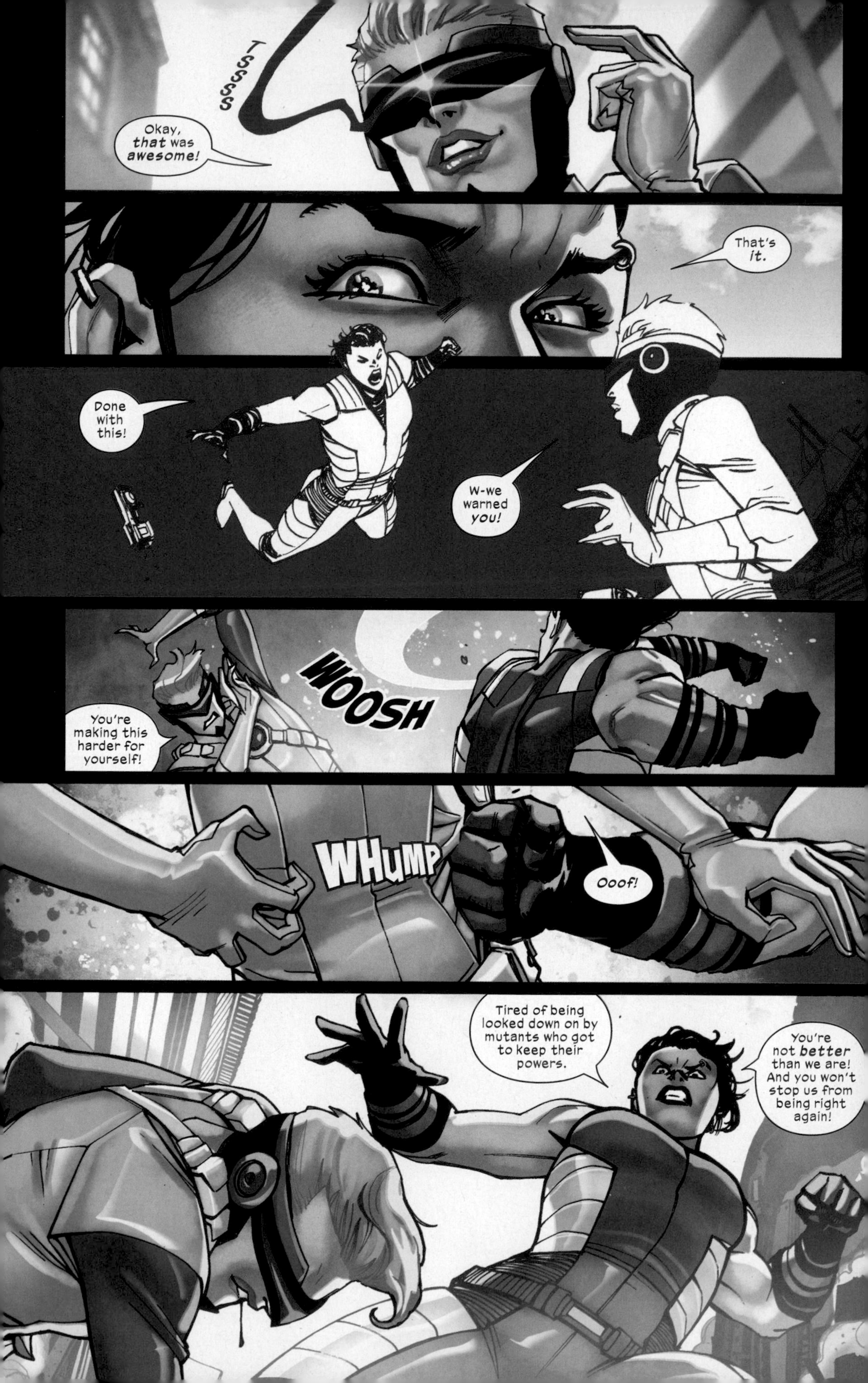
TSSSS
Okay, that was awesome!
That's it.
Done with this!
W-we warned you!
WOOSH
You're making this harder for yourself!
WHUMP
Ooof!
Tired of being looked down on by mutants who got to keep their powers.
You're not better than we are! And you won't stop us from being right again!

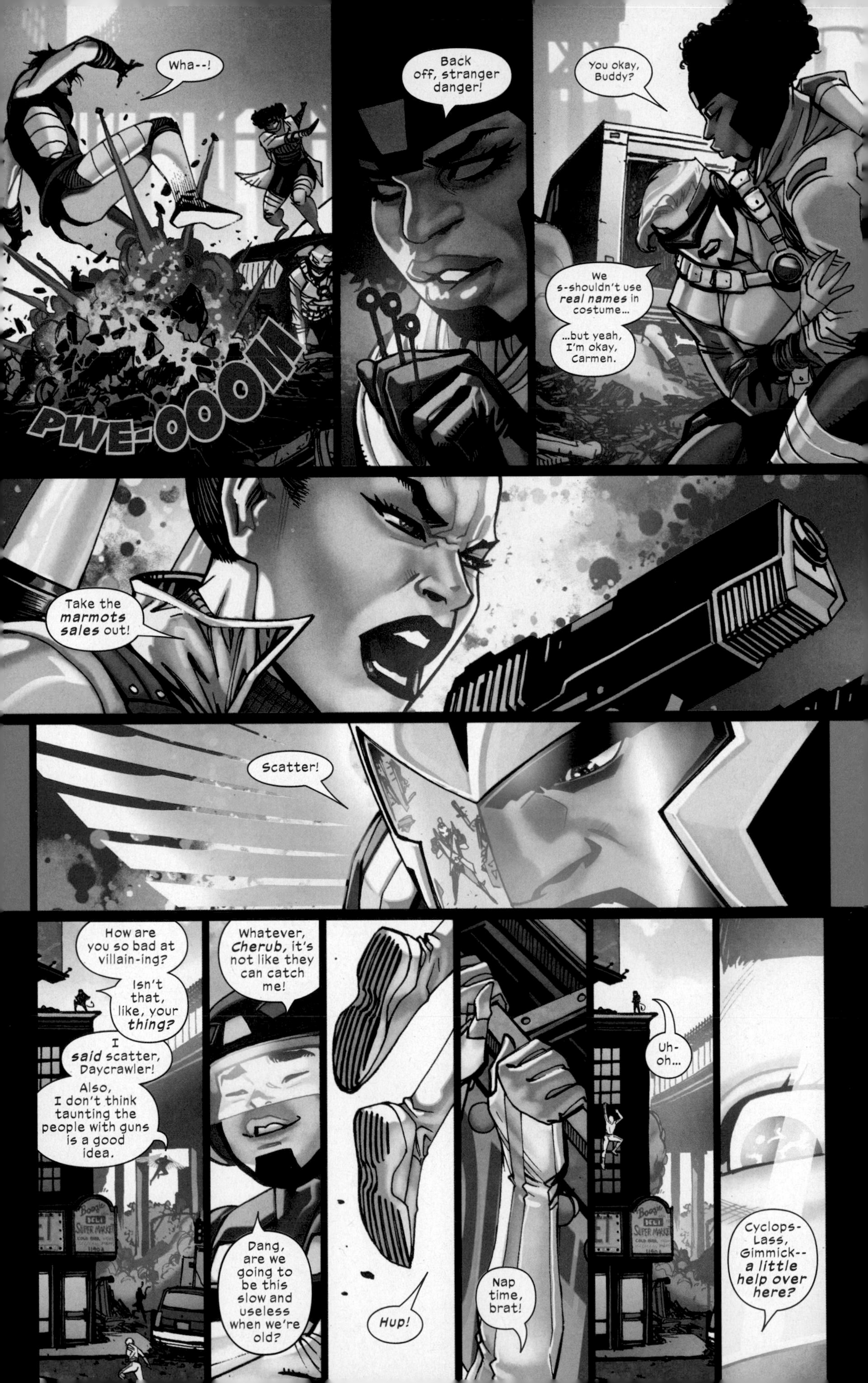
Wha--!
PWE-OOOM
Back off, stranger danger!
You okay, Buddy?
We s-shouldn't use *real names* in costume...
...but yeah, I'm okay, Carmen.
Take the *marmots sales* out!
Scatter!
How are you so bad at villain-ing?
Isn't that, like, your *thing?*
I *said* scatter, Daycrawler!
Also, I don't think taunting the people with guns is a good idea.
Whatever, *Cherub,* it's not like they can catch me!
Dang, are we going to be this slow and useless when we're old?
Hup!
Nap time, brat!
Uh-oh...
Cyclops-Lass, Gimmick-- *a little help over here?*

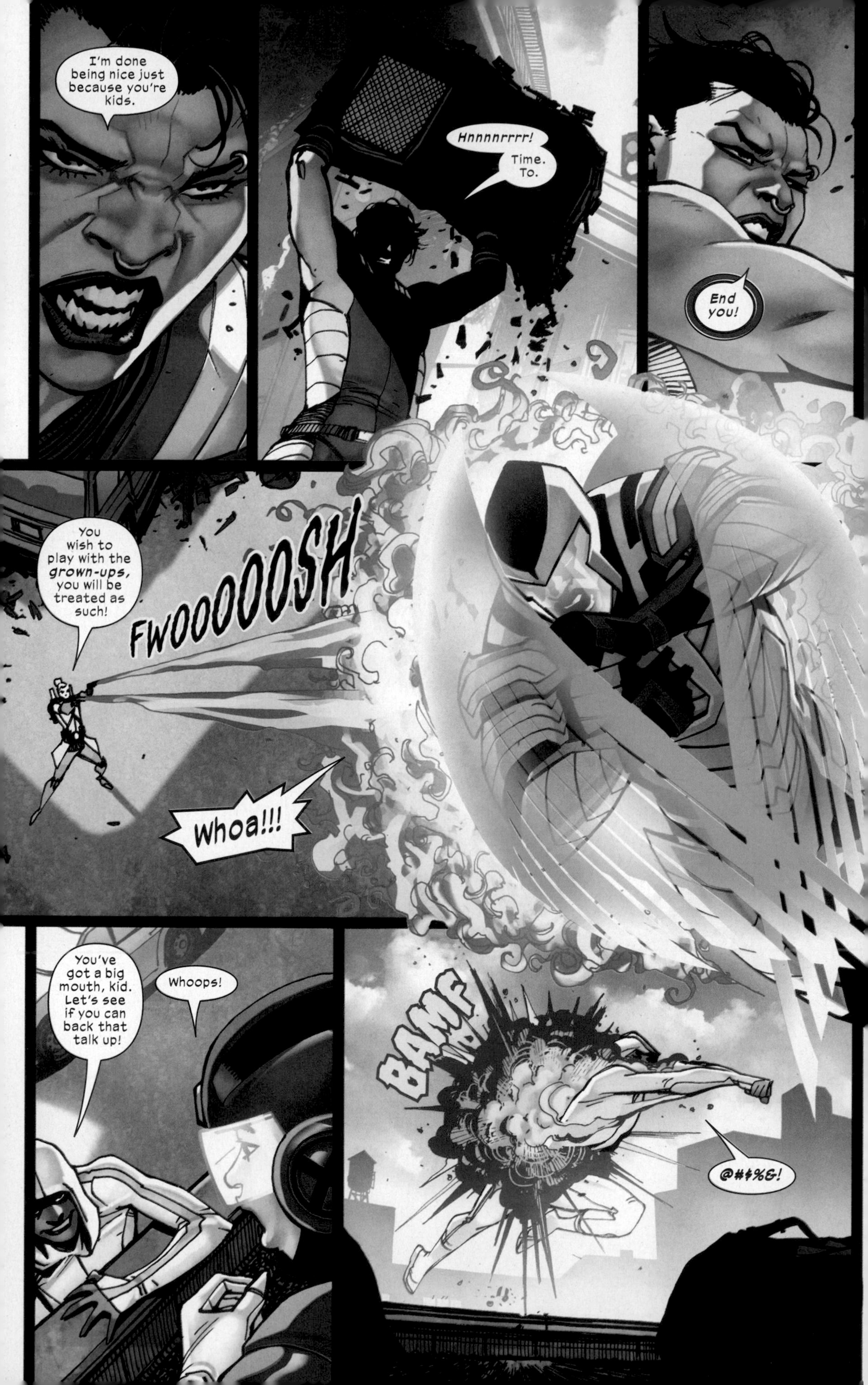
I'm done being nice just because you're kids.
Hnnnnrrrr!
Time. To.
End you!
You wish to play with the *grown-ups,* you will be treated as such!
FWOOOOOSH
Whoa!!!
You've got a big mouth, kid. Let's see if you can back that talk up!
Whoops!
BAMF
@#$%&!

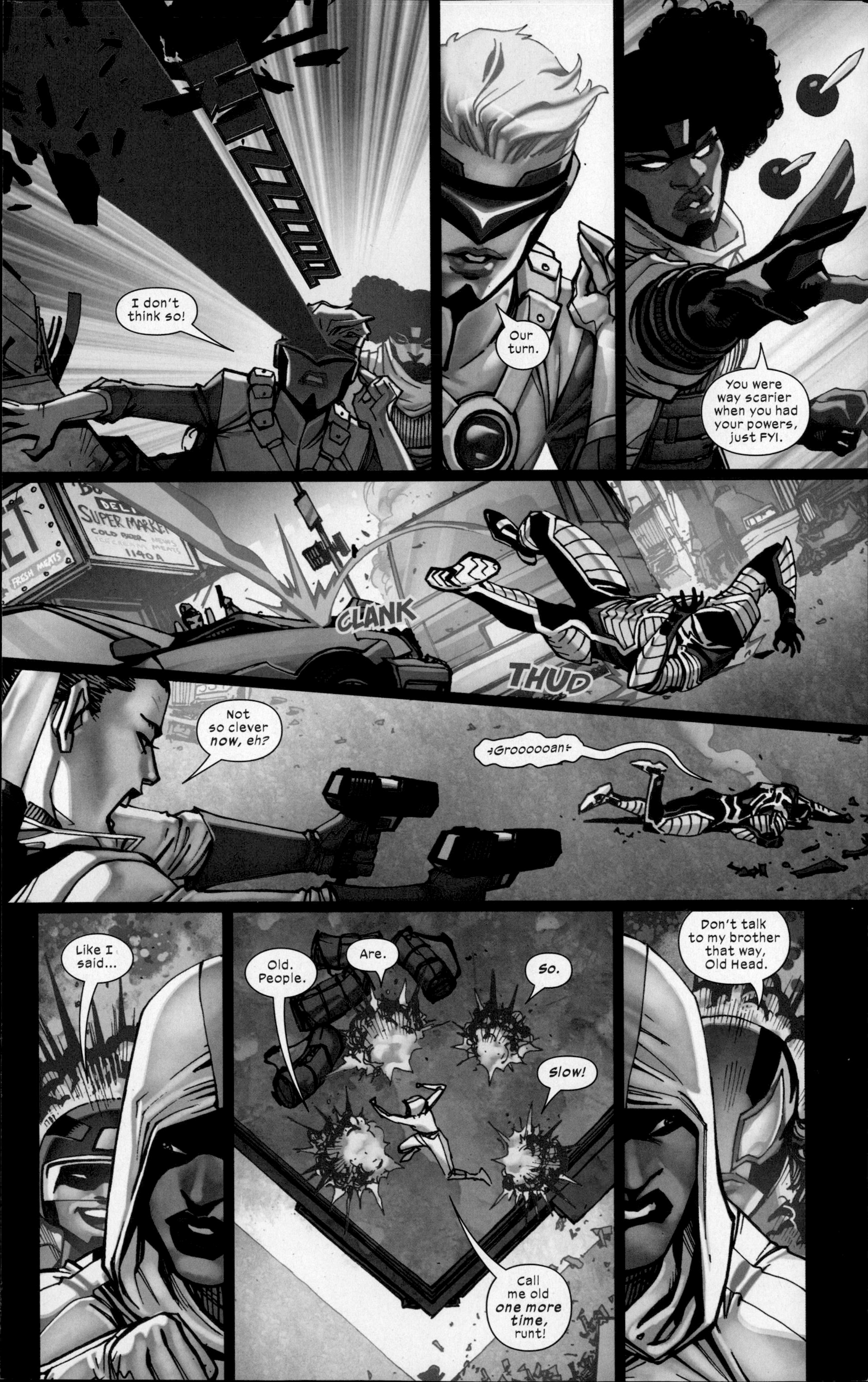
I don't think so!
Our turn.
You were way scarier when you had your powers, just FYI.
SUPER MARKET
DELI
COLD BEER
FRESH MEATS
1140A
CLANK
THUD
Not so clever now, eh?
-Groooooan-
Like I said...
Old. People.
Are.
So.
Slow!
Call me old one more time, runt!
Don't talk to my brother that way, Old Head.

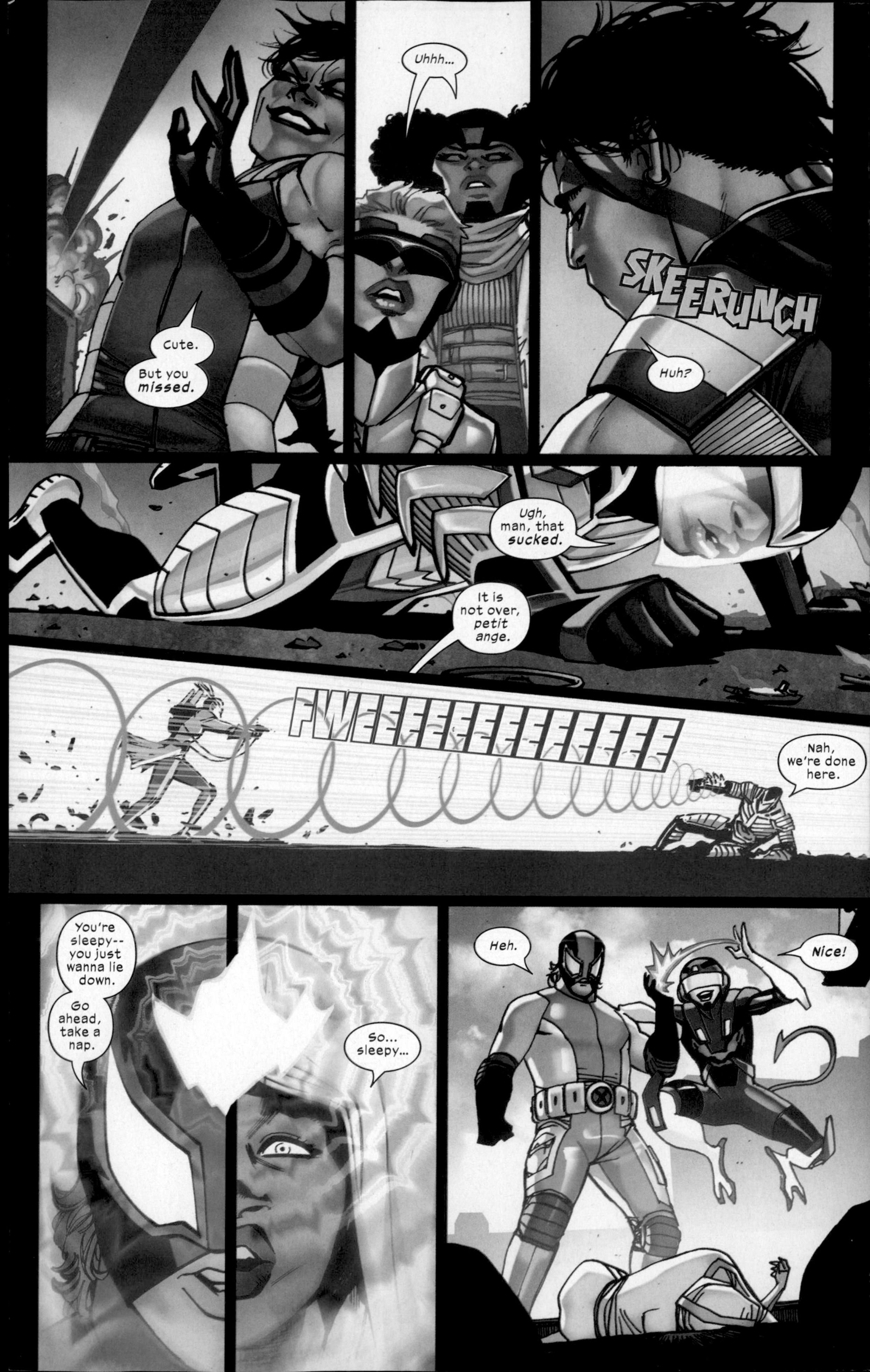
Uhhh...
Cute.
But you *missed.*
SKEERUNCH
Huh?
Ugh, man, that *sucked.*
It is not over, petit ange.
FWEEEEEEEEEEEEEE
Nah, we're done here.
You're sleepy-- you just wanna lie down.
Go ahead, take a nap.
So... sleepy...
Heh.
Nice!

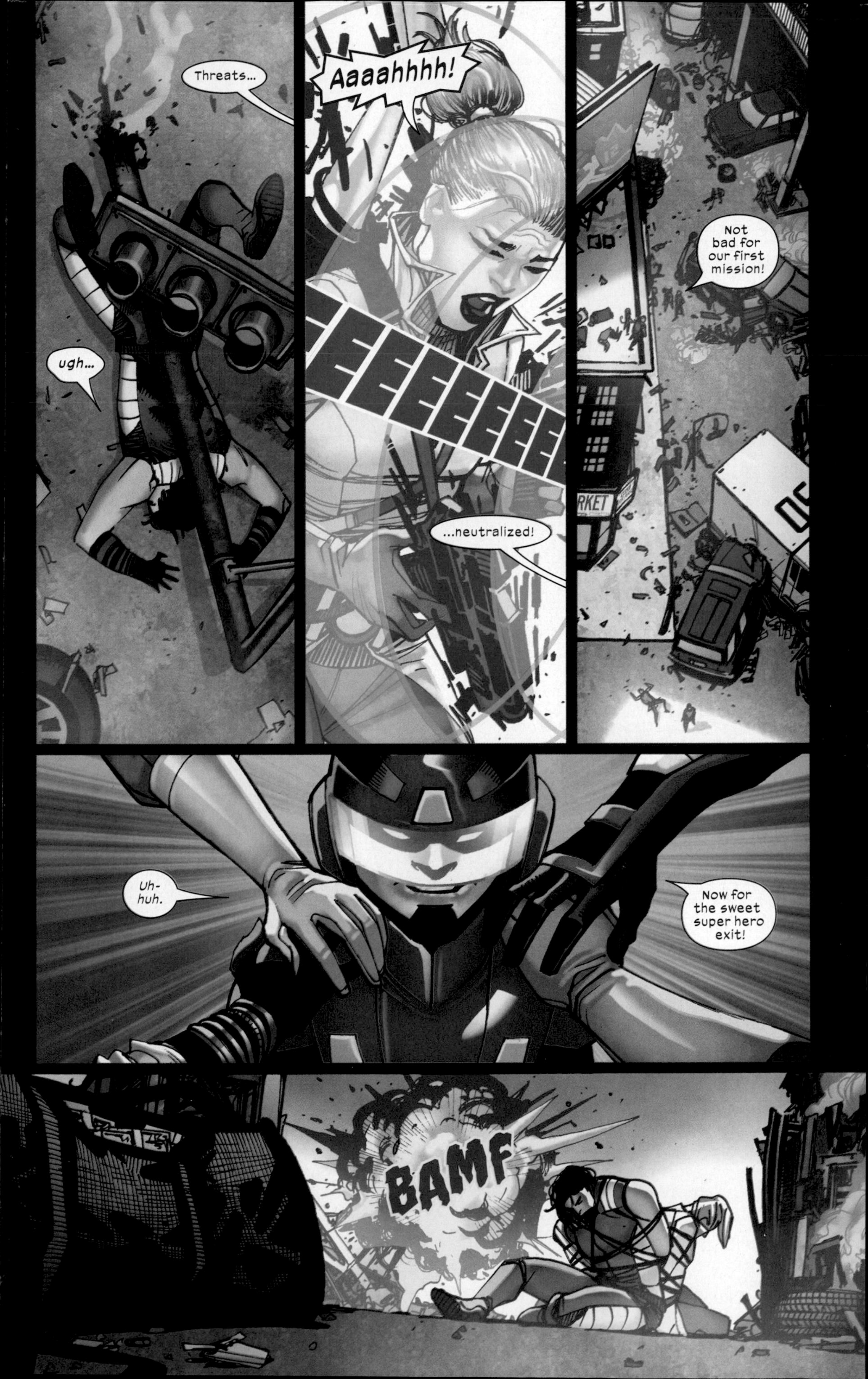
Threats...
ugh...
Aaaahhhh!
EEEEEEEEE
...neutralized!
Not bad for our first mission!
Uh-huh.
Now for the sweet super hero exit!
BAMF

mutantsunmuted.com/unc_uni/groups/hells_belles

THE HELL'S BELLES

original entry by: **ArchivistX**

The Hell's Belles were a group of mercenary mutant women under the direction of **Cyber*** and often affiliated with a large drug cartel[1].

The group consisted of **Briquette***, **Tremolo***, **Flambé*** and **Vague***.

The mutant **Shrew*** was originally part of the crew but quit and later agreed to testify against them in exchange for immunity. The remaining Hell's Belles came into conflict with X-Factor when they attempted to kill Shrew for her betrayal.

POWERS

Briquette – superhuman strength, molten-hot skin (can melt objects on contact), invulnerability, claws.

Tremolo – energy blasts, vibration waves.

Flambé – manipulates fire/flames by controlling oxygen molecules. Cannot produce flames, but once they are lit, can make them hotter and focus them into jets.

Vague – flight and invisibility.

WHERE ARE THEY NOW?

All of the Hell's Belles, with the exception of Briquette, were depowered on M-Day but still operate as career criminals.

* See individual entries on these mutants for more details on their histories and origins!
[1] Citation needed

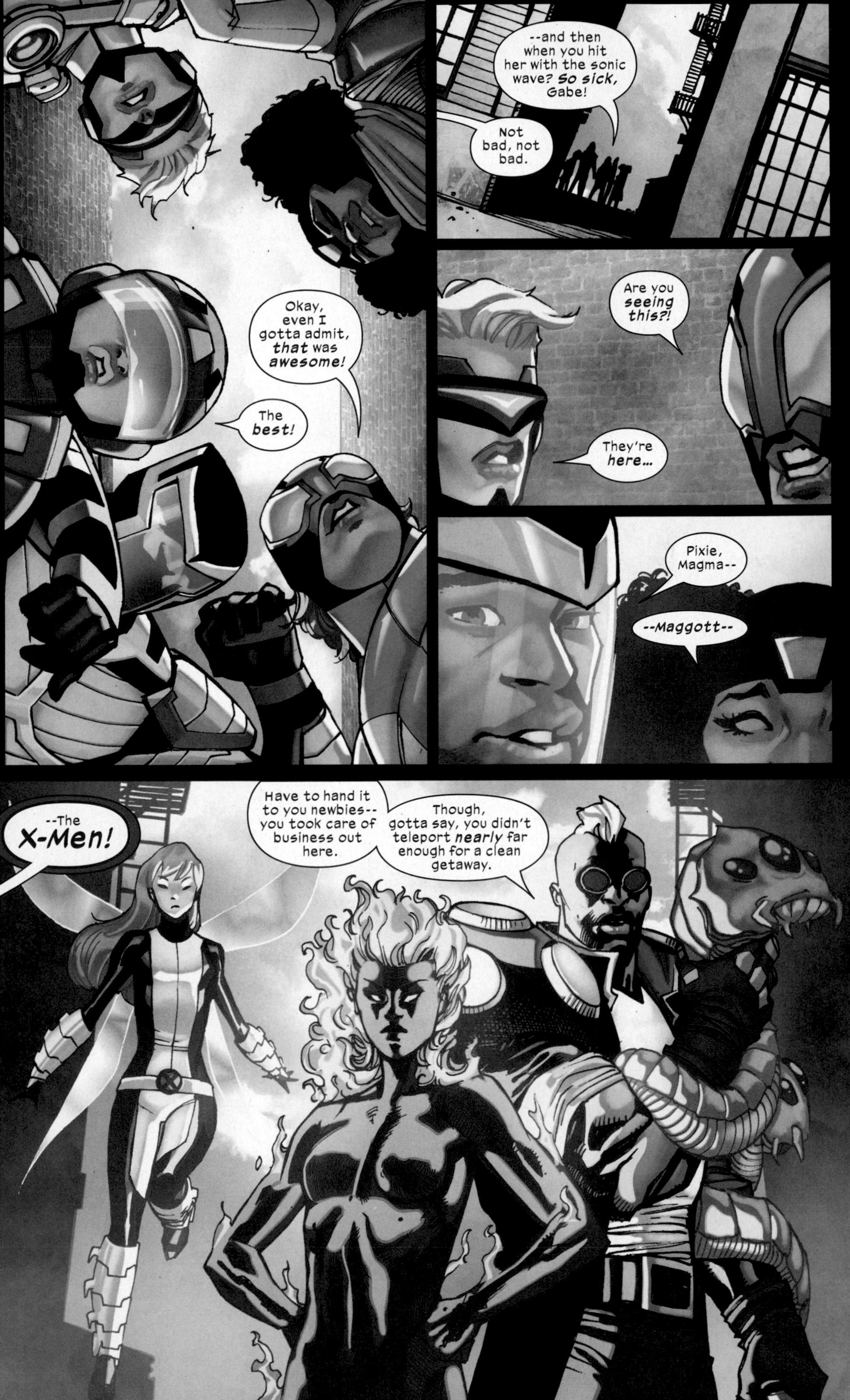

--and then when you hit her with the sonic wave? So sick, Gabe!
Not bad, not bad.
Okay, even I gotta admit, that was awesome!
The best!
Are you seeing this?!
They're here...
Pixie, Magma--
--Maggott--
--The X-Men!
Have to hand it to you newbies--you took care of business out here.
Though, gotta say, you didn't teleport nearly far enough for a clean getaway.

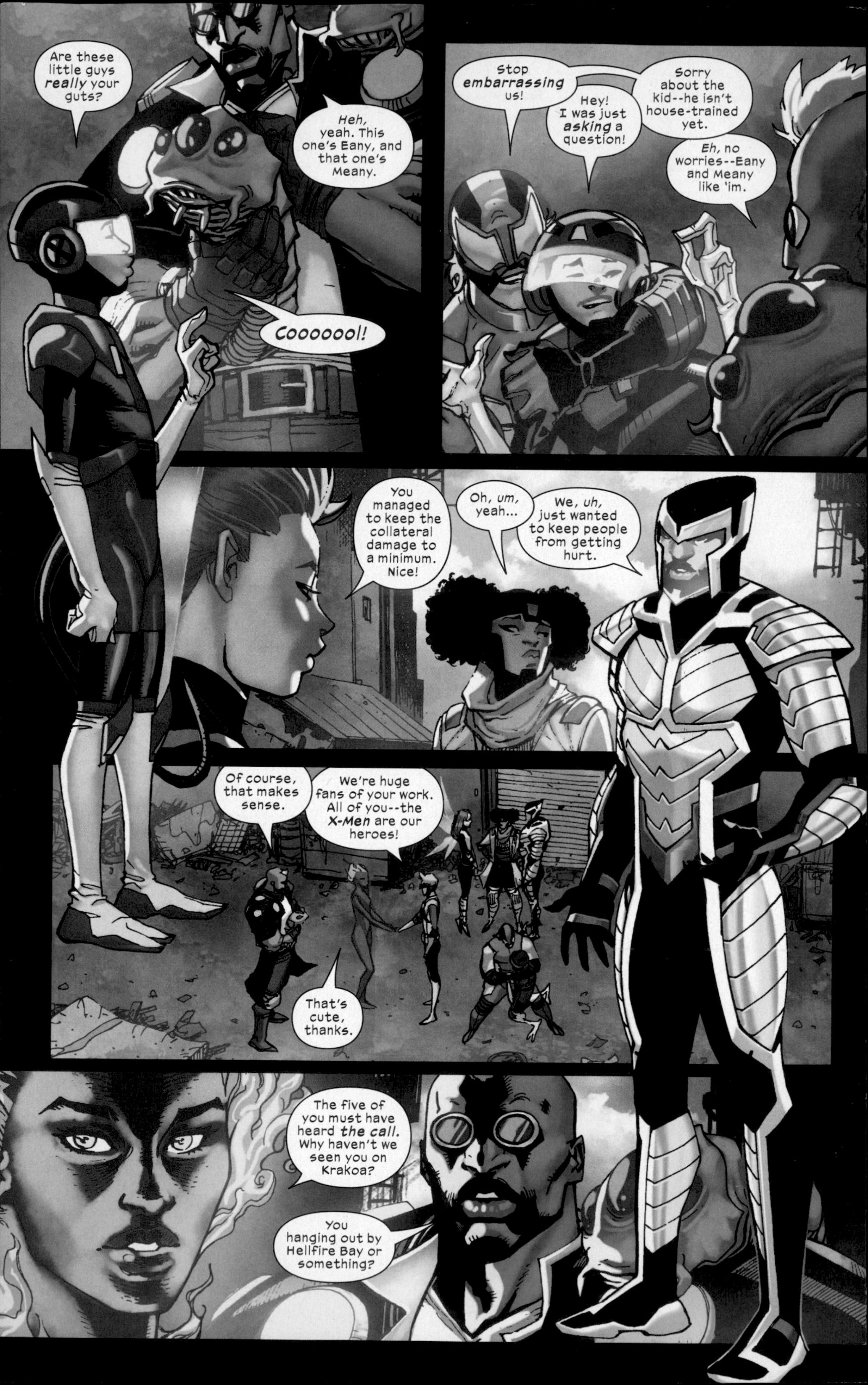
Are these little guys *really* your guts?
Heh, yeah. This one's Eany, and that one's Meany.
Cooooool!
Stop *embarrassing* us!
Hey! I was just *asking* a question!
Sorry about the kid--he isn't house-trained yet.
Eh, no worries--Eany and Meany like 'im.
You managed to keep the collateral damage to a minimum. Nice!
Oh, um, yeah...
We, *uh,* just wanted to keep people from getting hurt.
Of course, that makes sense.
We're huge fans of your work. All of you--the *X-Men* are our heroes!
That's cute, thanks.
The five of you must have heard *the call.* Why haven't we seen you on Krakoa?
You hanging out by Hellfire Bay or something?

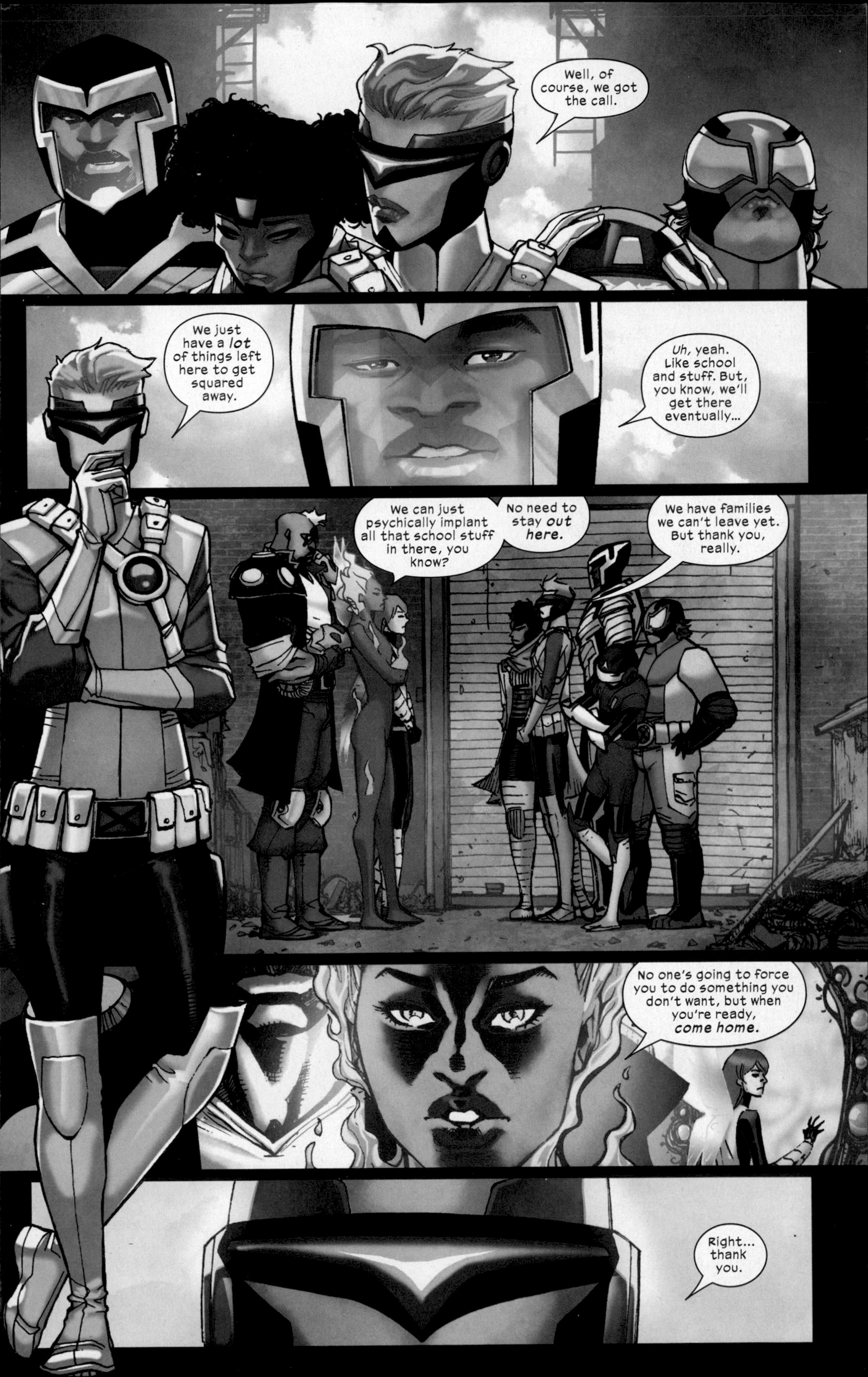

Well, of course, we got the call.
We just have a *lot* of things left here to get squared away.
Uh, yeah. Like school and stuff. But, you know, we'll get there eventually...
We can just psychically implant all that school stuff in there, you know?
No need to stay *out here.*
We have families we can't leave yet. But thank you, really.
No one's going to force you to do something you don't want, but when you're ready, **come home.**
Right... thank you.

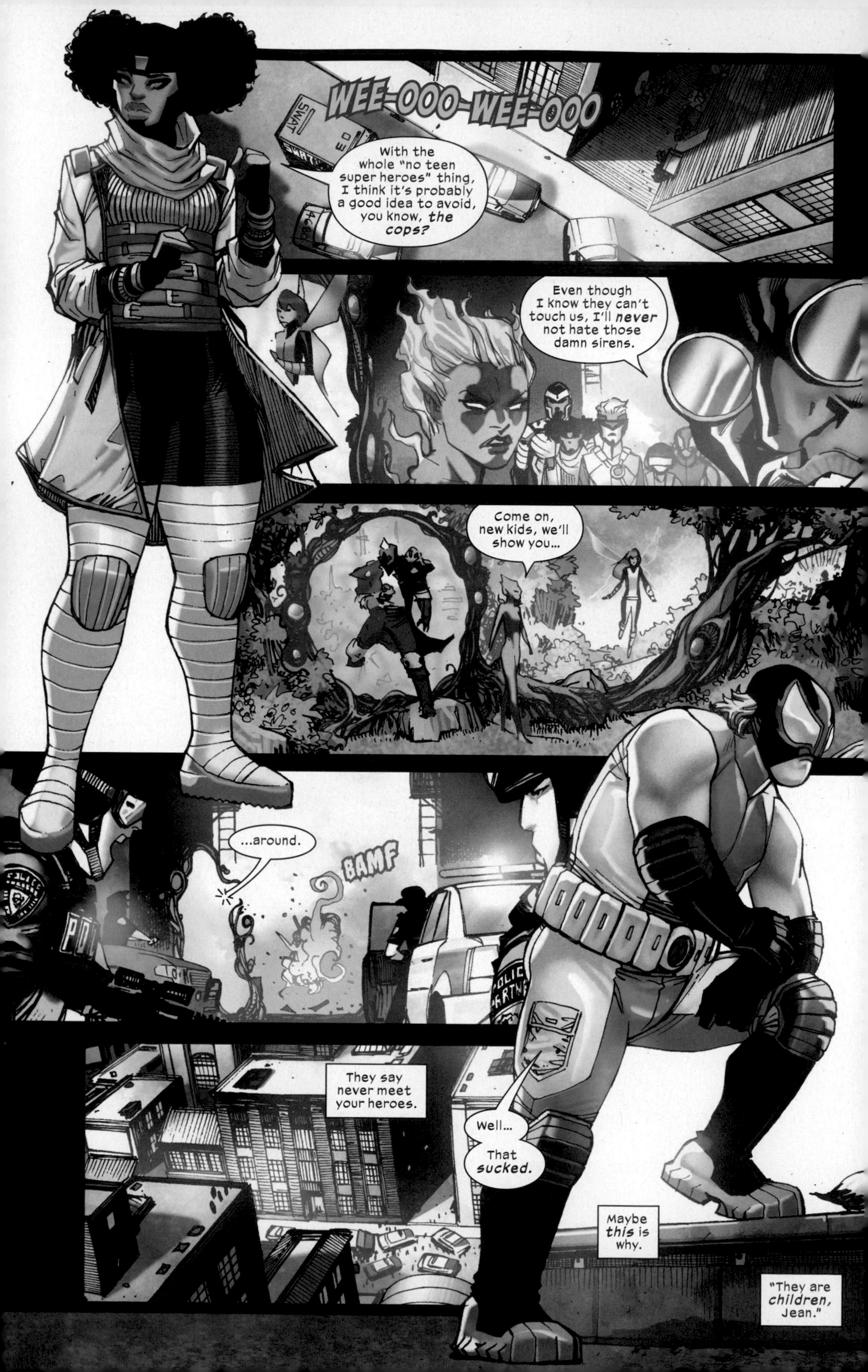
WEE-OOO-WEE-OOO
With the whole "no teen super heroes" thing, I think it's probably a good idea to avoid, you know, *the cops?*
Even though I know they can't touch us, I'll *never* not hate those damn sirens.
Come on, new kids, we'll show you...
...around.
BAMF
They say never meet your heroes.
Well...
That *sucked.*
Maybe *this* is why.
"They are *children,* Jean."

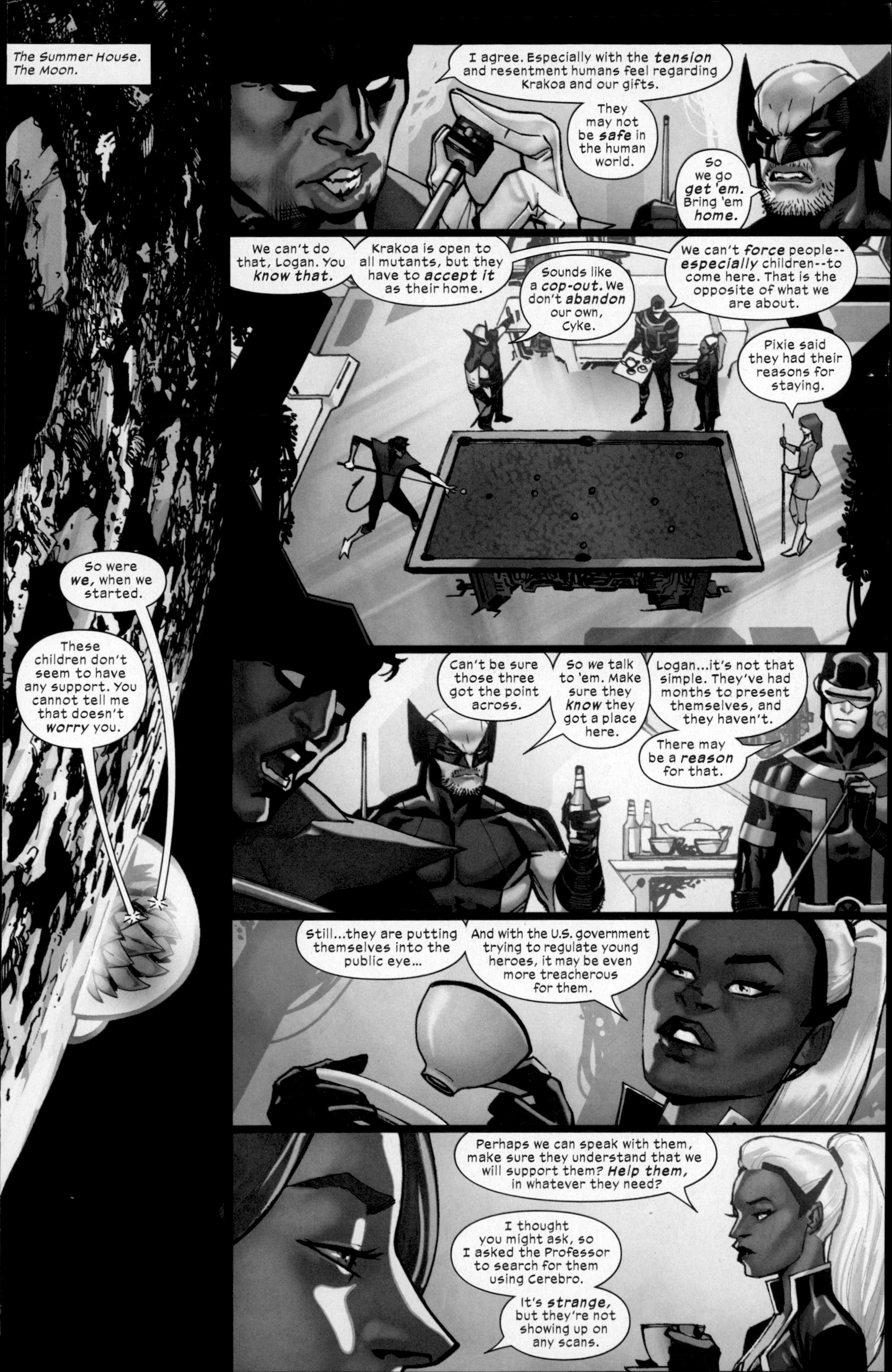
The Summer House. The Moon.
I agree. Especially with the tension and resentment humans feel regarding Krakoa and our gifts.
They may not be safe in the human world.
So we go get 'em. Bring 'em home.
We can't do that, Logan. You know that.
Krakoa is open to all mutants, but they have to accept it as their home.
Sounds like a cop-out. We don't abandon our own, Cyke.
We can't force people--especially children--to come here. That is the opposite of what we are about.
Pixie said they had their reasons for staying.
So were we, when we started.
These children don't seem to have any support. You cannot tell me that doesn't worry you.
Can't be sure those three got the point across.
So we talk to 'em. Make sure they know they got a place here.
Logan...it's not that simple. They've had months to present themselves, and they haven't.
There may be a reason for that.
Still...they are putting themselves into the public eye...
And with the U.S. government trying to regulate young heroes, it may be even more treacherous for them.
Perhaps we can speak with them, make sure they understand that we will support them? Help them, in whatever they need?
I thought you might ask, so I asked the Professor to search for them using Cerebro.
It's strange, but they're not showing up on any scans.

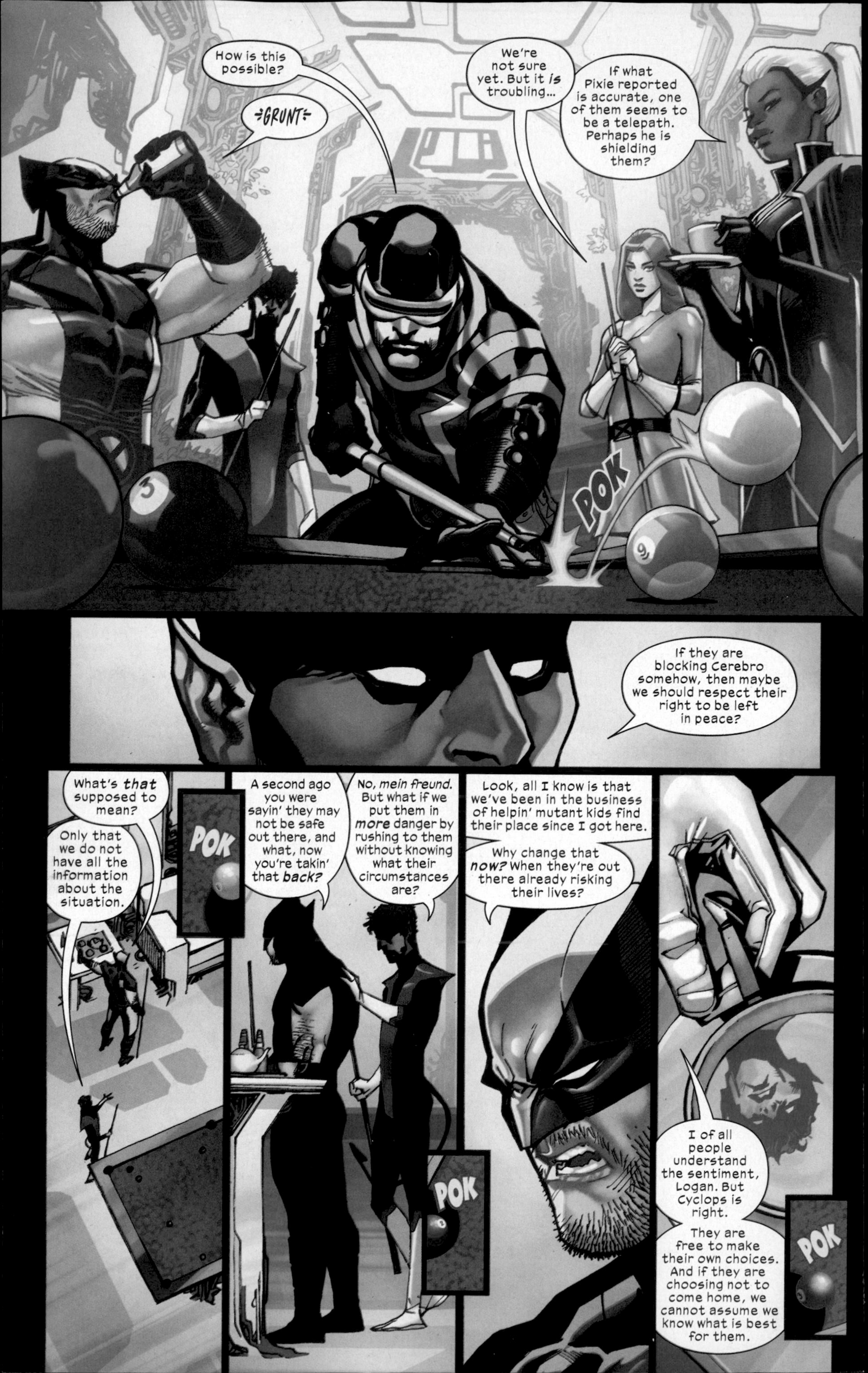

How is this possible?
GRUNT
We're not sure yet. But it *is* troubling...
If what Pixie reported is accurate, one of them seems to be a telepath. Perhaps he is shielding them?
POK
If they are blocking Cerebro somehow, then maybe we should respect their right to be left in peace?
What's *that* supposed to mean?
Only that we do not have all the information about the situation.
POK
A second ago you were sayin' they may not be safe out there, and what, now you're takin' that *back?*
No, *mein freund.* But what if we put them in *more* danger by rushing to them without knowing what their circumstances are?
POK
Look, all I know is that we've been in the business of helpin' mutant kids find their place since I got here.
Why change that *now?* When they're out there already risking their lives?
I of all people understand the sentiment, Logan. But Cyclops is right.
They are free to make their own choices. And if they are choosing not to come home, we cannot assume we know what is best for them.
POK

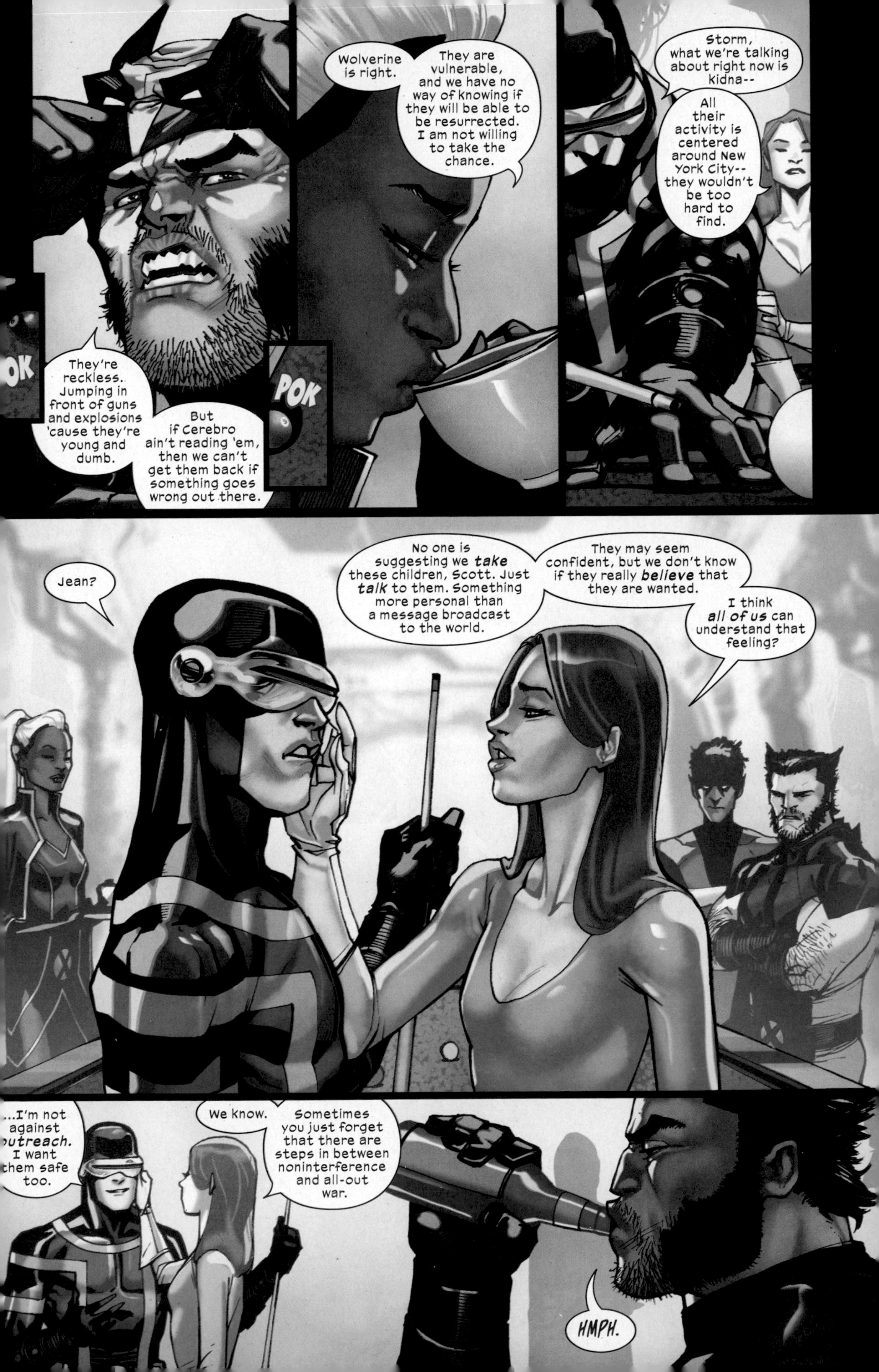
OK
They're reckless. Jumping in front of guns and explosions 'cause they're young and dumb.
But if Cerebro ain't reading 'em, then we can't get them back if something goes wrong out there.
POK
Wolverine is right.
They are vulnerable, and we have no way of knowing if they will be able to be resurrected. I am not willing to take the chance.
Storm, what we're talking about right now is kidna--
All their activity is centered around New York City-- they wouldn't be too hard to find.
Jean?
No one is suggesting we *take* these children, Scott. Just *talk* to them. Something more personal than a message broadcast to the world.
They may seem confident, but we don't know if they really *believe* that they are wanted.
I think *all of us* can understand that feeling?
...I'm not against outreach. I want them safe too.
We know.
Sometimes you just forget that there are steps in between noninterference and all-out war.
HMPH.

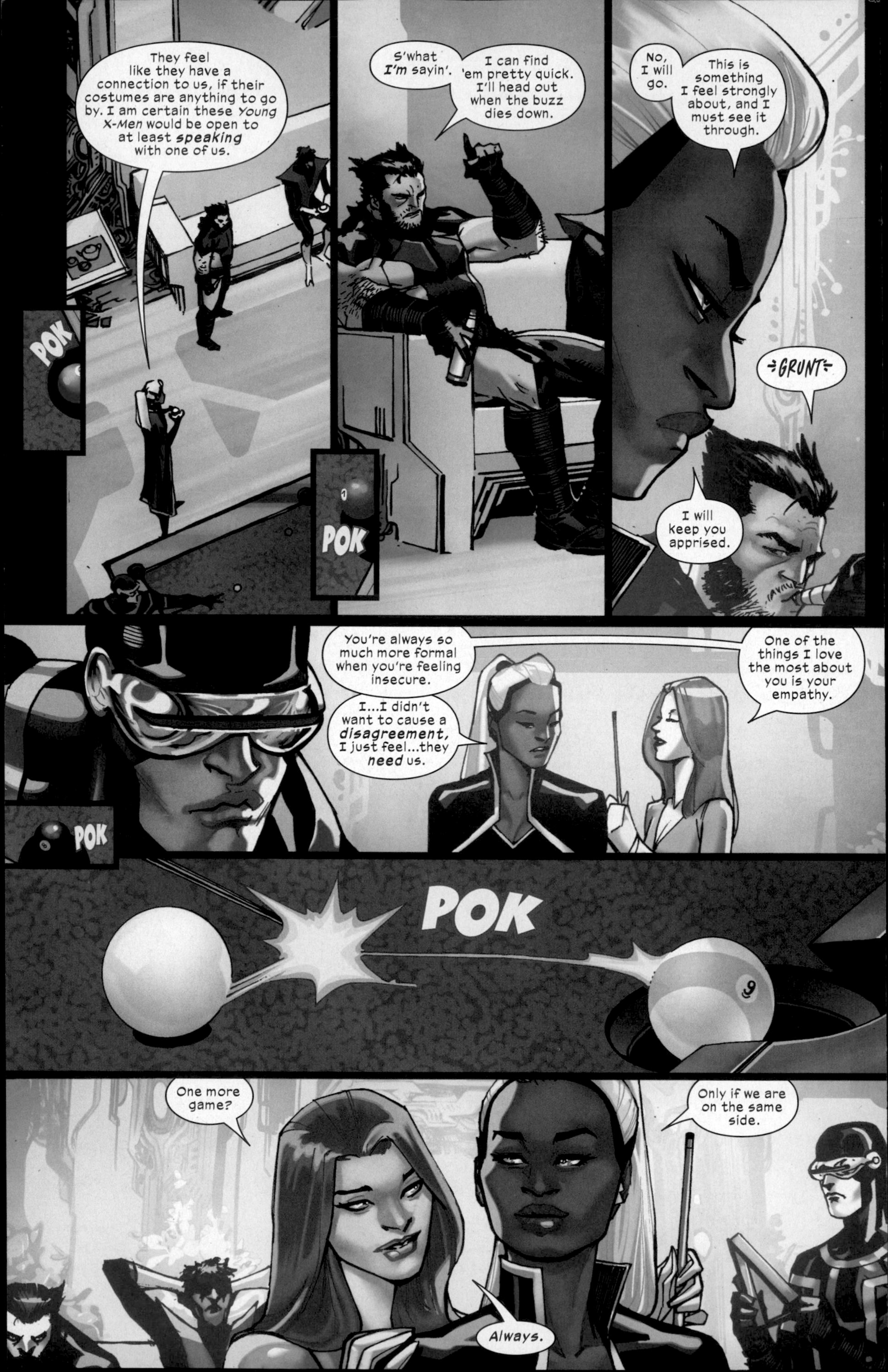
They feel like they have a connection to us, if their costumes are anything to go by. I am certain these *Young X-Men* would be open to at least *speaking* with one of us.
POK
S'what *I'm* sayin'.
I can find 'em pretty quick. I'll head out when the buzz dies down.
POK
No, I will go.
This is something I feel strongly about, and I must see it through.
GRUNT
I will keep you apprised.
You're always so much more formal when you're feeling insecure.
I...I didn't want to cause a *disagreement,* I just feel...they *need* us.
One of the things I love the most about you is your empathy.
POK
POK
One more game?
Only if we are on the same side.
Always.

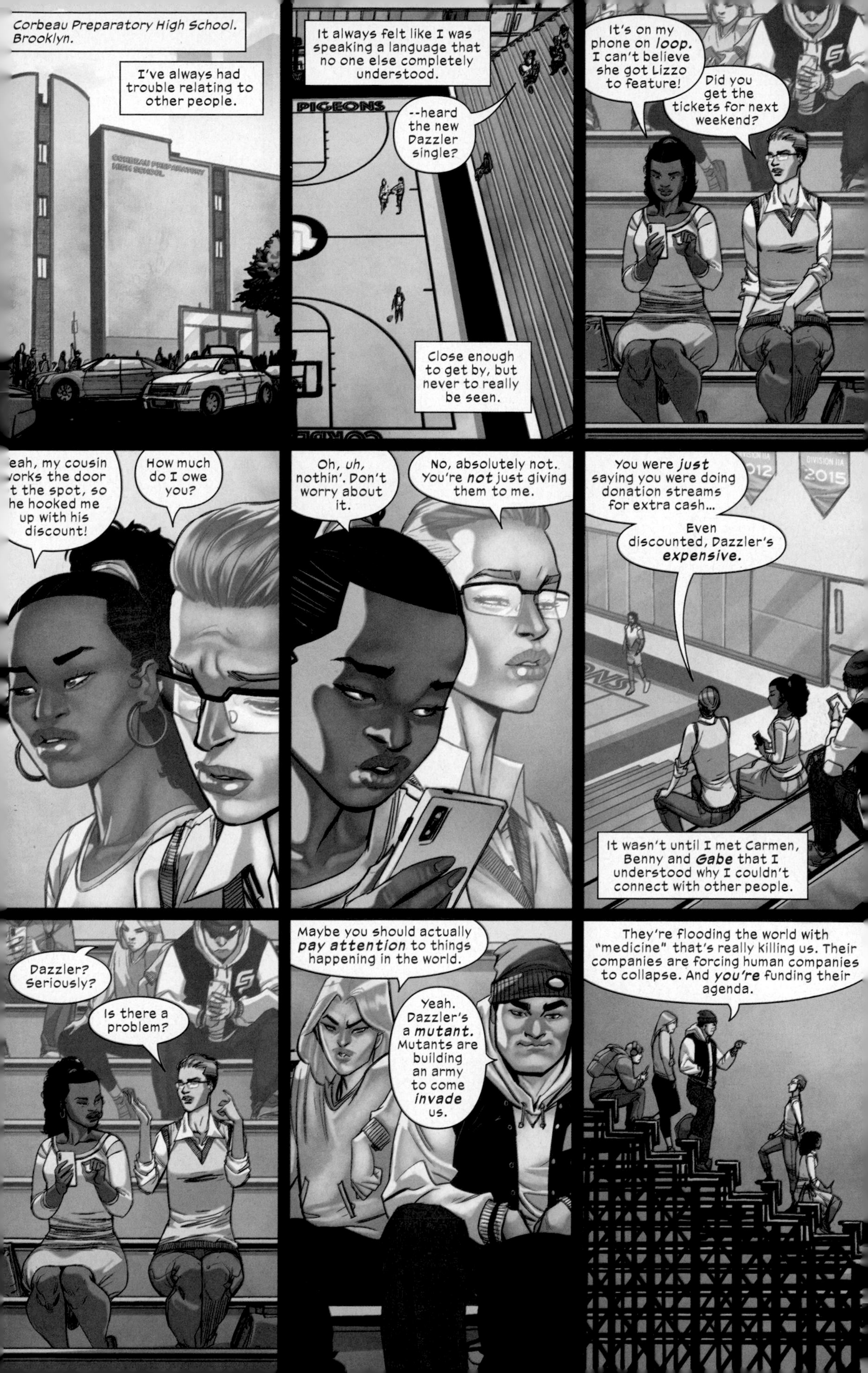
Corbeau Preparatory High School. Brooklyn.
I've always had trouble relating to other people.
It always felt like I was speaking a language that no one else completely understood.
--heard the new Dazzler single?
Close enough to get by, but never to really be seen.
It's on my phone on loop. I can't believe she got Lizzo to feature!
Did you get the tickets for next weekend?
eah, my cousin works the door t the spot, so he hooked me up with his discount!
How much do I owe you?
Oh, uh, nothin'. Don't worry about it.
No, absolutely not. You're not just giving them to me.
You were just saying you were doing donation streams for extra cash...
Even discounted, Dazzler's expensive.
It wasn't until I met Carmen, Benny and Gabe that I understood why I couldn't connect with other people.
Dazzler? Seriously?
Is there a problem?
Maybe you should actually pay attention to things happening in the world.
Yeah. Dazzler's a mutant. Mutants are building an army to come invade us.
They're flooding the world with "medicine" that's really killing us. Their companies are forcing human companies to collapse. And you're funding their agenda.

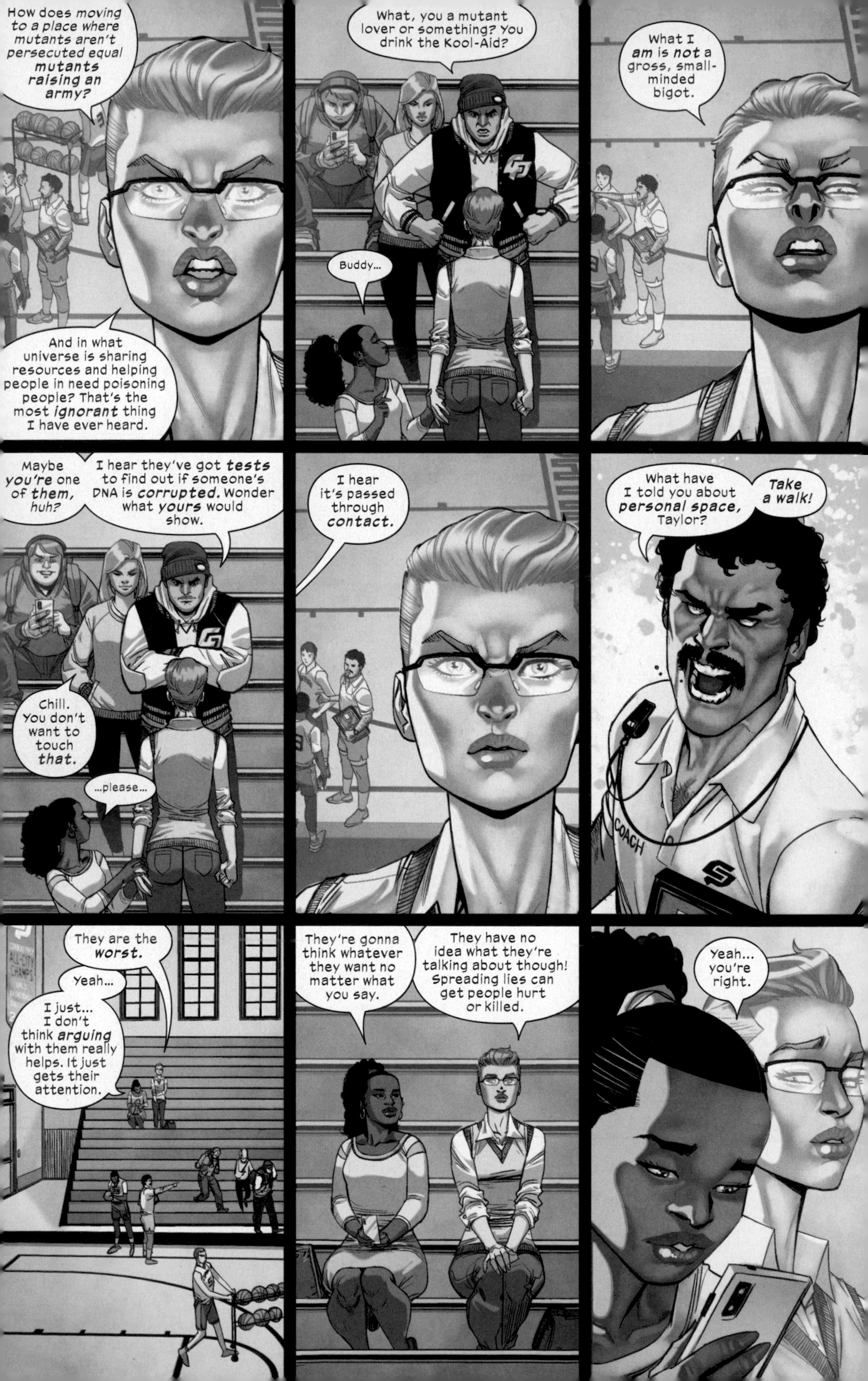
How does moving to a place where mutants aren't persecuted equal **mutants raising an army?**
And in what universe is sharing resources and helping people in need poisoning people? That's the most *ignorant* thing I have ever heard.
What, you a mutant lover or something? You drink the Kool-Aid?
Buddy...
What I **am** is **not** a gross, small-minded bigot.
Maybe *you're* one of *them,* huh?
I hear they've got *tests* to find out if someone's DNA is *corrupted.* Wonder what *yours* would show.
Chill. You don't want to touch *that.*
...please...
I hear it's passed through *contact.*
What have I told you about *personal space,* Taylor?
Take a walk!
COACH
They are the *worst.*
Yeah...
I just... I don't think *arguing* with them really helps. It just gets their attention.
They're gonna think whatever they want no matter what you say.
They have no idea what they're talking about though! Spreading lies can get people hurt or killed.
Yeah... you're right.

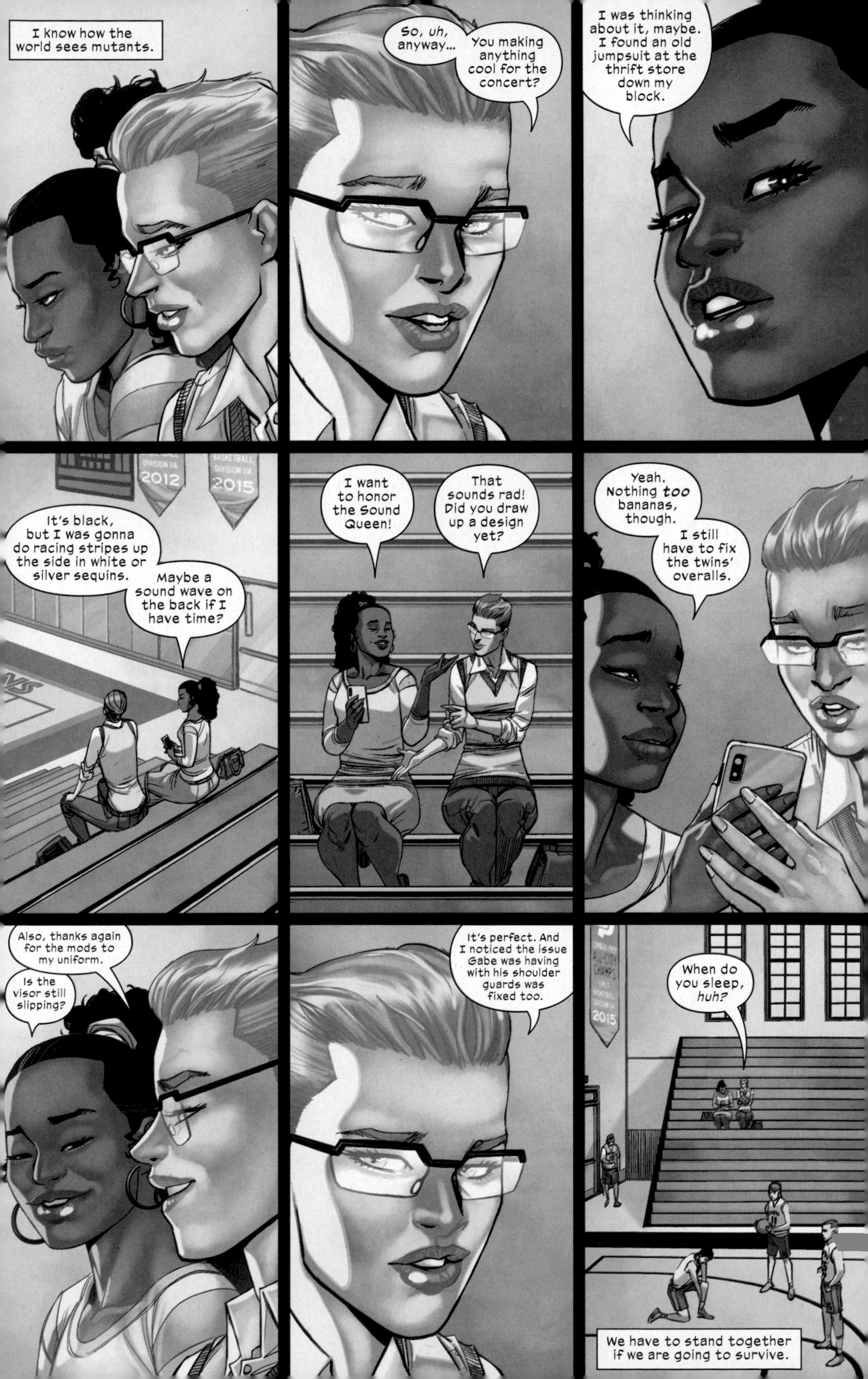
I know how the world sees mutants.
So, uh, anyway...
You making anything cool for the concert?
I was thinking about it, maybe. I found an old jumpsuit at the thrift store down my block.
DIVISION IIA 2012
BASKETBALL DIVISION IIA 2015
It's black, but I was gonna do racing stripes up the side in white or silver sequins.
Maybe a sound wave on the back if I have time?
I want to honor the Sound Queen!
That sounds rad! Did you draw up a design yet?
Yeah. Nothing *too* bananas, though.
I still have to fix the twins' overalls.
Also, thanks again for the mods to my uniform.
Is the visor still slipping?
It's perfect. And I noticed the issue Gabe was having with his shoulder guards was fixed too.
ALL-CITY CHAMPS
2015
When do you sleep, *huh?*
We have to stand together if we are going to survive.

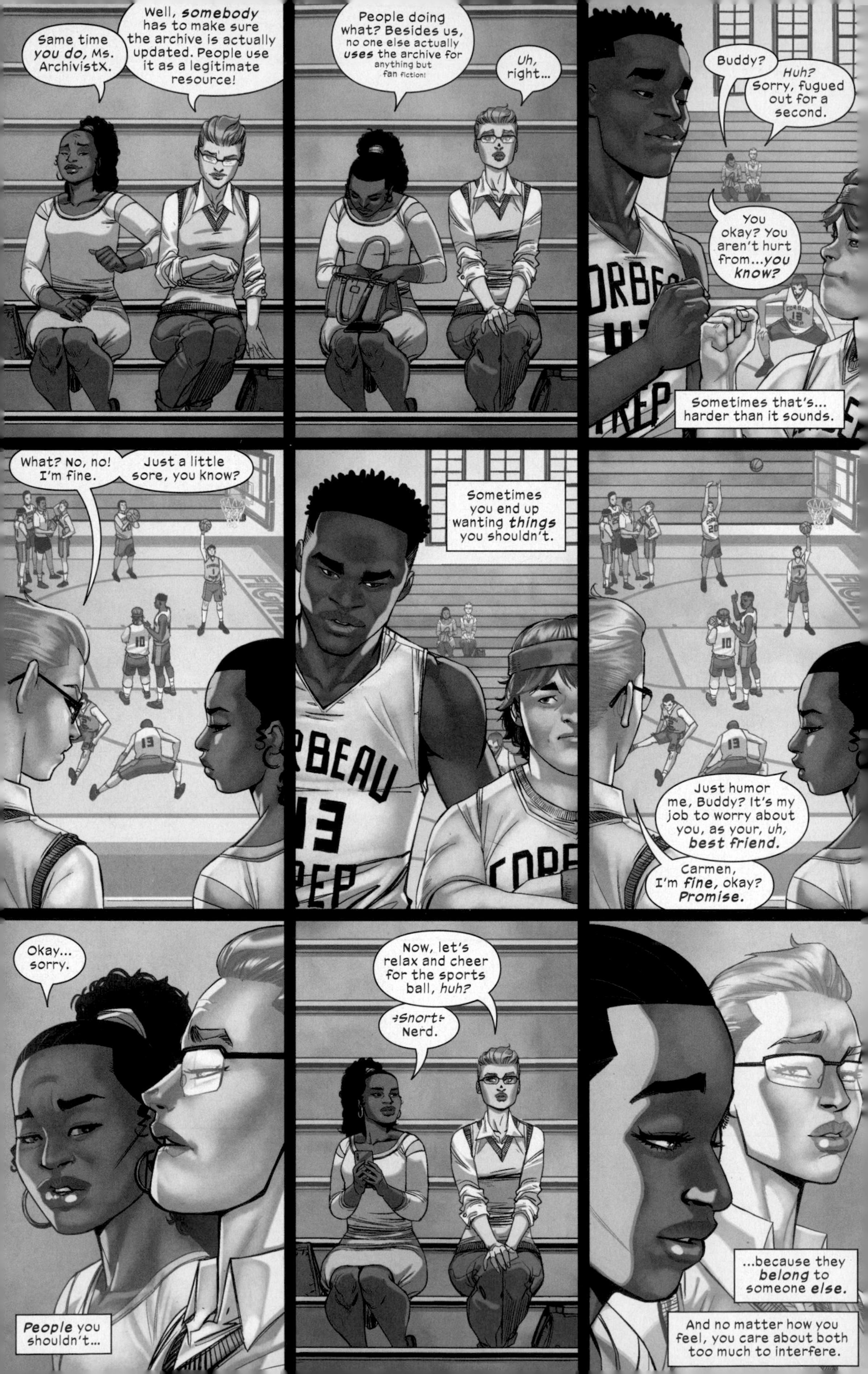

Same time *you do,* Ms. ArchivistX.
Well, ***somebody*** has to make sure the archive is actually updated. People use it as a legitimate resource!
People doing what? Besides us, no one else actually ***uses*** the archive for anything but fan fiction!
Uh, right...
Buddy?
Huh? Sorry, fugued out for a second.
You okay? You aren't hurt from...***you know?***
Sometimes that's... harder than it sounds.
What? No, no! I'm fine.
Just a little sore, you know?
Sometimes you end up wanting ***things*** you shouldn't.
Just humor me, Buddy? It's my job to worry about you, as your, *uh,* ***best friend.***
Carmen, I'm ***fine,*** okay? ***Promise.***
Okay... sorry.
People you shouldn't...
Now, let's relax and cheer for the sports ball, *huh?*
Snort Nerd.
...because they ***belong*** to someone ***else.***
And no matter how you feel, you care about both too much to interfere.

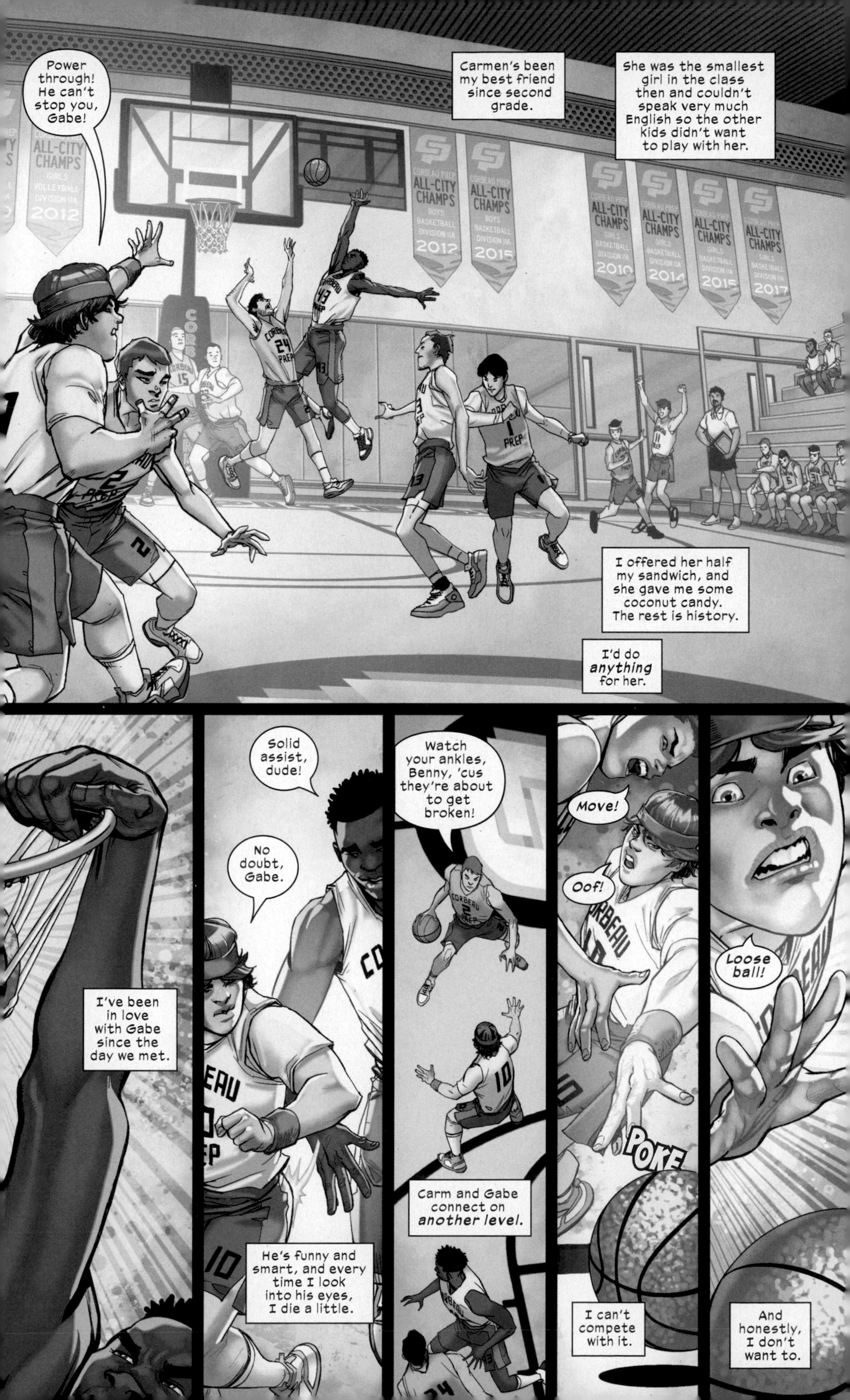

Power through! He can't stop you, Gabe!
Carmen's been my best friend since second grade.
She was the smallest girl in the class then and couldn't speak very much English so the other kids didn't want to play with her.
I offered her half my sandwich, and she gave me some coconut candy. The rest is history.
I'd do *anything* for her.
I've been in love with Gabe since the day we met.
Solid assist, dude!
No doubt, Gabe.
He's funny and smart, and every time I look into his eyes, I die a little.
Watch your ankles, Benny, 'cus they're about to get broken!
Carm and Gabe connect on *another level.*
Move!
Oof!
POKE
I can't compete with it.
Loose ball!
And honestly, I don't want to.

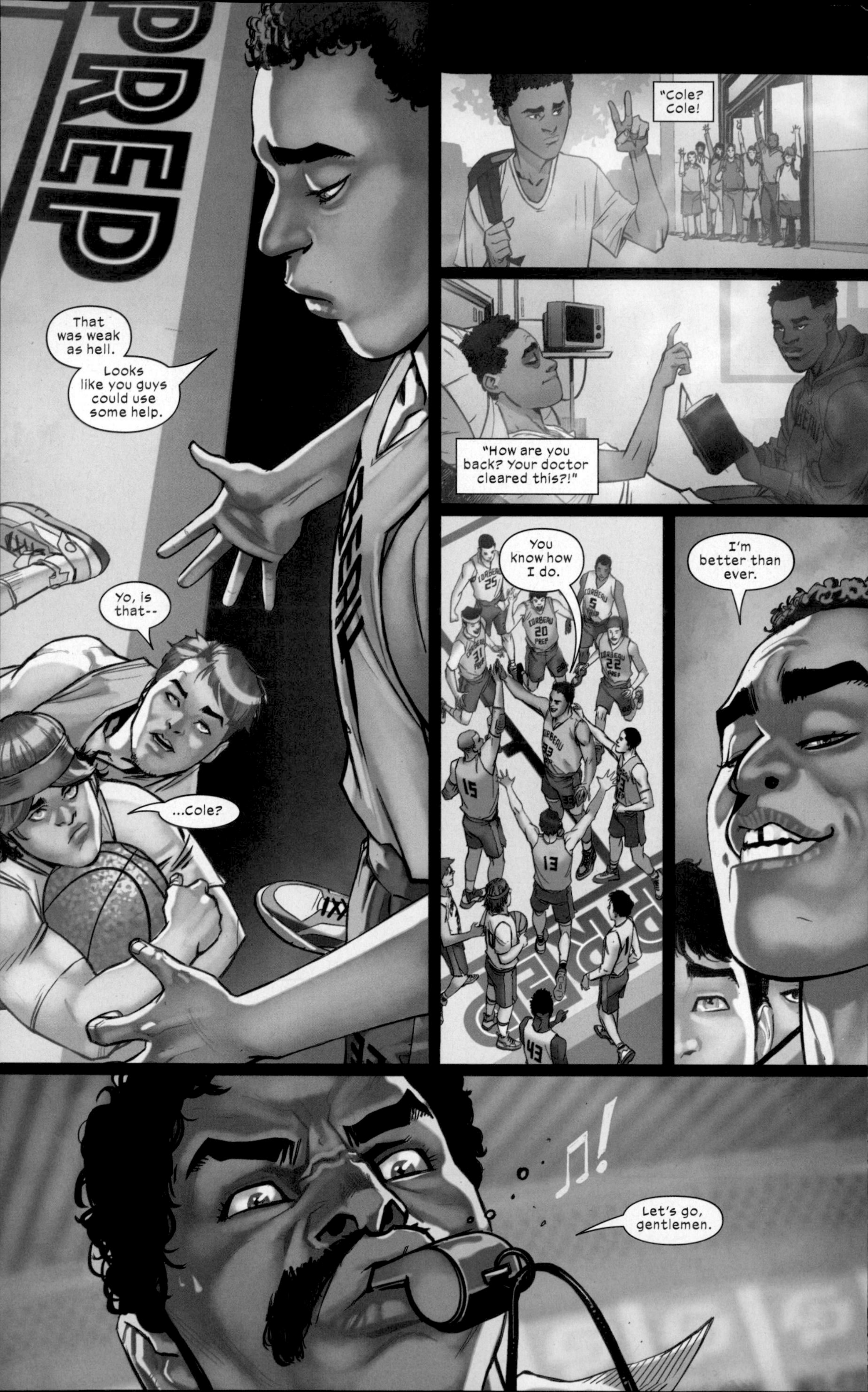

That was weak as hell.
Looks like you guys could use some help.
Yo, is that--
...Cole?
"Cole? Cole!
"How are you back? Your doctor cleared this?!"
You know how I do.
I'm better than ever.
Let's go, gentlemen.

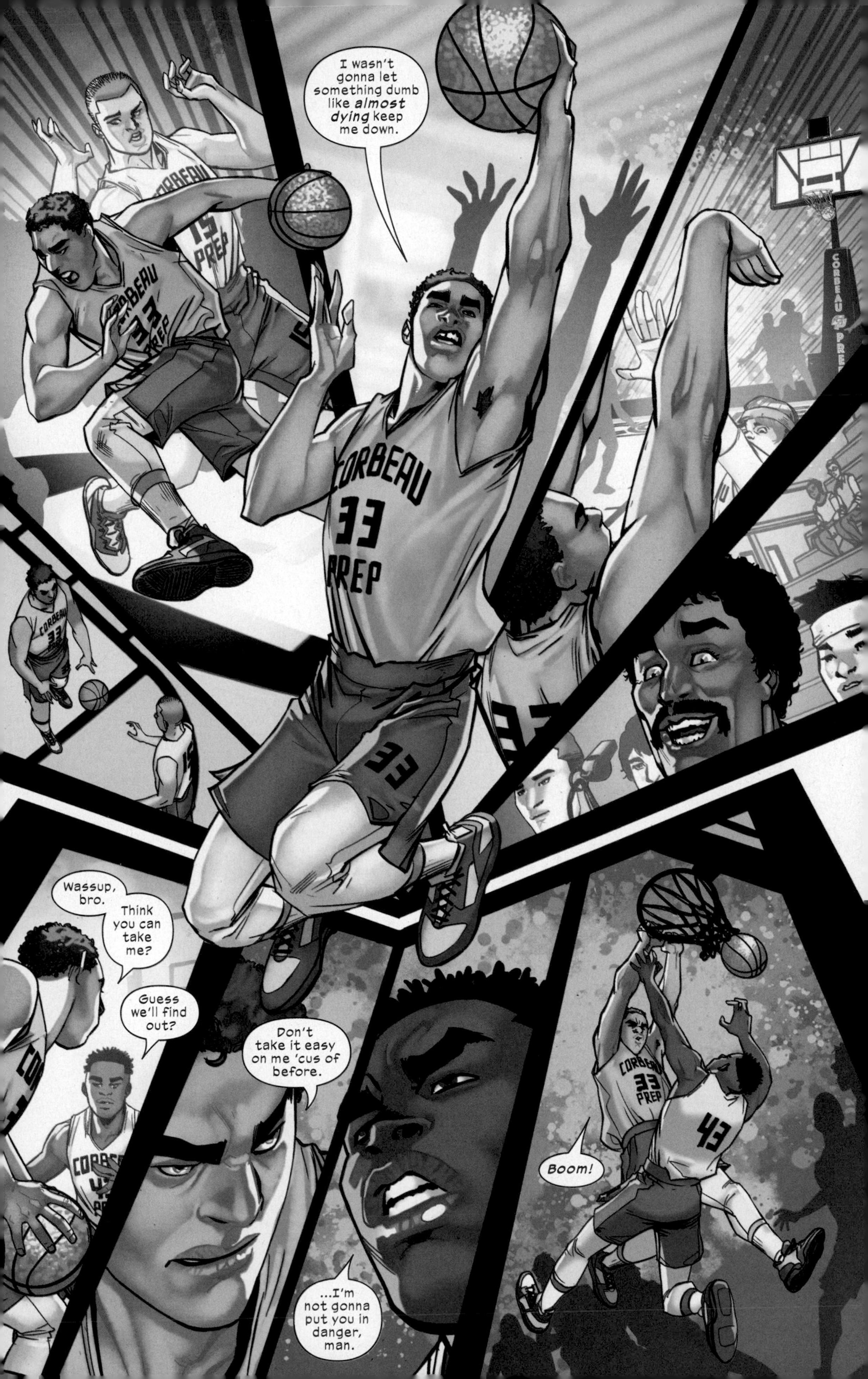
I wasn't gonna let something dumb like *almost dying* keep me down.
CORBEAU 33 PREP
Wassup, bro.
Think you can take me?
Guess we'll find out?
Don't take it easy on me 'cus of before.
...I'm not gonna put you in danger, man.
Boom!

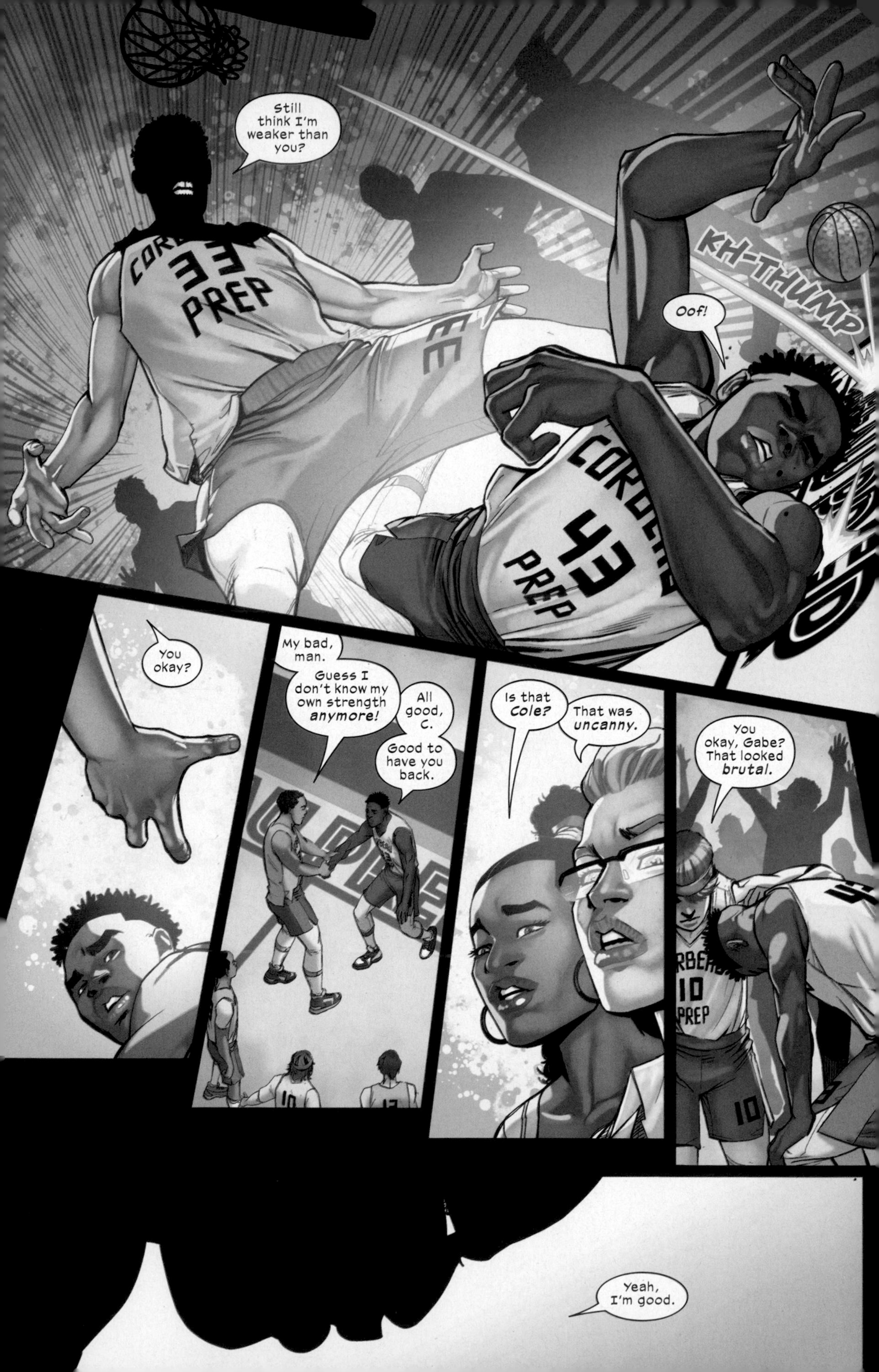

Still think I'm weaker than you?
KH-THUMP
Oof!
You okay?
My bad, man.
Guess I don't know my own strength *anymore!*
All good, C.
Good to have you back.
Is that *Cole?*
That was *uncanny.*
You okay, Gabe? That looked *brutal.*
Yeah, I'm good.

mutantsunmuted.com/

A site dedicated to archiving all footage involving mutants!

NEWEST VIDEO

 Wolverine Spotted Fighting Ghost Rider Wearing a Cape?

FEATURED VIDEO

 Jumbo Carnation & Dazzler Spotted in Tribeca – New Collab?

IN THE NEWS

Footage from the media.

MUTANT FIGHTS

Your faves wrecking the government, battling each other, and causing general carnage!

SIGHTINGS

Mutant sightings all over the world, uploaded by members!

FAN ENCOUNTERS

Mutants walk among us and apparently love to sign autographs!

FORUM

> But how do the gates work???

> I tried the one in Washington Square Park and nothing happened! I was still in Manhattan.

> They only work for muties. My neighbor walked through one and disappeared.

As long as I could remember, there's been a part of me that felt *different*.

Even at home, I couldn't be myself.

My father loves me--has done his best--but there are parts of me that he can't ever *understand*.

It's not that I'm afraid he wouldn't accept me.

He's *always* supported me, even when he didn't get it.

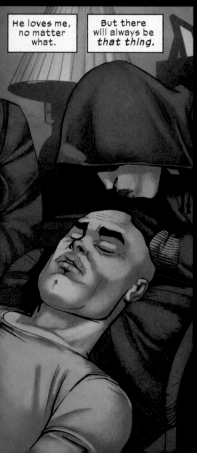

He loves me, no matter what.

But there will always be *that thing*.

He'd want me to be happy...

He'd want me to be with *them*.

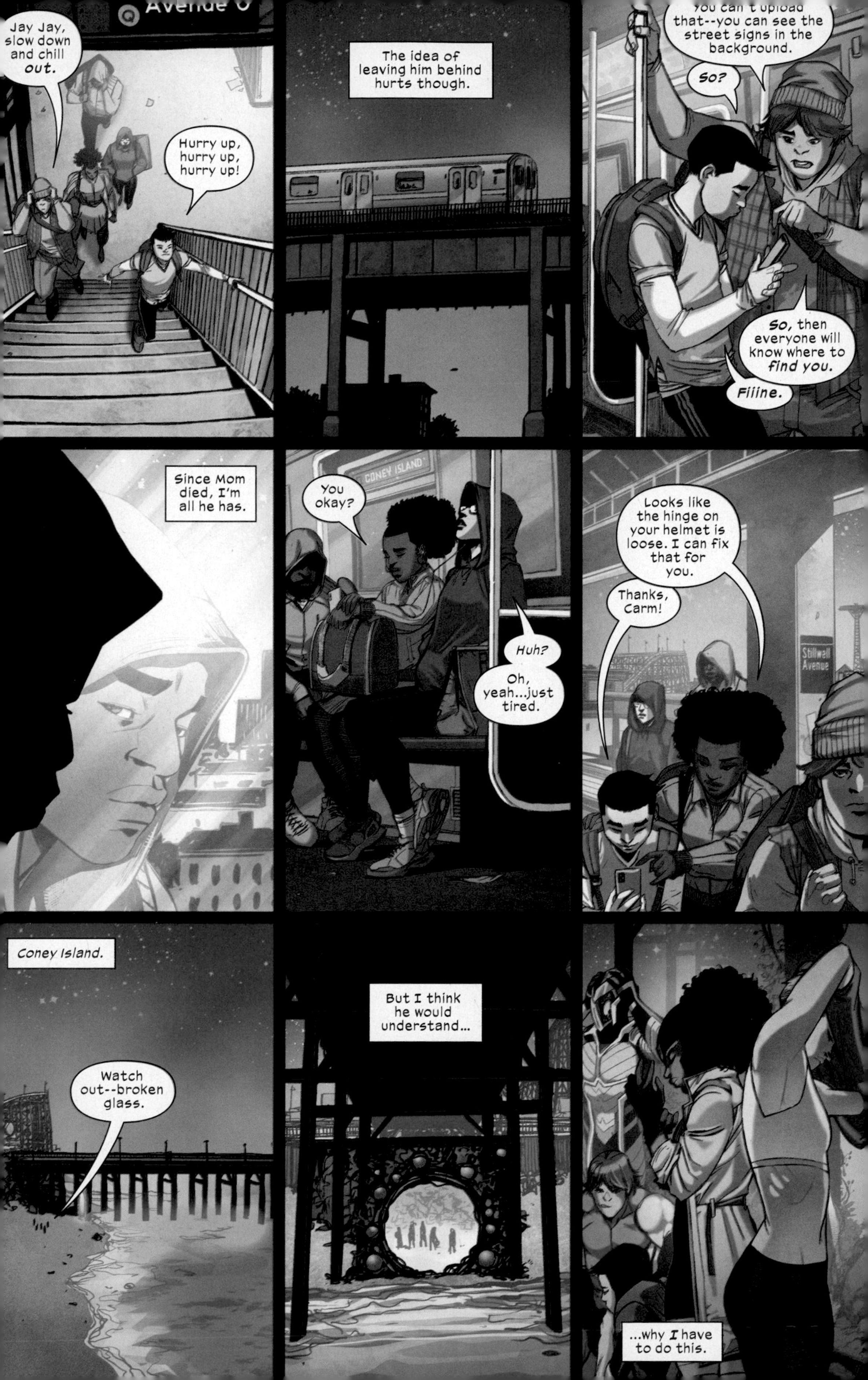
Avenue U
Jay Jay, slow down and chill out.
Hurry up, hurry up, hurry up!
The idea of leaving him behind hurts though.
You can't upload that--you can see the street signs in the background.
So?
So, then everyone will know where to find you.
Fiiine.
Since Mom died, I'm all he has.
CONEY ISLAND
You okay?
Huh?
Oh, yeah...just tired.
Looks like the hinge on your helmet is loose. I can fix that for you.
Thanks, Carm!
Stillwell Avenue
Coney Island.
Watch out--broken glass.
But I think he would understand...
...why I have to do this.

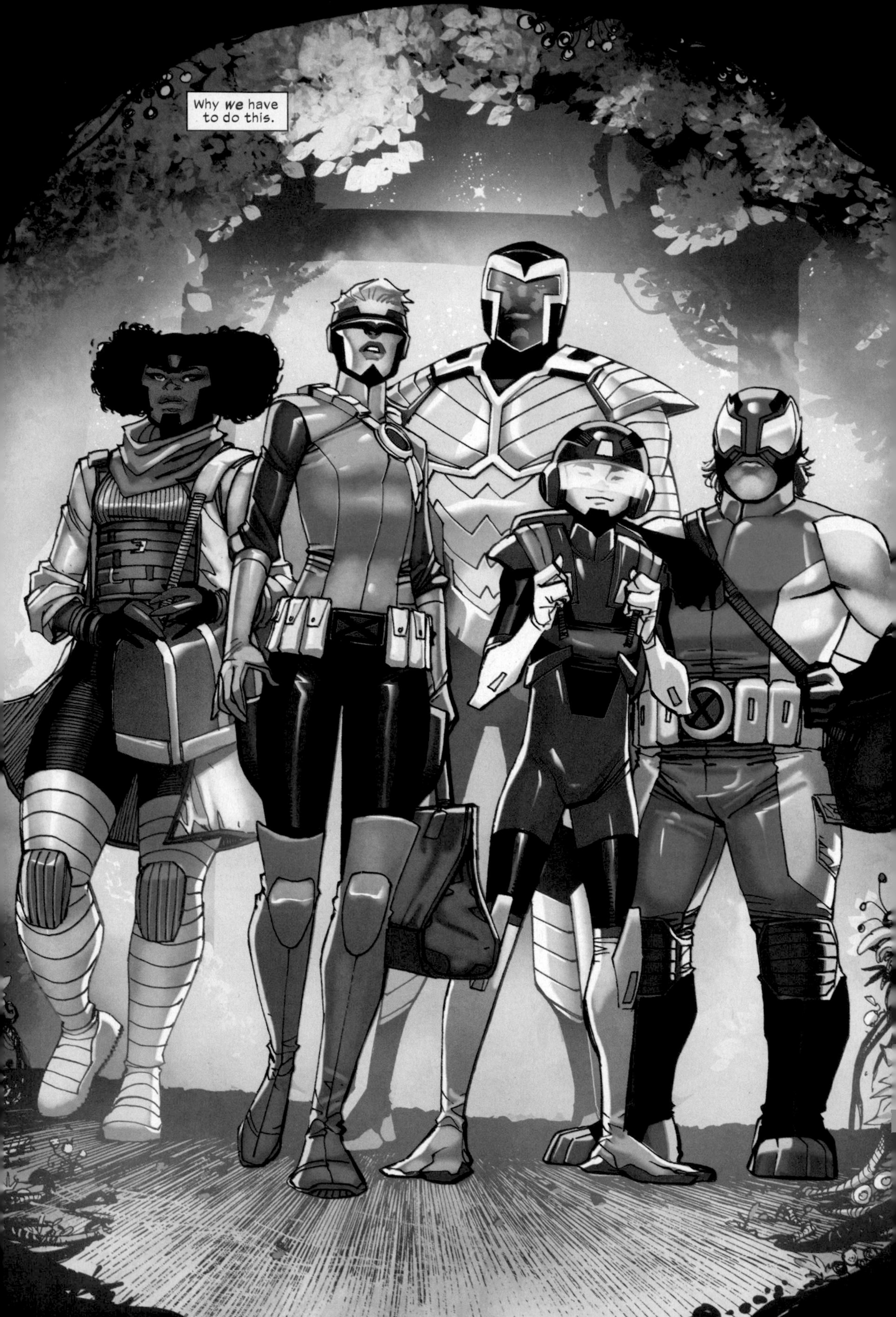

Why we have to do this.

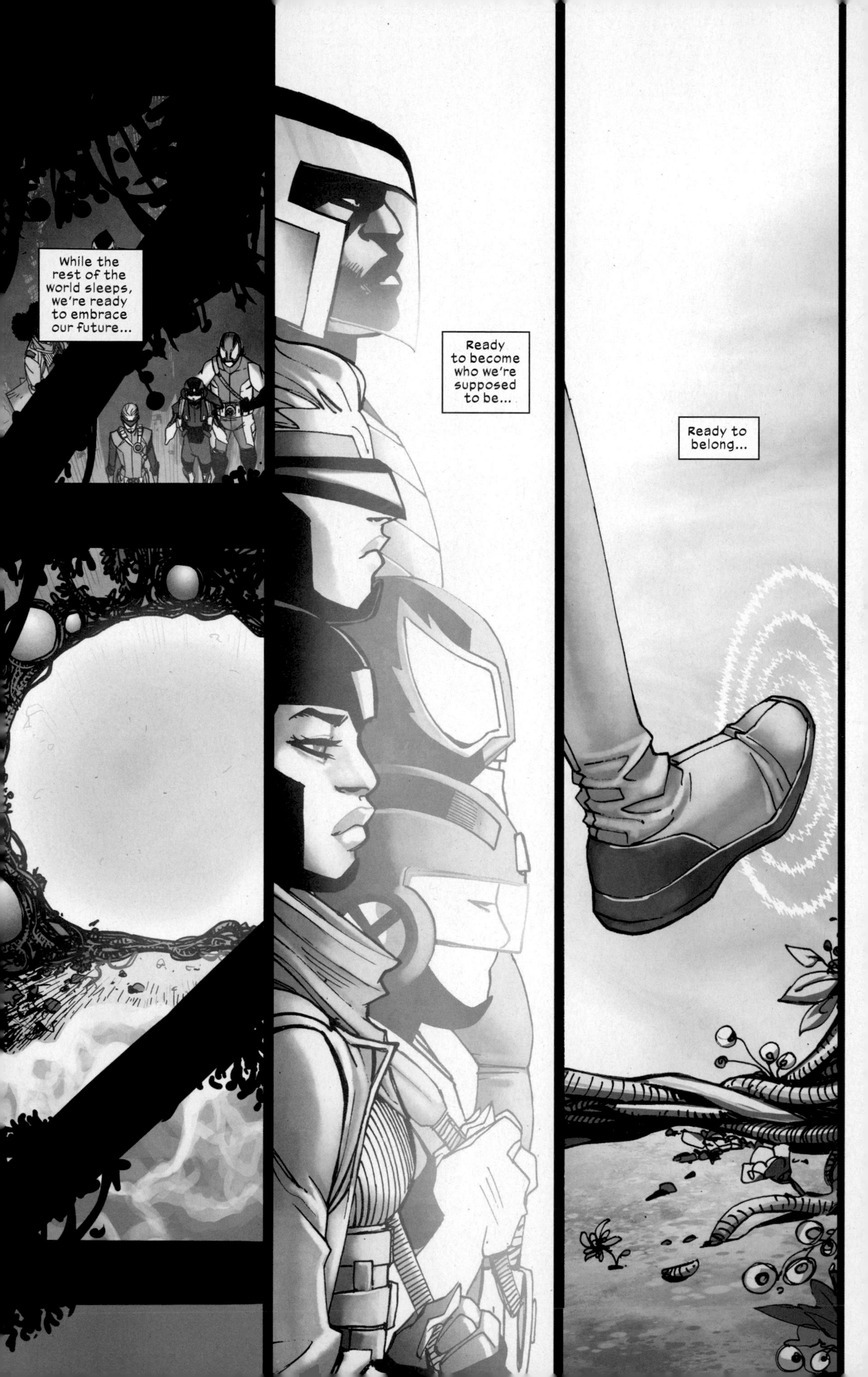
While the rest of the world sleeps, we're ready to embrace our future...
Ready to become who we're supposed to be...
Ready to belong...

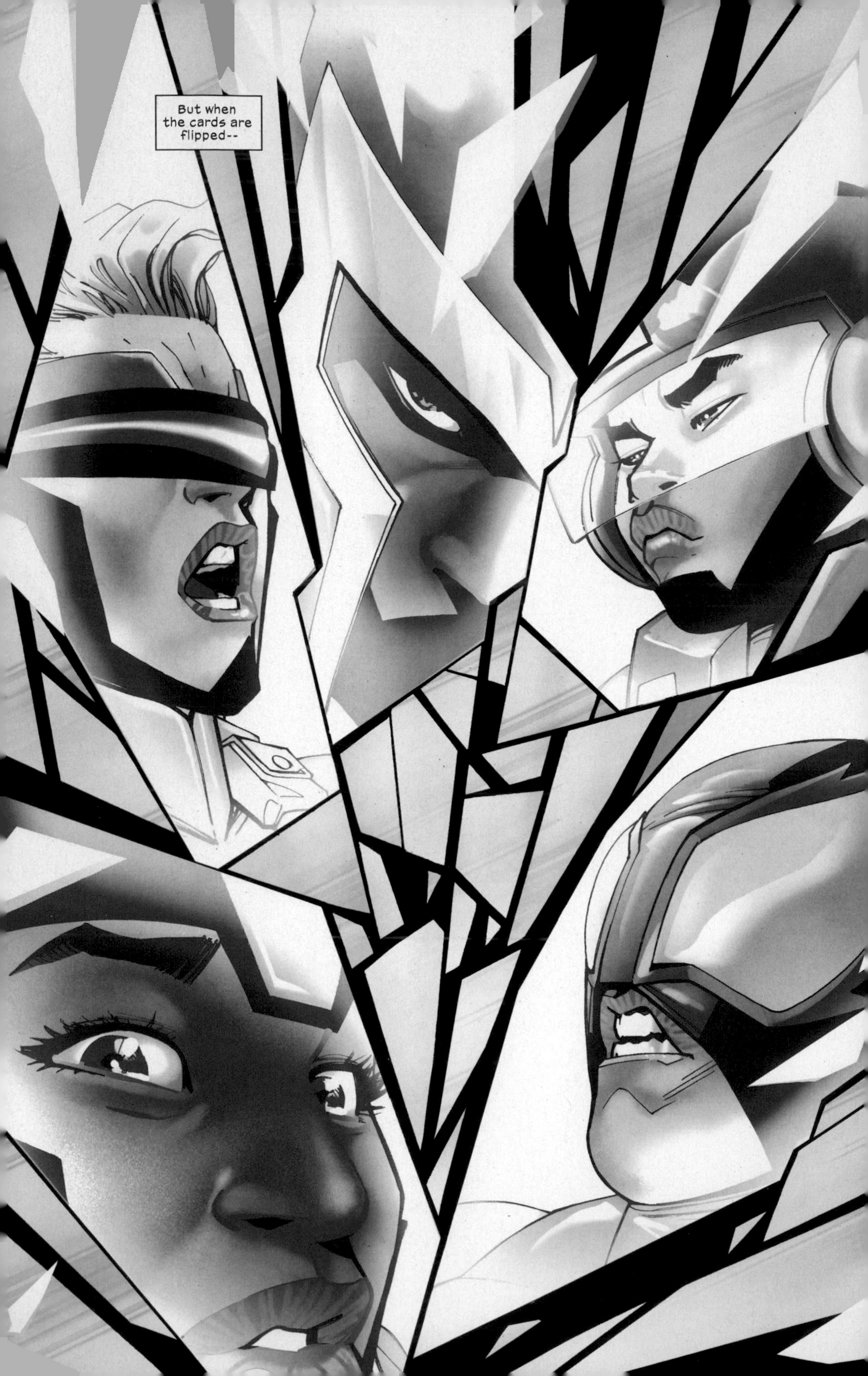
But when the cards are flipped--

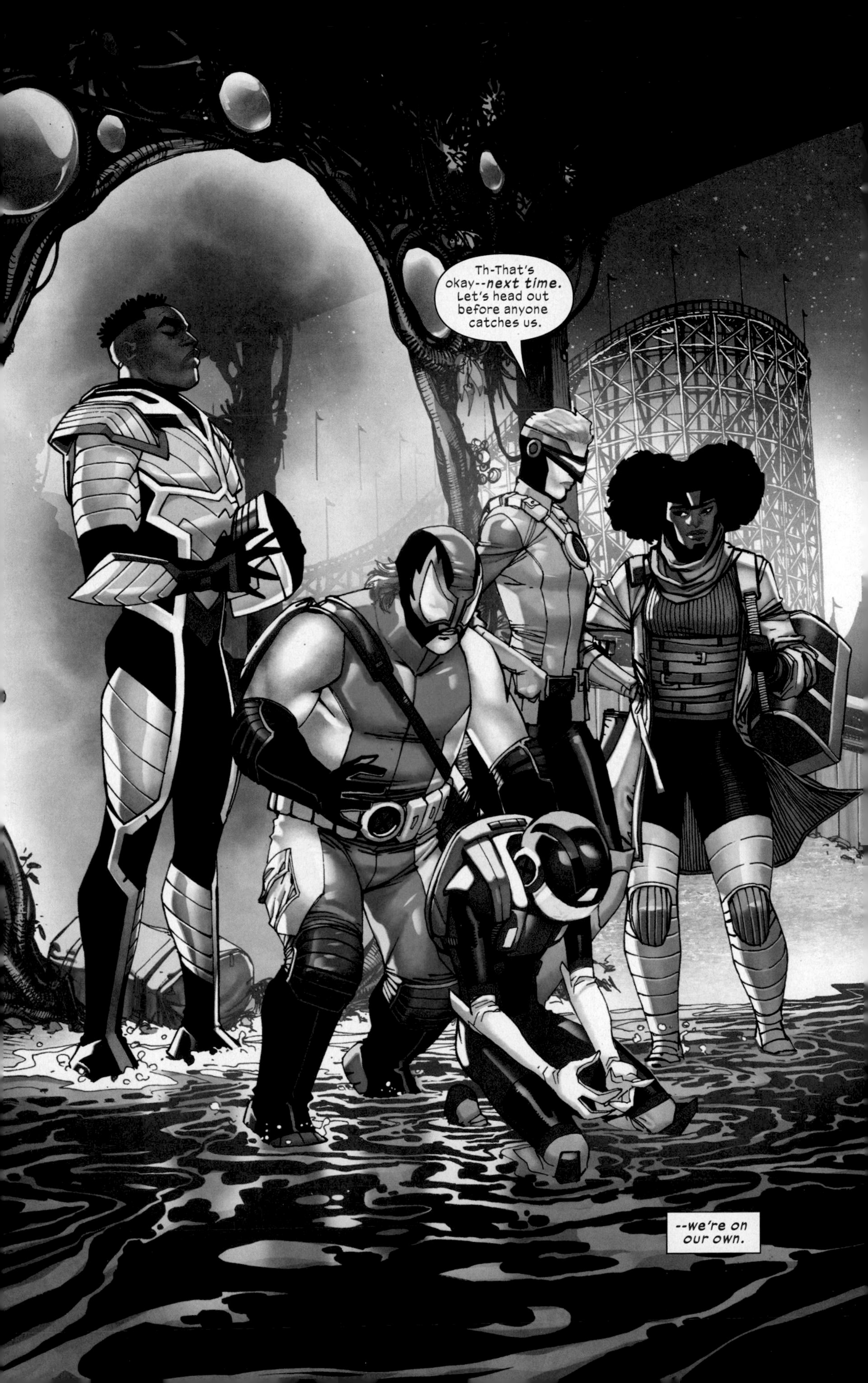
Th-That's okay--*next time.* Let's head out before anyone catches us.
--we're on our own.

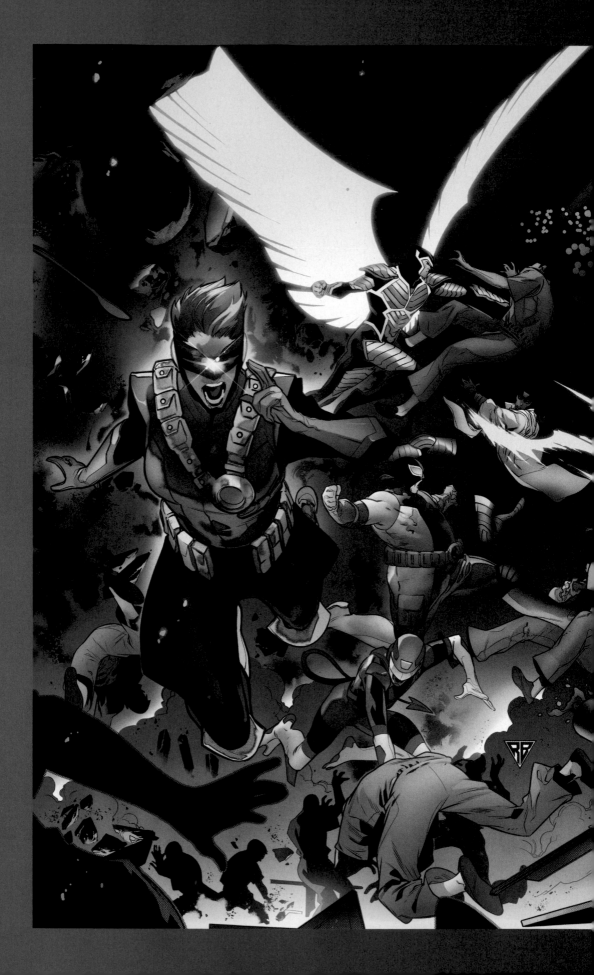

Prison Break

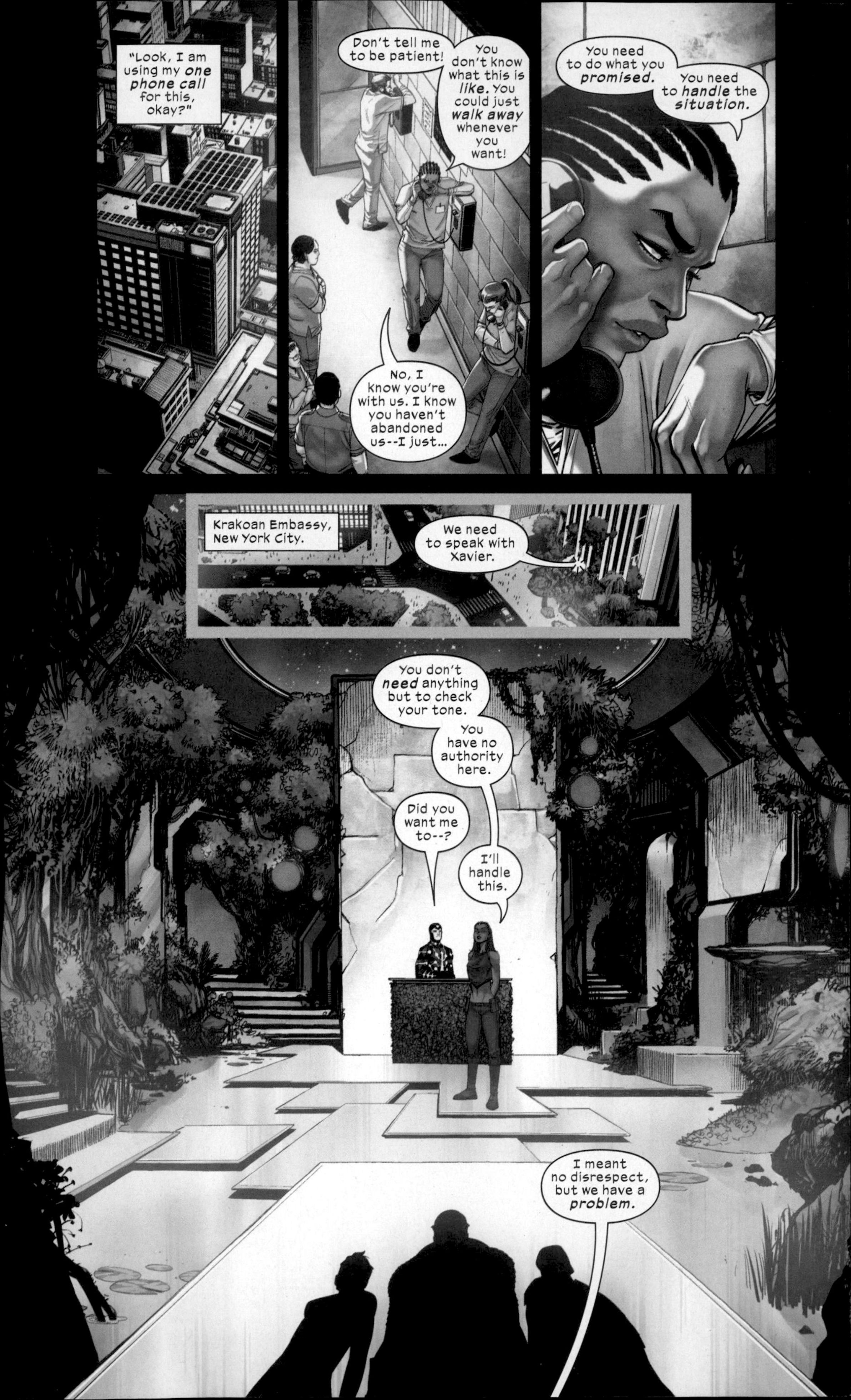
"Look, I am using my *one phone call* for this, okay?"
Don't tell me to be patient!
You don't know what this is *like.* You could just *walk away* whenever you want!
No, I know you're with us. I know you haven't abandoned us--I just...
You need to do what you *promised.*
You need to *handle* the *situation.*
Krakoan Embassy, New York City.
We need to speak with Xavier.
You don't *need* anything but to check your tone.
You have no authority here.
Did you want me to--?
I'll handle this.
I meant no disrespect, but we have a *problem.*

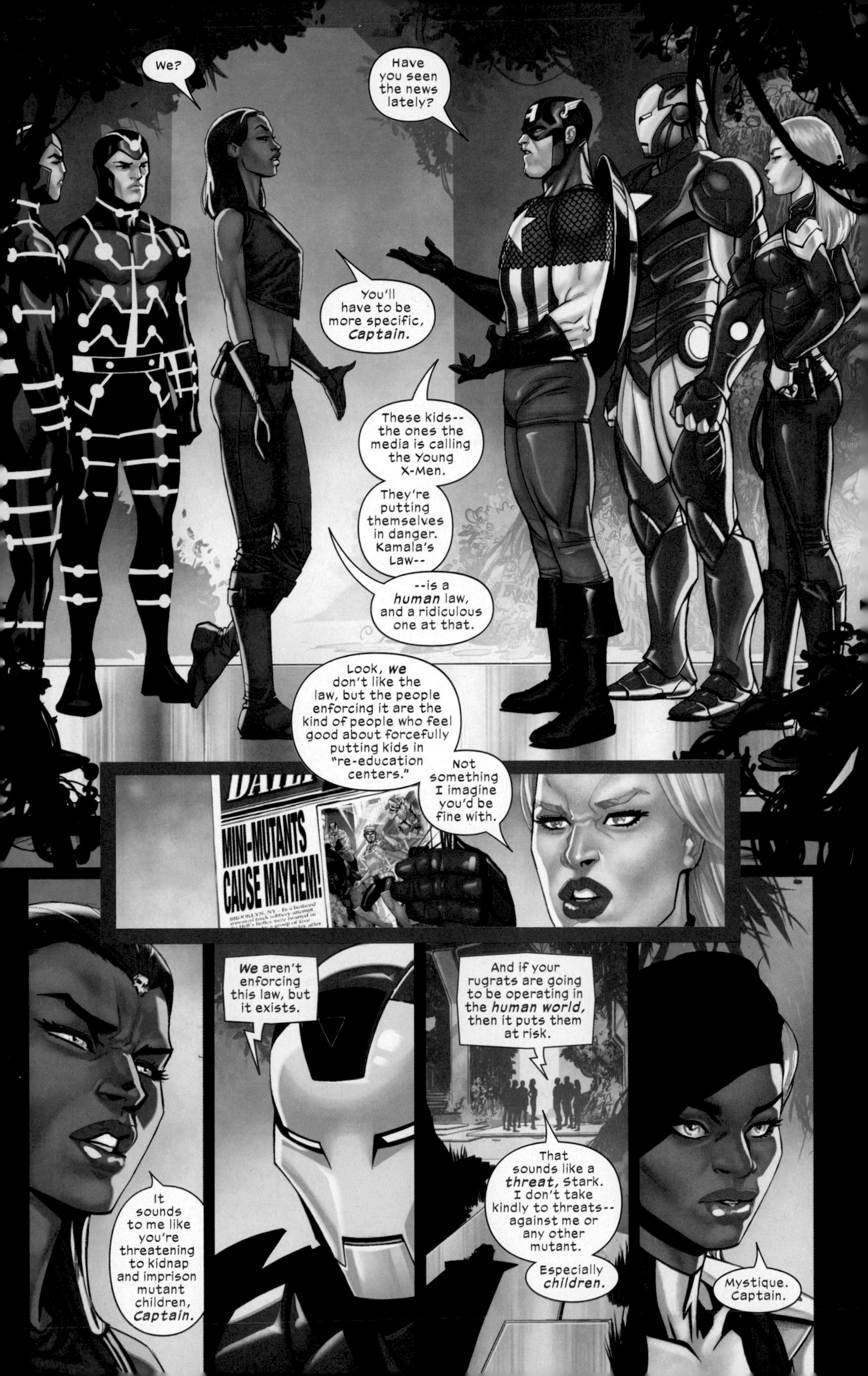
We?
Have you seen the news lately?
You'll have to be more specific, Captain.
These kids--the ones the media is calling the Young X-Men.
They're putting themselves in danger. Kamala's Law--
--is a human law, and a ridiculous one at that.
Look, we don't like the law, but the people enforcing it are the kind of people who feel good about forcefully putting kids in "re-education centers."
Not something I imagine you'd be fine with.
DAILY
MINI-MUTANTS CAUSE MAYHEM!
It sounds to me like you're threatening to kidnap and imprison mutant children, Captain.
We aren't enforcing this law, but it exists.
And if your rugrats are going to be operating in the human world, then it puts them at risk.
That sounds like a threat, Stark. I don't take kindly to threats--against me or any other mutant.
Especially children.
Mystique. Captain.

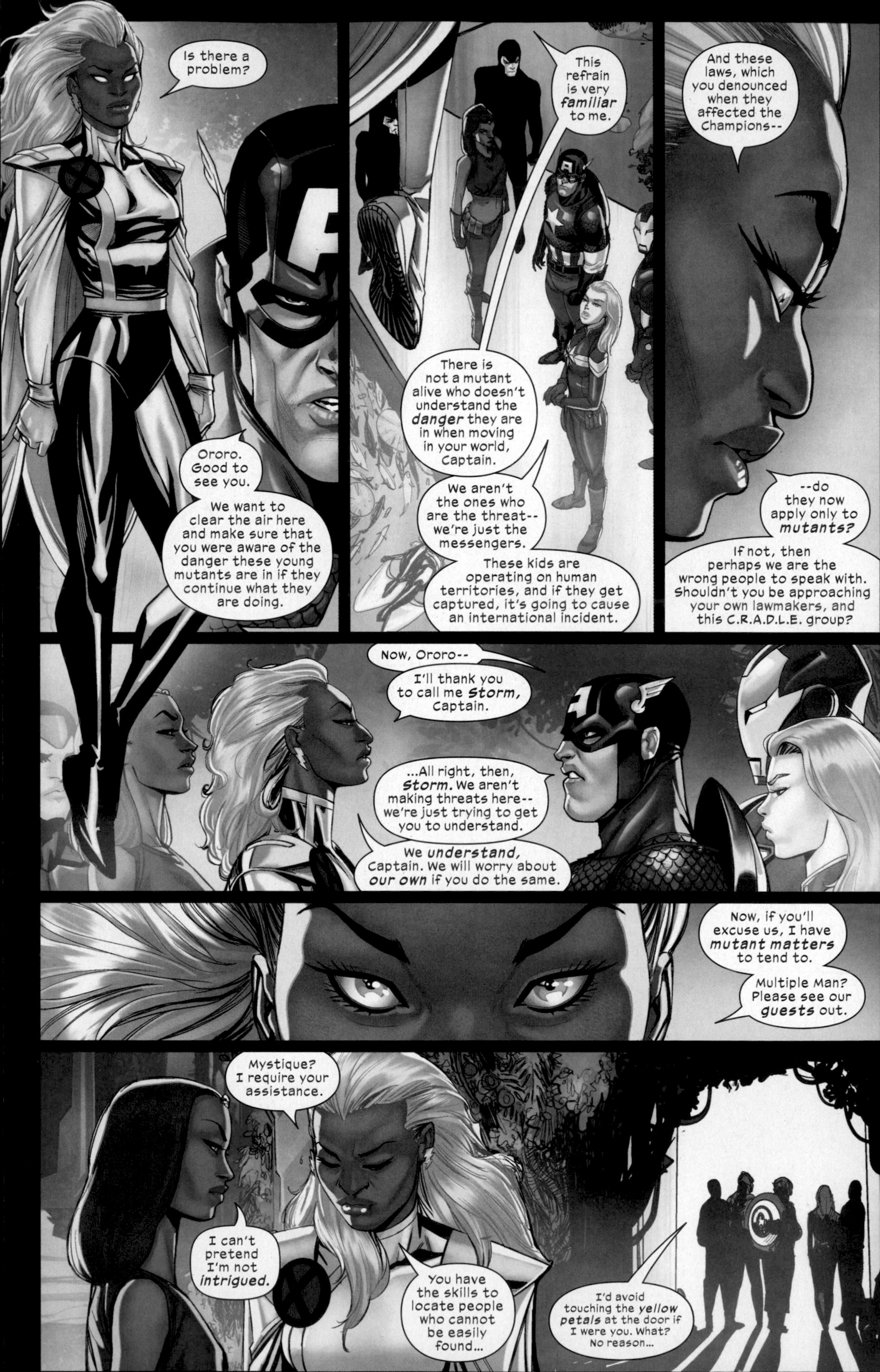
Is there a problem?
Ororo. Good to see you.
We want to clear the air here and make sure that you were aware of the danger these young mutants are in if they continue what they are doing.
This refrain is very *familiar* to me.
There is not a mutant alive who doesn't understand the *danger* they are in when moving in your world, Captain.
We aren't the ones who are the threat--we're just the messengers.
These kids are operating on human territories, and if they get captured, it's going to cause an international incident.
And these laws, which you denounced when they affected the Champions--
--do they now apply only to *mutants?*
If not, then perhaps we are the wrong people to speak with. Shouldn't you be approaching your own lawmakers, and this C.R.A.D.L.E. group?
Now, Ororo--
I'll thank you to call me *Storm,* Captain.
...All right, then, *Storm.* We aren't making threats here--we're just trying to get you to understand.
We *understand,* Captain. We will worry about *our own* if you do the same.
Now, if you'll excuse us, I have *mutant matters* to tend to.
Multiple Man? Please see our *guests* out.
Mystique? I require your assistance.
I can't pretend I'm not *intrigued.*
You have the skills to locate people who cannot be easily found...
I'd avoid touching the *yellow petals* at the door if I were you. What? No reason...

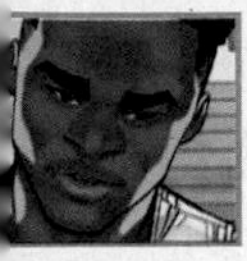

FINNA_FIGHT
Gabe Brathwaite

FOLLOWED

"YOU MUST BE A MUTANT TO HAVE ABS LIKE THAT" WORKOUT
(Intermediate)

I get asked about core workouts all the time, and the one thing that always comes up is that people "want the abs but don't have the time." You ***make*** time for the things you think are important!

This workout will have you cut like Wolverine's claws got a grudge.

Remember the motto: hustle smarter, so you can go harder.

(Also, remember to rest 60 seconds between sets.)

WARM-UP

Home: 20 jumping jacks (2 sets)/Gym: treadmill for half a mile, at 4 mph.

WORKOUT

- 16 elbow-to-knee crunches (2 sets)
- 1-minute star plank hold (2 sets per arm)
- 8 clapping push-ups (2 sets)
- 16 Russian twists (2 sets)
- 12 butt-ups (2 sets)
- 12 raised leg circles (2 sets)
- 16 mountain climbers (2 sets)

COOLDOWN

Stretching, at least 5 minutes.

REWARD FOOD:

Swole-Search Smoothie*

*click the link to check it out!

1,024 fist bumps

APRIL #mutant #abs #workout #mutantabs #swolesearchsmoothie

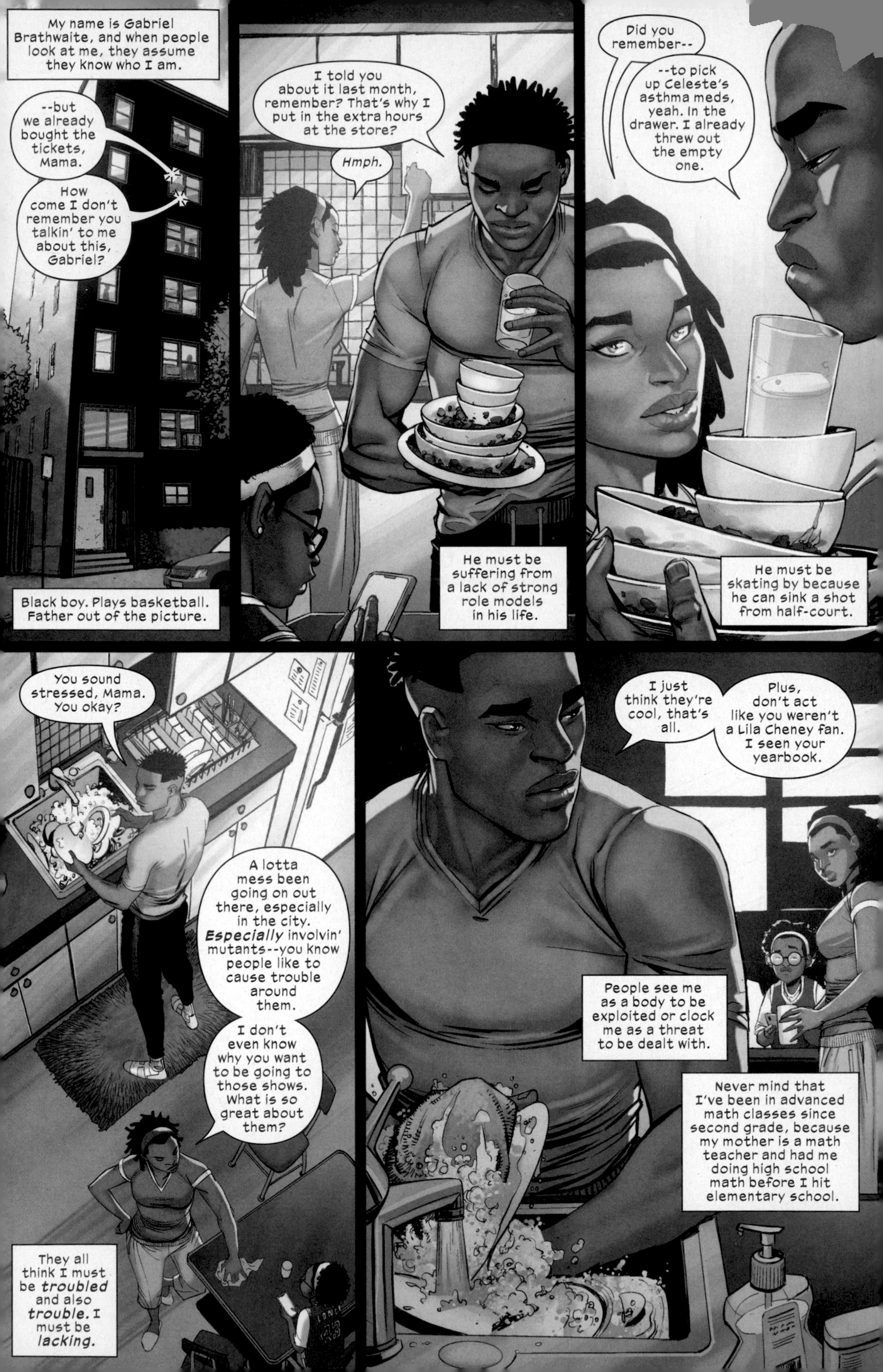

My name is Gabriel Brathwaite, and when people look at me, they assume they know who I am.
--but we already bought the tickets, Mama.
How come I don't remember you talkin' to me about this, Gabriel?
Black boy. Plays basketball. Father out of the picture.
I told you about it last month, remember? That's why I put in the extra hours at the store?
Hmph.
He must be suffering from a lack of strong role models in his life.
Did you remember--
--to pick up Celeste's asthma meds, yeah. In the drawer. I already threw out the empty one.
He must be skating by because he can sink a shot from half-court.
You sound stressed, Mama. You okay?
A lotta mess been going on out there, especially in the city. *Especially* involvin' mutants--you know people like to cause trouble around them.
I don't even know why you want to be going to those shows. What is so great about them?
They all think I must be *troubled* and also *trouble.* I must be *lacking.*
I just think they're cool, that's all.
Plus, don't act like you weren't a Lila Cheney fan. I seen your yearbook.
People see me as a body to be exploited or clock me as a threat to be dealt with.
Never mind that I've been in advanced math classes since second grade, because my mother is a math teacher and had me doing high school math before I hit elementary school.

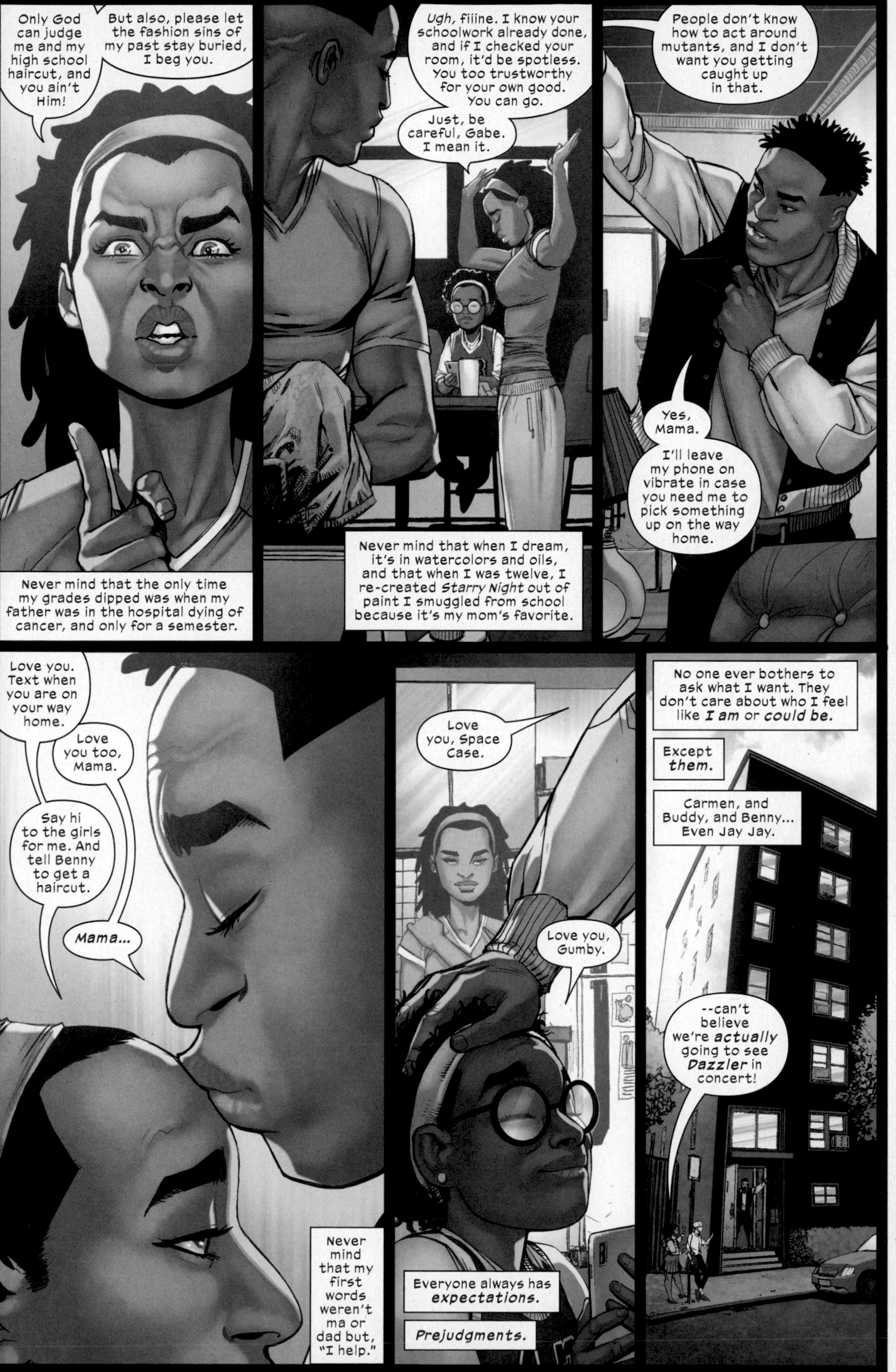
Only God can judge me and my high school haircut, and you ain't Him!
But also, please let the fashion sins of my past stay buried, I beg you.
Never mind that the only time my grades dipped was when my father was in the hospital dying of cancer, and only for a semester.
Ugh, fiiine. I know your schoolwork already done, and if I checked your room, it'd be spotless. You too trustworthy for your own good. You can go.
Just, be careful, Gabe. I mean it.
Never mind that when I dream, it's in watercolors and oils, and that when I was twelve, I re-created Starry Night out of paint I smuggled from school because it's my mom's favorite.
People don't know how to act around mutants, and I don't want you getting caught up in that.
Yes, Mama.
I'll leave my phone on vibrate in case you need me to pick something up on the way home.
Love you. Text when you are on your way home.
Love you too, Mama.
Say hi to the girls for me. And tell Benny to get a haircut.
Mama...
Never mind that my first words weren't ma or dad but, "I help."
Love you, Space Case.
Love you, Gumby.
Everyone always has expectations.
Prejudgments.
No one ever bothers to ask what I want. They don't care about who I feel like I am or could be.
Except them.
Carmen, and Buddy, and Benny... Even Jay Jay.
--can't believe we're actually going to see Dazzler in concert!

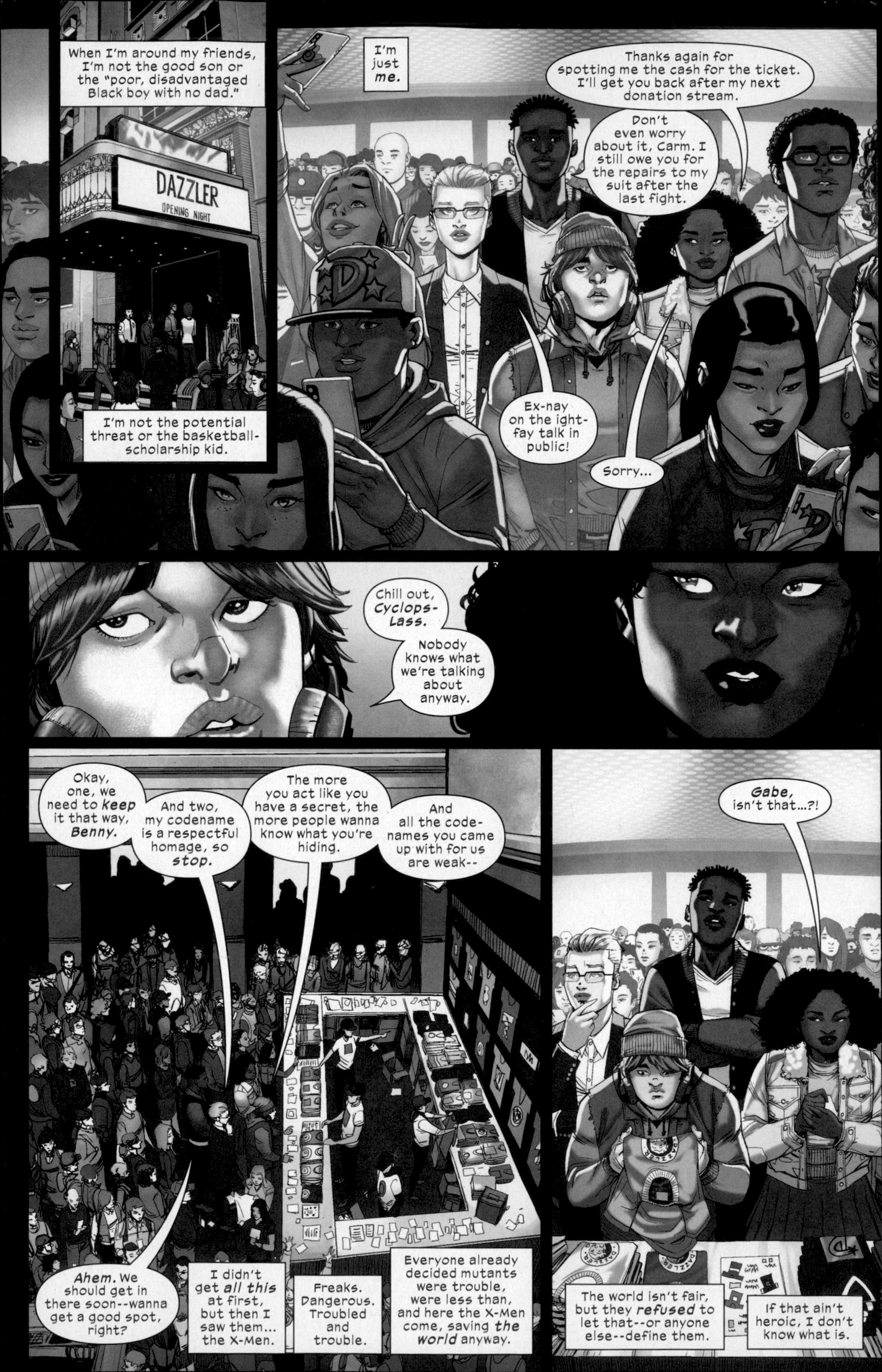
When I'm around my friends, I'm not the good son or the "poor, disadvantaged Black boy with no dad."
DAZZLER
OPENING NIGHT
I'm not the potential threat or the basketball-scholarship kid.
I'm just me.
Thanks again for spotting me the cash for the ticket. I'll get you back after my next donation stream.
Don't even worry about it, Carm. I still owe you for the repairs to my suit after the last fight.
Ex-nay on the ight-fay talk in public!
Sorry...
Chill out, Cyclops-Lass.
Nobody knows what we're talking about anyway.
Okay, one, we need to keep it that way, Benny.
And two, my codename is a respectful homage, so stop.
The more you act like you have a secret, the more people wanna know what you're hiding.
And all the code-names you came up with for us are weak--
Ahem. We should get in there soon--wanna get a good spot, right?
I didn't get all this at first, but then I saw them... the X-Men.
Freaks. Dangerous. Troubled and trouble.
Everyone already decided mutants were trouble, were less than, and here the X-Men come, saving the world anyway.
Gabe, isn't that...?!
The world isn't fair, but they refused to let that--or anyone else--define them.
If that ain't heroic, I don't know what is.

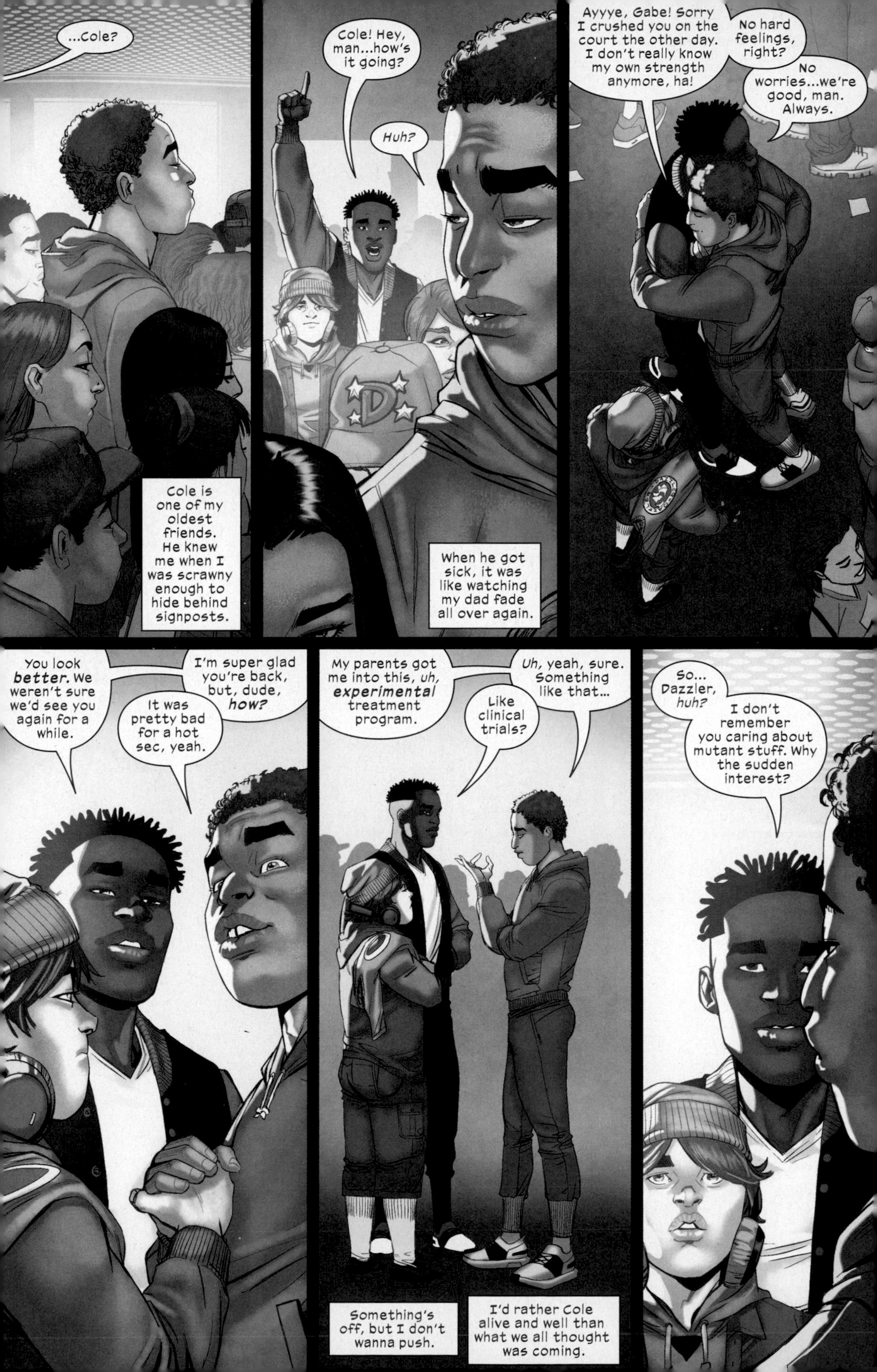
...Cole?
Cole is one of my oldest friends. He knew me when I was scrawny enough to hide behind signposts.
Cole! Hey, man...how's it going?
Huh?
When he got sick, it was like watching my dad fade all over again.
Ayyye, Gabe! Sorry I crushed you on the court the other day. I don't really know my own strength anymore, ha!
No hard feelings, right?
No worries...we're good, man. Always.
You look *better.* We weren't sure we'd see you again for a while.
I'm super glad you're back, but, dude, *how?*
It was pretty bad for a hot sec, yeah.
My parents got me into this, *uh,* ***experimental*** treatment program.
Like clinical trials?
Uh, yeah, sure. Something like that...
Something's off, but I don't wanna push.
I'd rather Cole alive and well than what we all thought was coming.
So... Dazzler, *huh?*
I don't remember you caring about mutant stuff. Why the sudden interest?

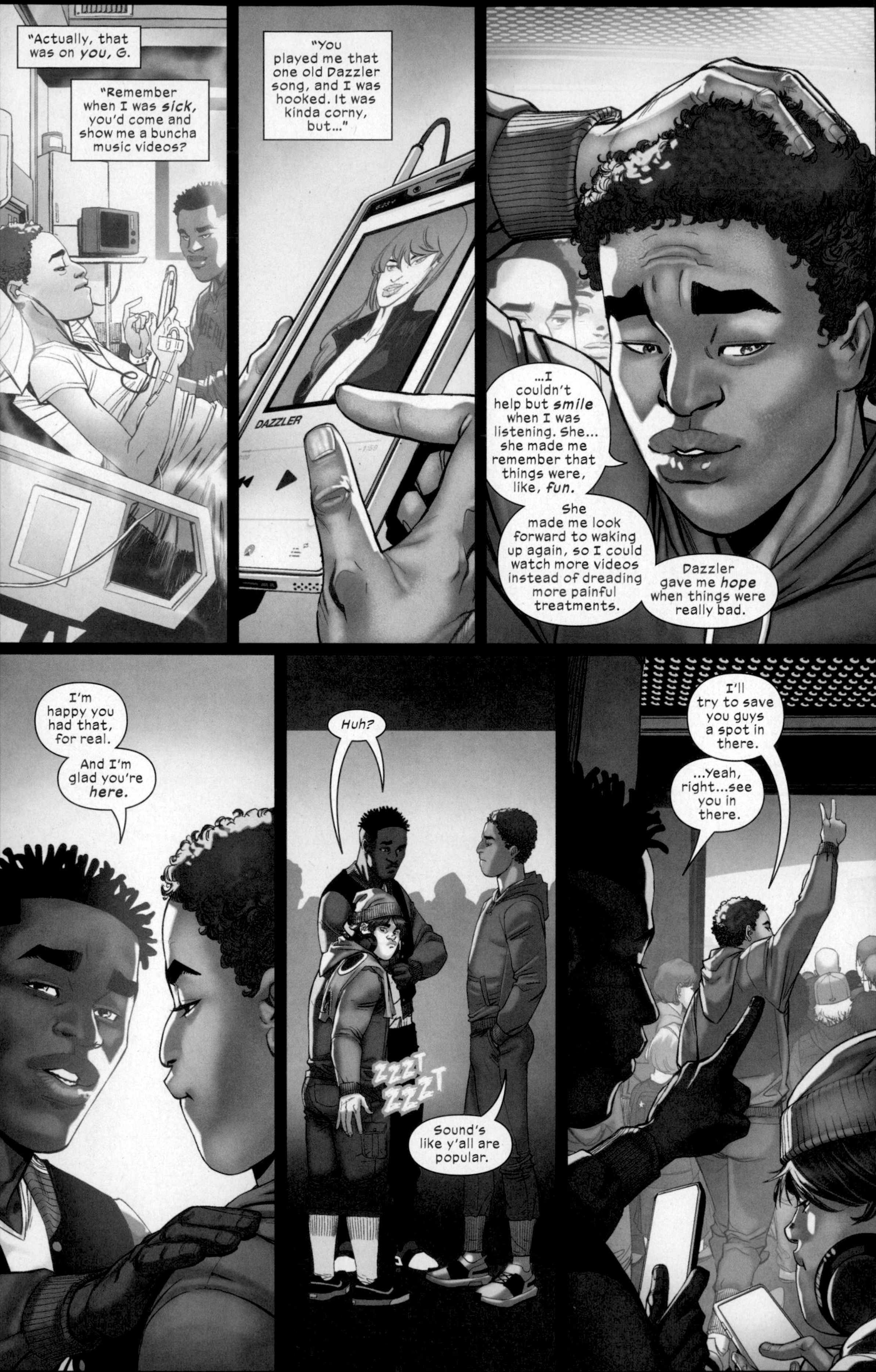
"Actually, that was on you, G.
"Remember when I was sick, you'd come and show me a buncha music videos?
"You played me that one old Dazzler song, and I was hooked. It was kinda corny, but..."
DAZZLER
...I couldn't help but smile when I was listening. She... she made me remember that things were, like, fun.
She made me look forward to waking up again, so I could watch more videos instead of dreading more painful treatments.
Dazzler gave me hope when things were really bad.
I'm happy you had that, for real.
And I'm glad you're here.
Huh?
ZZZT ZZZT
Sound's like y'all are popular.
I'll try to save you guys a spot in there.
...Yeah, right...see you in there.

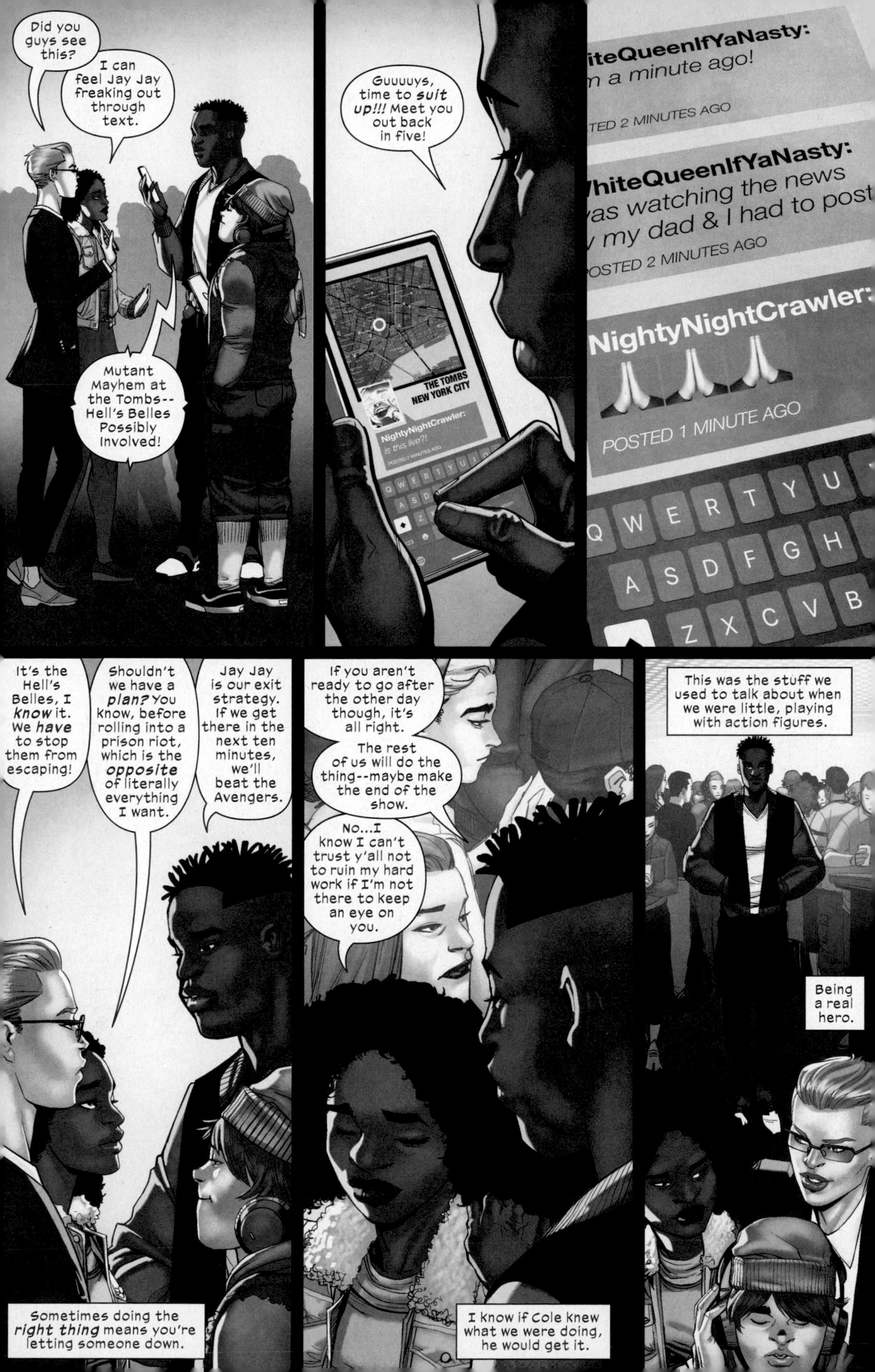

Did you guys see this?
I can feel Jay Jay freaking out through text.
Mutant Mayhem at the Tombs-- Hell's Belles Possibly Involved!
Guuuuys, time to *suit up!!!* Meet you out back in five!
THE TOMBS
NEW YORK CITY
NightyNightCrawler:
is this live?!
iteQueenIfYaNasty:
n a minute ago!
TED 2 MINUTES AGO
WhiteQueenIfYaNasty:
vas watching the news
y my dad & I had to post
OSTED 2 MINUTES AGO
NightyNightCrawler:
POSTED 1 MINUTE AGO
It's the Hell's Belles, I *know* it. We *have* to stop them from escaping!
Shouldn't we have a *plan?* You know, before rolling into a prison riot, which is the *opposite* of literally everything I want.
Jay Jay is our exit strategy. If we get there in the next ten minutes, we'll beat the Avengers.
Sometimes doing the *right thing* means you're letting someone down.
If you aren't ready to go after the other day though, it's all right.
The rest of us will do the thing--maybe make the end of the show.
No...I know I can't trust y'all not to ruin my hard work if I'm not there to keep an eye on you.
I know if Cole knew what we were doing, he would get it.
This was the stuff we used to talk about when we were little, playing with action figures.
Being a real hero.

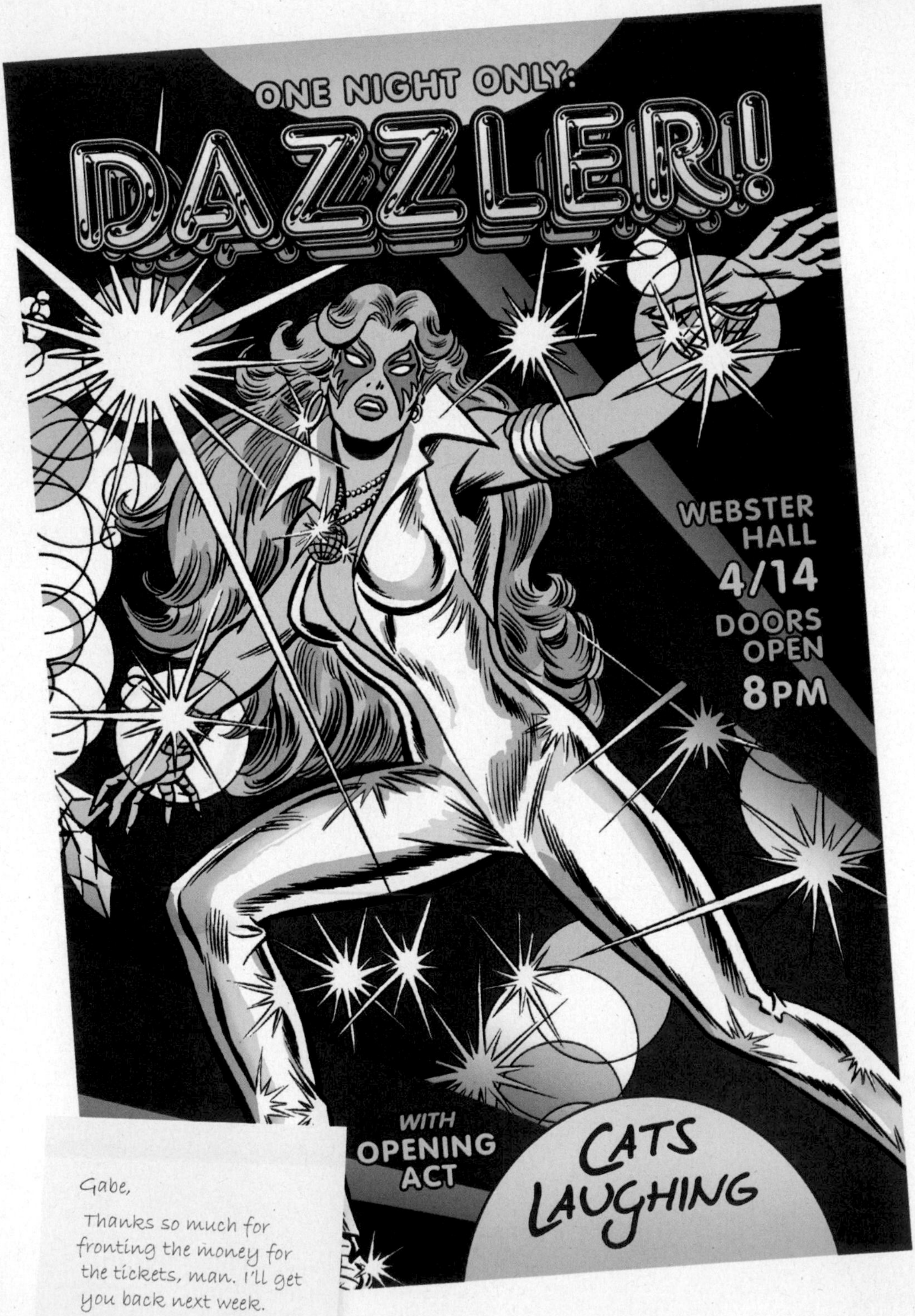
ONE NIGHT ONLY:
DAZZLER!
WEBSTER HALL
4/14
DOORS OPEN
8PM
WITH OPENING ACT
CATS LAUGHING

Gabe,

Thanks so much for fronting the money for the tickets, man. I'll get you back next week.

--Benny

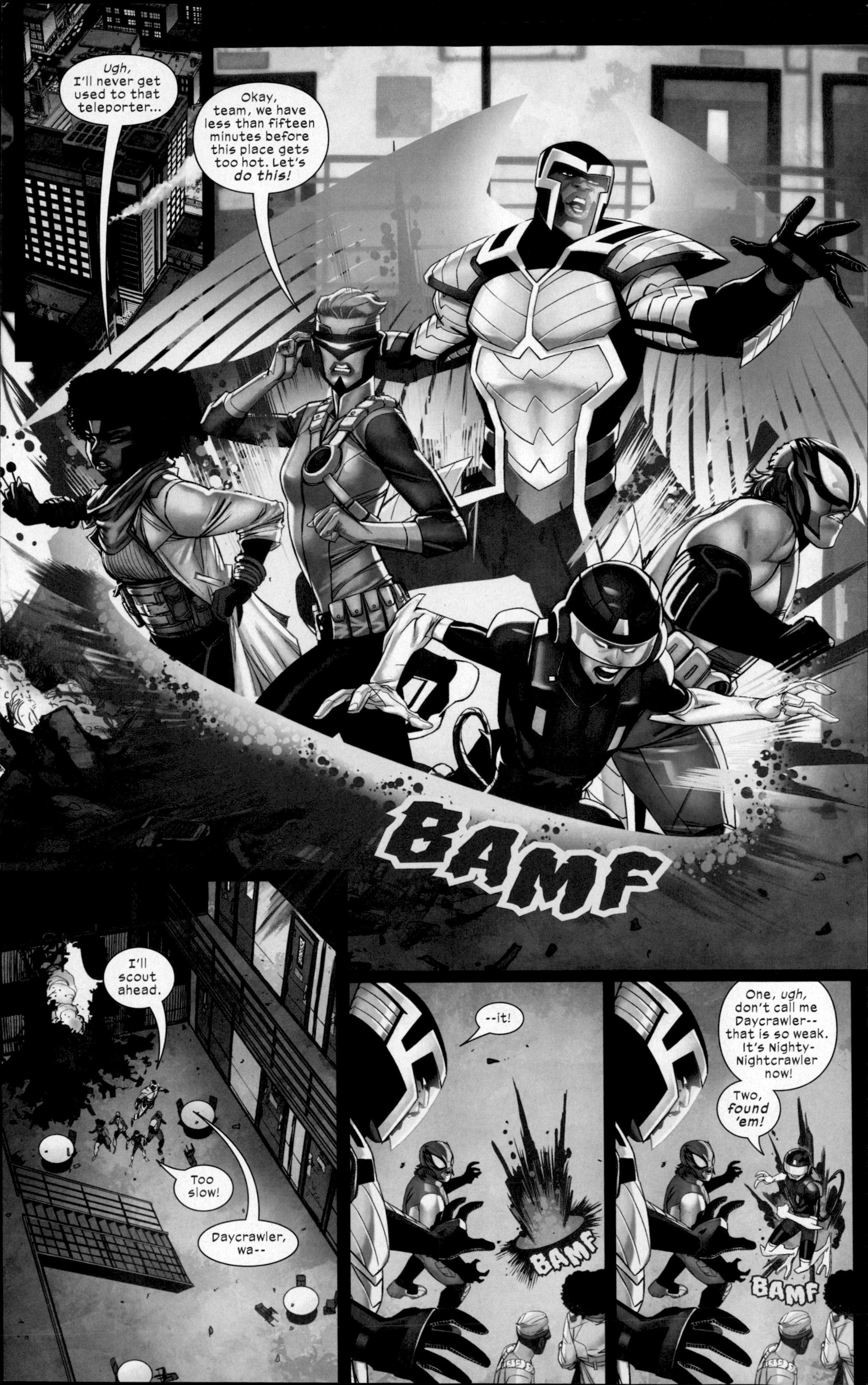
Ugh, I'll never get used to that teleporter...
Okay, team, we have less than fifteen minutes before this place gets too hot. Let's do this!
BAMF
I'll scout ahead.
Too slow!
Daycrawler, wa--
--it!
BAMF
One, ugh, don't call me Daycrawler-- that is so weak. It's Nighty-Nightcrawler now!
Two, found 'em!
BAMF

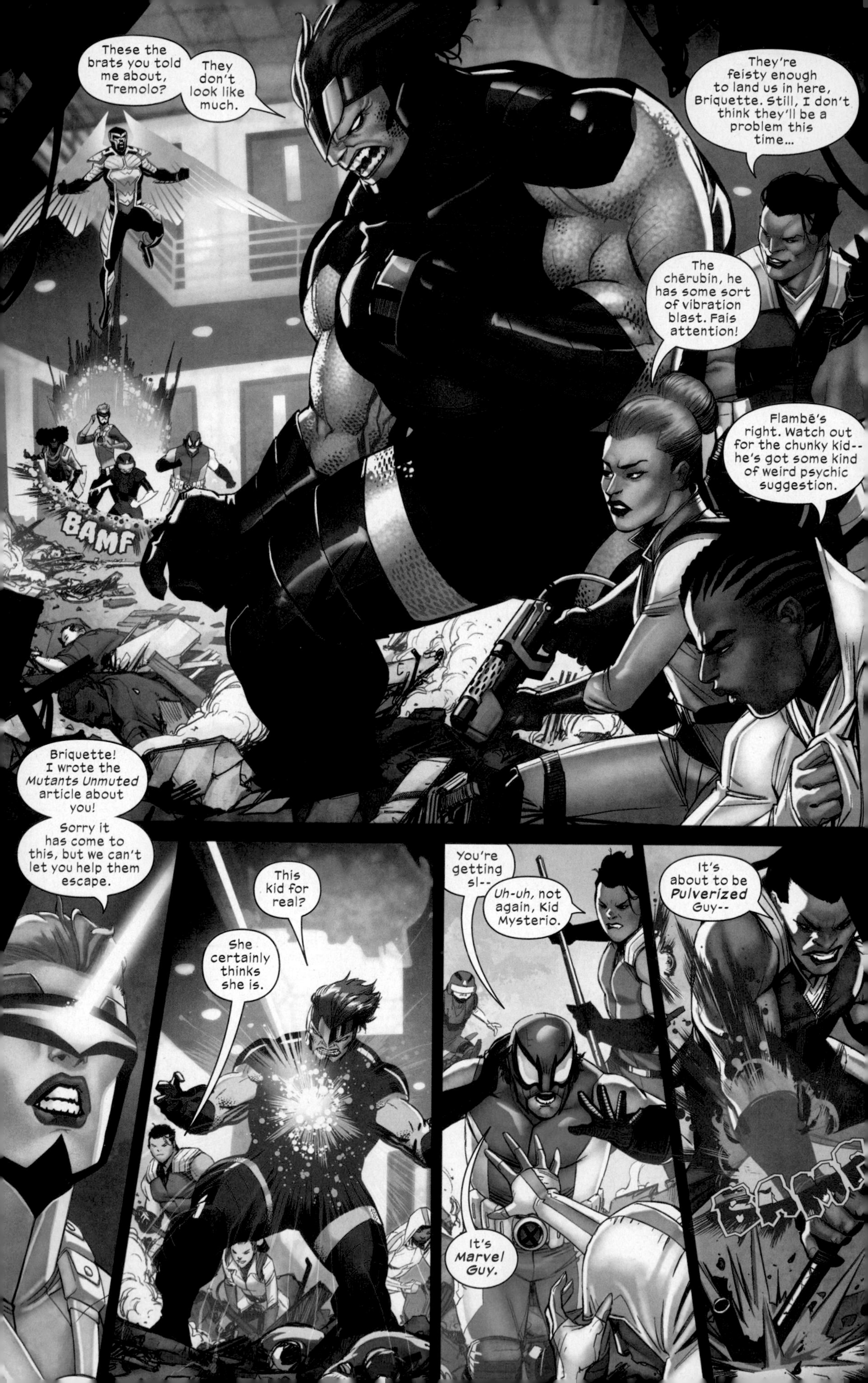
These the brats you told me about, Tremolo?
They don't look like much.
They're feisty enough to land us in here, Briquette. Still, I don't think they'll be a problem this time...
The chērubin, he has some sort of vibration blast. Fais attention!
Flambé's right. Watch out for the chunky kid-- he's got some kind of weird psychic suggestion.
BAMF
Briquette! I wrote the *Mutants Unmuted* article about you!
Sorry it has come to this, but we can't let you help them escape.
This kid for real?
She certainly thinks she is.
You're getting sl--
Uh-uh, not again, Kid Mysterio.
It's *Marvel Guy*.
It's about to be *Pulverized* Guy--

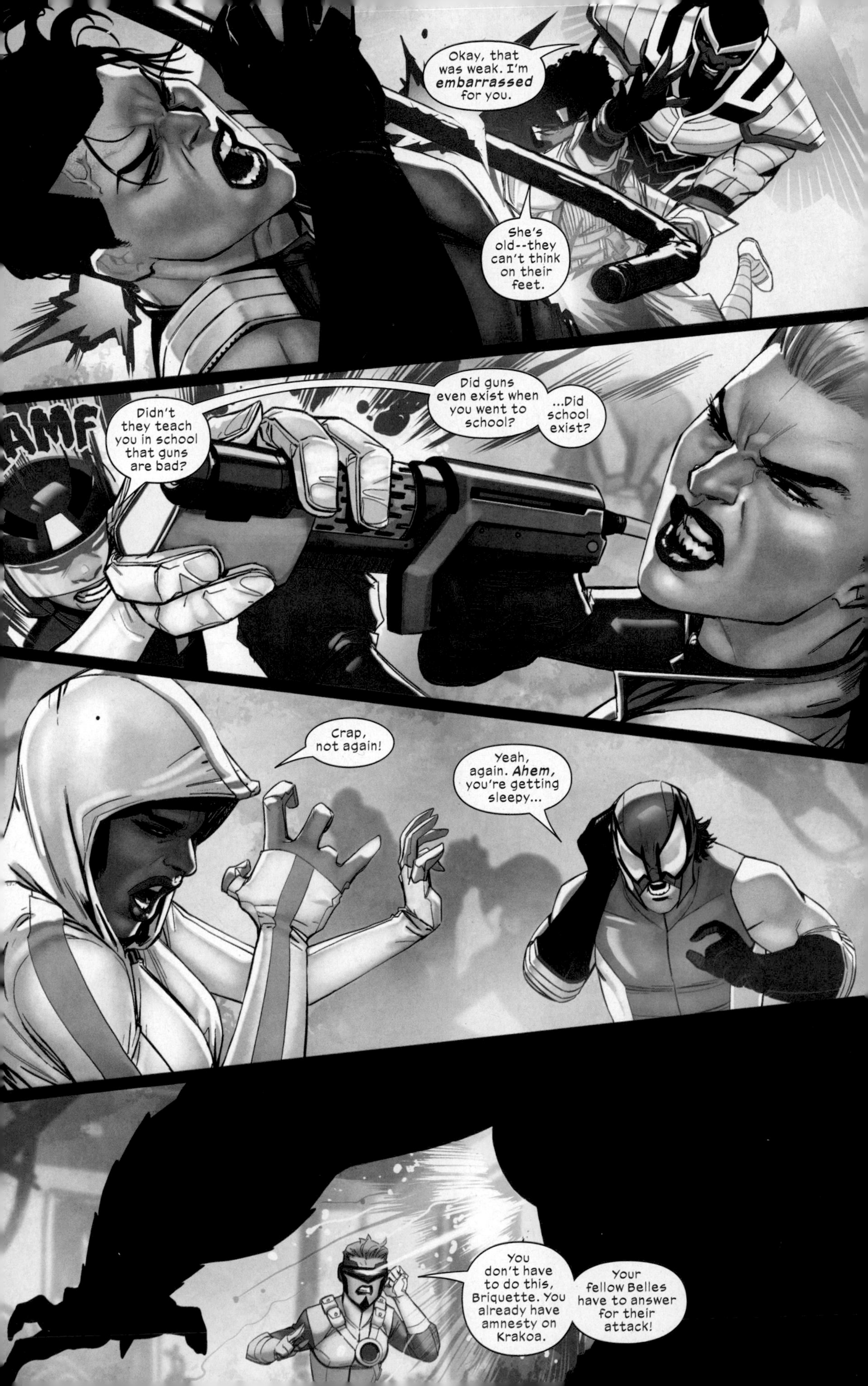
Okay, that was weak. I'm *embarrassed* for you.
She's old--they can't think on their feet.
AMF
Didn't they teach you in school that guns are bad?
Did guns even exist when you went to school?
...Did school exist?
Crap, not again!
Yeah, again. *Ahem,* you're getting sleepy...
You don't have to do this, Briquette. You already have amnesty on Krakoa.
Your fellow Belles have to answer for their attack!

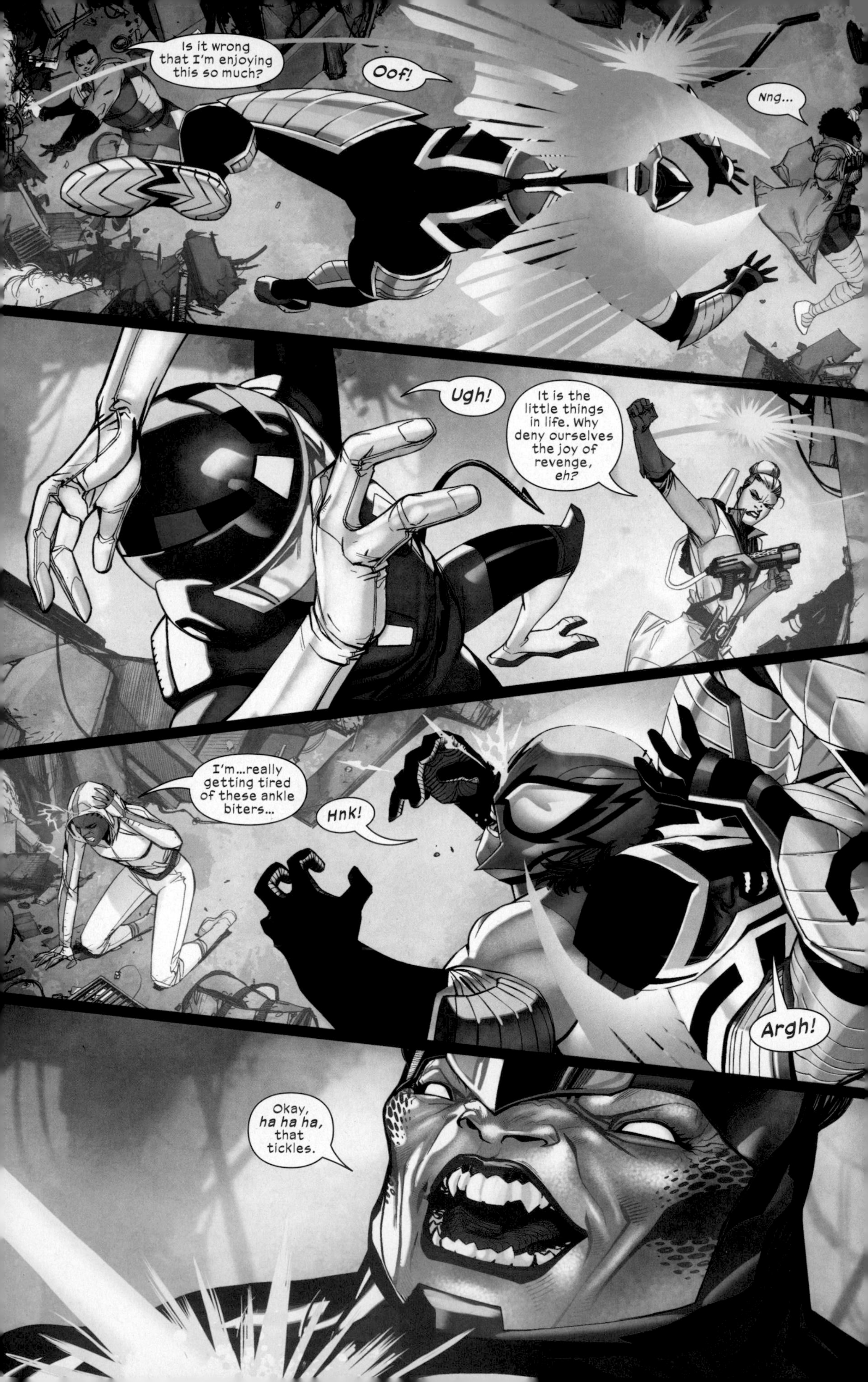
Is it wrong that I'm enjoying this so much?
Oof!
Nng...
Ugh!
It is the little things in life. Why deny ourselves the joy of revenge, eh?
I'm...really getting tired of these ankle biters...
Hnk!
Argh!
Okay, ha ha ha, that tickles.

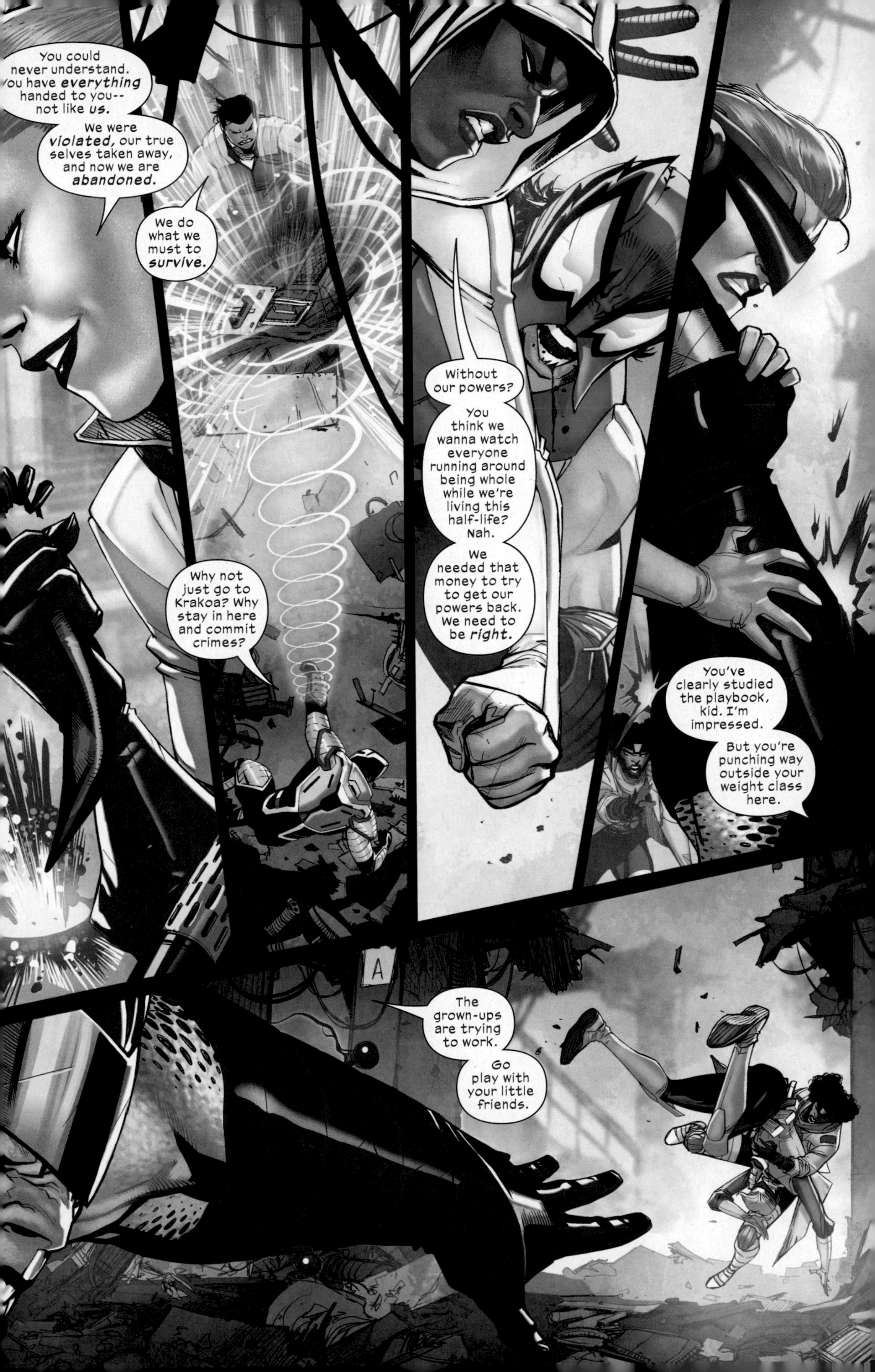

You could never understand. You have everything handed to you-- not like us.
We were violated, our true selves taken away, and now we are abandoned.
We do what we must to survive.
Why not just go to Krakoa? Why stay in here and commit crimes?
Without our powers?
You think we wanna watch everyone running around being whole while we're living this half-life? Nah.
We needed that money to try to get our powers back. We need to be right.
You've clearly studied the playbook, kid. I'm impressed.
But you're punching way outside your weight class here.
A
The grown-ups are trying to work.
Go play with your little friends.

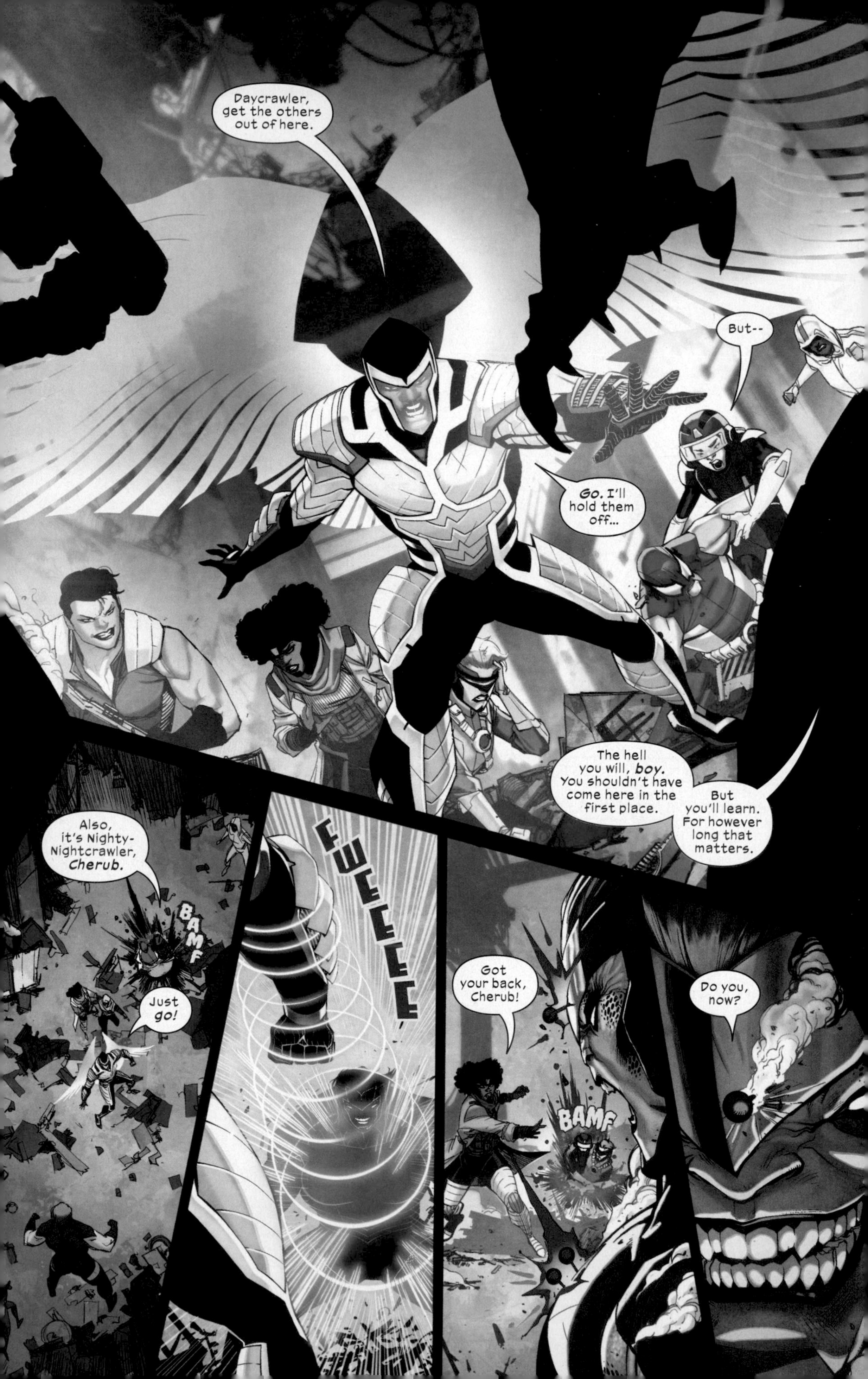
Daycrawler, get the others out of here.
But--
Go. I'll hold them off...
The hell you will, boy. You shouldn't have come here in the first place.
But you'll learn. For however long that matters.
Also, it's Nighty-Nightcrawler, Cherub.
BAMF
Just go!
FWEEEE
Got your back, Cherub!
BAMF
Do you, now?

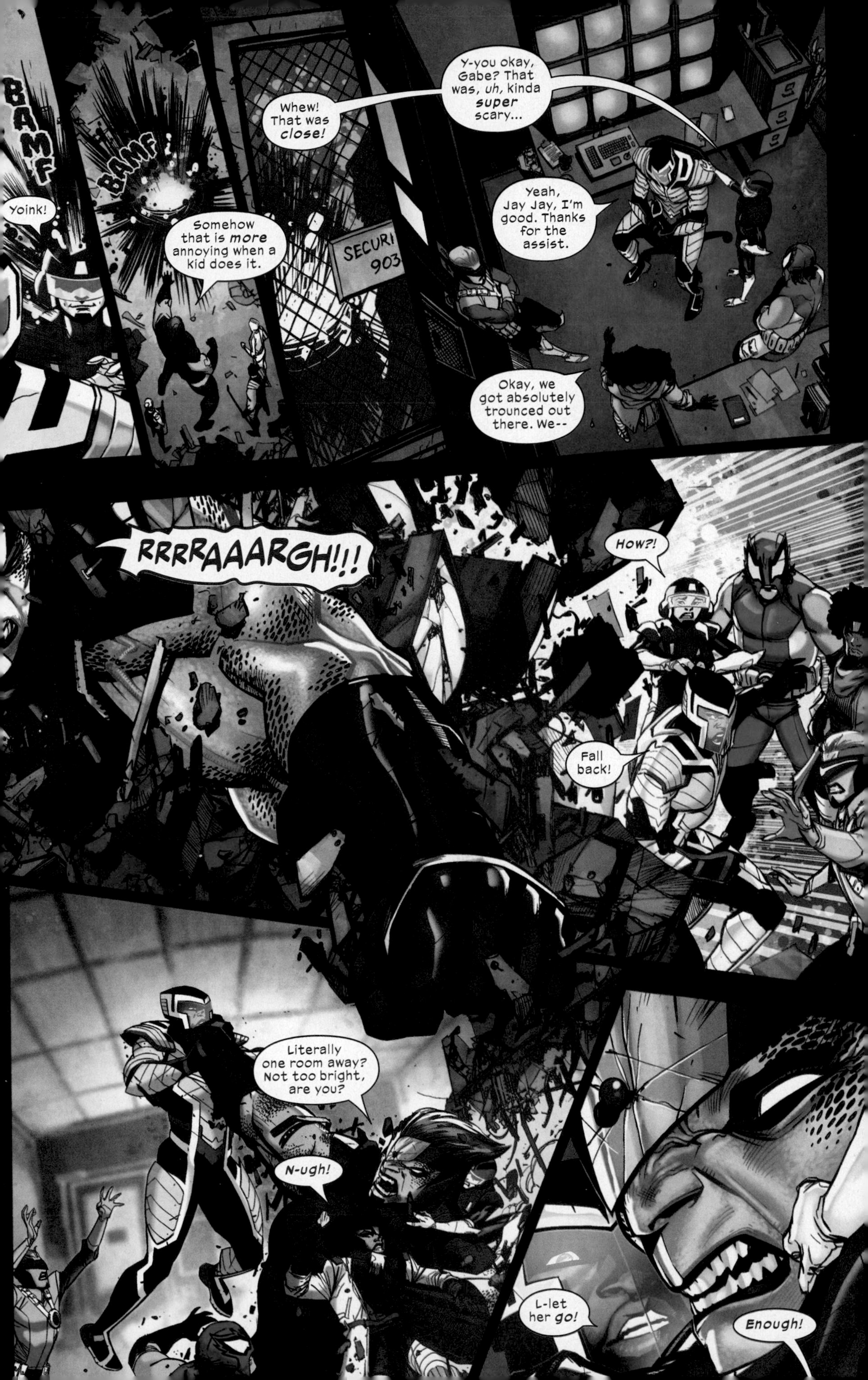
BAMF
Yoink!
BAMF!
Somehow that is more annoying when a kid does it.
SECURI 903
Whew! That was close!
Y-you okay, Gabe? That was, uh, kinda super scary...
Yeah, Jay Jay, I'm good. Thanks for the assist.
Okay, we got absolutely trounced out there. We--
RRRRAAARGH!!!
How?!
Fall back!
Literally one room away? Not too bright, are you?
N-ugh!
L-let her go!
Enough!

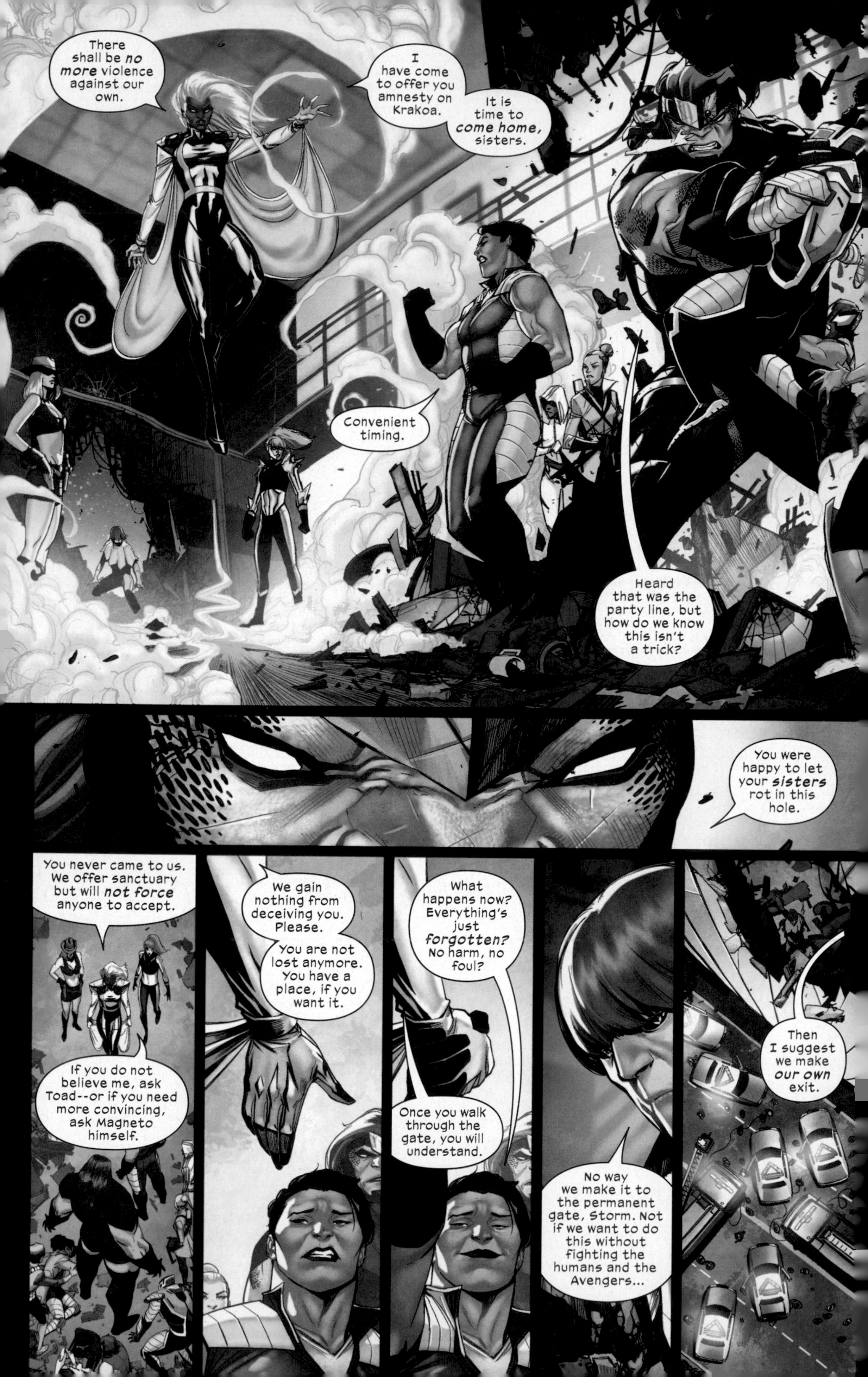
There shall be no more violence against our own.
I have come to offer you amnesty on Krakoa.
It is time to come home, sisters.
Convenient timing.
Heard that was the party line, but how do we know this isn't a trick?
You were happy to let your sisters rot in this hole.
You never came to us. We offer sanctuary but will not force anyone to accept.
If you do not believe me, ask Toad--or if you need more convincing, ask Magneto himself.
We gain nothing from deceiving you. Please.
You are not lost anymore. You have a place, if you want it.
What happens now? Everything's just forgotten? No harm, no foul?
Once you walk through the gate, you will understand.
No way we make it to the permanent gate, Storm. Not if we want to do this without fighting the humans and the Avengers...
Then I suggest we make our own exit.

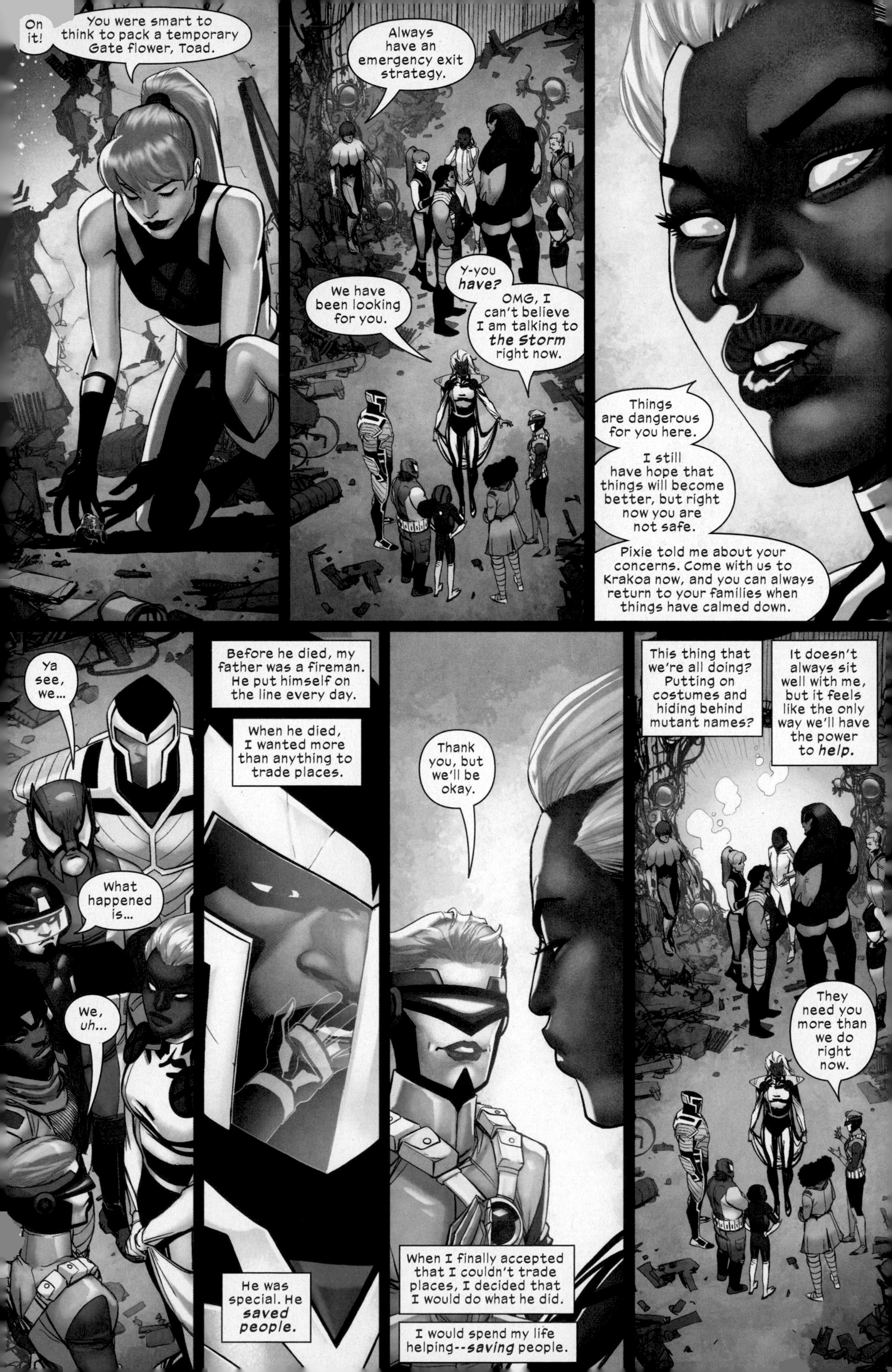
On it!
You were smart to think to pack a temporary Gate flower, Toad.
Always have an emergency exit strategy.
We have been looking for you.
Y-you *have?*
OMG, I can't believe I am talking to *the Storm* right now.
Things are dangerous for you here.
I still have hope that things will become better, but right now you are not safe.
Pixie told me about your concerns. Come with us to Krakoa now, and you can always return to your families when things have calmed down.
Ya see, we...
What happened is...
We, uh...
Before he died, my father was a fireman. He put himself on the line every day.
When he died, I wanted more than anything to trade places.
He was special. He *saved people.*
Thank you, but we'll be okay.
When I finally accepted that I couldn't trade places, I decided that I would do what he did.
I would spend my life helping--*saving* people.
This thing that we're all doing? Putting on costumes and hiding behind mutant names?
It doesn't always sit well with me, but it feels like the only way we'll have the power to *help.*
They need you more than we do right now.

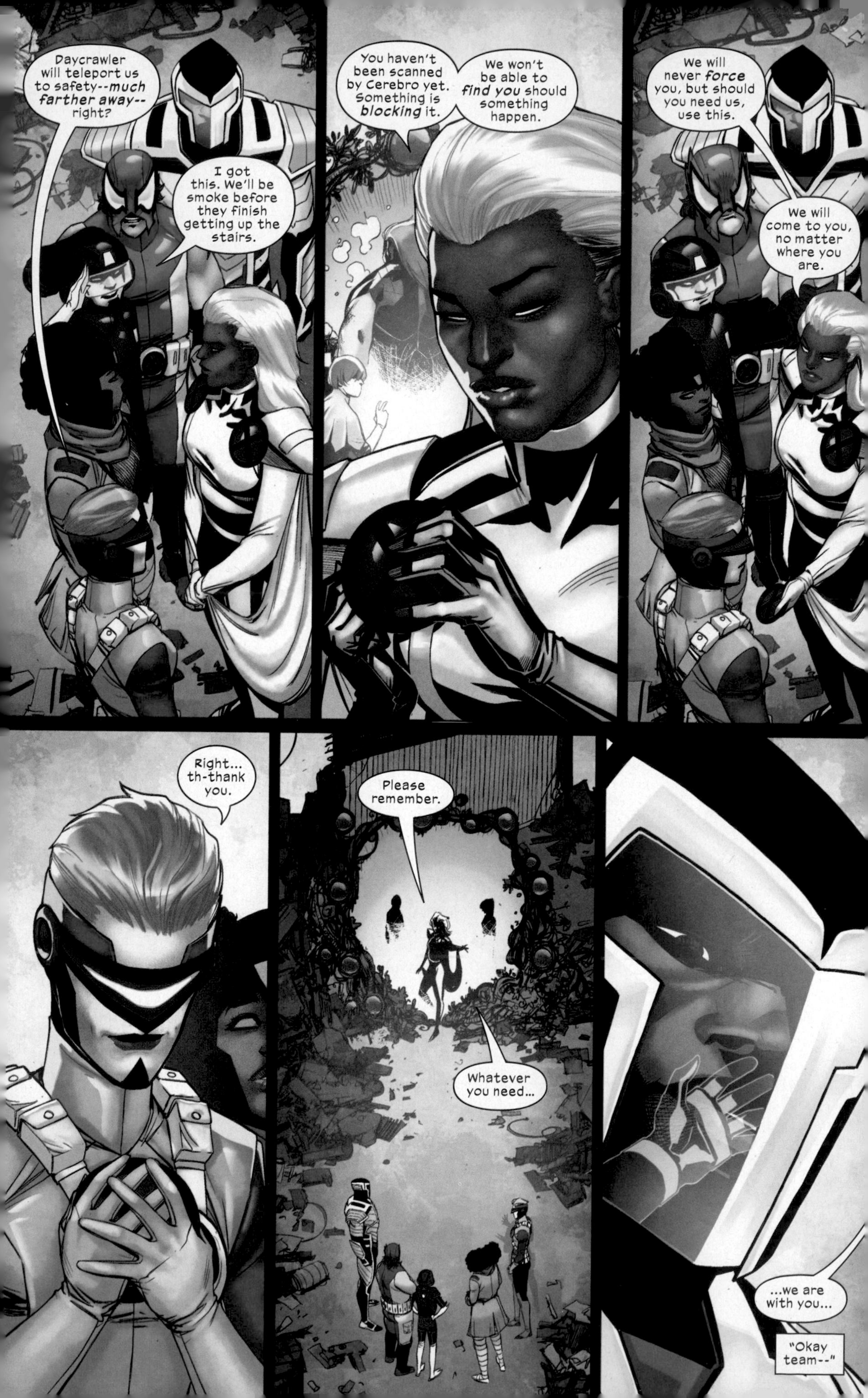

Daycrawler will teleport us to safety--*much farther away*--right?
I got this. We'll be smoke before they finish getting up the stairs.
You haven't been scanned by Cerebro yet. Something is *blocking* it.
We won't be able to *find you* should something happen.
We will never *force* you, but should you need us, use this.
We will come to you, no matter where you are.
Right... th-thank you.
Please remember.
Whatever you need...
...we are with you...
"Okay team--"

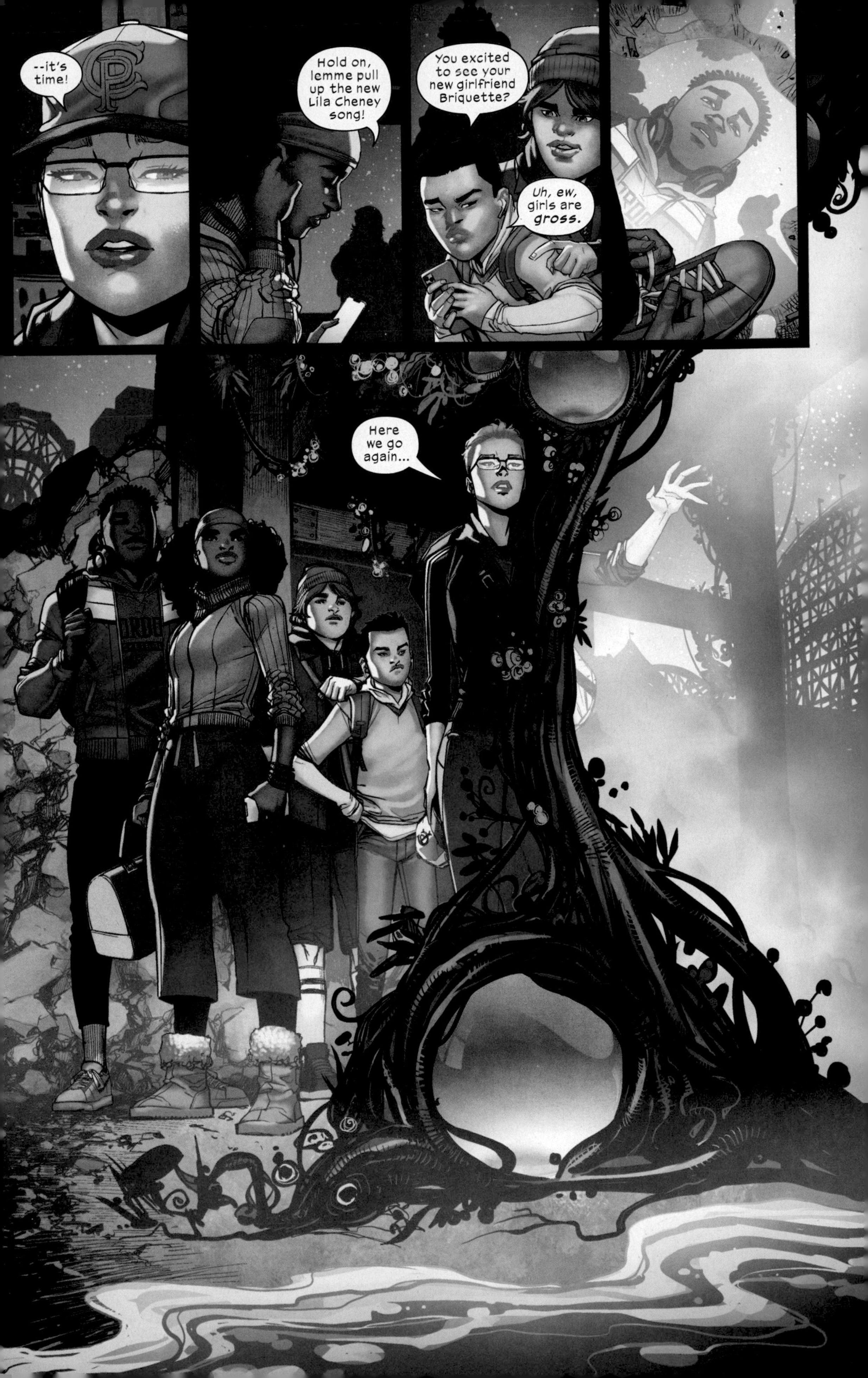
--it's time!
Hold on, lemme pull up the new Lila Cheney song!
You excited to see your new girlfriend Briquette?
Uh, ew, girls are gross.
Here we go again...

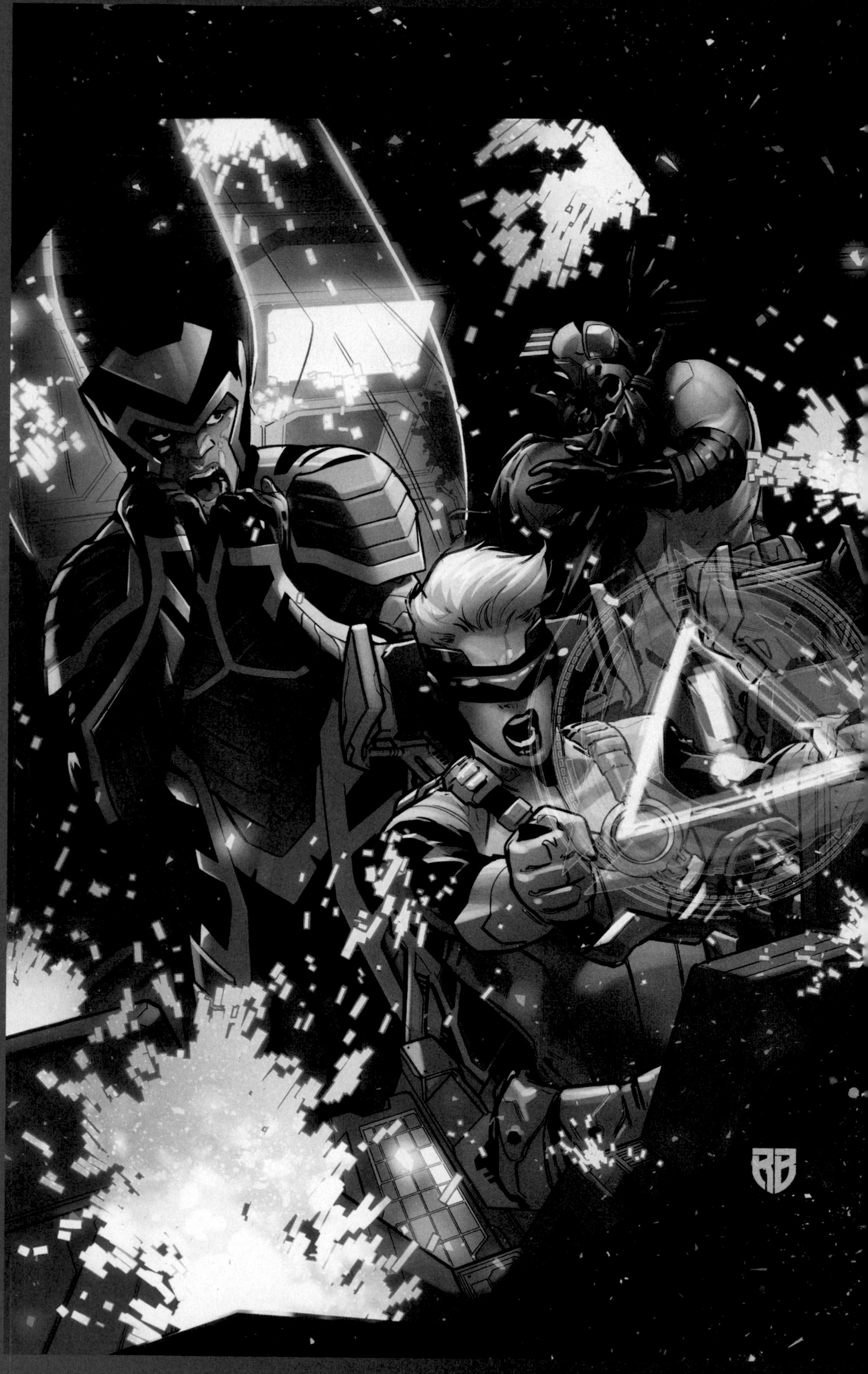

Unusual Dinner Guests

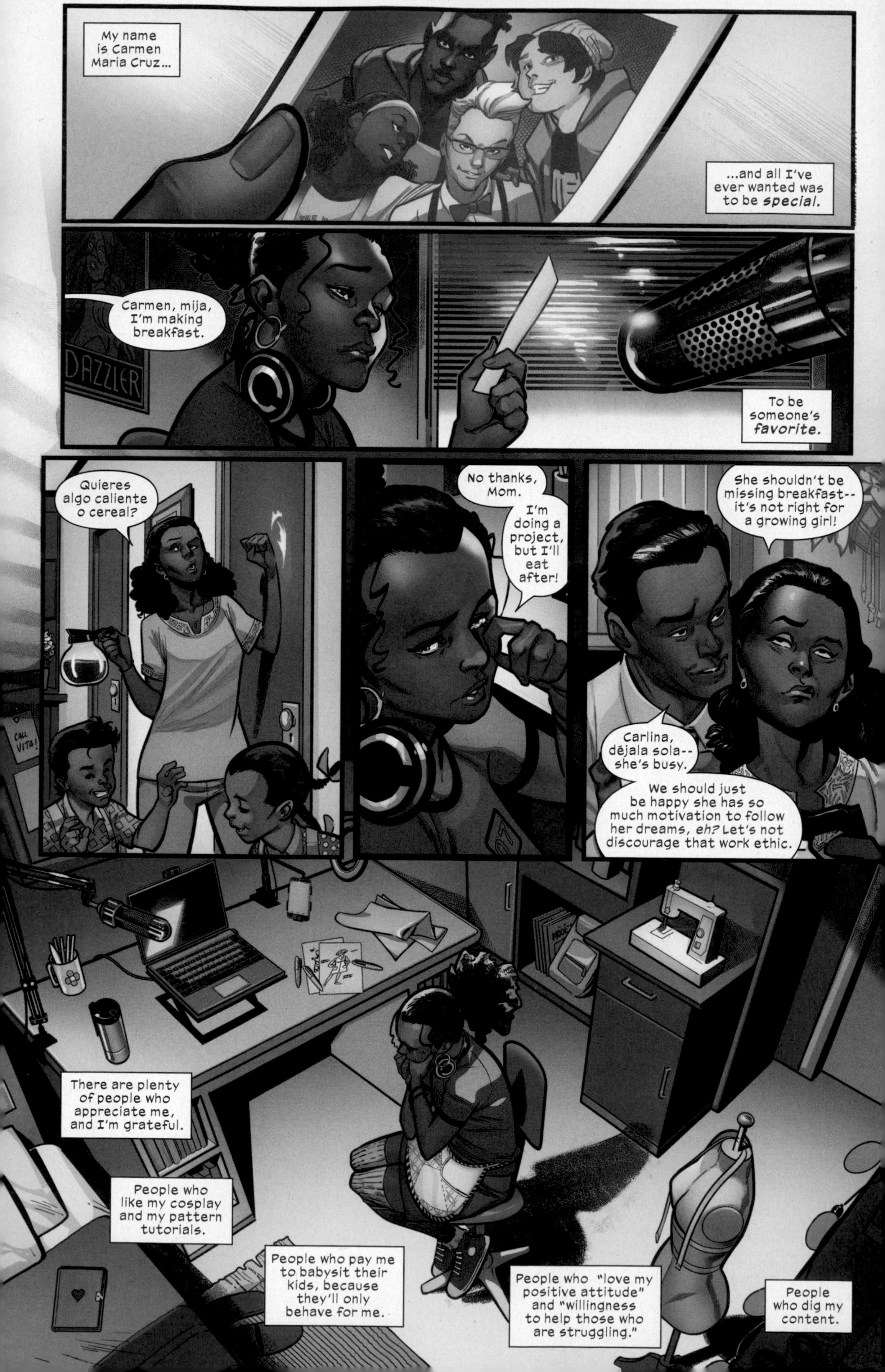
My name is Carmen Maria Cruz...
...and all I've ever wanted was to be *special.*
Carmen, mija, I'm making breakfast.
To be someone's *favorite.*
Quieres algo caliente o cereal?
No thanks, Mom.
I'm doing a project, but I'll eat after!
She shouldn't be missing breakfast-- it's not right for a growing girl!
Carlina, déjala sola-- she's busy.
We should just be happy she has so much motivation to follow her dreams, *eh?* Let's not discourage that work ethic.
There are plenty of people who appreciate me, and I'm grateful.
People who like my cosplay and my pattern tutorials.
People who pay me to babysit their kids, because they'll only behave for me.
People who "love my positive attitude" and "willingness to help those who are struggling."
People who dig my content.

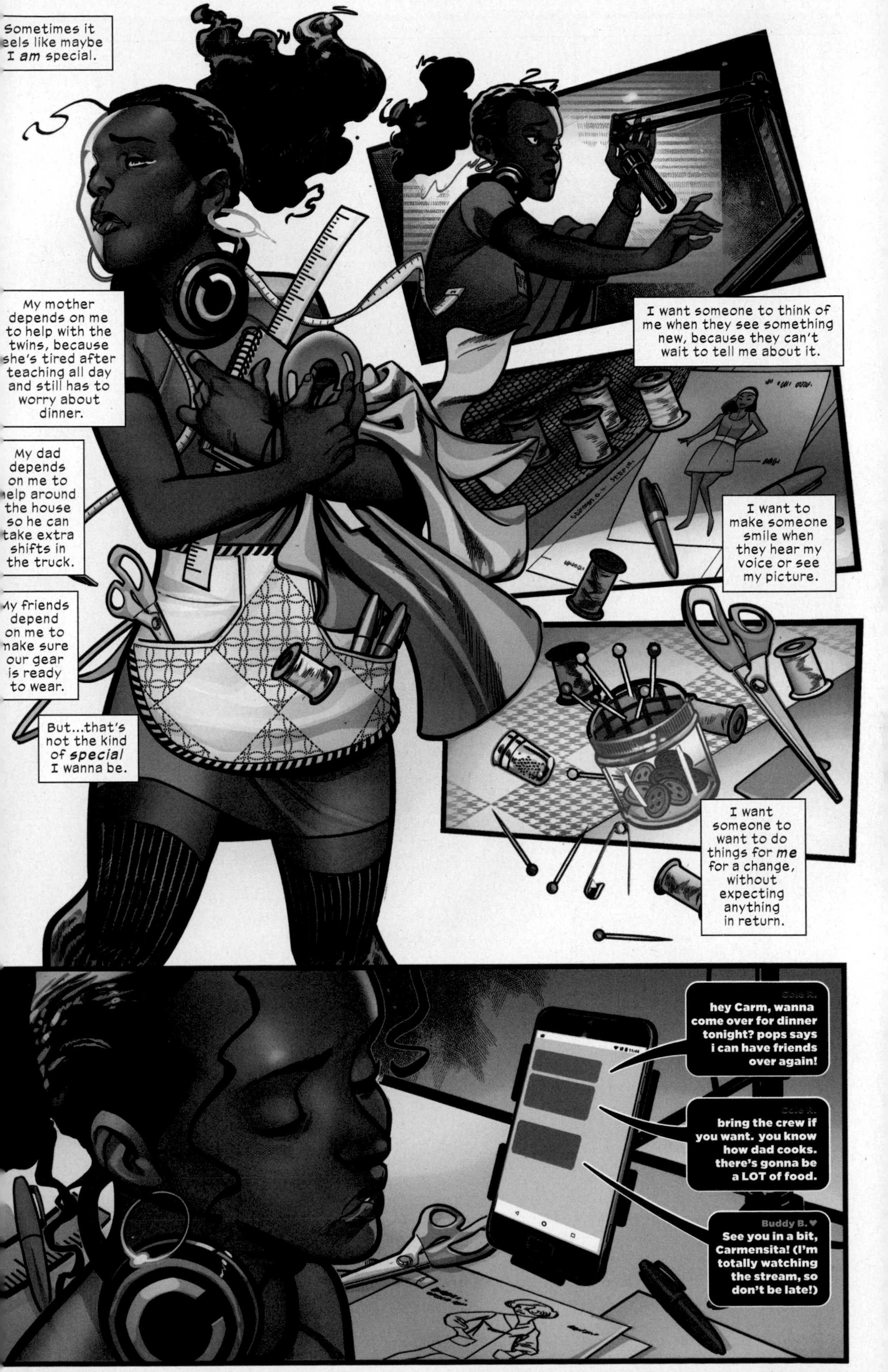
Sometimes it eels like maybe I *am* special.
My mother depends on me to help with the twins, because she's tired after teaching all day and still has to worry about dinner.
My dad depends on me to elp around the house so he can take extra shifts in the truck.
My friends depend on me to make sure our gear is ready to wear.
But...that's not the kind of *special* I wanna be.
I want someone to think of me when they see something new, because they can't wait to tell me about it.
I want to make someone smile when they hear my voice or see my picture.
I want someone to want to do things for *me* for a change, without expecting anything in return.
Cole R.
hey Carm, wanna come over for dinner tonight? pops says i can have friends over again!
Cole R.
bring the crew if you want. you know how dad cooks. there's gonna be a LOT of food.
Buddy B. ♥
See you in a bit, Carmensita! (I'm totally watching the stream, so don't be late!)

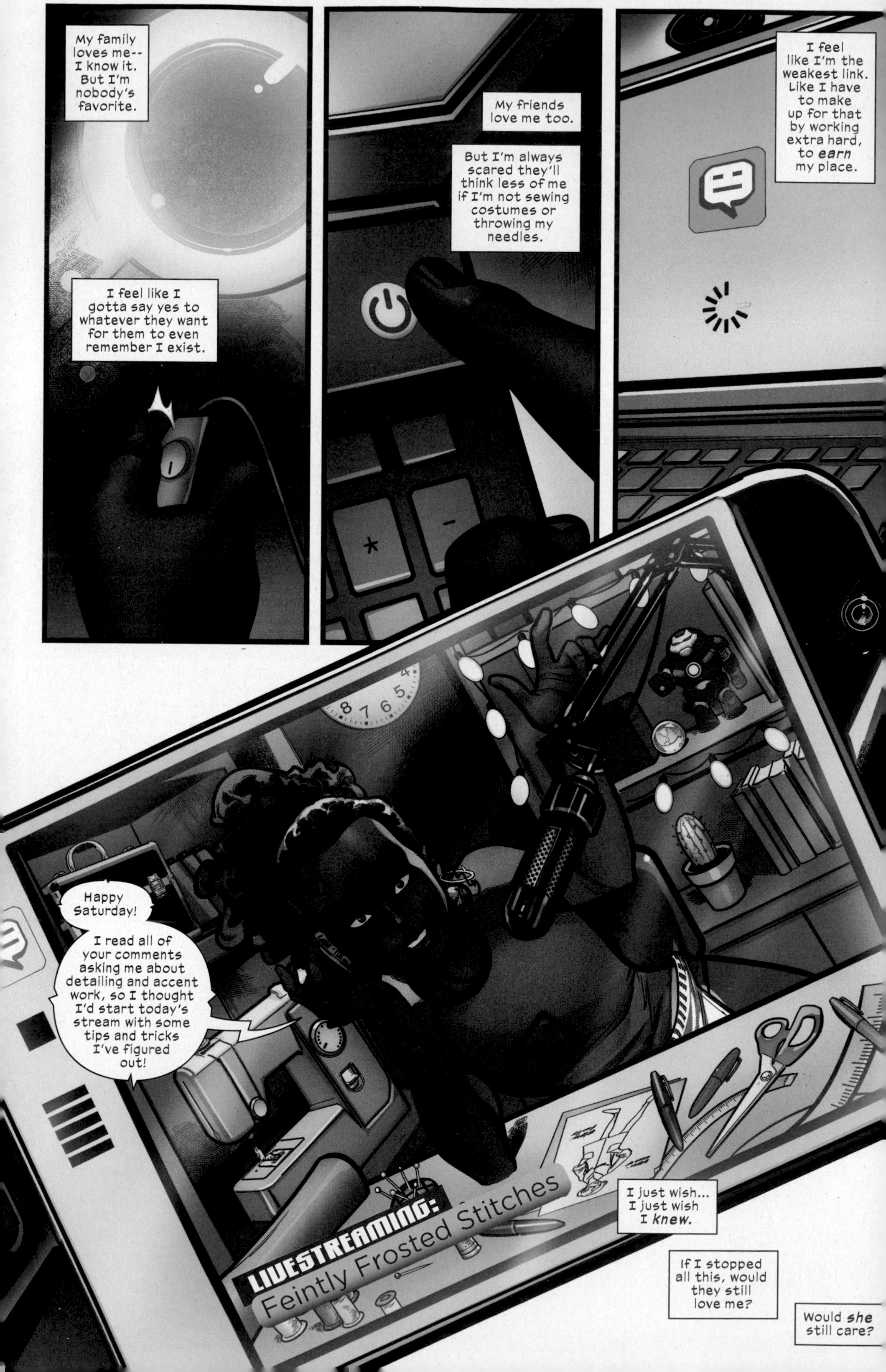
My family loves me-- I know it. But I'm nobody's favorite.
I feel like I gotta say yes to whatever they want for them to even remember I exist.
My friends love me too.
But I'm always scared they'll think less of me if I'm not sewing costumes or throwing my needles.
I feel like I'm the weakest link. Like I have to make up for that by working extra hard, to *earn* my place.
Happy Saturday!
I read all of your comments asking me about detailing and accent work, so I thought I'd start today's stream with some tips and tricks I've figured out!
LIVESTREAMING:
Feintly Frosted Stitches
I just wish... I just wish I *knew*.
If I stopped all this, would they still love me?
Would *she* still care?

X-Change

Shop ▼ | Search

X-Change > Costumes > Headgear > Magneto >

Broken Helmet. Six Pieces Recovered from Attack on NYC

PRICE:

$500.00 USD OR **BEST OFFER**

SHIPPING:

$19.99 USD

DESCRIPTION:

Pre-Krakoa! Authentic artifact from the Master of Magnetism's attack on New York City, damaged in battle with the X-Men! Six pieces from Magneto's iconic helmet, as photographed. The helmet/metal repels telepathic attack/probes!

BUY

* * [SOLD TO USER: FeintlyFrostedStitches] * * *

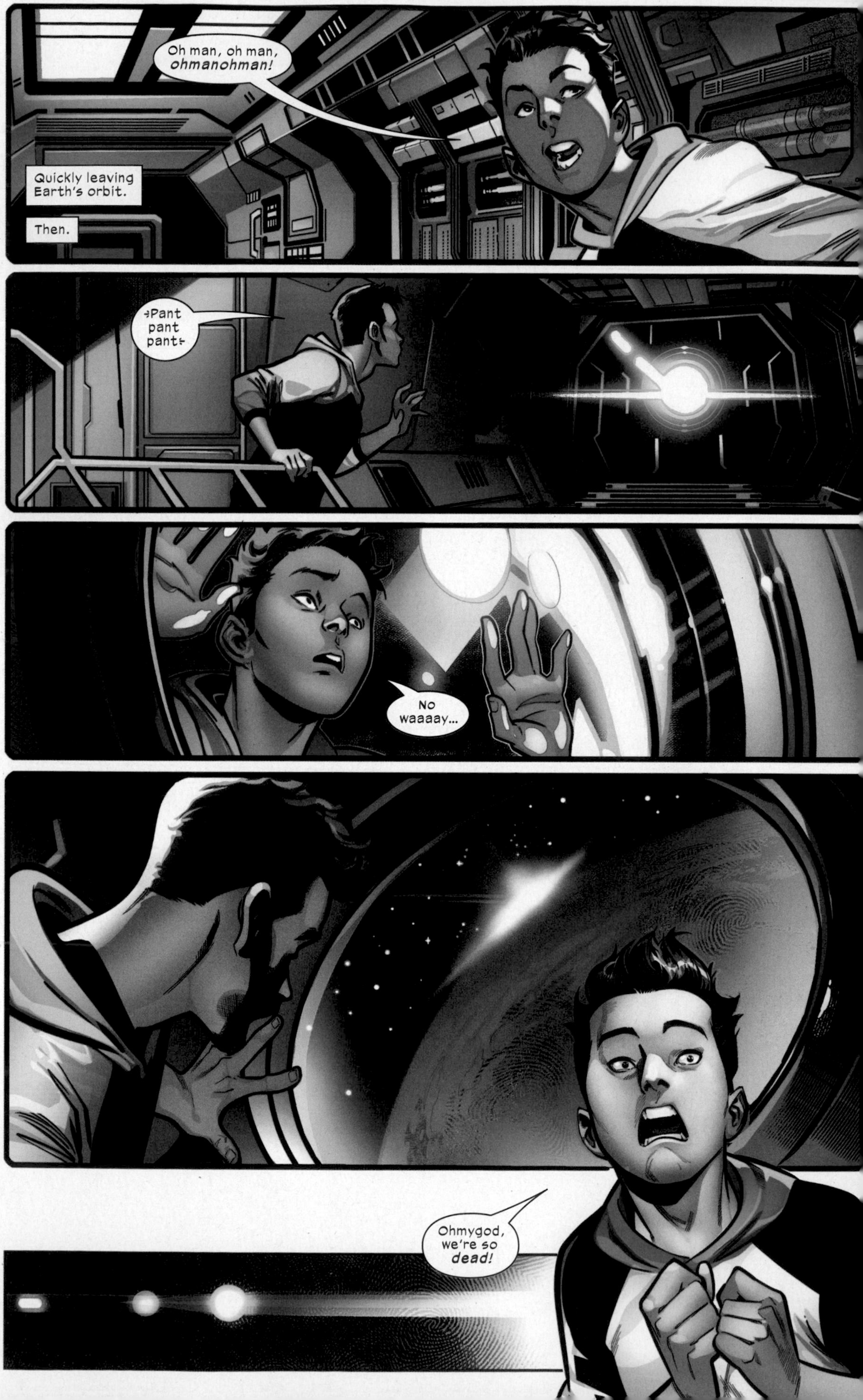
Quickly leaving Earth's orbit.
Then.
Oh man, oh man, *ohmanohman!*
⸗Pant pant pant⸗
No waaaay...
Ohmygod, we're so *dead!*

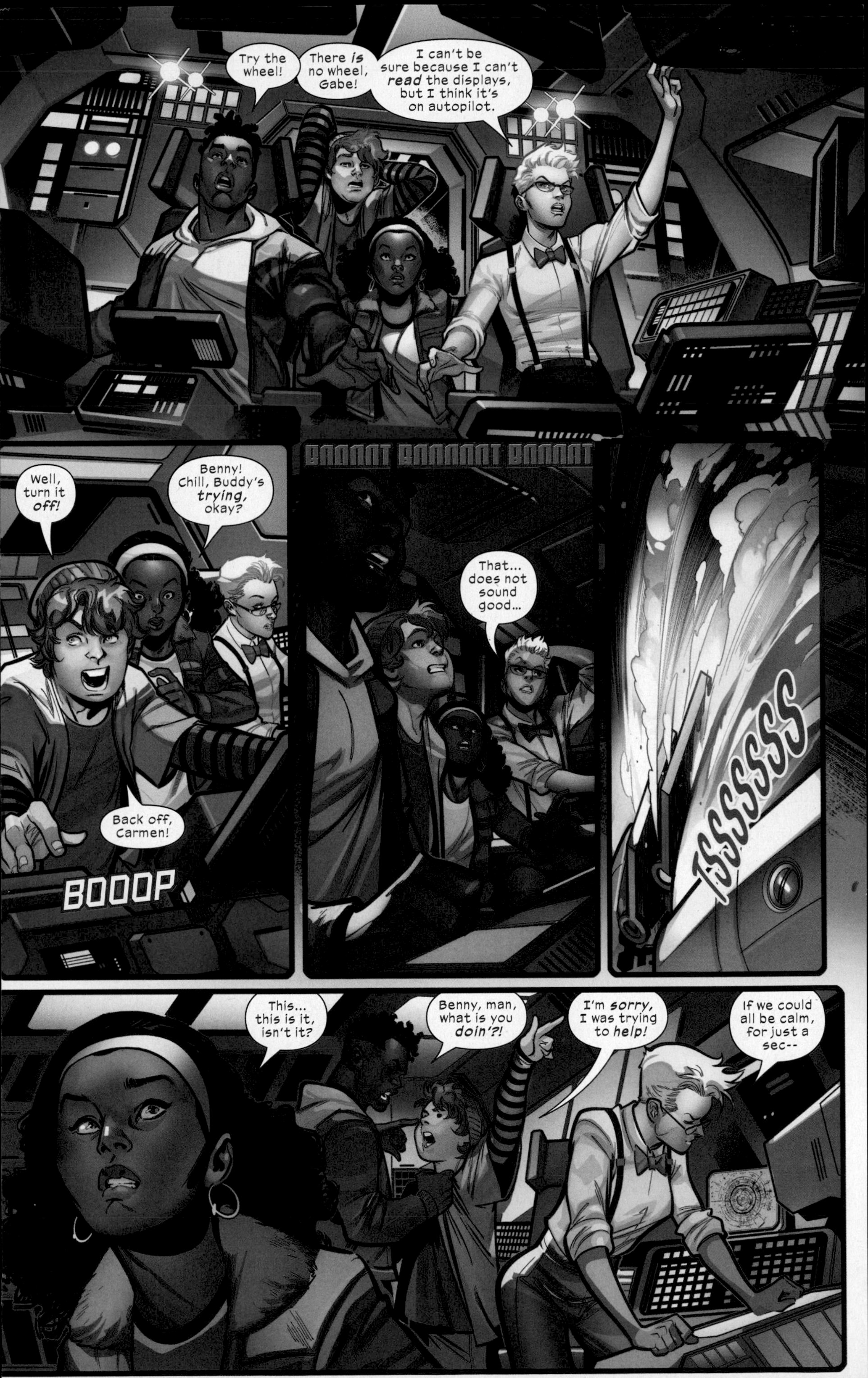
Try the wheel!
There *is* no wheel, Gabe!
I can't be sure because I can't *read* the displays, but I think it's on autopilot.
Well, turn it *off!*
Benny! Chill, Buddy's *trying,* okay?
Back off, Carmen!
BOOOP
BAAAAT BAAAAAT BAAAAT
That... does not sound good...
TSSSSSSS
This... this is it, isn't it?
Benny, man, what is you *doin'?!*
I'm *sorry,* I was trying to *help!*
If we could all be calm, for just a sec--

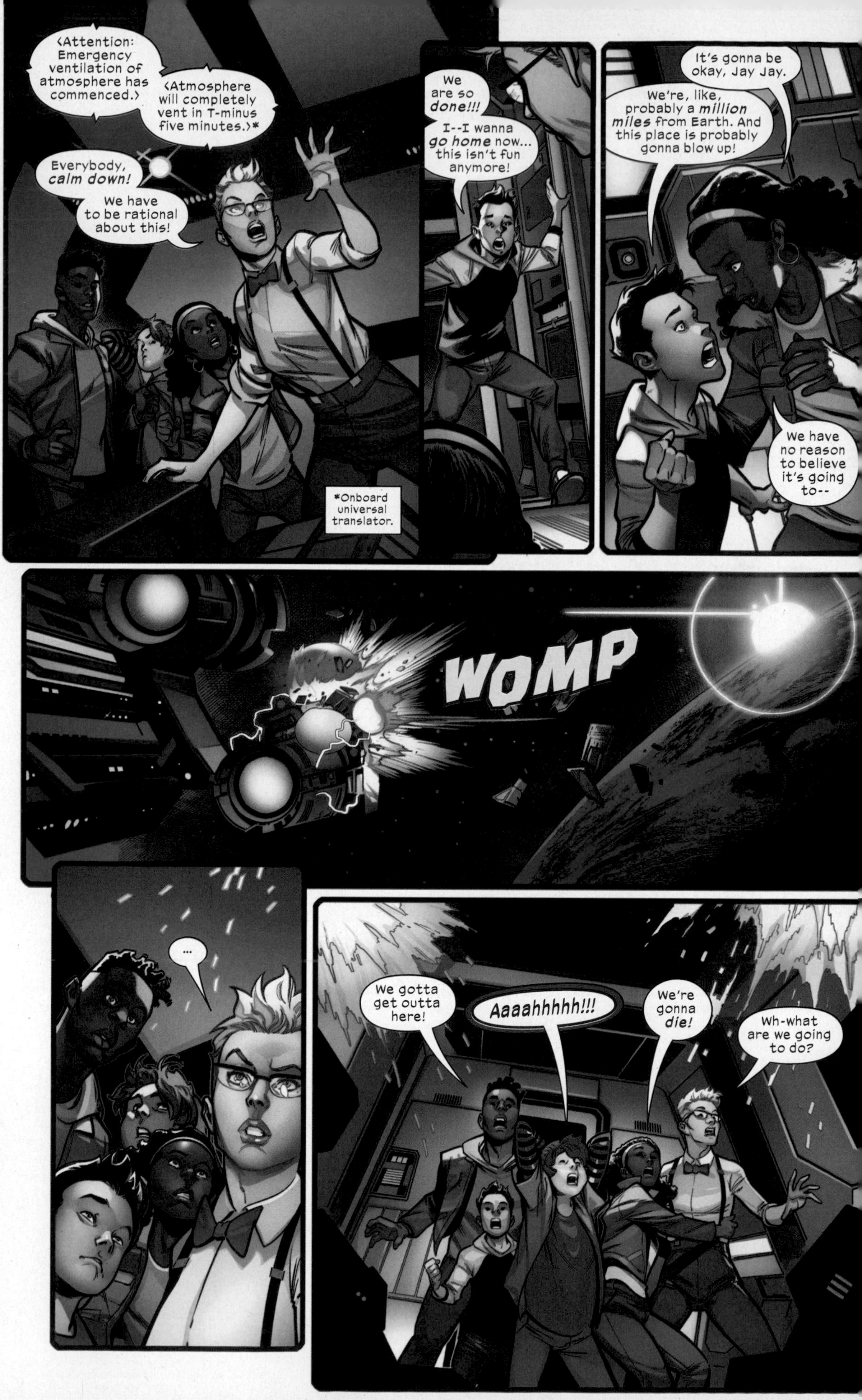
<Attention: Emergency ventilation of atmosphere has commenced.>
<Atmosphere will completely vent in T-minus five minutes.>*
Everybody, calm down!
We have to be rational about this!
*Onboard universal translator.
We are so done!!!
I--I wanna go home now... this isn't fun anymore!
It's gonna be okay, Jay Jay.
We're, like, probably a million miles from Earth. And this place is probably gonna blow up!
We have no reason to believe it's going to--
WOMP
...
We gotta get outta here!
Aaaahhhhh!!!
We're gonna die!
Wh-what are we going to do?

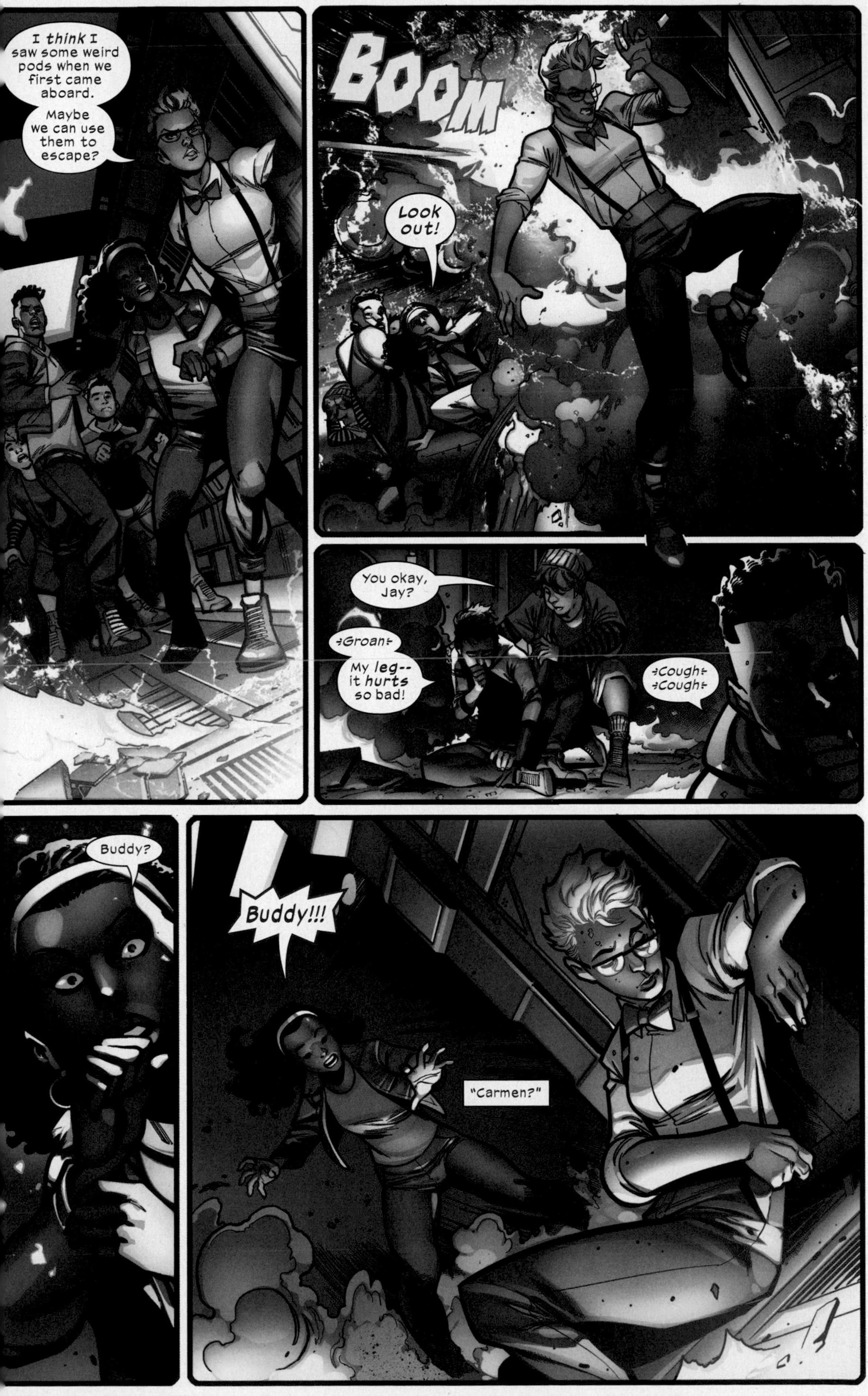

I think I saw some weird pods when we first came aboard.
Maybe we can use them to escape?
BOOM
Look out!
You okay, Jay?
Groan
My leg-- it hurts so bad!
Cough Cough
Buddy?
Buddy!!!
"Carmen?"

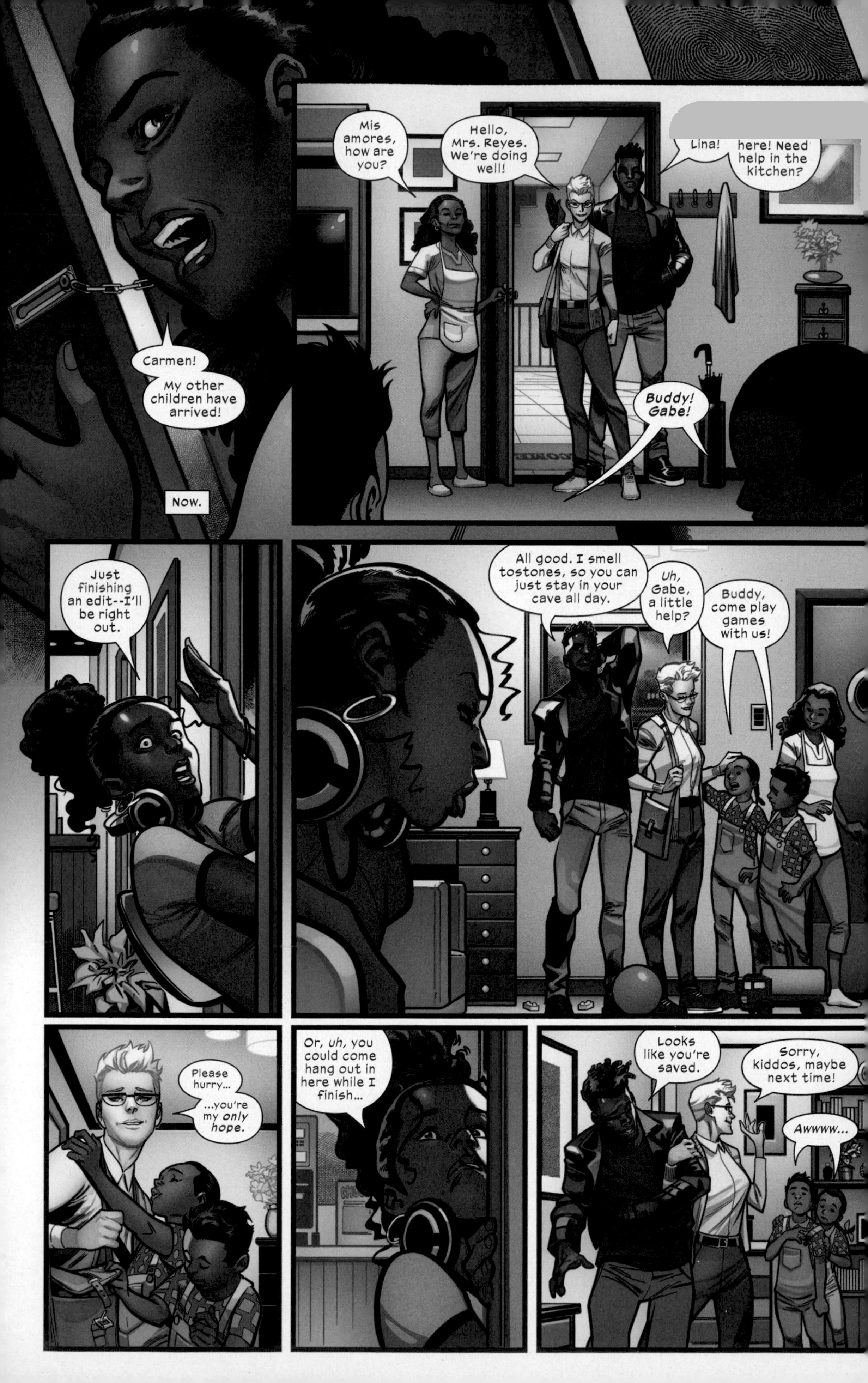
Carmen!
My other children have arrived!
Now.
Mis amores, how are you?
Hello, Mrs. Reyes. We're doing well!
Lina!
here! Need help in the kitchen?
Buddy! Gabe!
Just finishing an edit--I'll be right out.
All good. I smell tostones, so you can just stay in your cave all day.
Uh, Gabe, a little help?
Buddy, come play games with us!
Please hurry...
...you're my only hope.
Or, uh, you could come hang out in here while I finish...
Looks like you're saved.
Sorry, kiddos, maybe next time!
Awwww...

FEINTLY FROSTED STITCHES UPDATE

DETAILS AND ACCENTS

I've gotten a bunch of comments praising (thank you!!!) the accents on some of my more recent pieces and asking all kinds of questions about my process.

I decided to do a live Q and A on my stream and break down my thinking on the issue. Check out the video.

I think something that isn't discussed enough in conversations about cosplay -- and making your own clothes from patterns in general -- is that the details that make a piece unique are what makes a piece shine.

*** TO BE CLEAR: There is NOTHING wrong with replicating things exactly or with wanting something to be exactly like the original! ***

BUT, that being said, I see a lot of y'all talking about reproducing things exactly -- how that's what makes a piece valid. And while that works for some people, I think the strength of DIY is that makers put themselves in their work! The little details and accents that speak to you? That set your piece apart? That's what makes it special!

The reason I got into this wasn't just because learning to repair and repurpose old clothes is cheaper than buying (though that is important) or because I wanted to make money (I wish!!!), but also because sewing and cosplay give people a place to express themselves and to play. Sometimes this is the only way folks can be completely open -- to be themselves -- and I want to encourage that!

SO! I hope that anyone reading this who may have been nervous to put themselves into their work gets a boost in confidence. You are what makes your work special! Celebrate that!

And to folks who were asking what my next pattern is/when I'm dropping it, watch this space!

[Hint: Drip worthy of a queen! :3]

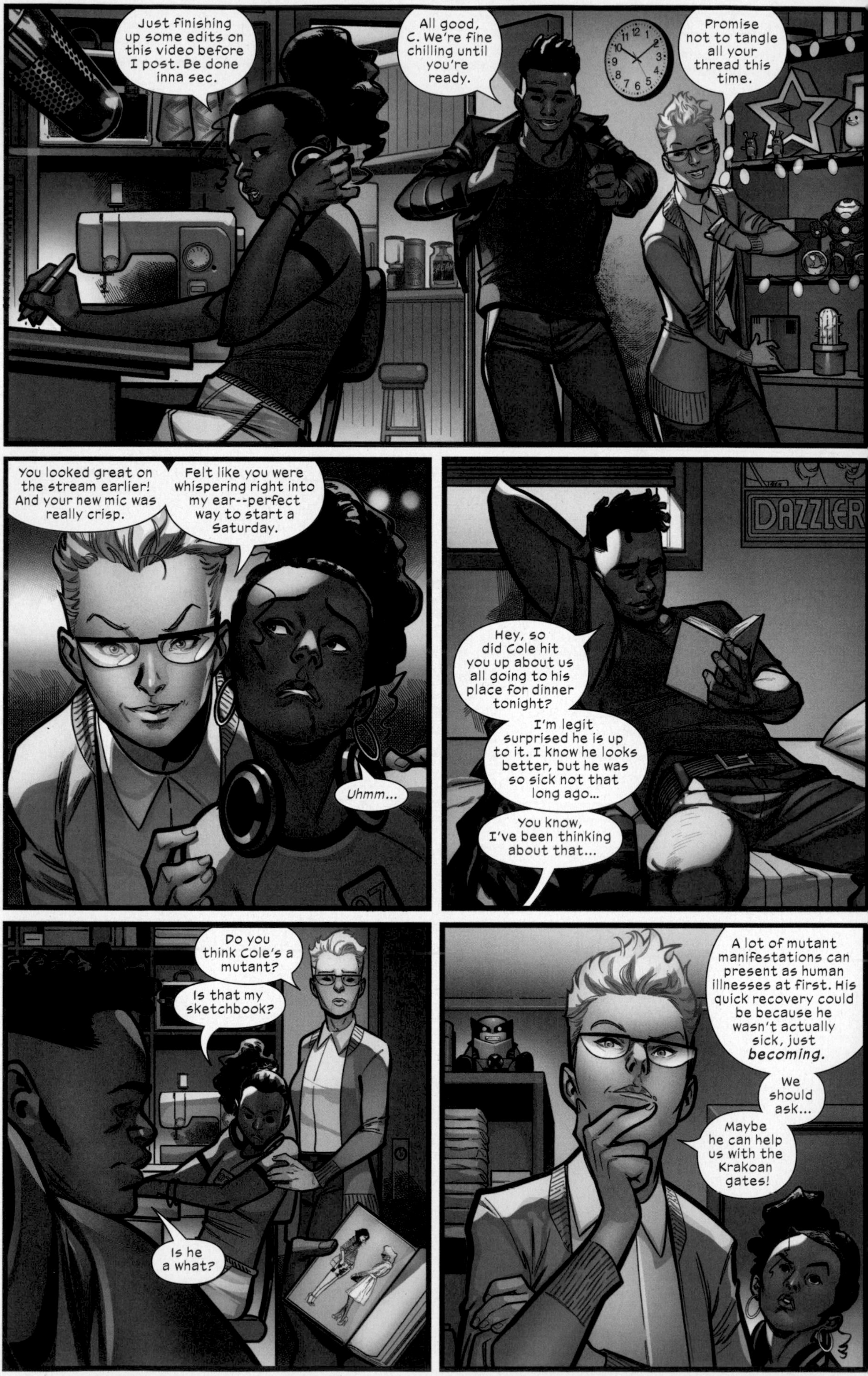
Just finishing up some edits on this video before I post. Be done inna sec.
All good, C. We're fine chilling until you're ready.
Promise not to tangle all your thread this time.
You looked great on the stream earlier! And your new mic was really crisp.
Felt like you were whispering right into my ear--perfect way to start a Saturday.
Uhmm...
DAZZLER
Hey, so did Cole hit you up about us all going to his place for dinner tonight?
I'm legit surprised he is up to it. I know he looks better, but he was so sick not that long ago...
You know, I've been thinking about that...
Do you think Cole's a mutant?
Is that my sketchbook?
Is he a what?
A lot of mutant manifestations can present as human illnesses at first. His quick recovery could be because he wasn't actually sick, just *becoming.*
We should ask...
Maybe he can help us with the Krakoan gates!

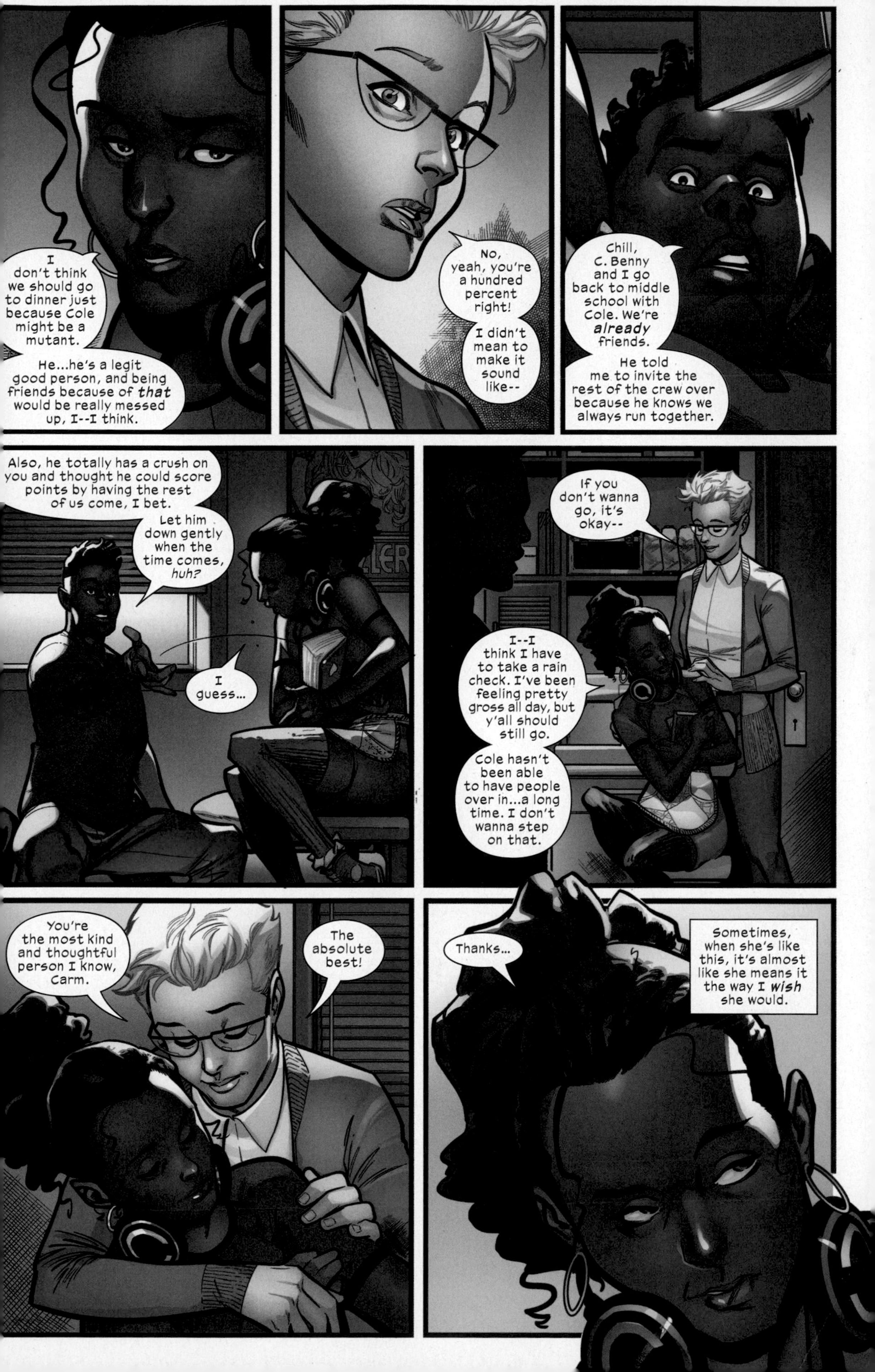
I don't think we should go to dinner just because Cole might be a mutant.
He...he's a legit good person, and being friends because of *that* would be really messed up, I--I think.
No, yeah, you're a hundred percent right!
I didn't mean to make it sound like--
Chill, C. Benny and I go back to middle school with Cole. We're *already* friends.
He told me to invite the rest of the crew over because he knows we always run together.
Also, he totally has a crush on you and thought he could score points by having the rest of us come, I bet.
Let him down gently when the time comes, *huh?*
I guess...
If you don't wanna go, it's okay--
I--I think I have to take a rain check. I've been feeling pretty gross all day, but y'all should still go.
Cole hasn't been able to have people over in...a long time. I don't wanna step on that.
You're the most kind and thoughtful person I know, Carm.
The absolute best!
Thanks...
Sometimes, when she's like this, it's almost like she means it the way I *wish* she would.

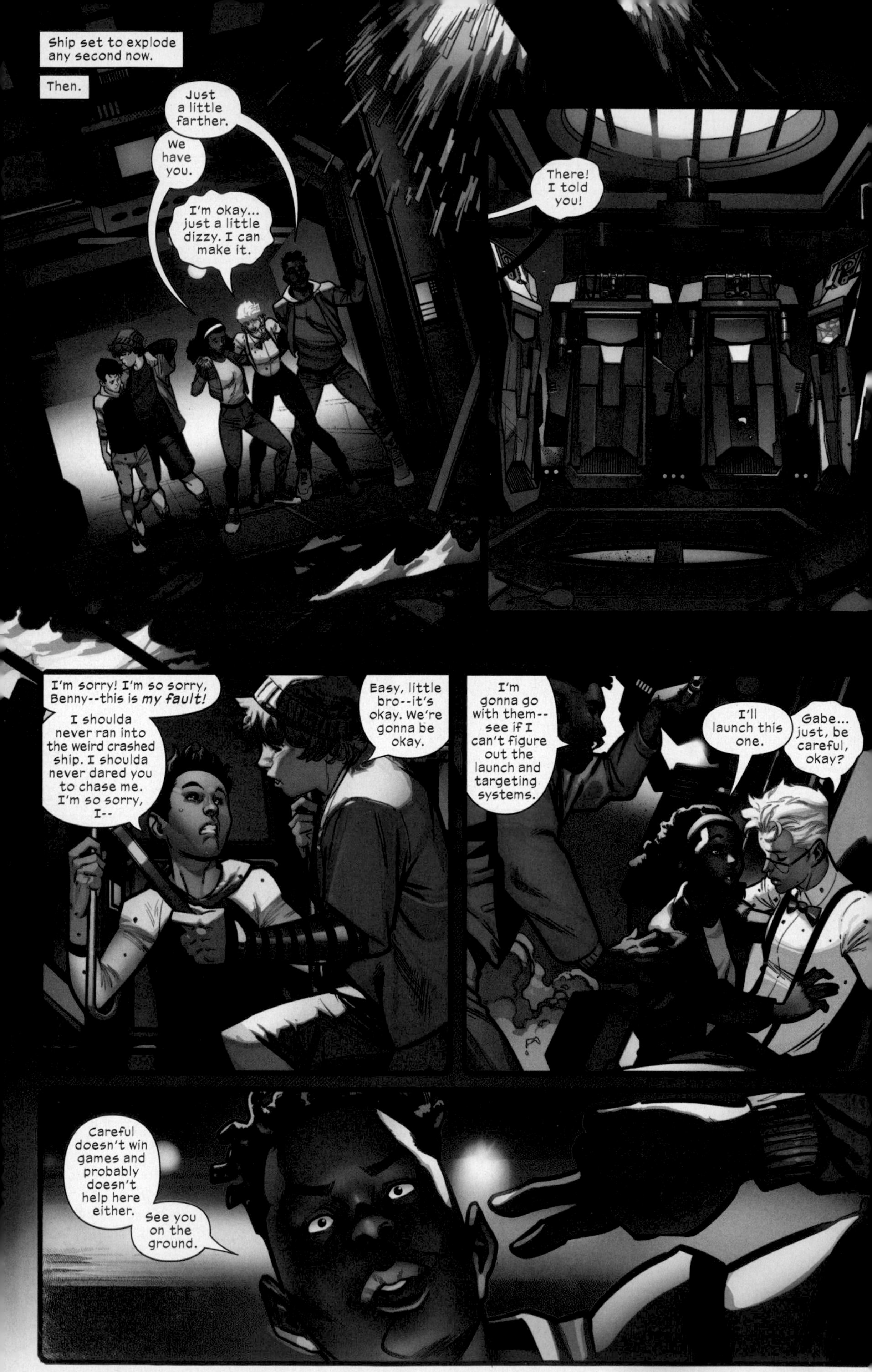
Ship set to explode any second now.
Then.
Just a little farther.
We have you.
I'm okay... just a little dizzy. I can make it.
There! I told you!
I'm sorry! I'm so sorry, Benny--this is *my fault!*
I shoulda never ran into the weird crashed ship. I shoulda never dared you to chase me. I'm so sorry, I--
Easy, little bro--it's okay. We're gonna be okay.
I'm gonna go with them--see if I can't figure out the launch and targeting systems.
I'll launch this one.
Gabe... just, be careful, okay?
Careful doesn't win games and probably doesn't help here either.
See you on the ground.

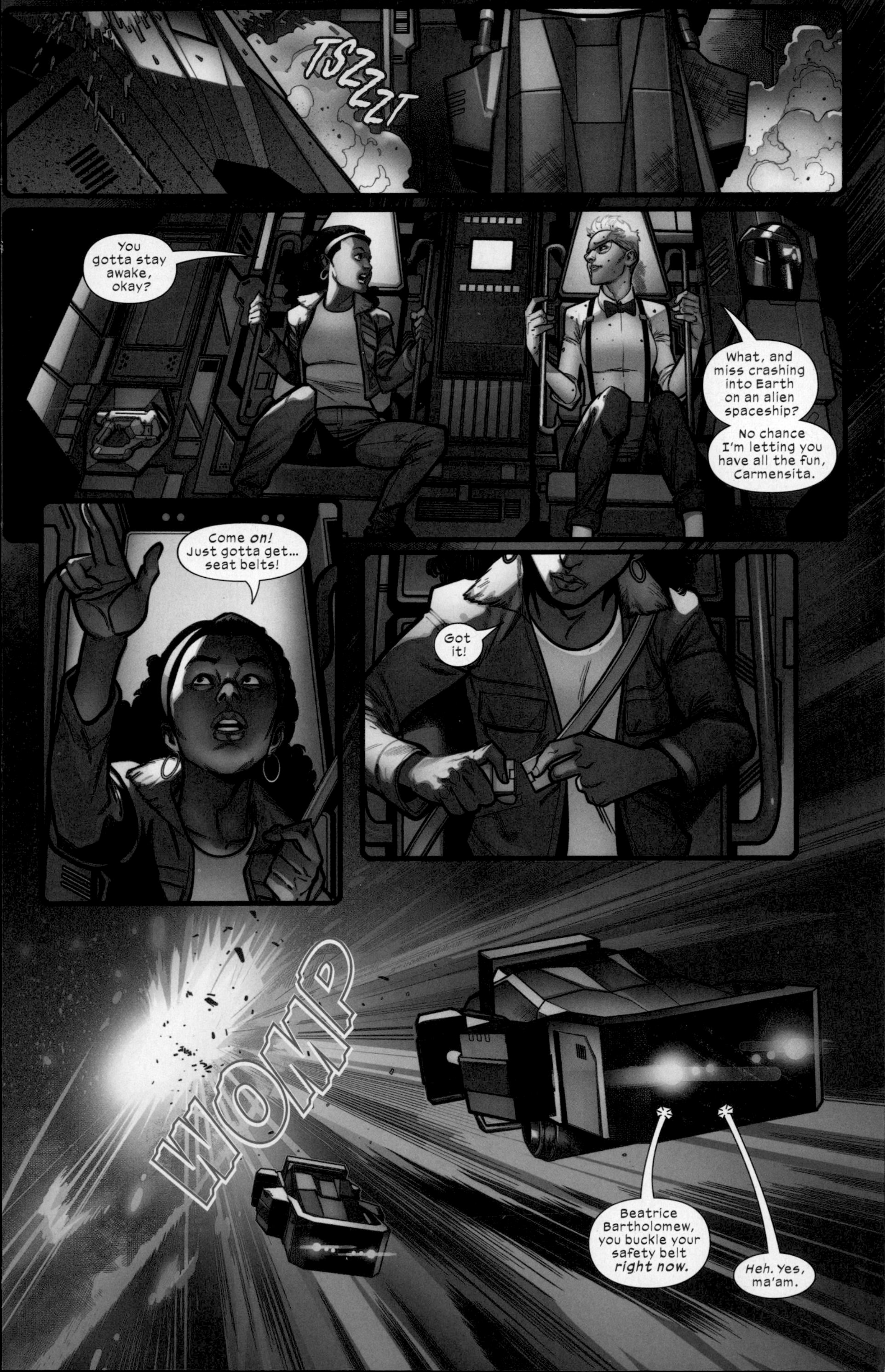
TSZZZT
You gotta stay awake, okay?
What, and miss crashing into Earth on an alien spaceship?
No chance I'm letting you have all the fun, Carmensita.
Come on! Just gotta get... seat belts!
Got it!
WOMP
Beatrice Bartholomew, you buckle your safety belt right now.
Heh. Yes, ma'am.

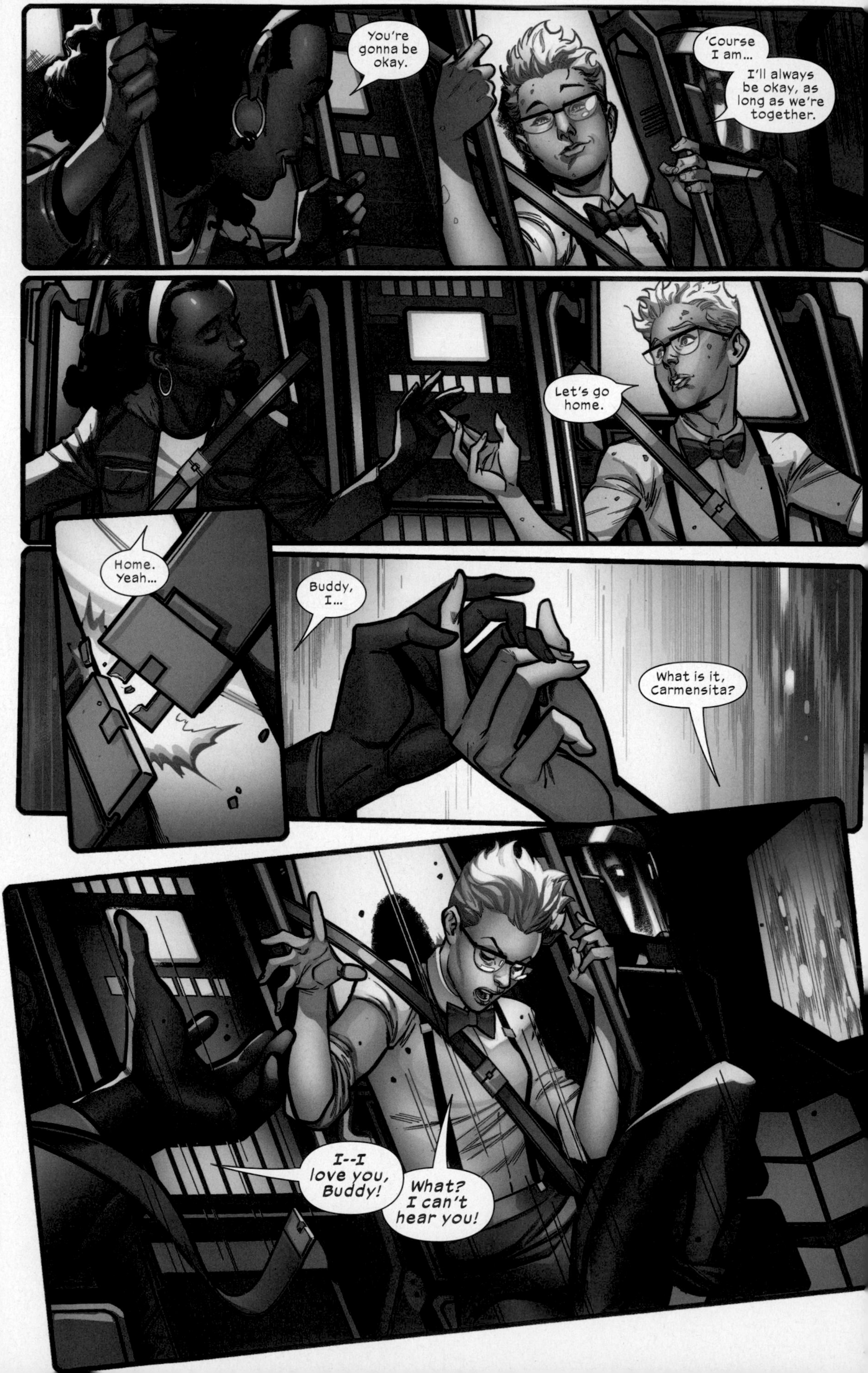
You're gonna be okay.
'Course I am...
I'll always be okay, as long as we're together.
Let's go home.
Home. Yeah...
Buddy, I...
What is it, Carmensita?
I--I love you, Buddy!
What? I can't hear you!

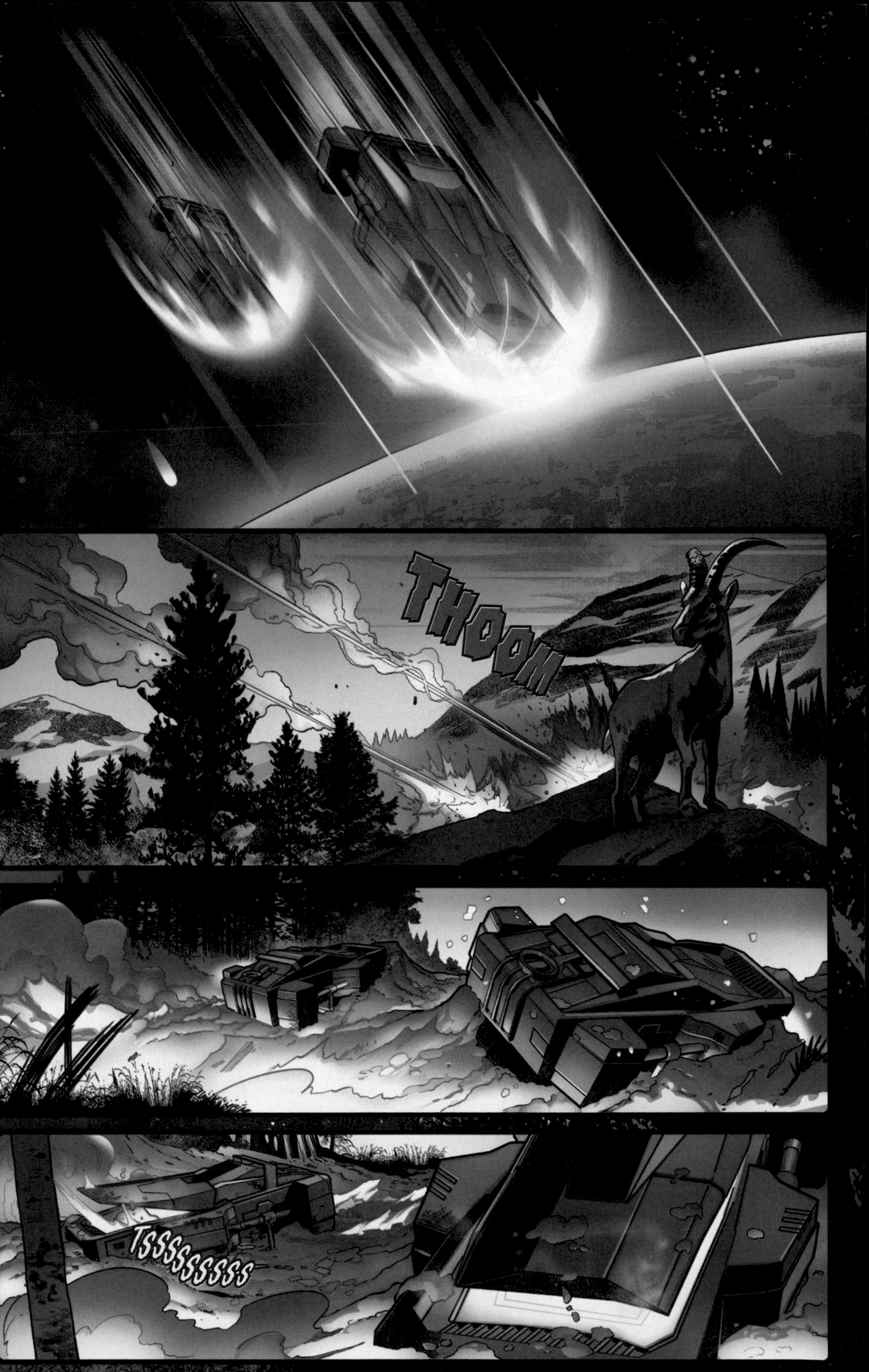
THOOM
TSSSSSSSSS

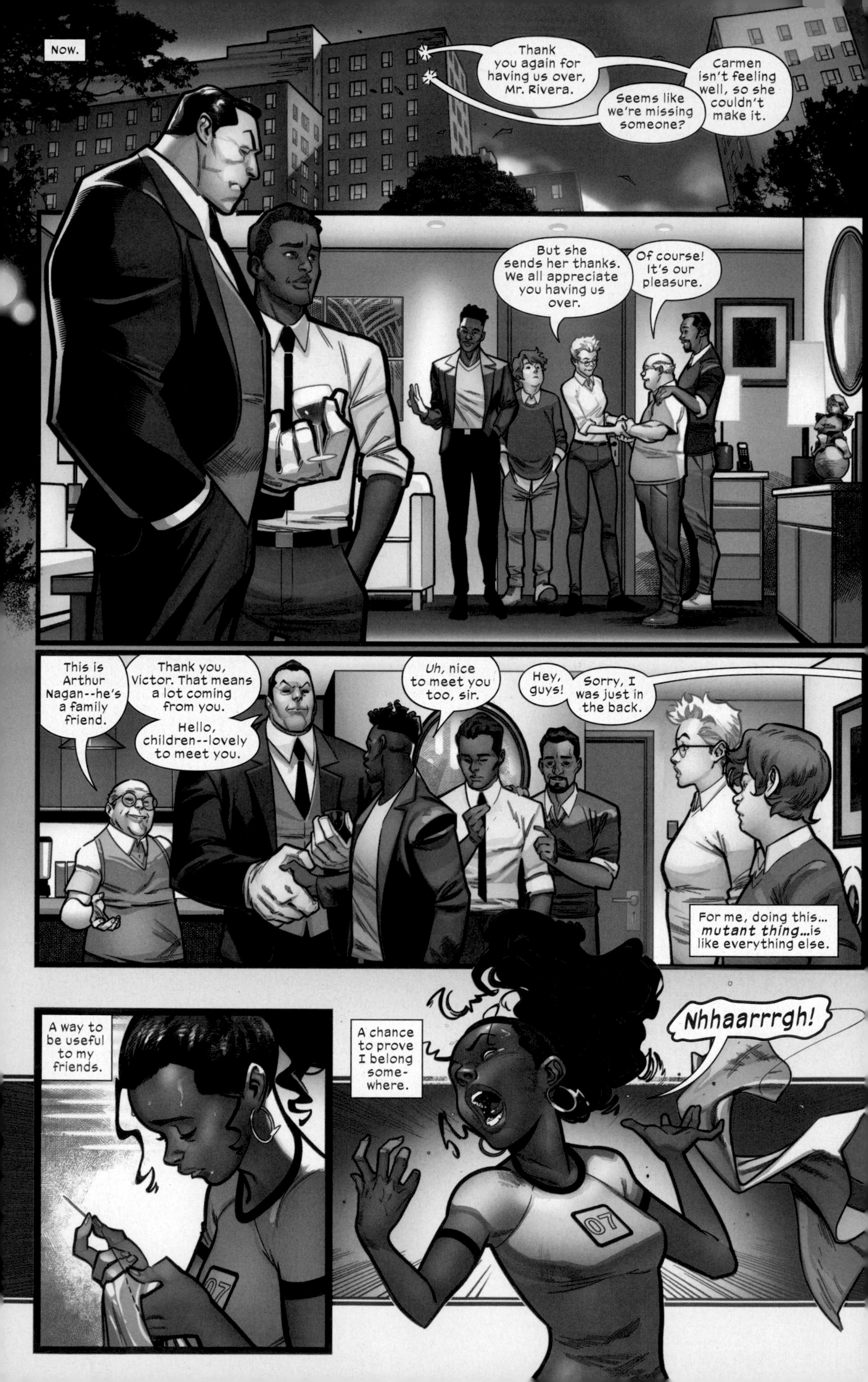

Now.
Thank you again for having us over, Mr. Rivera.
Seems like we're missing someone?
Carmen isn't feeling well, so she couldn't make it.
But she sends her thanks. We all appreciate you having us over.
Of course! It's our pleasure.
This is Arthur Nagan--he's a family friend.
Thank you, Victor. That means a lot coming from you.
Hello, children--lovely to meet you.
Uh, nice to meet you too, sir.
Hey, guys!
Sorry, I was just in the back.
For me, doing this... *mutant thing*...is like everything else.
A way to be useful to my friends.
A chance to prove I belong some- where.
Nhhaarrrgh!

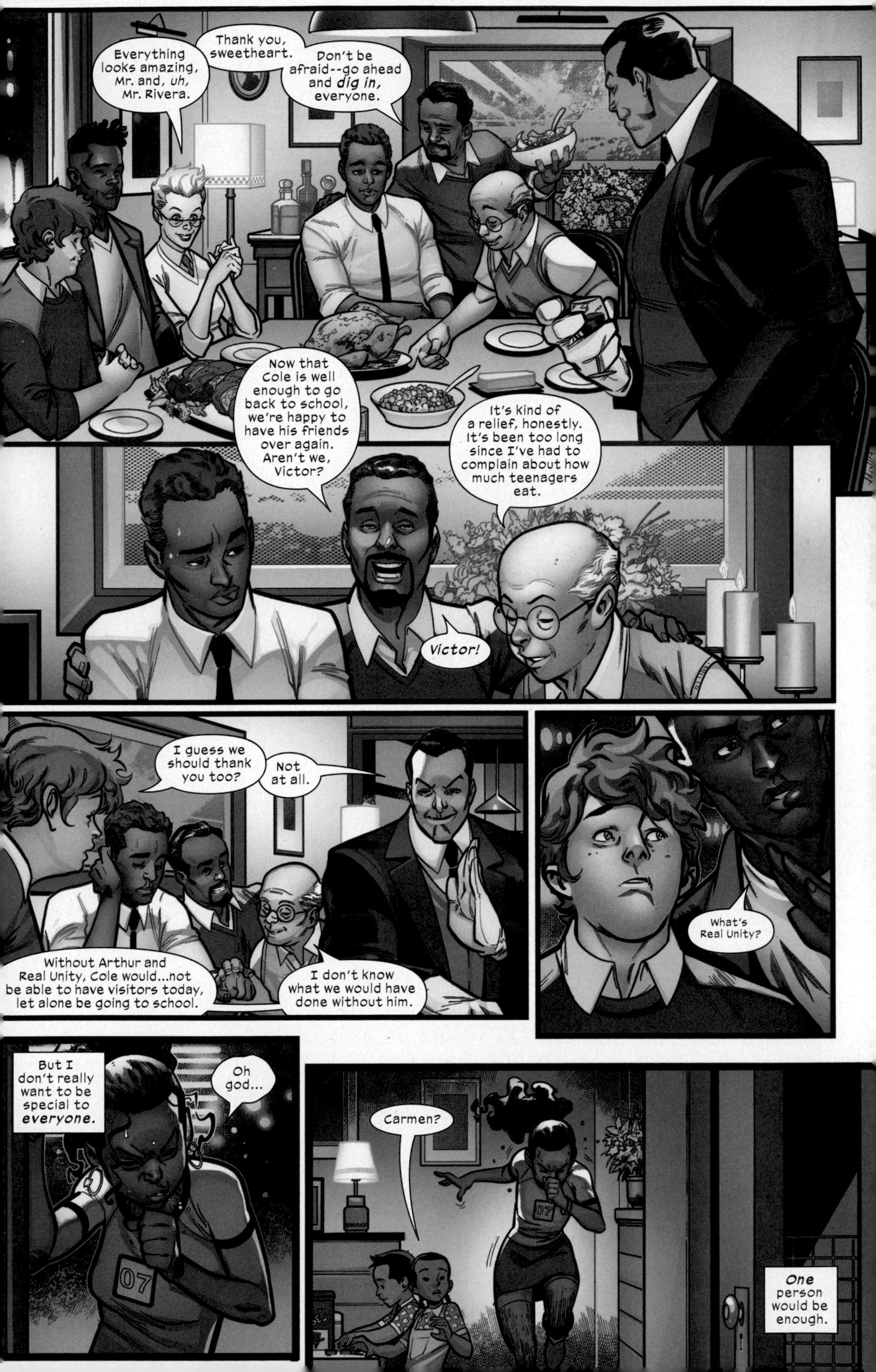
Everything looks amazing, Mr. and, *uh,* Mr. Rivera.
Thank you, sweetheart.
Don't be afraid--go ahead and ***dig in,*** everyone.
Now that Cole is well enough to go back to school, we're happy to have his friends over again. Aren't we, Victor?
It's kind of a relief, honestly. It's been too long since I've had to complain about how much teenagers eat.
Victor!
I guess we should thank you too?
Not at all.
Without Arthur and Real Unity, Cole would...not be able to have visitors today, let alone be going to school.
I don't know what we would have done without him.
What's Real Unity?
But I don't really want to be special to ***everyone.***
Oh god...
Carmen?
One person would be enough.

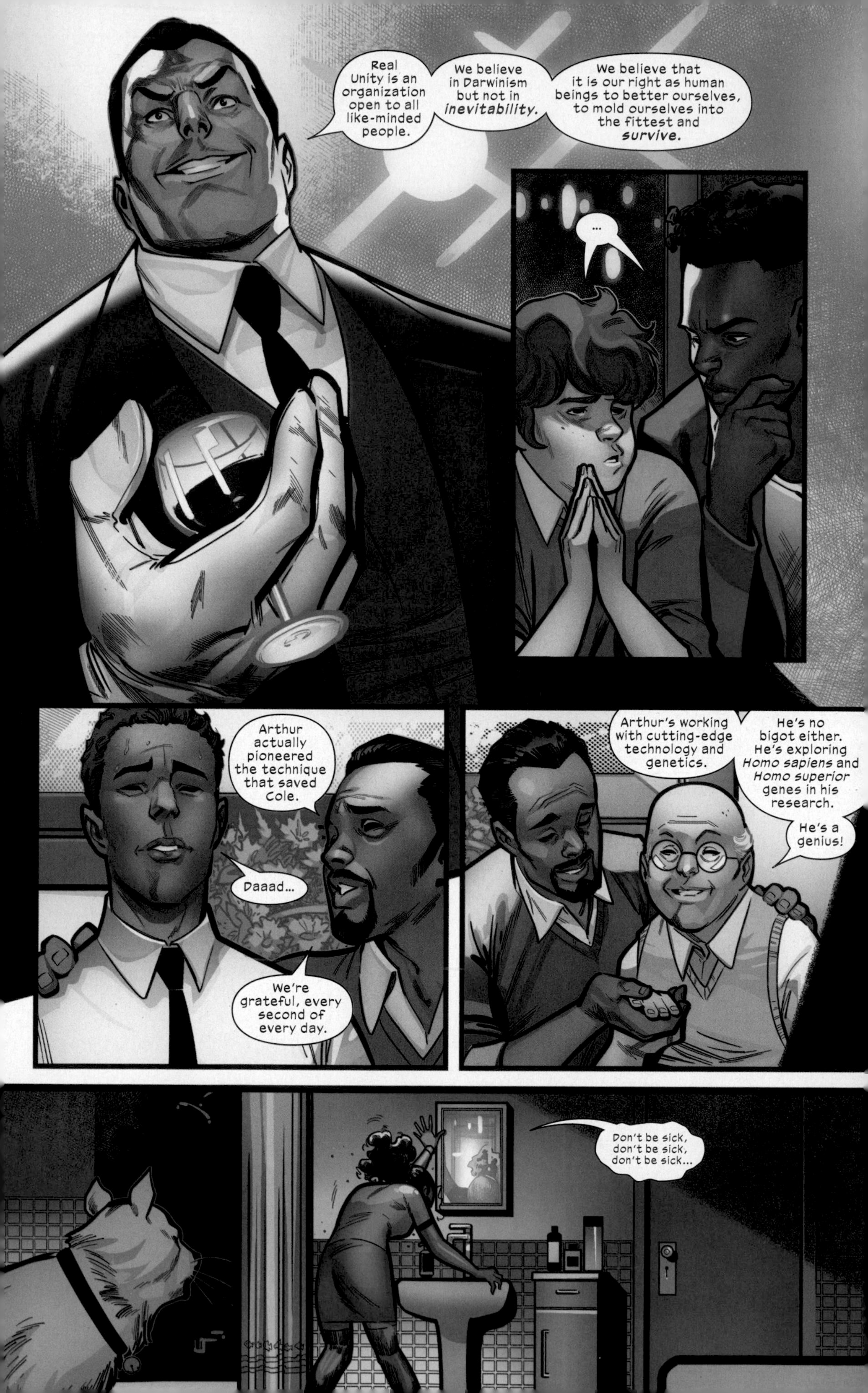
Real Unity is an organization open to all like-minded people.
We believe in Darwinism but not in *inevitability.*
We believe that it is our right as human beings to better ourselves, to mold ourselves into the fittest and *survive.*
...
Arthur actually pioneered the technique that saved Cole.
Daaad...
We're grateful, every second of every day.
Arthur's working with cutting-edge technology and genetics.
He's no bigot either. He's exploring *Homo sapiens* and *Homo superior* genes in his research.
He's a genius!
Don't be sick, don't be sick, don't be sick...

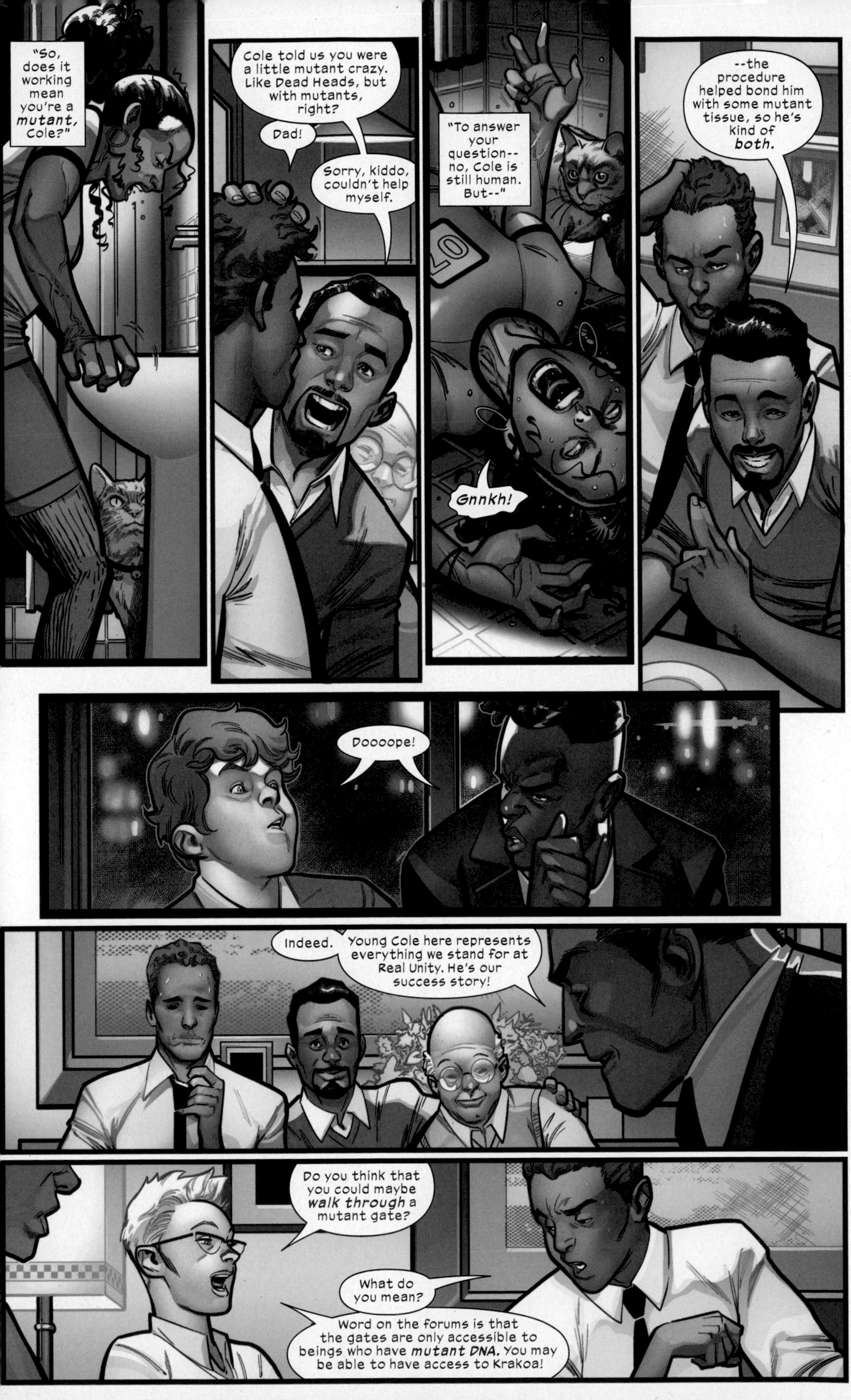
"So, does it working mean you're a mutant, Cole?"
Cole told us you were a little mutant crazy. Like Dead Heads, but with mutants, right?
Dad!
Sorry, kiddo, couldn't help myself.
"To answer your question--no, Cole is still human. But--"
Gnnkh!
--the procedure helped bond him with some mutant tissue, so he's kind of both.
Doooope!
Indeed.
Young Cole here represents everything we stand for at Real Unity. He's our success story!
Do you think that you could maybe walk through a mutant gate?
What do you mean?
Word on the forums is that the gates are only accessible to beings who have mutant DNA. You may be able to have access to Krakoa!

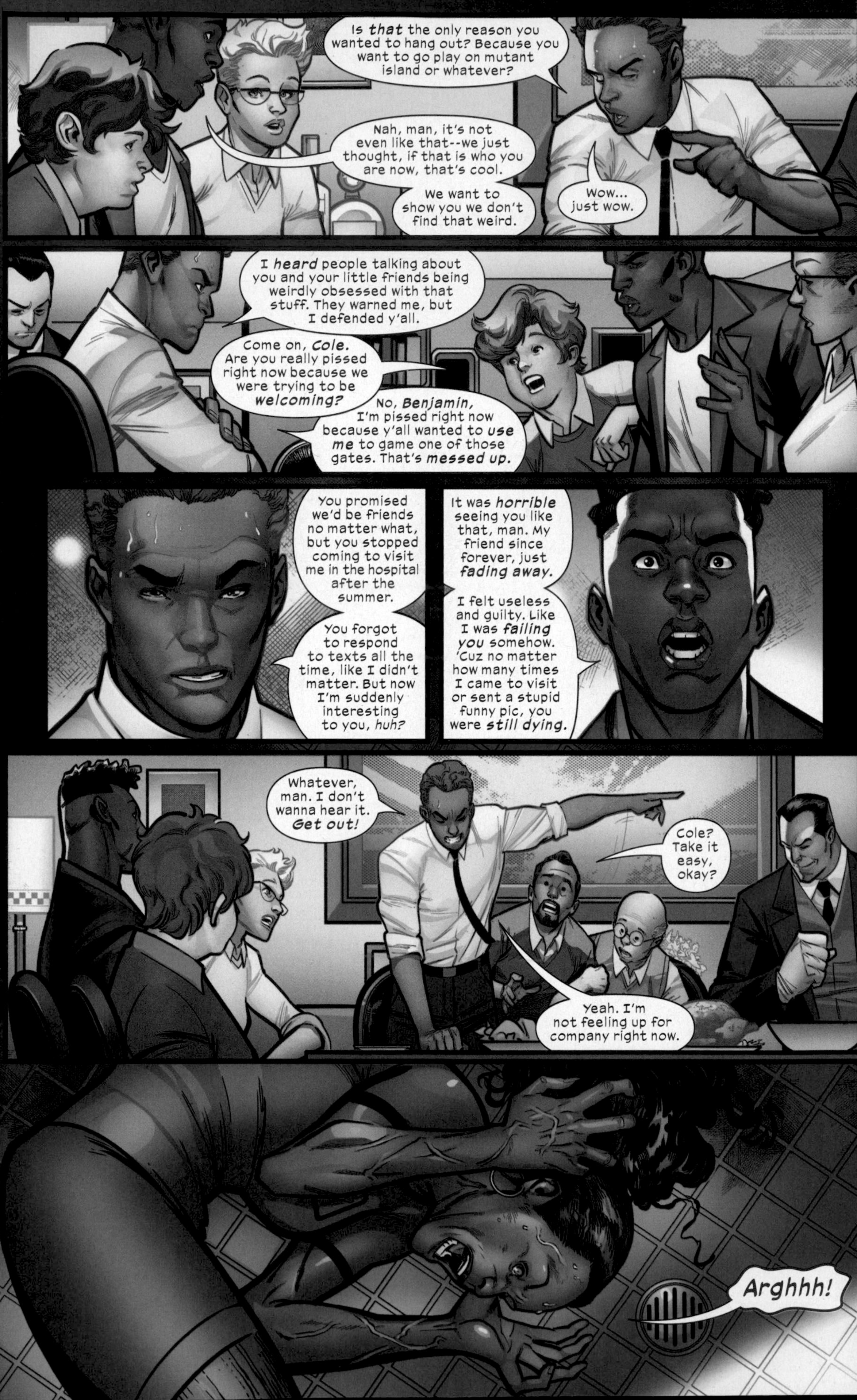
Is that the only reason you wanted to hang out? Because you want to go play on mutant island or whatever?
Nah, man, it's not even like that--we just thought, if that is who you are now, that's cool.
We want to show you we don't find that weird.
Wow... just wow.
I heard people talking about you and your little friends being weirdly obsessed with that stuff. They warned me, but I defended y'all.
Come on, Cole. Are you really pissed right now because we were trying to be welcoming?
No, Benjamin, I'm pissed right now because y'all wanted to use me to game one of those gates. That's messed up.
You promised we'd be friends no matter what, but you stopped coming to visit me in the hospital after the summer.
You forgot to respond to texts all the time, like I didn't matter. But now I'm suddenly interesting to you, huh?
It was horrible seeing you like that, man. My friend since forever, just fading away.
I felt useless and guilty. Like I was failing you somehow. 'Cuz no matter how many times I came to visit or sent a stupid funny pic, you were still dying.
Whatever, man. I don't wanna hear it. Get out!
Cole? Take it easy, okay?
Yeah. I'm not feeling up for company right now.
Arghhh!

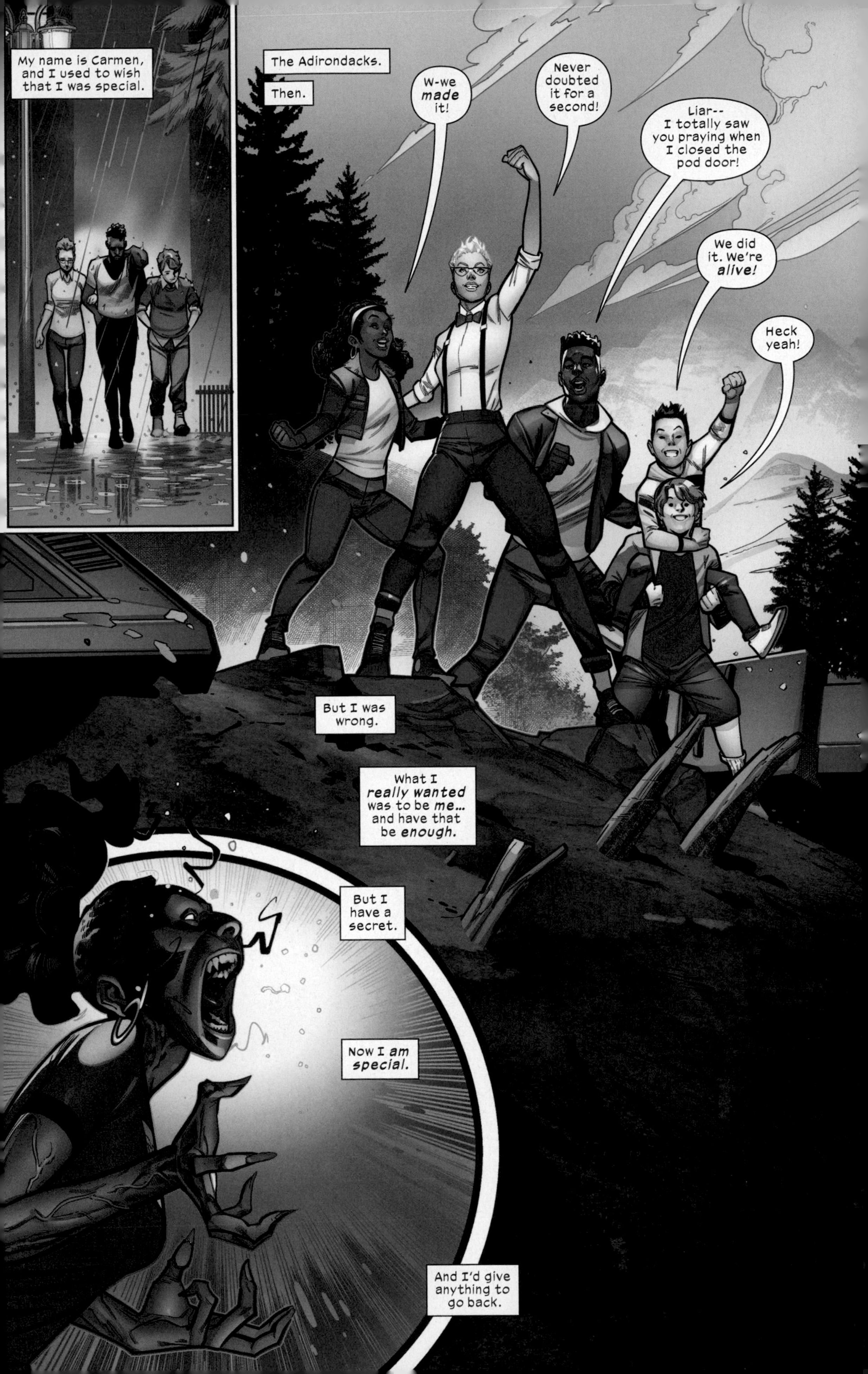

My name is Carmen, and I used to wish that I was special.
The Adirondacks.
Then.
W-we *made* it!
Never doubted it for a second!
Liar-- I totally saw you praying when I closed the pod door!
We did it. We're *alive!*
Heck yeah!
But I was wrong.
What I *really wanted* was to be *me*... and have that be *enough.*
But I have a secret.
Now I *am special.*
And I'd give anything to go back.

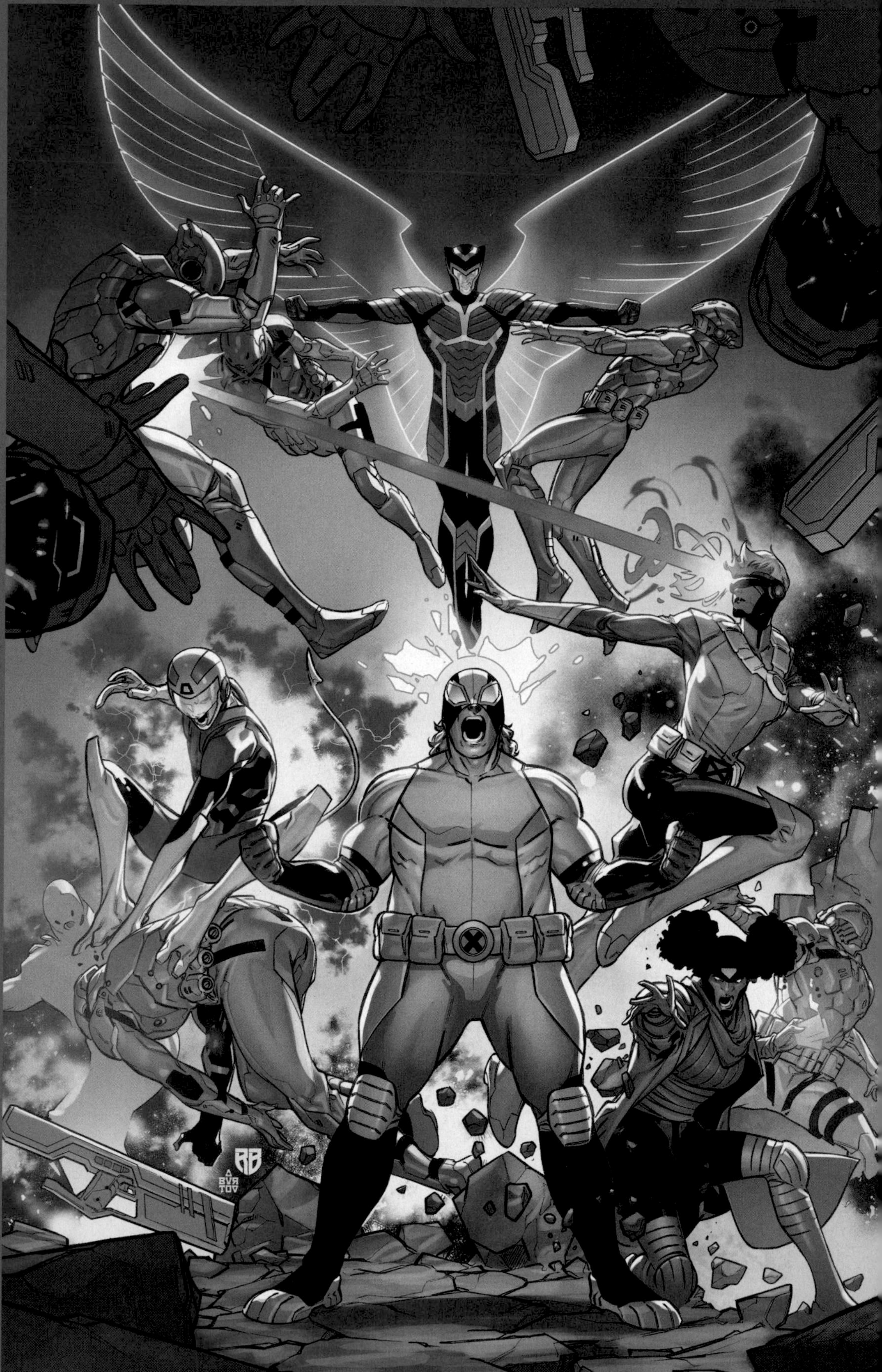

Captured

[Child[REN]_of]
[____the_A[TOM]

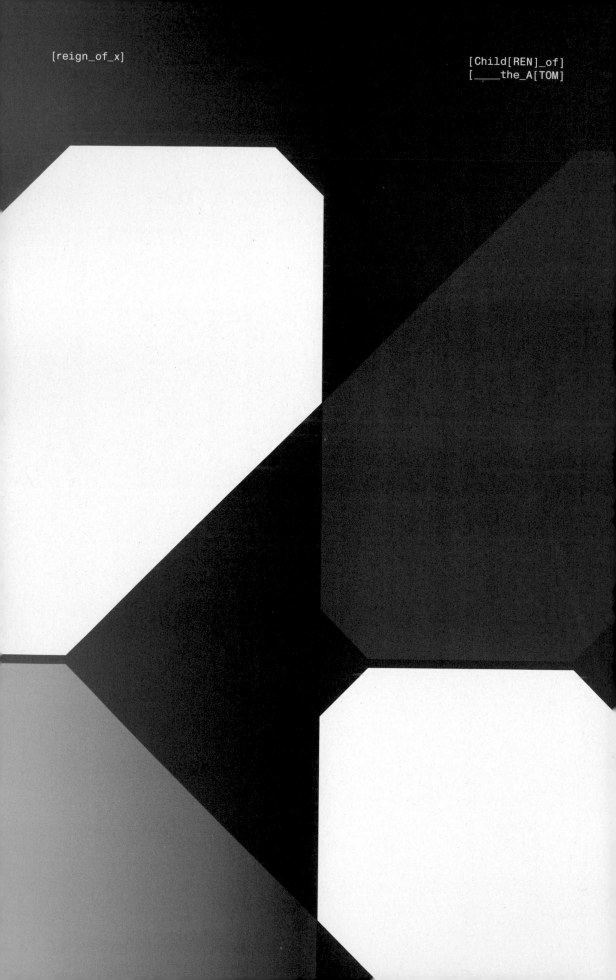

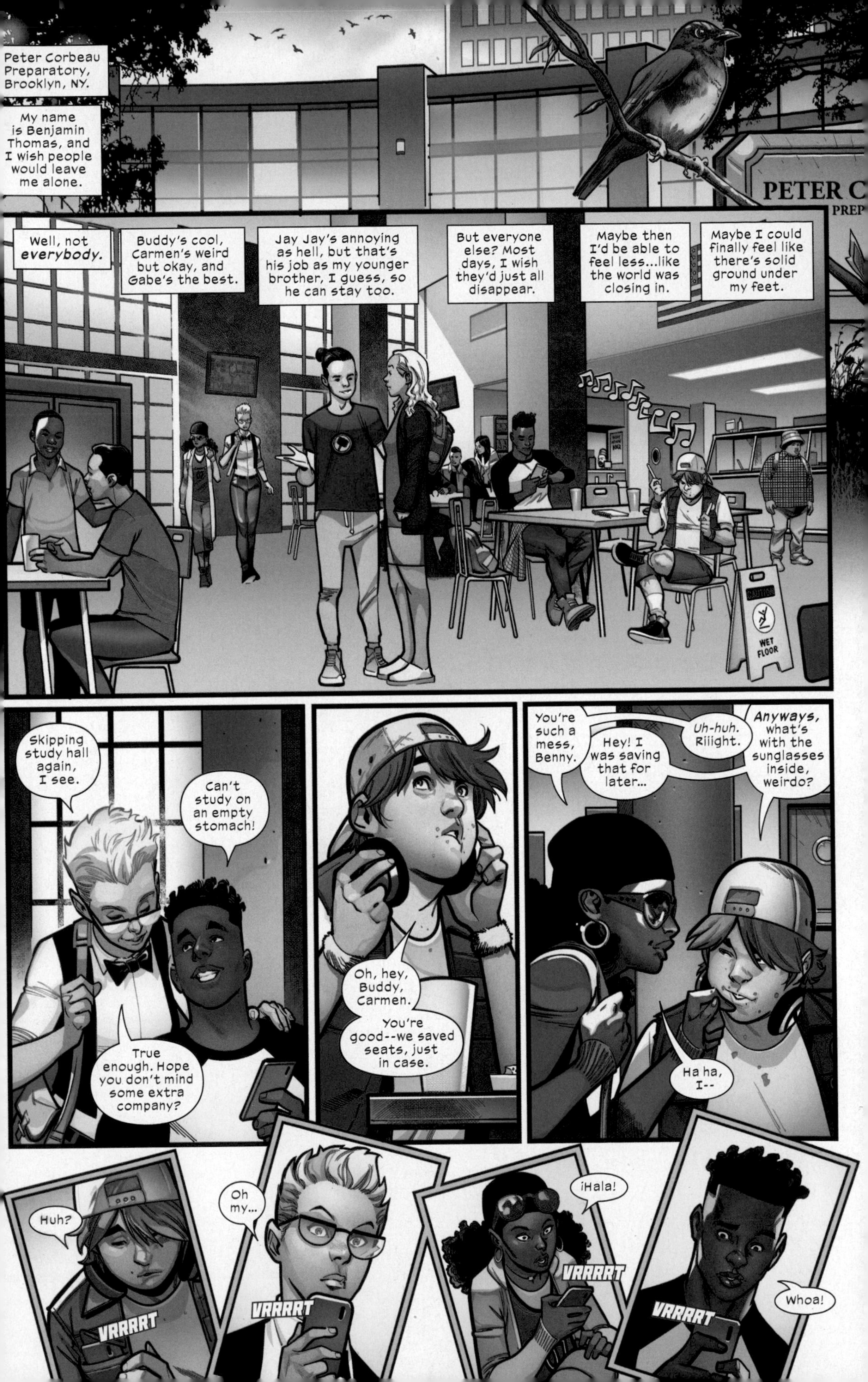
Peter Corbeau Preparatory, Brooklyn, NY.
My name is Benjamin Thomas, and I wish people would leave me alone.
PETER C
PREP
Well, not *everybody.*
Buddy's cool, Carmen's weird but okay, and Gabe's the best.
Jay Jay's annoying as hell, but that's his job as my younger brother, I guess, so he can stay too.
But everyone else? Most days, I wish they'd just all disappear.
Maybe then I'd be able to feel less...like the world was closing in.
Maybe I could finally feel like there's solid ground under my feet.
CAUTION
WET FLOOR
Skipping study hall again, I see.
Can't study on an empty stomach!
True enough. Hope you don't mind some extra company?
Oh, hey, Buddy, Carmen.
You're good--we saved seats, just in case.
You're such a mess, Benny.
Hey! I was saving that for later...
Uh-huh. Riiight.
Anyways, what's with the sunglasses inside, weirdo?
Ha ha, I--
Huh?
VRRRRT
Oh my...
VRRRRT
¡Hala!
VRRRRT
VRRRRT
Whoa!

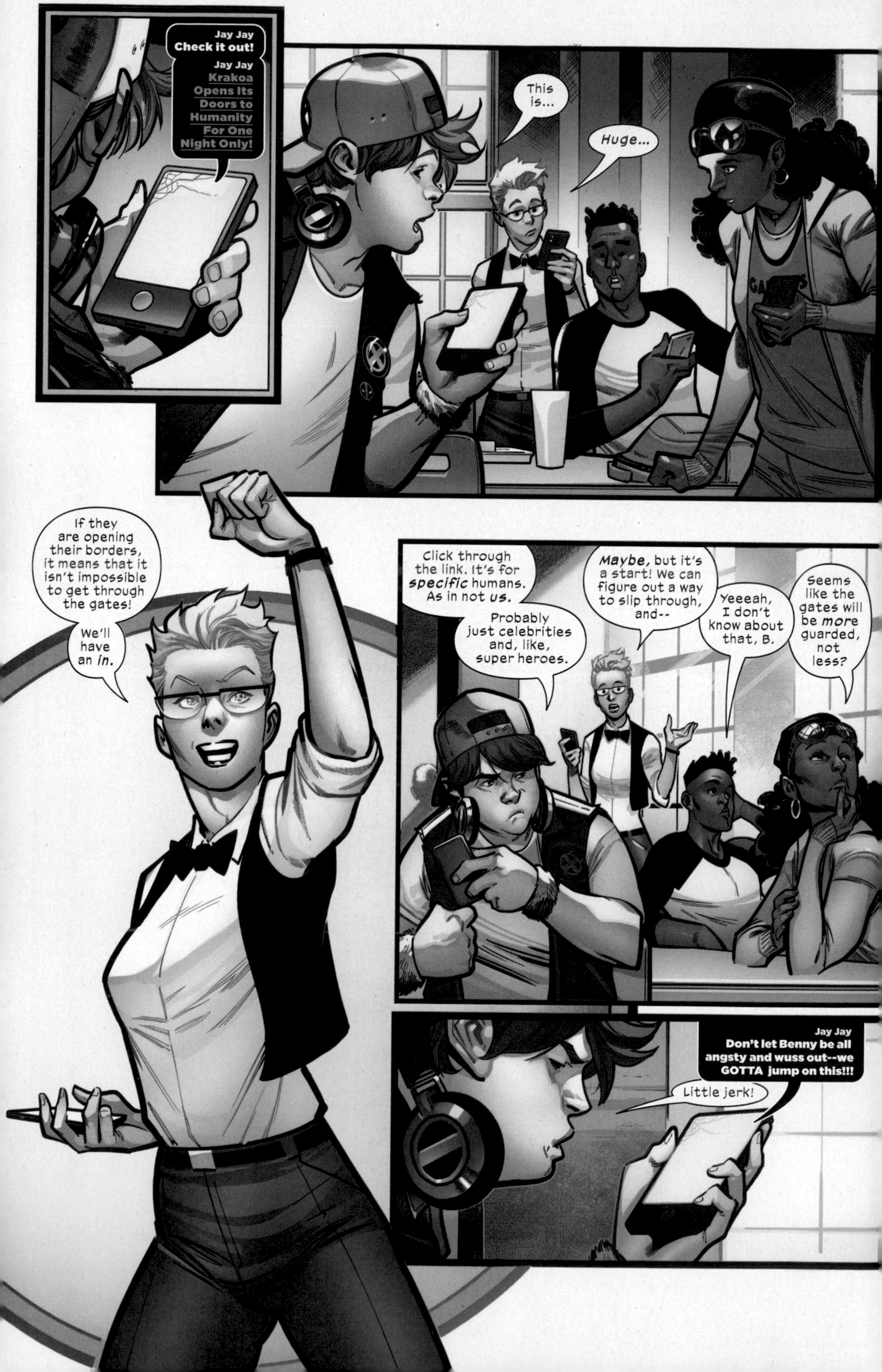
Jay Jay
Check it out!
Jay Jay
Krakoa Opens Its Doors to Humanity For One Night Only!
This is...
Huge...
If they are opening their borders, it means that it isn't impossible to get through the gates!
We'll have an *in.*
Click through the link. It's for *specific* humans. As in not *us.*
Probably just celebrities and, like, super heroes.
Maybe, but it's a start! We can figure out a way to slip through, and--
Yeeeah, I don't know about that, B.
Seems like the gates will be *more* guarded, not less?
Jay Jay
Don't let Benny be all angsty and wuss out--we GOTTA jump on this!!!
Little jerk!

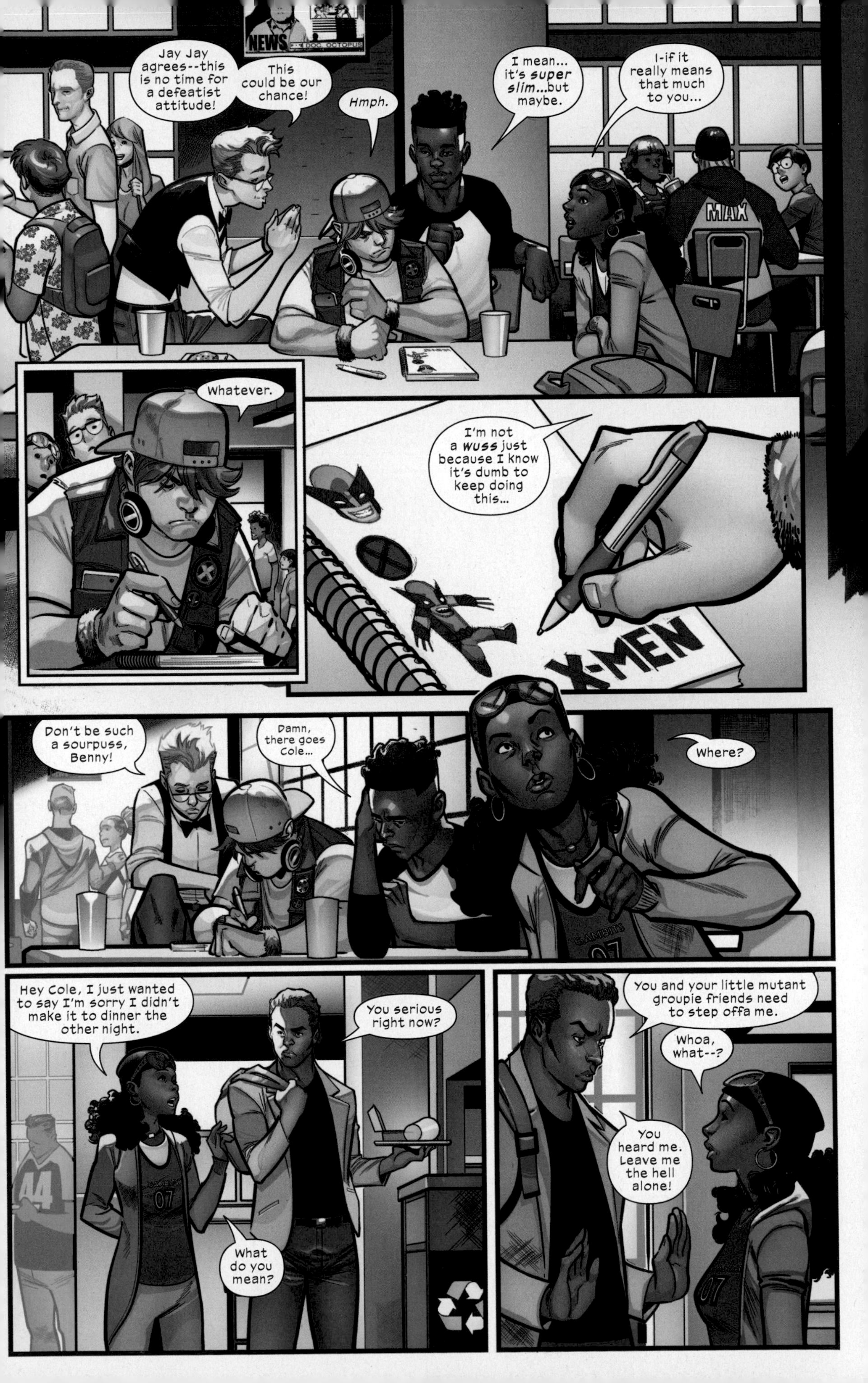
NEWS
DOC OCTOPUS
Jay Jay agrees--this is no time for a defeatist attitude!
This could be our chance!
Hmph.
I mean... it's super slim...but maybe.
I-if it really means that much to you...
MAX
Whatever.
I'm not a WUSS just because I know it's dumb to keep doing this...
X-MEN
Don't be such a sourpuss, Benny!
Damn, there goes Cole...
Where?
Hey Cole, I just wanted to say I'm sorry I didn't make it to dinner the other night.
You serious right now?
What do you mean?
You and your little mutant groupie friends need to step offa me.
Whoa, what--?
You heard me. Leave me the hell alone!

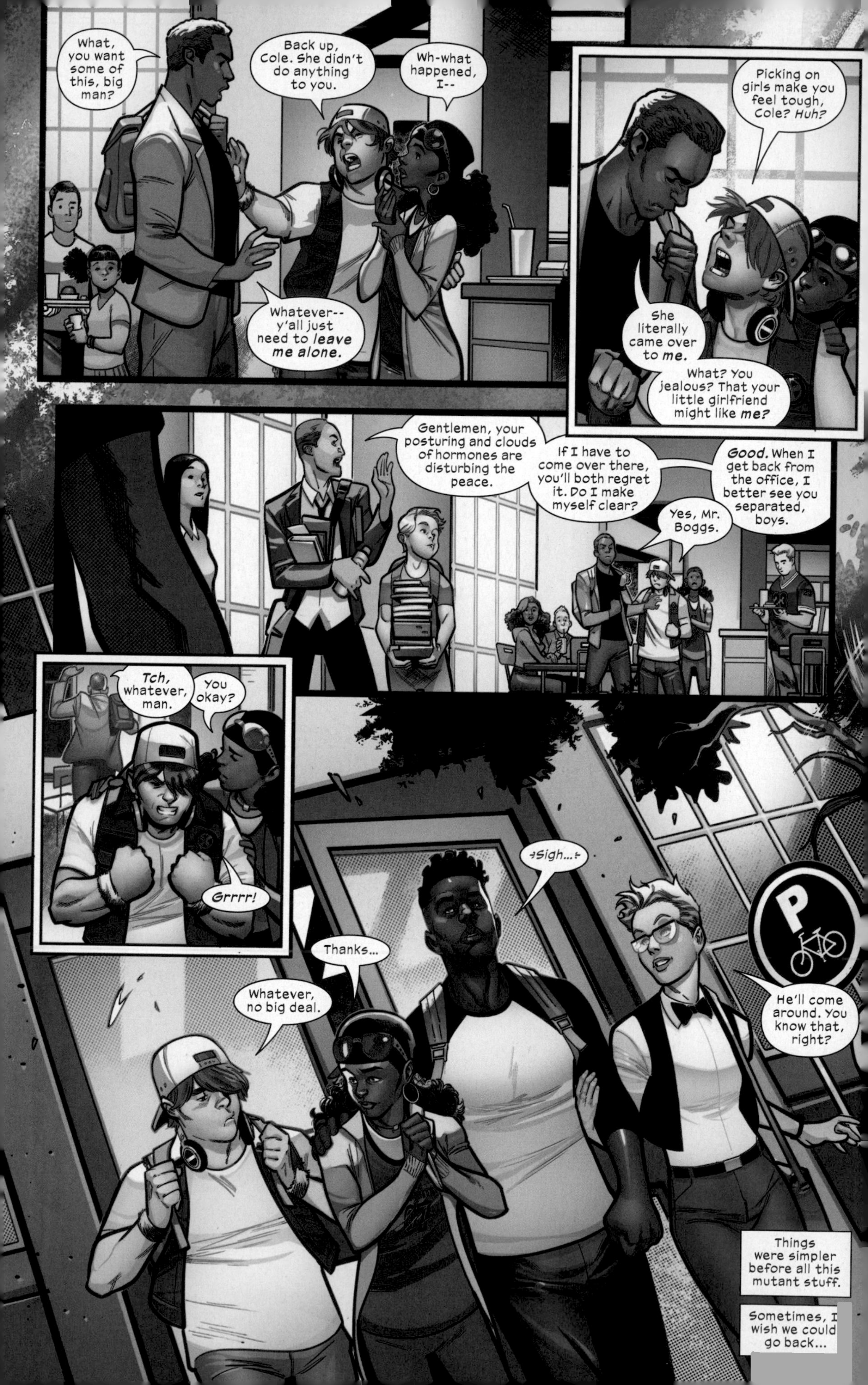
What, you want some of this, big man?
Back up, Cole. She didn't do anything to you.
Wh-what happened, I--
Whatever-- y'all just need to *leave me alone.*
Picking on girls make you feel tough, Cole? *Huh?*
She literally came over to *me.*
What? You jealous? That your little girlfriend might like *me?*
Gentlemen, your posturing and clouds of hormones are disturbing the peace.
If I have to come over there, you'll both regret it. Do I make myself clear?
Yes, Mr. Boggs.
Good. When I get back from the office, I better see you separated, boys.
Tch, whatever, man.
You okay?
Grrrr!
Sigh...
Thanks...
Whatever, no big deal.
He'll come around. You know that, right?
Things were simpler before all this mutant stuff.
Sometimes, I wish we could go back...

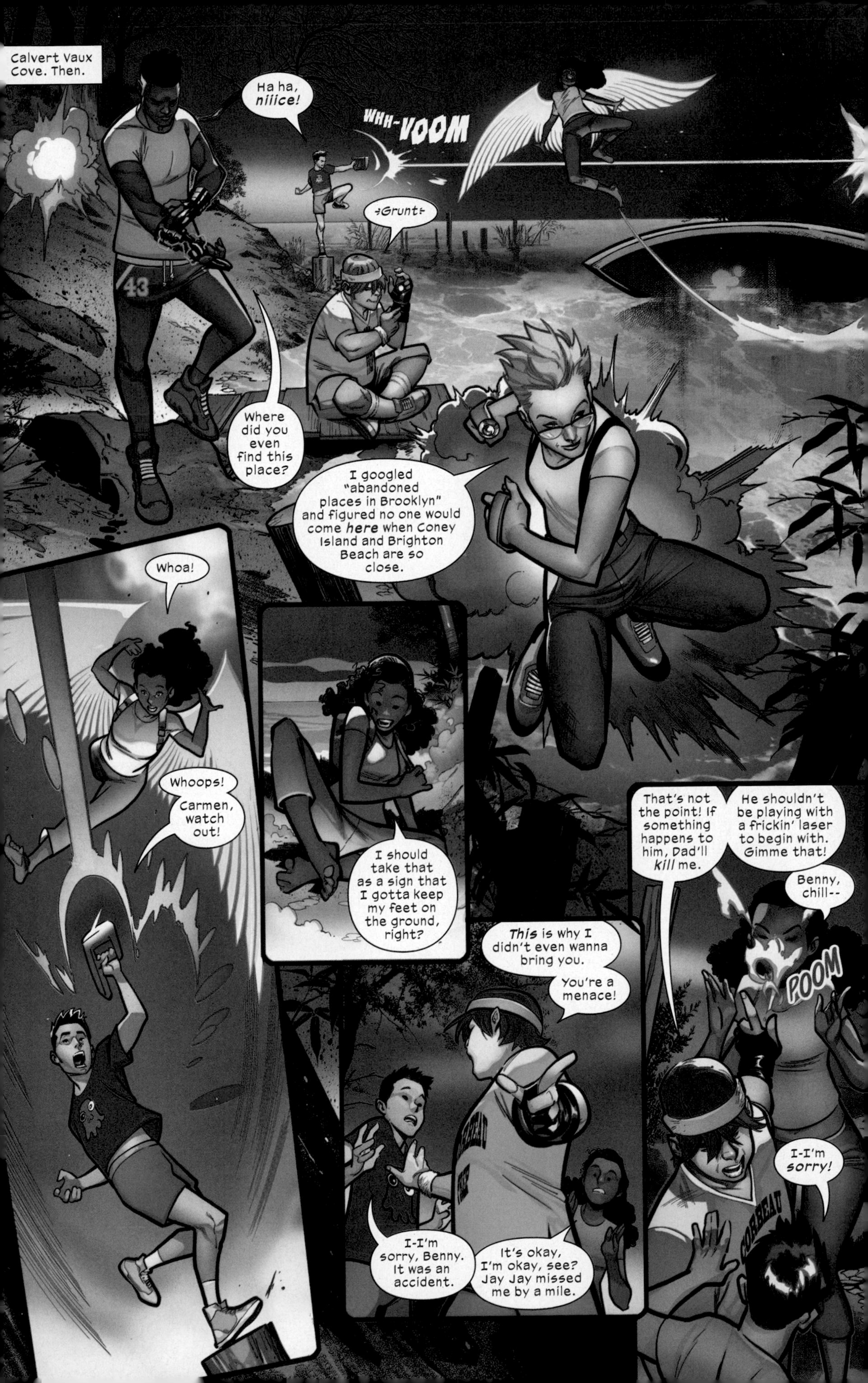
Calvert Vaux Cove. Then.
Ha ha, niiice!
WHH-VOOM
-Grunt-
Where did you even find this place?
I googled "abandoned places in Brooklyn" and figured no one would come here when Coney Island and Brighton Beach are so close.
Whoa!
Whoops!
Carmen, watch out!
I should take that as a sign that I gotta keep my feet on the ground, right?
This is why I didn't even wanna bring you.
You're a menace!
I-I'm sorry, Benny. It was an accident.
It's okay, I'm okay, see? Jay Jay missed me by a mile.
That's not the point! If something happens to him, Dad'll kill me.
He shouldn't be playing with a frickin' laser to begin with. Gimme that!
Benny, chill--
POOM
I-I'm sorry!

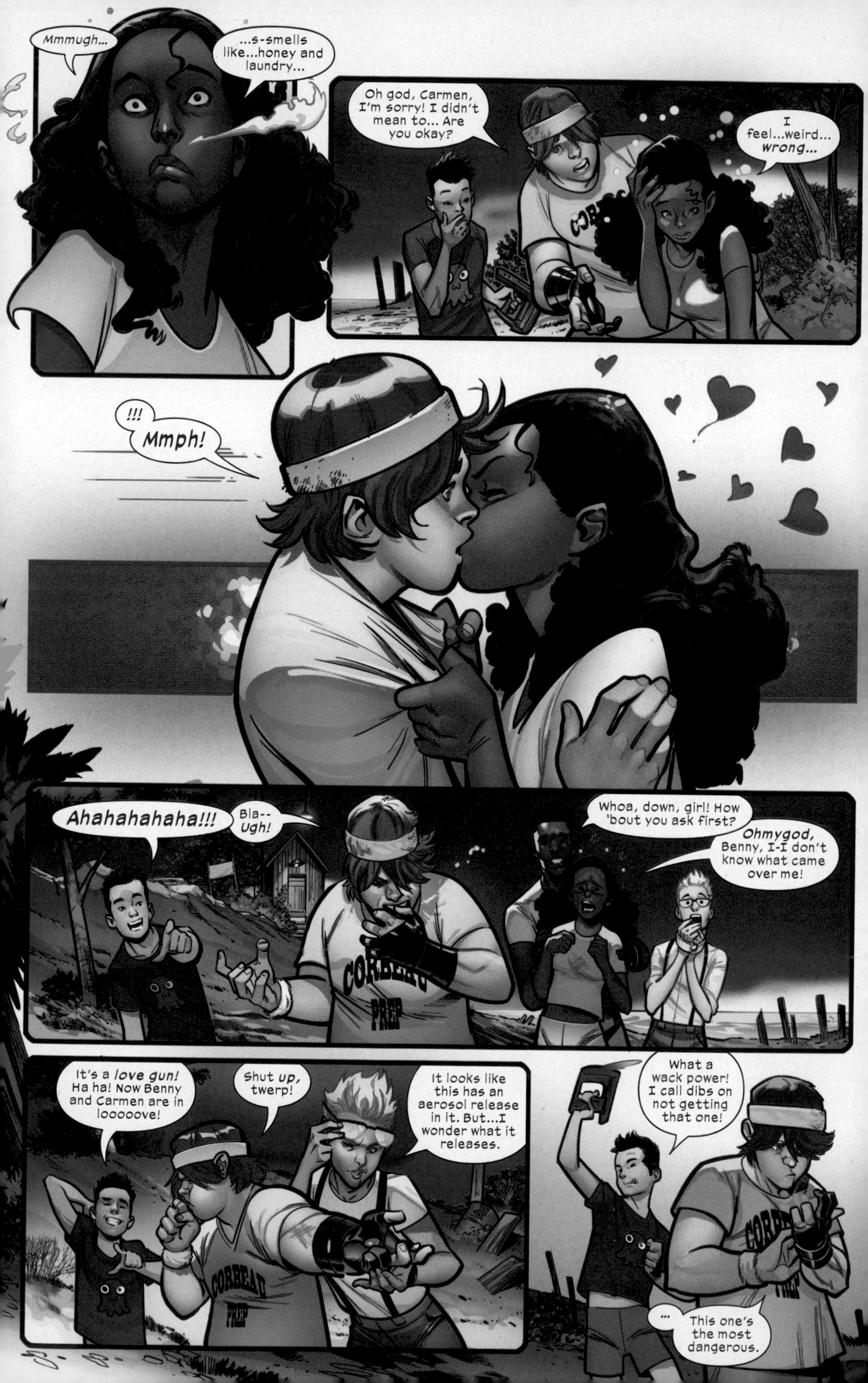
Mmmugh...
...s-smells like...honey and laundry...
Oh god, Carmen, I'm sorry! I didn't mean to... Are you okay?
I feel...weird... wrong...
!!! Mmph!
Ahahahahaha!!!
Bla-- Ugh!
Whoa, down, girl! How 'bout you ask first?
Ohmygod, Benny, I-I don't know what came over me!
It's a love gun! Ha ha! Now Benny and Carmen are in looooove!
Shut up, twerp!
It looks like this has an aerosol release in it. But...I wonder what it releases.
What a wack power! I call dibs on not getting that one!
...
This one's the most dangerous.

[VIBE...00]
[CLOUD..04]

VIBECLOUD/WEAPONXTRA

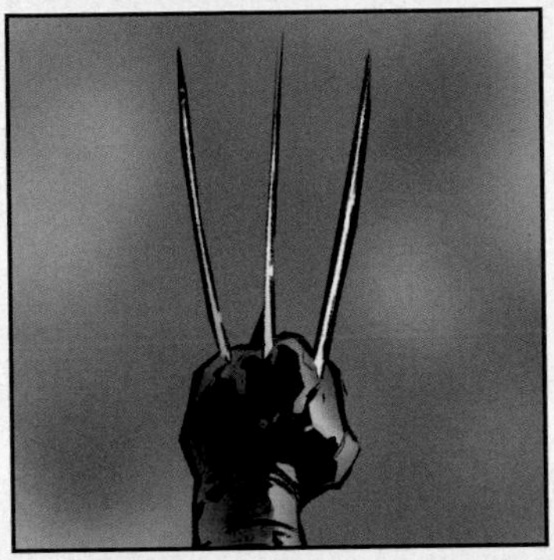

SNIKT SNAKT FT. DARK COLOSSUS & FEINTLY FROSTED STITCHES

WEAPON XTRA

First single off of the "Grim-Dark Past" EP! Weapon Xtra shreds on guitar and lead vocals, with a verse from Dark Colossus and backups and hook by Feintly Frosted Stitches!

TAGS: {Rock} {Metal} {Punk} {Hip Hop} {Thrash}

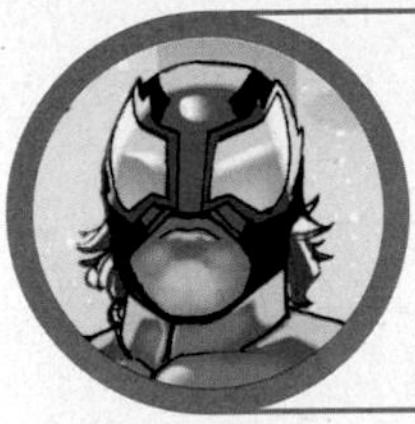

WEAPON XTRA

7K

712

1

MUSIC STATION

Follow

••• More

Share

Comments:

LadyMrSinistyr: This absolutely WHIPS!

XGaveItToYa: wrong wolverine costume, but p cool trak

PapaH: Hope you kids gets signed

DazzlersGlitterLipgloss: yoooo, that DC verse thooooo

LNEx: When am I getting a feature, tho? Lemme know!

ArchivistX: <3

RoboRevolution: Lila Cheney's bettr

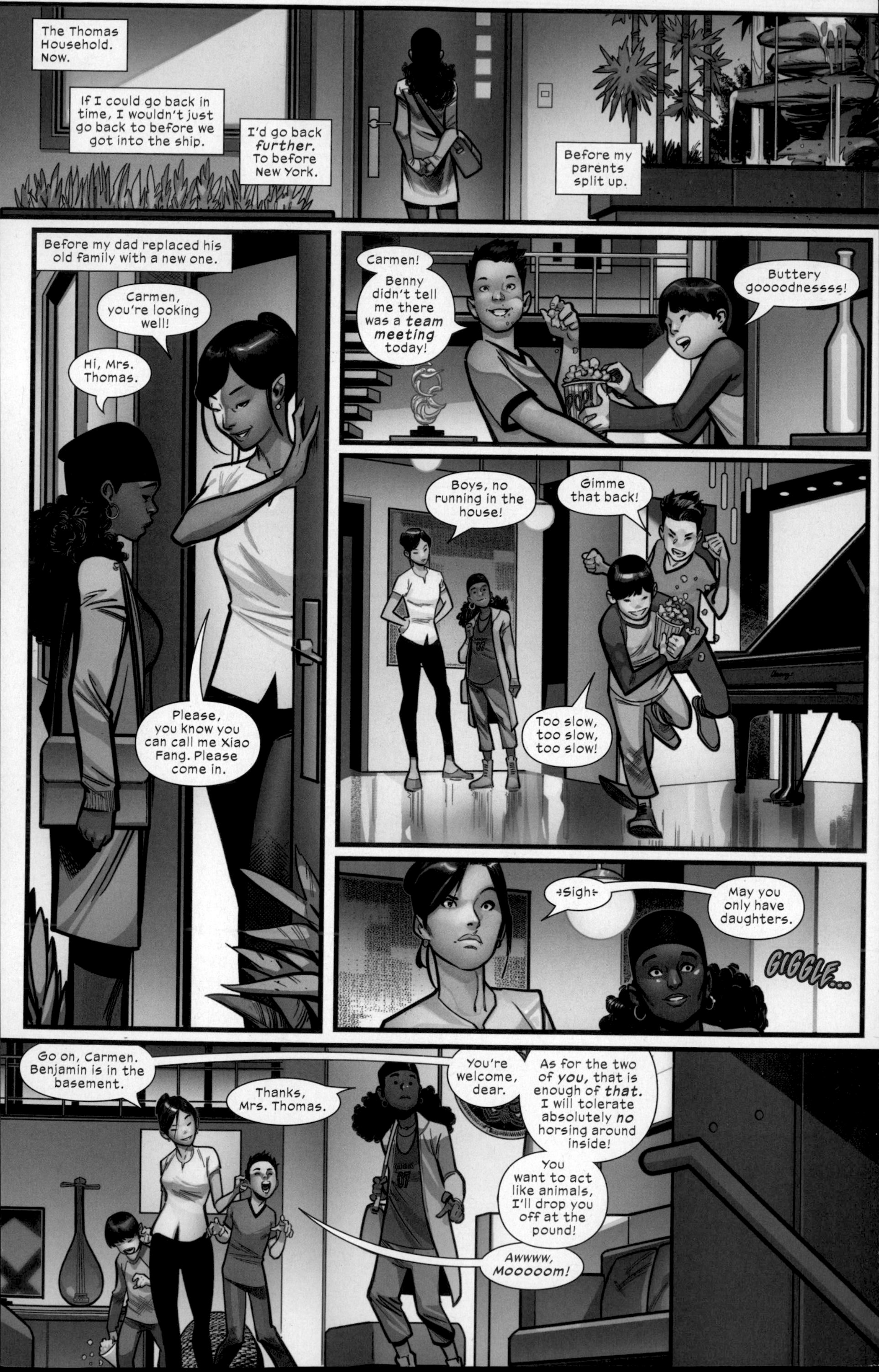
The Thomas Household. Now.
If I could go back in time, I wouldn't just go back to before we got into the ship.
I'd go back *further.* To before New York.
Before my parents split up.
Before my dad replaced his old family with a new one.
Carmen, you're looking well!
Hi, Mrs. Thomas.
Please, you know you can call me Xiao Fang. Please come in.
Carmen! Benny didn't tell me there was a *team meeting* today!
Buttery gooodnessss!
Boys, no running in the house!
Gimme that back!
Too slow, too slow, too slow!
-Sigh-
May you only have daughters.
GIGGLE...
Go on, Carmen. Benjamin is in the basement.
Thanks, Mrs. Thomas.
You're welcome, dear.
As for the two of *you,* that is enough of *that.* I will tolerate absolutely *no* horsing around inside!
You want to act like animals, I'll drop you off at the pound!
Awwww, Mooooom!

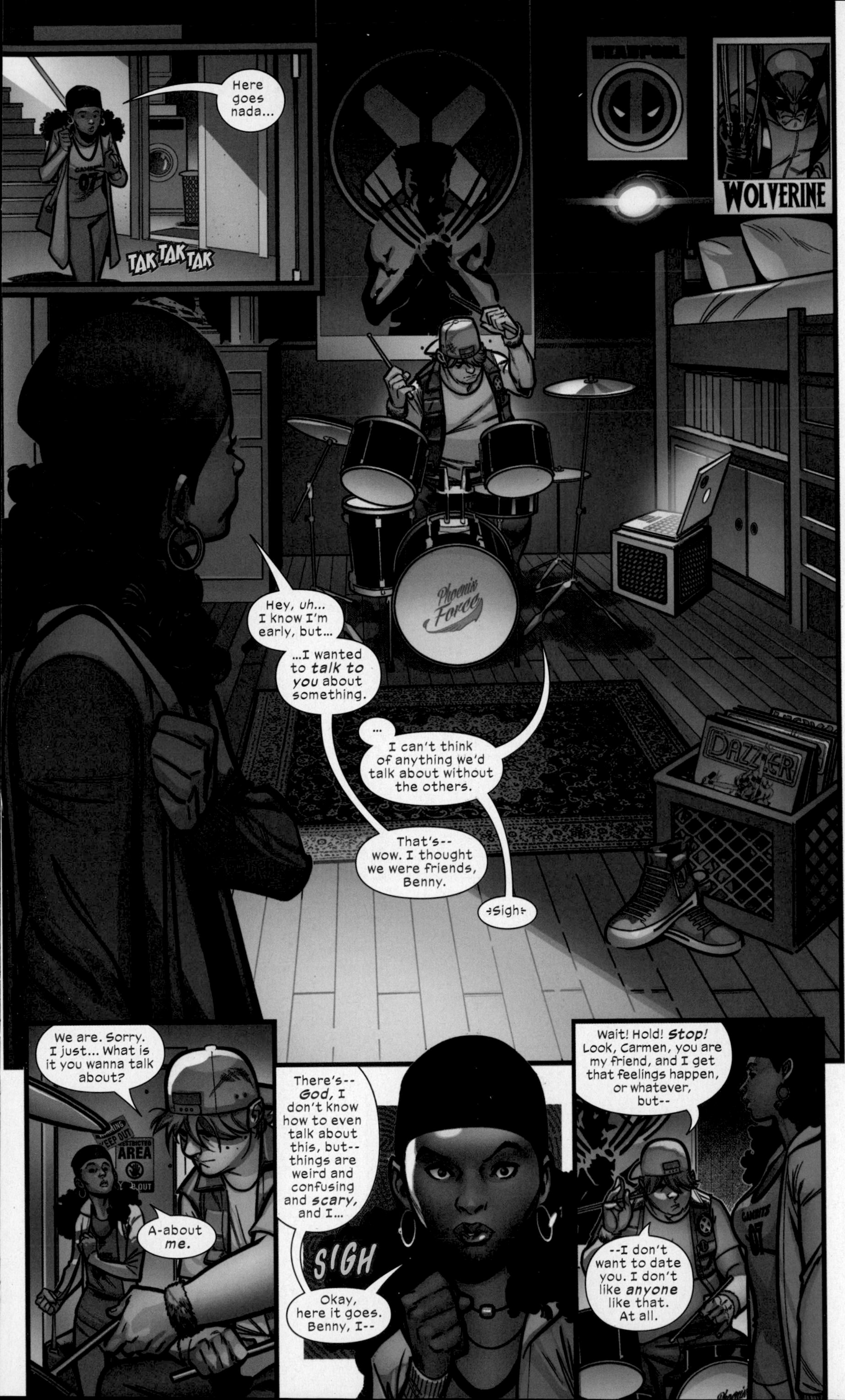
Here goes nada...
TAK TAK TAK
WOLVERINE
Hey, uh... I know I'm early, but...
...I wanted to talk to you about something.
...
I can't think of anything we'd talk about without the others.
That's-- wow. I thought we were friends, Benny.
-Sigh-
DAZZLER
We are. Sorry. I just... What is it you wanna talk about?
A-about me.
There's-- God, I don't know how to even talk about this, but-- things are weird and confusing and scary, and I...
SIGH
Okay, here it goes. Benny, I--
Wait! Hold! Stop! Look, Carmen, you are my friend, and I get that feelings happen, or whatever, but--
--I don't want to date you. I don't like anyone like that. At all.

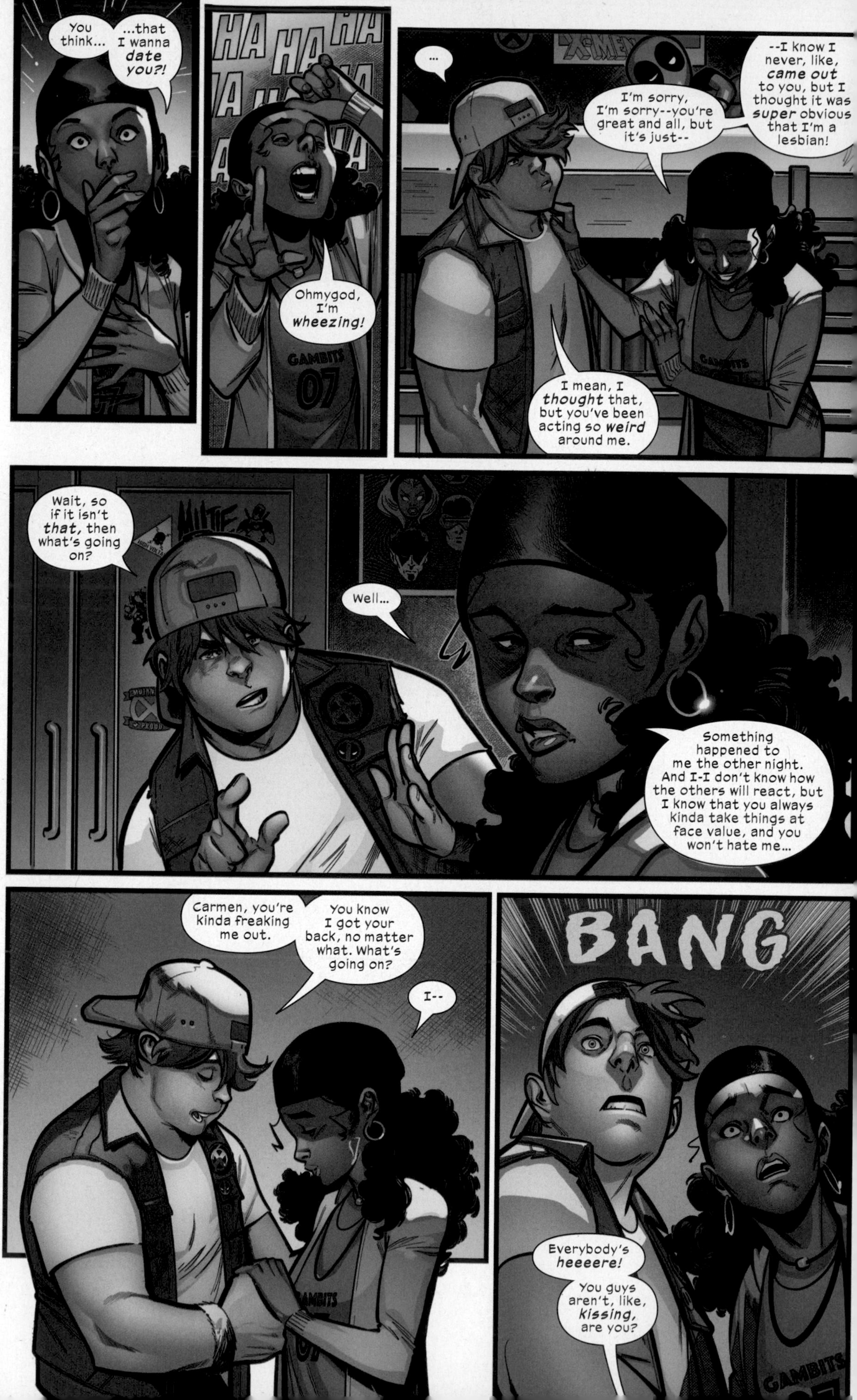
You think...
...that I wanna *date* you?!
HA HA HA HA HA HA
Ohmygod, I'm *wheezing!*
...
I'm sorry, I'm sorry--you're great and all, but it's just--
--I know I never, like, *came out* to you, but I thought it was *super* obvious that I'm a lesbian!
I mean, I *thought* that, but you've been acting so *weird* around me.
Wait, so if it isn't *that,* then what's going on?
Well...
Something happened to me the other night. And I-I don't know how the others will react, but I know that you always kinda take things at face value, and you won't hate me...
Carmen, you're kinda freaking me out.
You know I got your back, no matter what. What's going on?
I--
BANG
Everybody's *heeeere!*
You guys aren't, like, *kissing,* are you?

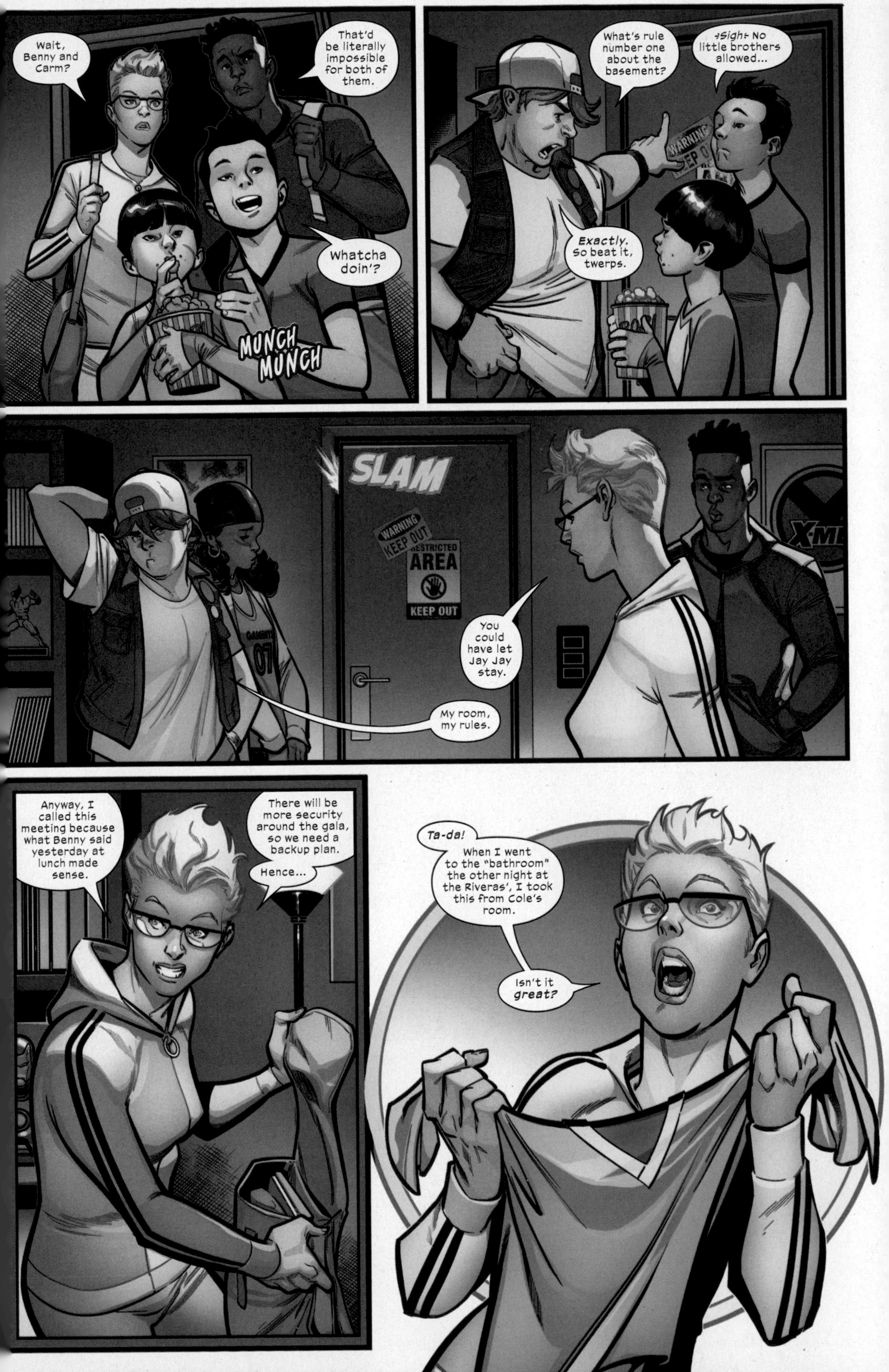

Wait, Benny and Carm?
That'd be literally impossible for both of them.
Whatcha doin'?
MUNCH MUNCH
What's rule number one about the basement?
-Sigh- No little brothers allowed...
WARNING KEEP O
Exactly. So beat it, twerps.
SLAM
WARNING KEEP OUT
RESTRICTED AREA
KEEP OUT
X-M
07
You could have let Jay Jay stay.
My room, my rules.
Anyway, I called this meeting because what Benny said yesterday at lunch made sense.
There will be more security around the gala, so we need a backup plan.
Hence...
Ta-da!
When I went to the "bathroom" the other night at the Riveras', I took this from Cole's room.
Isn't it great?

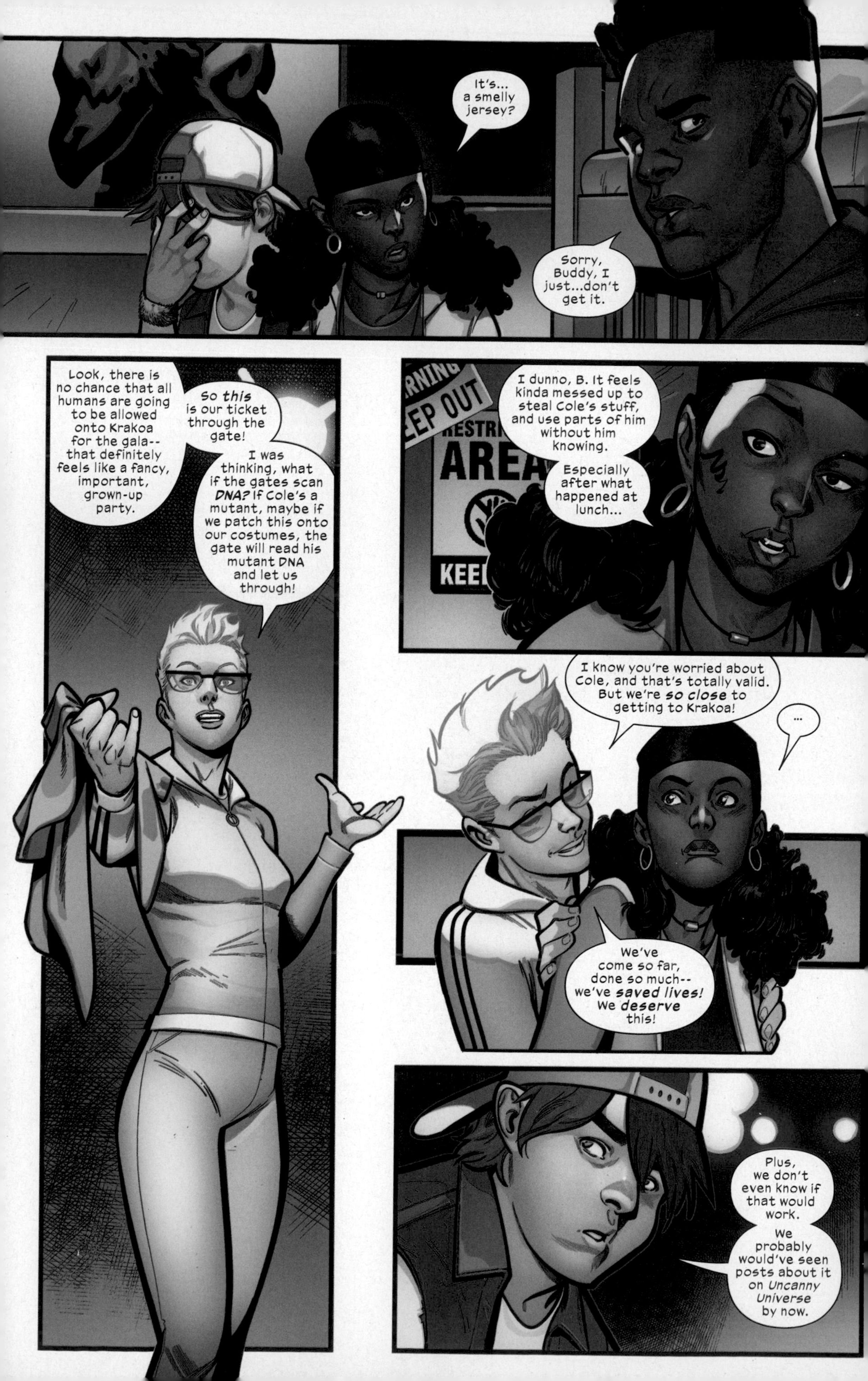
It's... a smelly jersey?
Sorry, Buddy, I just...don't get it.
Look, there is no chance that all humans are going to be allowed onto Krakoa for the gala-- that definitely feels like a fancy, important, grown-up party.
So *this* is our ticket through the gate!
I was thinking, what if the gates scan *DNA?* If Cole's a mutant, maybe if we patch this onto our costumes, the gate will read his mutant DNA and let us through!
WARNING
KEEP OUT
RESTRI
AREA
KEE
I dunno, B. It feels kinda messed up to steal Cole's stuff, and use parts of him without him knowing.
Especially after what happened at lunch...
I know you're worried about Cole, and that's totally valid. But we're *so close* to getting to Krakoa!
...
We've come so far, done so much-- we've *saved lives!* We *deserve* this!
Plus, we don't even know if that would work.
We probably would've seen posts about it on *Uncanny Universe* by now.

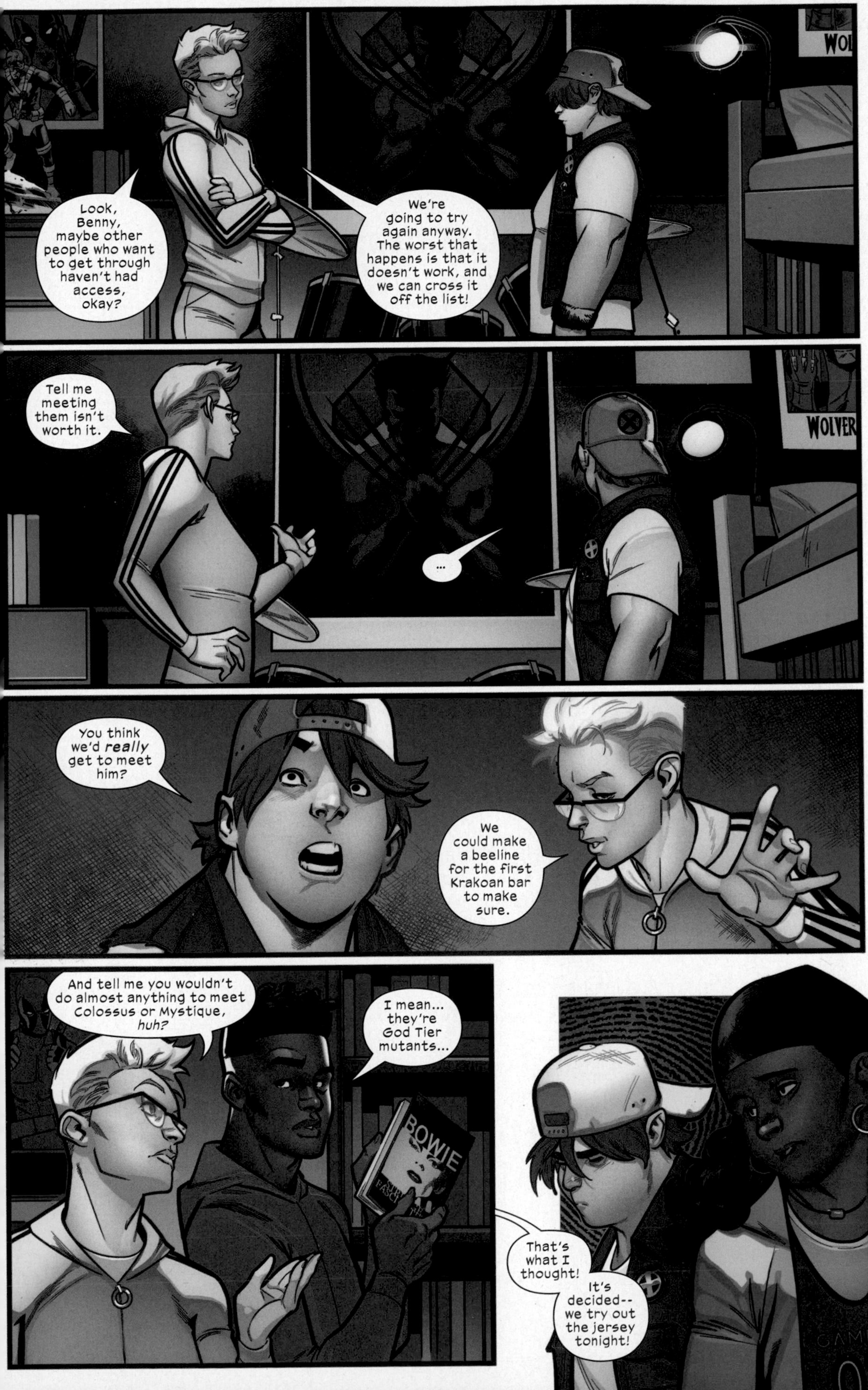
WOL
Look, Benny, maybe other people who want to get through haven't had access, okay?
We're going to try again anyway. The worst that happens is that it doesn't work, and we can cross it off the list!
Tell me meeting them isn't worth it.
WOLVER
...
You think we'd *really* get to meet him?
We could make a beeline for the first Krakoan bar to make sure.
And tell me you wouldn't do almost anything to meet Colossus or Mystique, *huh?*
I mean... they're God Tier mutants...
BOWIE
That's what I thought!
It's decided-- we try out the jersey tonight!
GAMBIT

Login/ Sign up

X-STREAM

Search

Newest Video | Featured Video | News | Forum | Contact Us

UNCANNY UNIVERSE/COLLECTIONS/SIGHTINGS/THEYOUNGXMEN

WHO are the Young X-Men?

Description:
The New Kids On The Block Caught Brawling!

A new group of mutants has been seen saving cats from trees and stopping purse-snatchings, but it looks like the wunderkind squad have upgraded to super-powered beefs with D-list villains.

Who are these baby X-Men? Drop any tips in the comments!

9:59

CURRENTLY PLAYING

Hellfire Gala
The Hellfire Trading Company
8:39

KRAKOA OPENING ITS DOORS TO HUMANS! MOD REACTION VID

300K VIEWS
X-POSTER

?
3:45

WHAT'S UP WITH THE X-MEN AND SWORDS?

487K VIEWS
MEDIA GAL

!!!!!
5:32

WHICH HEAVY-HITTIN X-MEN HAVE BEEN SEEN CUDDLING IN PUBLIC? THE ANSWER MAY SHOCK YOU!

1.1M VIEWS
KRAKOA VIEWER

3:45

UP NEXT

1.3M VIEWS
KRAKOA VIEWER

Comments:

ArchivistX: Their code names are - Marvel Guy, Cyclops-Lass, Cherub, Daycrawler, and Gimmick!

NightyNightCrawler: It's actually NightyNightCrawler, not Daycrawler, just fyi.

GeneJunk007: Those are the dumbest names I've ever heard! (Except Cherub, that's pretty legit...)

C.R.A.D.L.E.Official: If anyone has any information as to the whereabouts of these children, please follow this link and let us know. There is a small reward offered. We just want to make sure they are safe.

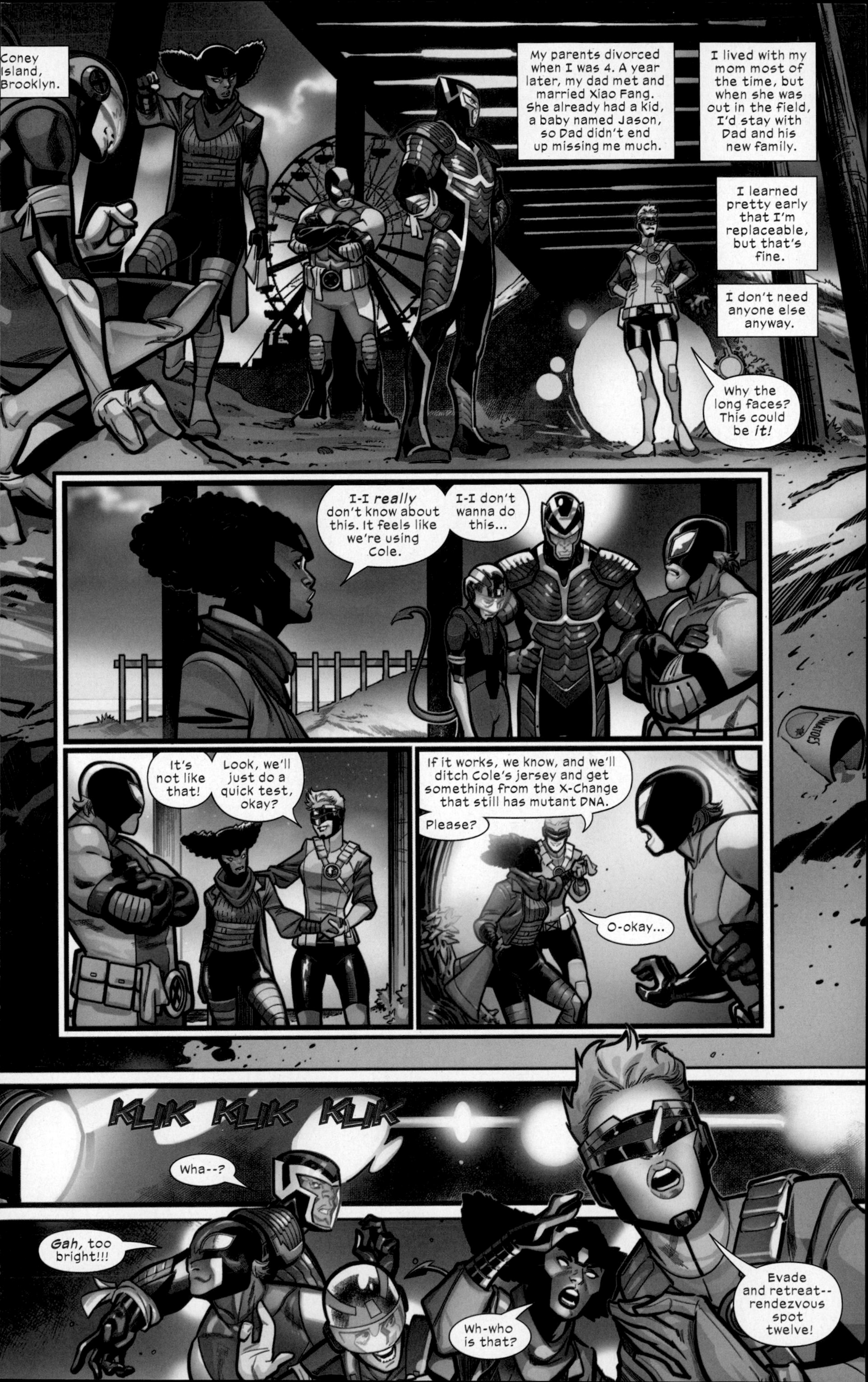

Coney Island, Brooklyn.
My parents divorced when I was 4. A year later, my dad met and married Xiao Fang. She already had a kid, a baby named Jason, so Dad didn't end up missing me much.
I lived with my mom most of the time, but when she was out in the field, I'd stay with Dad and his new family.
I learned pretty early that I'm replaceable, but that's fine.
I don't need anyone else anyway.
Why the long faces? This could be *it!*
I-I *really* don't know about this. It feels like we're using Cole.
I-I don't wanna do this...
It's not like that!
Look, we'll just do a quick test, okay?
If it works, we know, and we'll ditch Cole's jersey and get something from the X-Change that still has mutant DNA.
Please?
O-okay...
KLIK KLIK KLIK
Wha--?
Gah, too bright!!!
Wh-who is that?
Evade and retreat--rendezvous spot twelve!

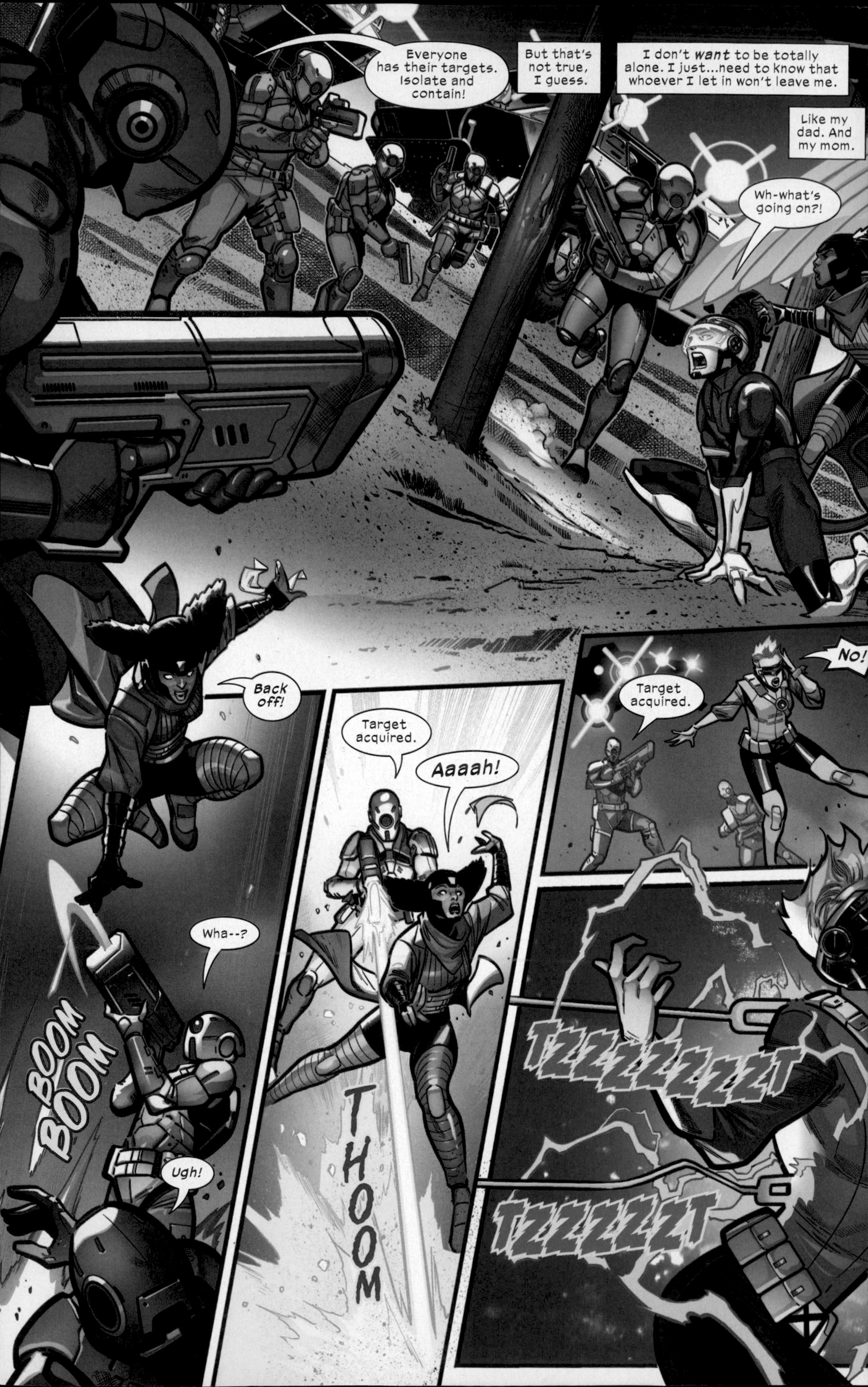
Everyone has their targets. Isolate and contain!
But that's not true, I guess.
I don't *want* to be totally alone. I just...need to know that whoever I let in won't leave me.
Like my dad. And my mom.
Wh-what's going on?!
Back off!
Wha--?
BOOM BOOM
Ugh!
Target acquired.
Aaaah!
THOOM
Target acquired.
No!
TZZZZZZZZT
TZZZZZZT

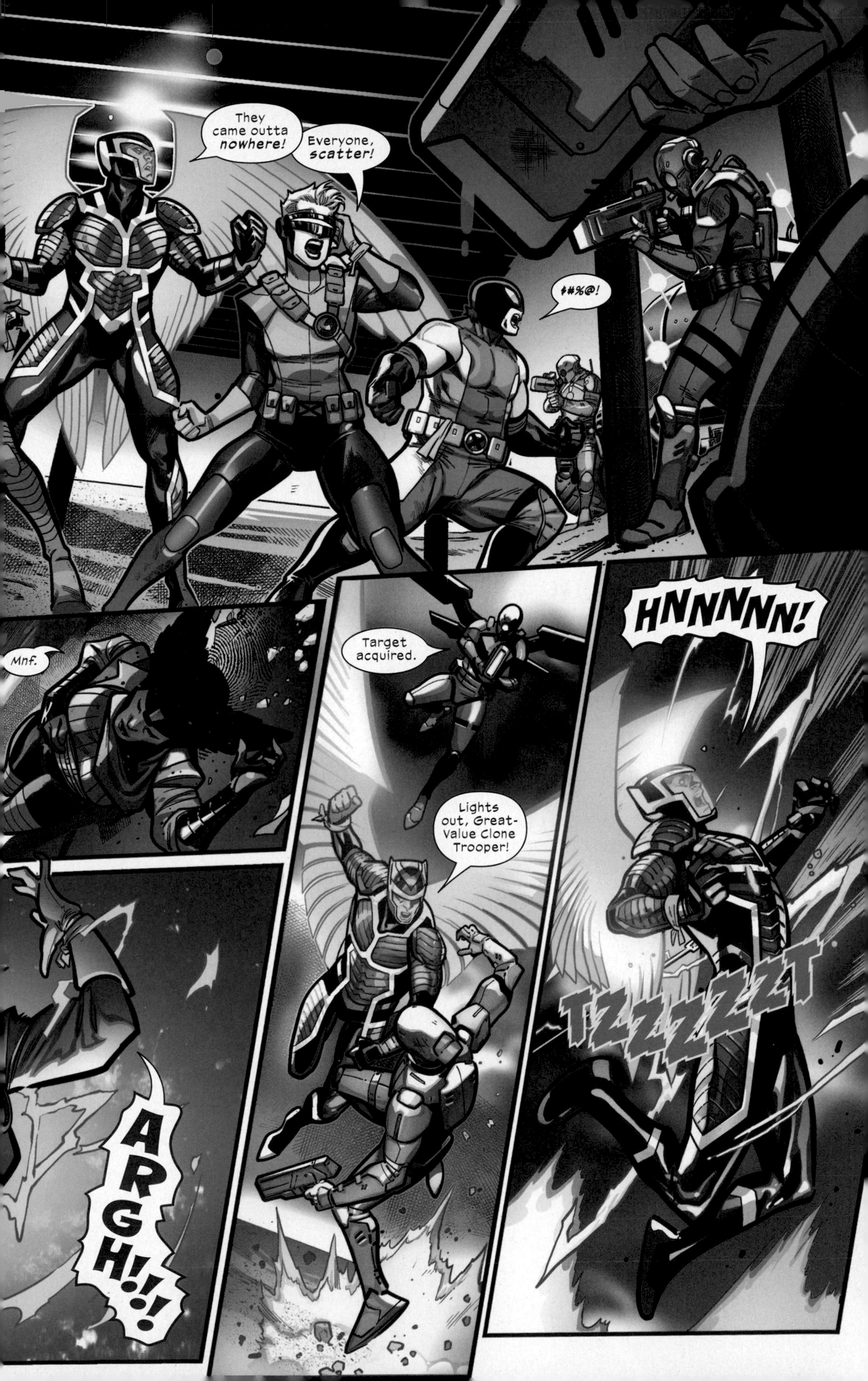
They came outta nowhere!
Everyone, scatter!
$#%@!
Mnf.
Target acquired.
HNNNNN!
Lights out, Great-Value Clone Trooper!
TZZZZZT
ARGH!!!

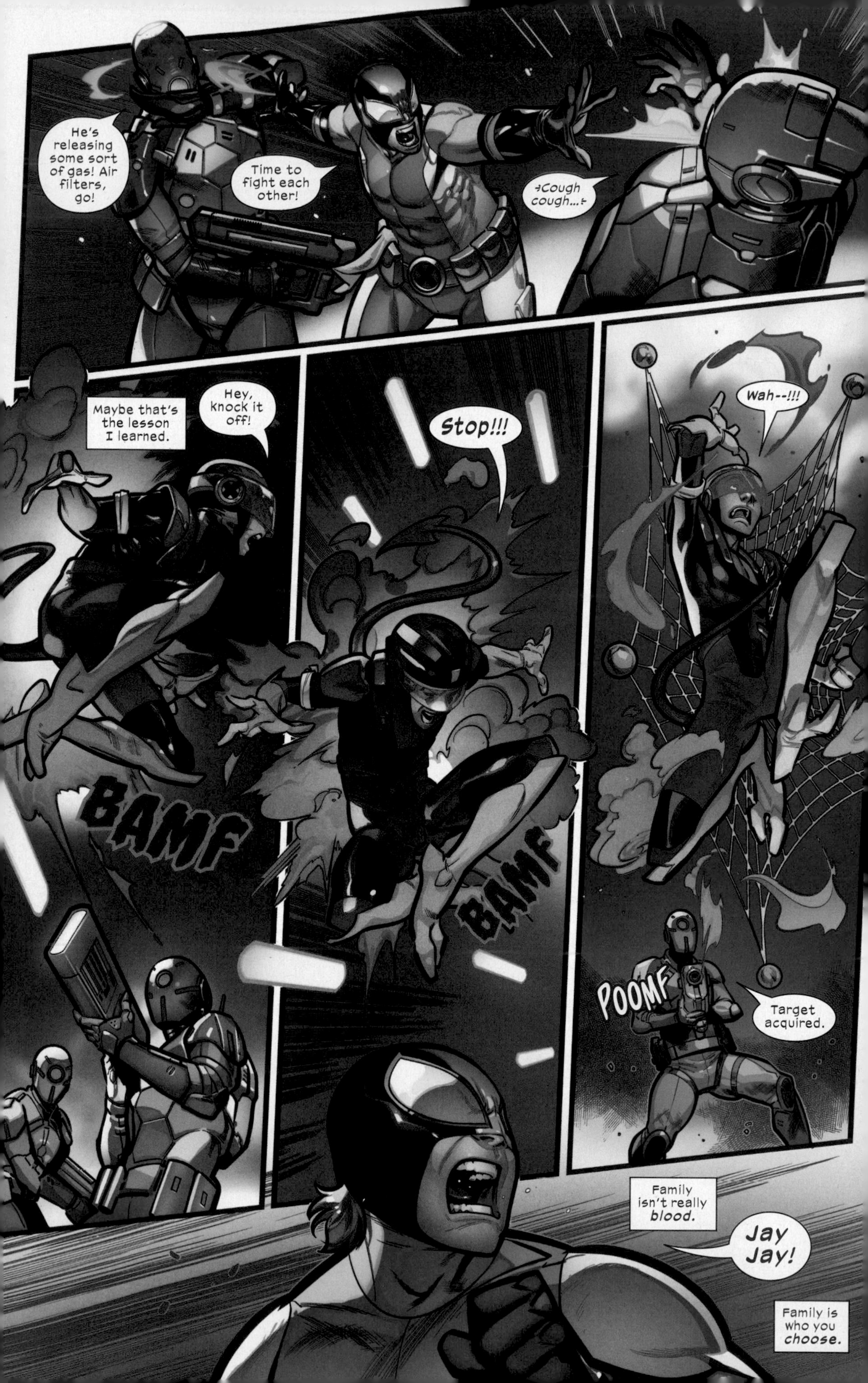

He's releasing some sort of gas! Air filters, go!
Time to fight each other!
Cough cough...
Maybe that's the lesson I learned.
Hey, knock it off!
Stop!!!
Wah--!!!
BAMF
BAMF
POOMF
Target acquired.
Family isn't really *blood.*
Jay Jay!
Family is who you *choose.*

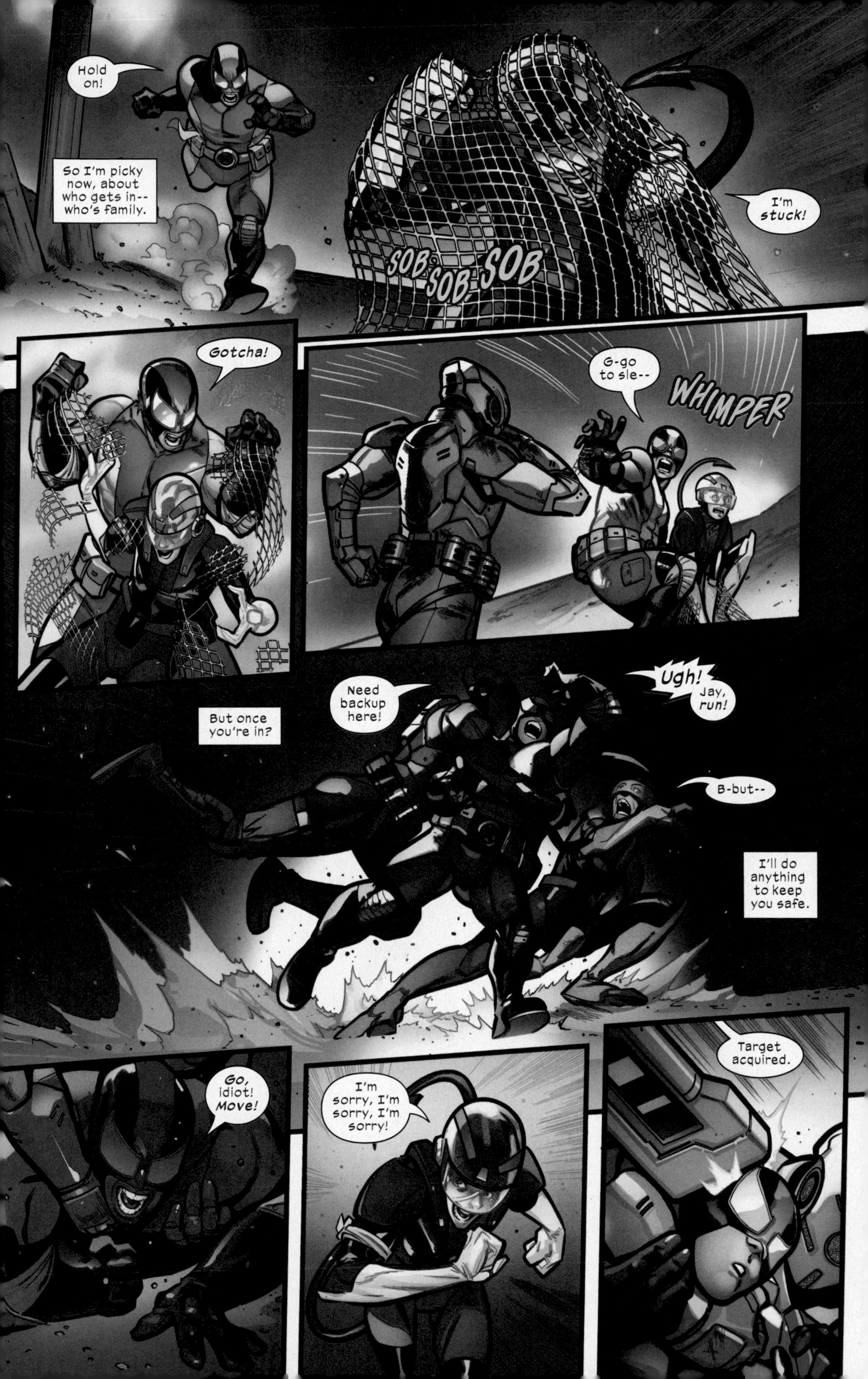
Hold on!
So I'm picky now, about who gets in-- who's family.
I'm stuck!
SOB SOB SOB
Gotcha!
G-go to sle--
WHIMPER
But once you're in?
Need backup here!
Ugh! Jay, run!
B-but--
I'll do anything to keep you safe.
Go, idiot! Move!
I'm sorry, I'm sorry, I'm sorry!
Target acquired.

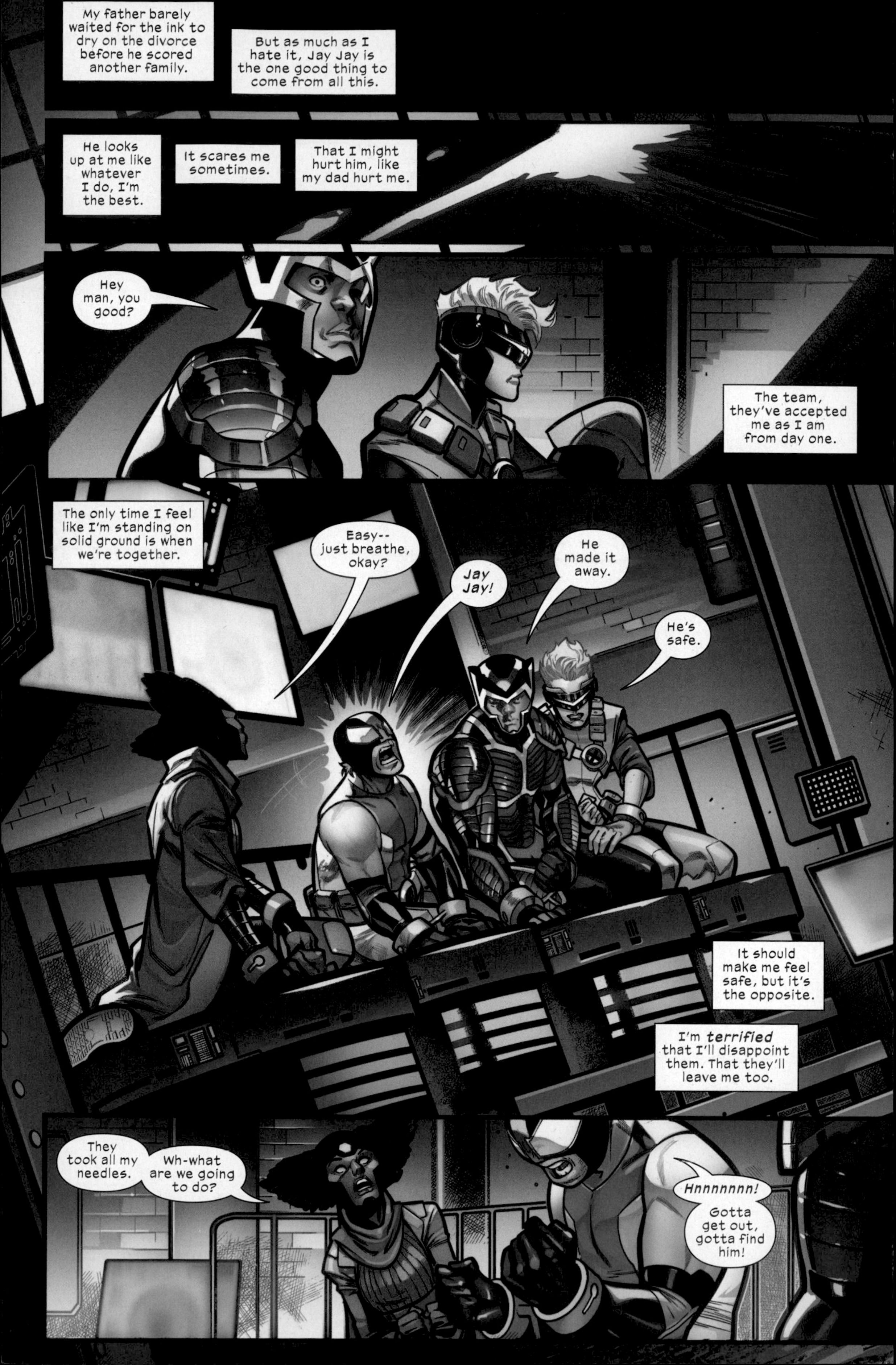
My father barely waited for the ink to dry on the divorce before he scored another family.
But as much as I hate it, Jay Jay is the one good thing to come from all this.
He looks up at me like whatever I do, I'm the best.
It scares me sometimes.
That I might hurt him, like my dad hurt me.
Hey man, you good?
The team, they've accepted me as I am from day one.
The only time I feel like I'm standing on solid ground is when we're together.
Easy-- just breathe, okay?
Jay Jay!
He made it away.
He's safe.
It should make me feel safe, but it's the opposite.
I'm *terrified* that I'll disappoint them. That they'll leave me too.
They took all my needles.
Wh-what are we going to do?
Hnnnnnnn!
Gotta get out, gotta find him!

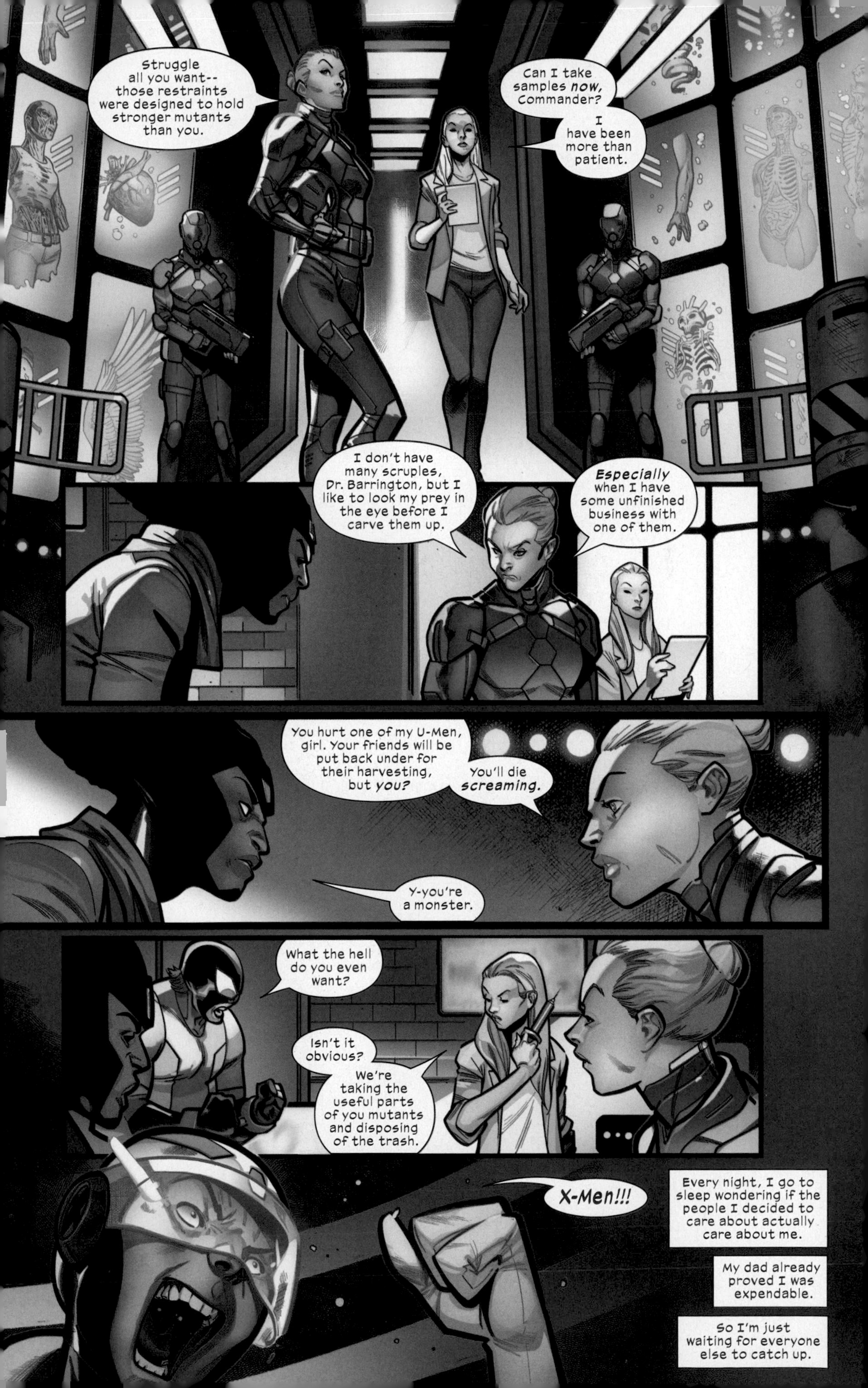
Struggle all you want-- those restraints were designed to hold stronger mutants than you.
Can I take samples now, Commander?
I have been more than patient.
I don't have many scruples, Dr. Barrington, but I like to look my prey in the eye before I carve them up.
Especially when I have some unfinished business with one of them.
You hurt one of my U-Men, girl. Your friends will be put back under for their harvesting, but you?
You'll die screaming.
Y-you're a monster.
What the hell do you even want?
Isn't it obvious?
We're taking the useful parts of you mutants and disposing of the trash.
X-Men!!!
Every night, I go to sleep wondering if the people I decided to care about actually care about me.
My dad already proved I was expendable.
So I'm just waiting for everyone else to catch up.

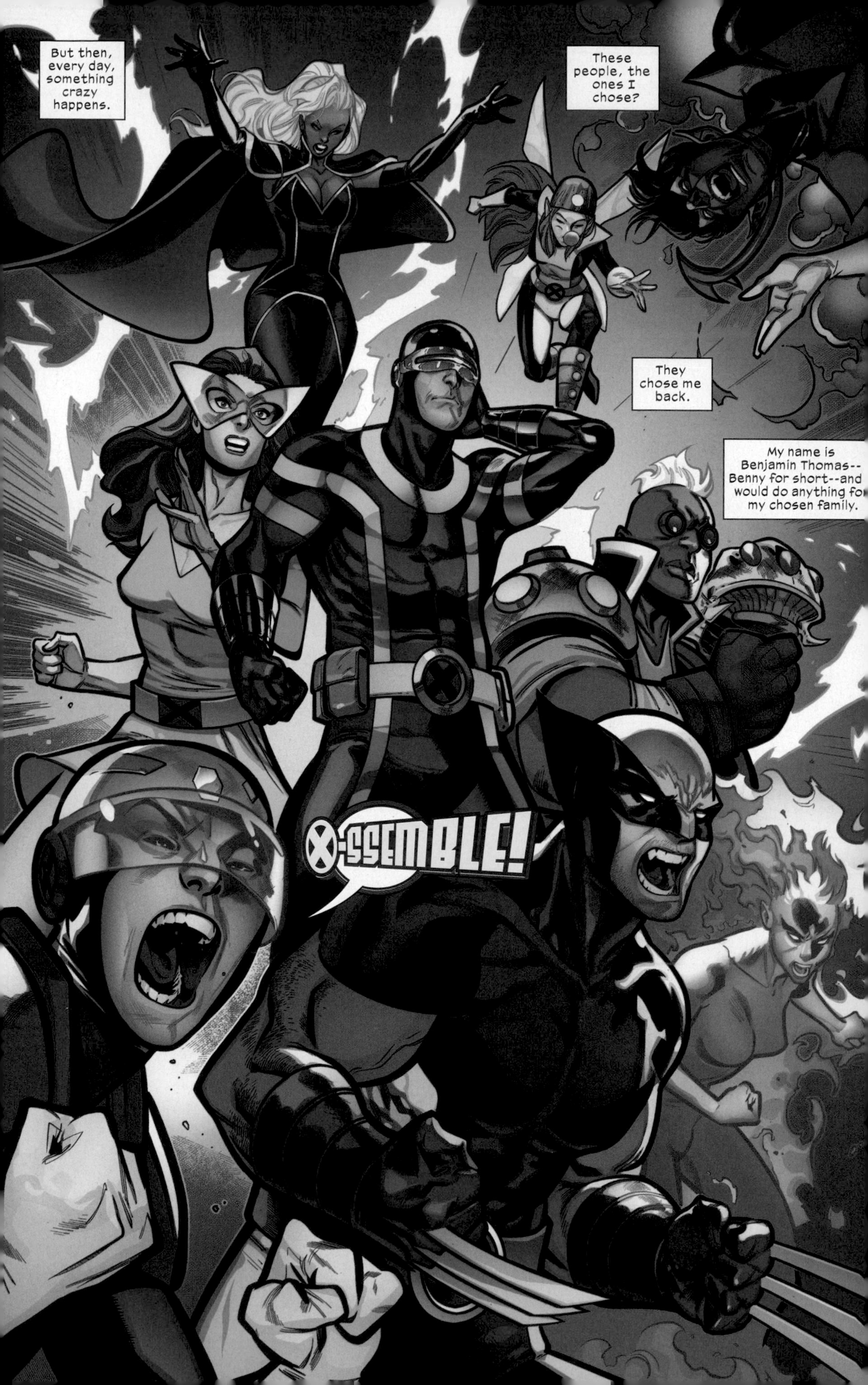
But then, every day, something crazy happens.
These people, the ones I chose?
They chose me back.
My name is Benjamin Thomas--Benny for short--and would do anything fo my chosen family.
X-SSEMBLE!

[Child[REN]_of]
[____the_A[TOM]

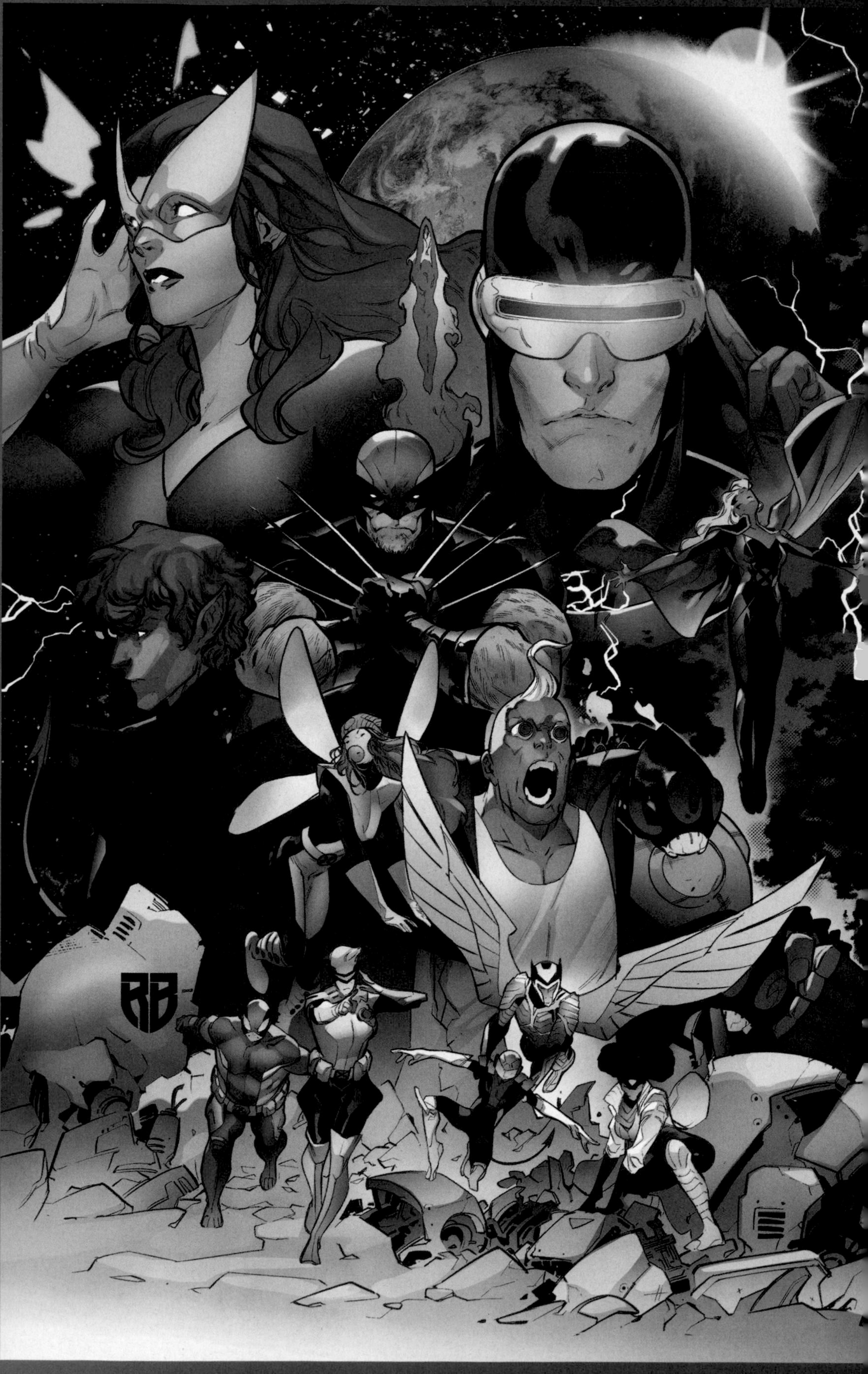

Reinforcements

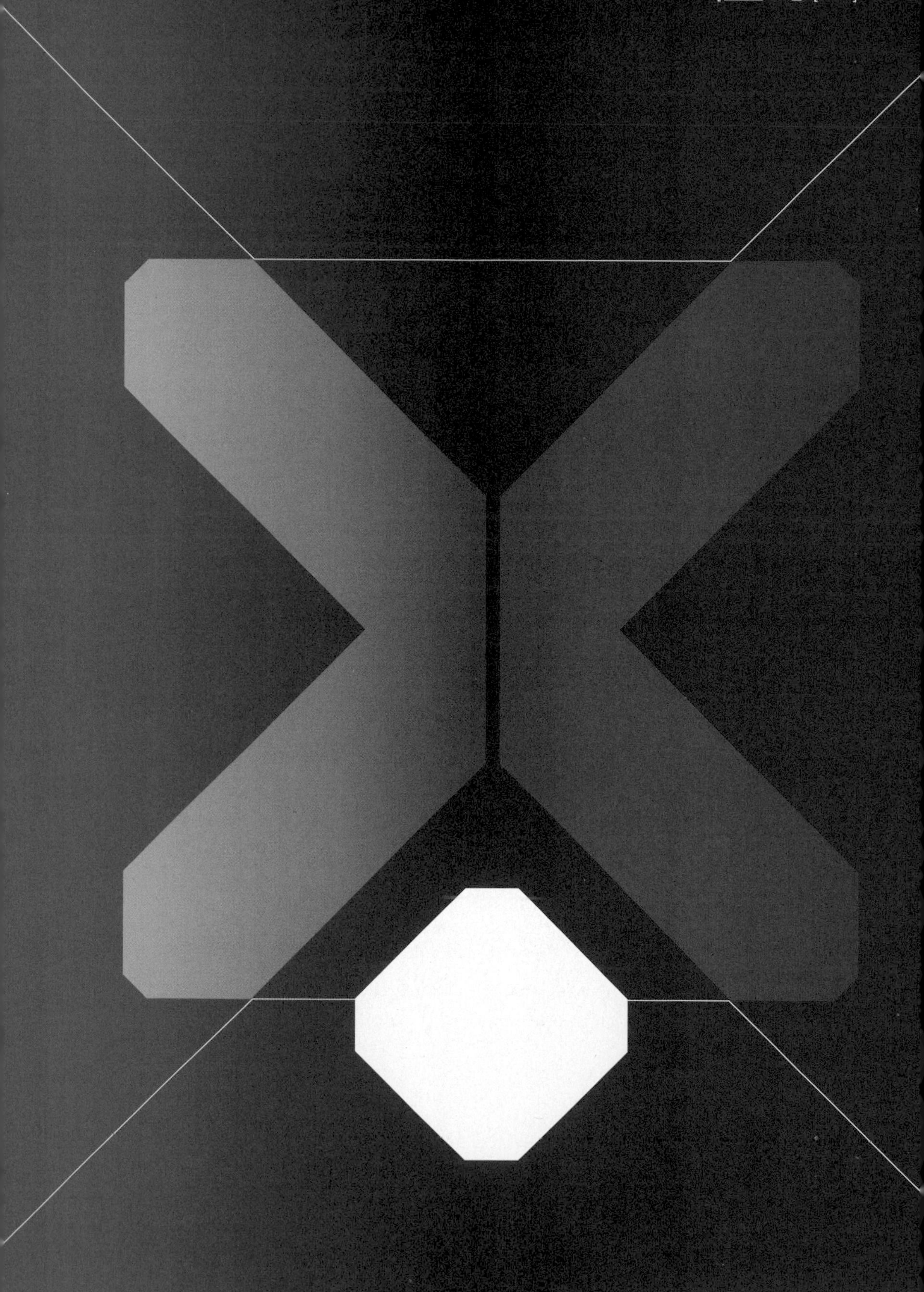

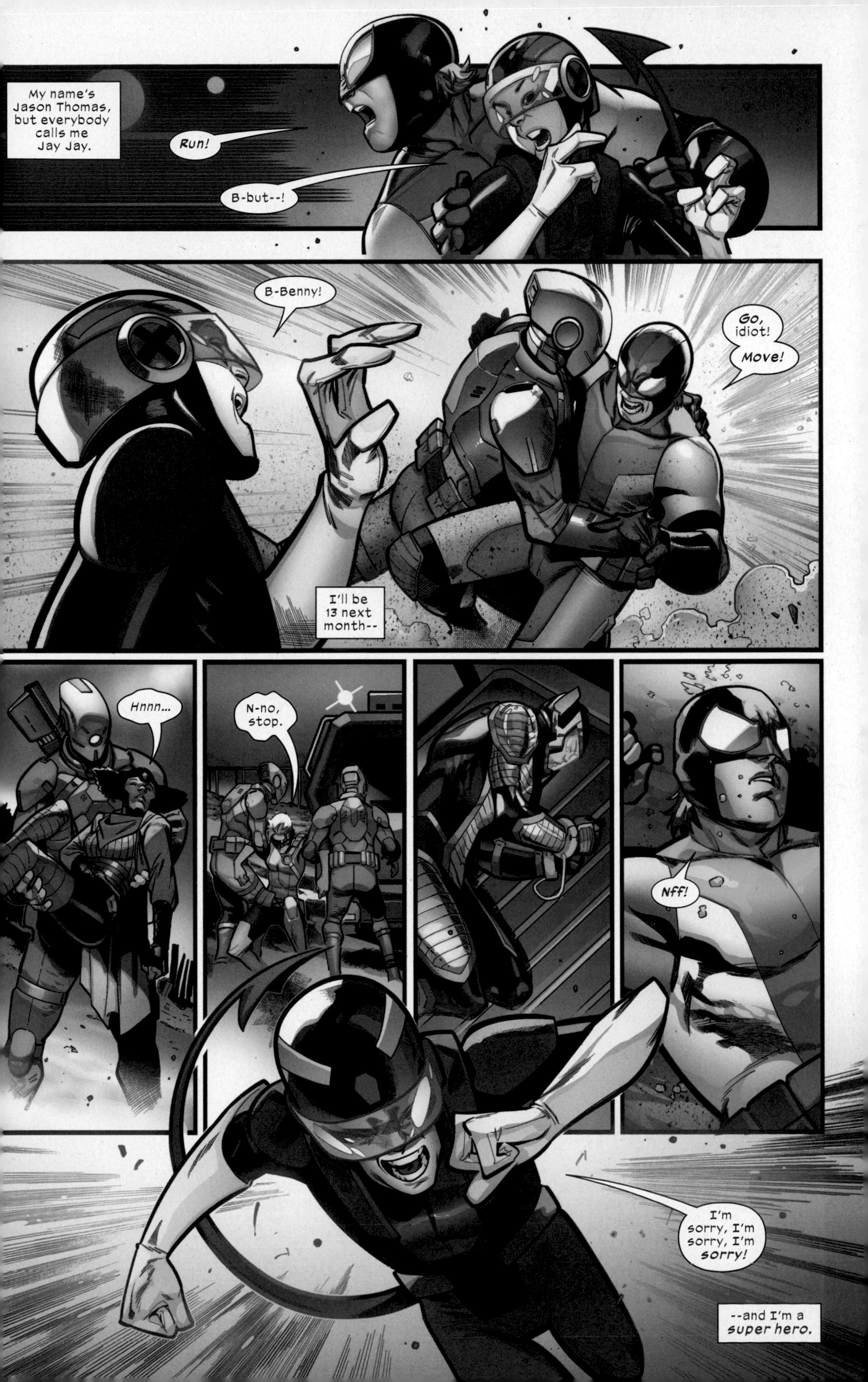

My name's Jason Thomas, but everybody calls me Jay Jay.
Run!
B-but--!
B-Benny!
Go, idiot!
Move!
I'll be 13 next month--
Hnnn...
N-no, stop.
Nff!
I'm sorry, I'm sorry, I'm sorry!
--and I'm a super hero.

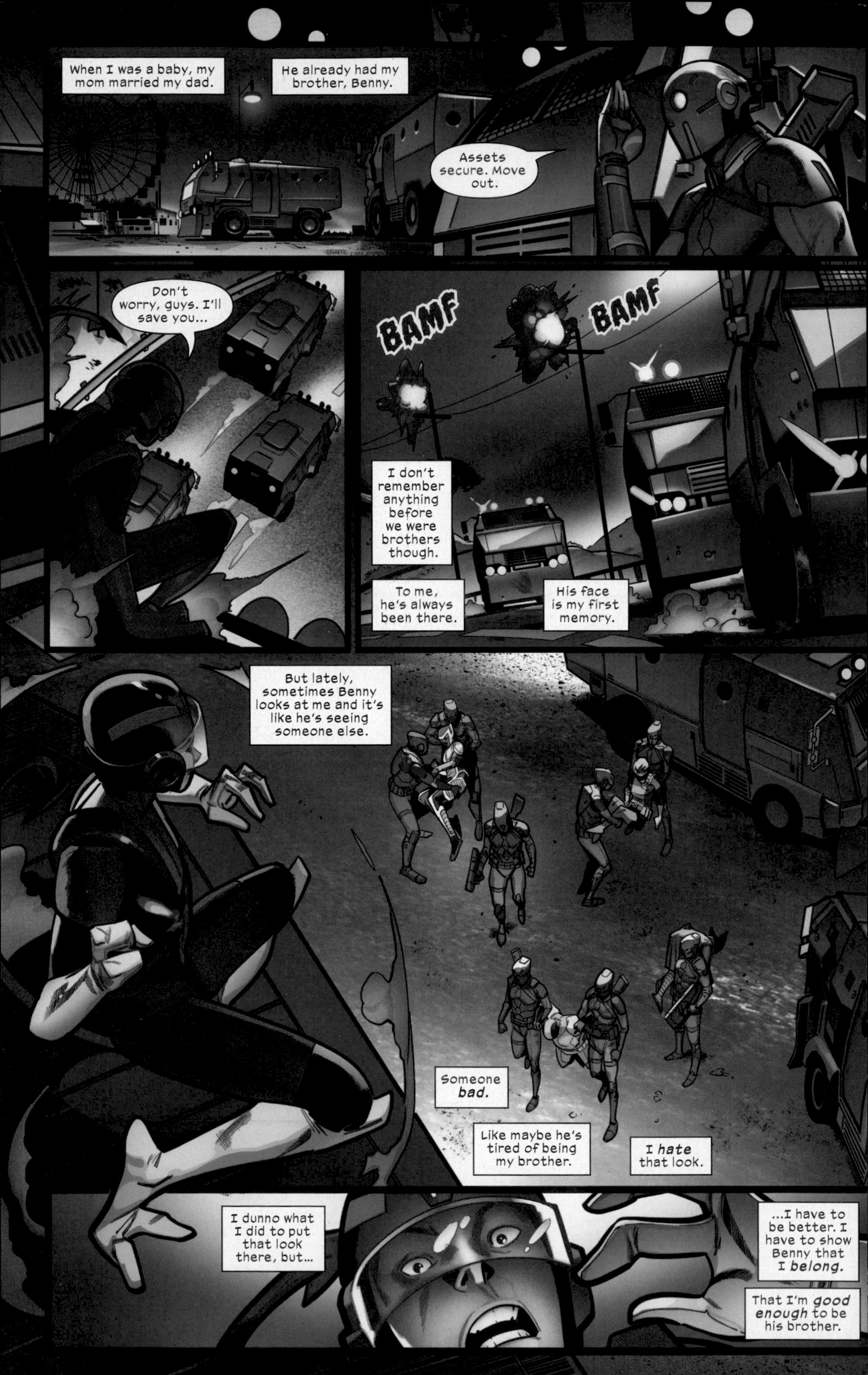

When I was a baby, my mom married my dad.
He already had my brother, Benny.
Assets secure. Move out.
Don't worry, guys. I'll save you...
BAMF
BAMF
I don't remember anything before we were brothers though.
To me, he's always been there.
His face is my first memory.
But lately, sometimes Benny looks at me and it's like he's seeing someone else.
Someone *bad.*
Like maybe he's tired of being my brother.
I *hate* that look.
I dunno what I did to put that look there, but...
...I have to be better. I have to show Benny that I *belong.*
That I'm *good enough* to be his brother.

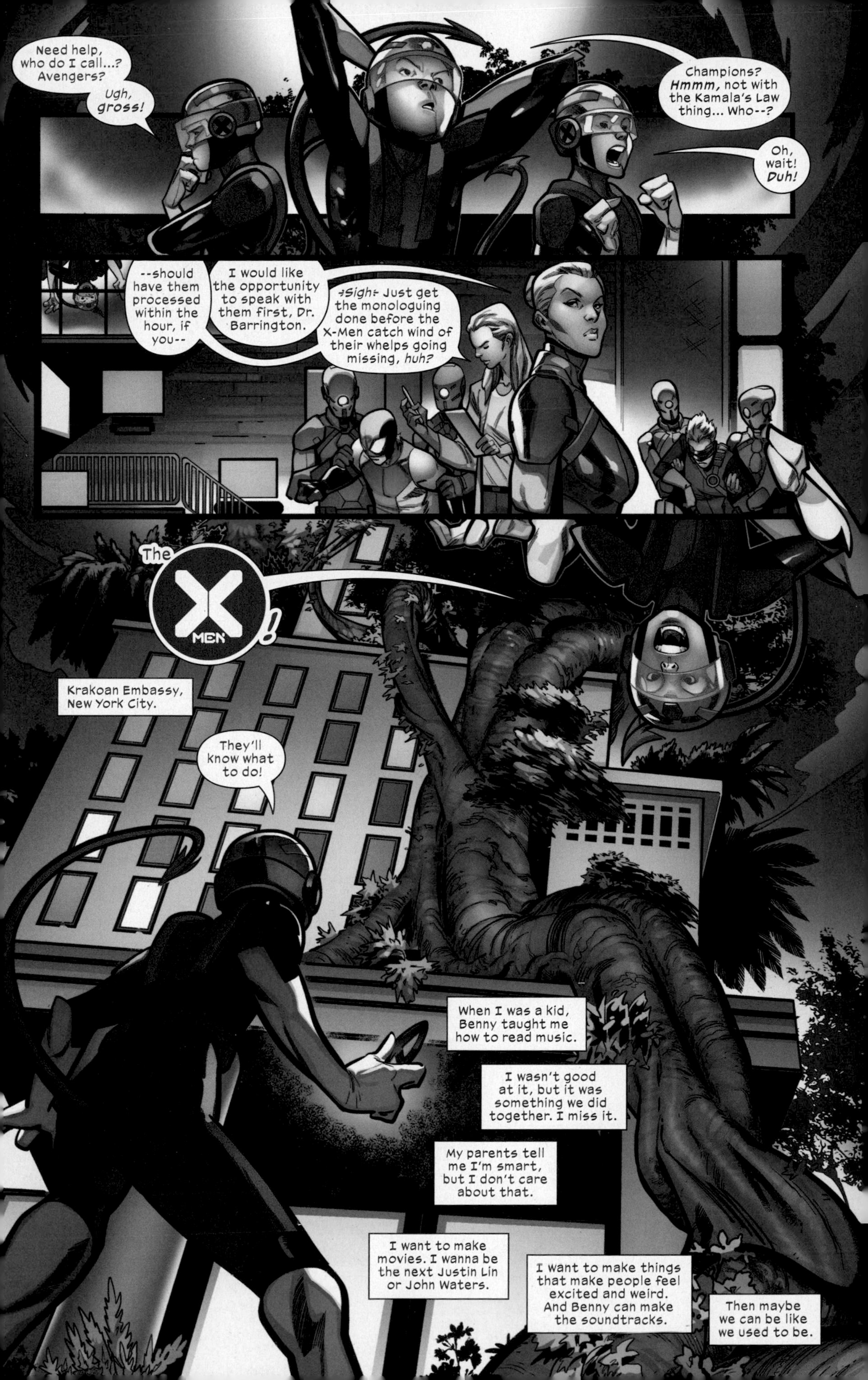

Need help, who do I call...? Avengers?
Ugh, gross!
Champions? Hmmm, not with the Kamala's Law thing... Who--?
Oh, wait! Duh!
--should have them processed within the hour, if you--
I would like the opportunity to speak with them first, Dr. Barrington.
-Sigh- Just get the monologuing done before the X-Men catch wind of their whelps going missing, huh?
The X-Men!
Krakoan Embassy, New York City.
They'll know what to do!
When I was a kid, Benny taught me how to read music.
I wasn't good at it, but it was something we did together. I miss it.
My parents tell me I'm smart, but I don't care about that.
I want to make movies. I wanna be the next Justin Lin or John Waters.
I want to make things that make people feel excited and weird. And Benny can make the soundtracks.
Then maybe we can be like we used to be.

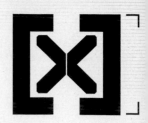

A STUDY OF THE POWERFUL GEAR USED BY THE CHILDREN OF THE ATOM

Source: Alien technology of unknown origin

Beatrice "Buddy" Bartholomew, A.K.A. Cyclops-Lass

Heat beam/laser-cutting tech inside her visor. The kids theorize that this is welding technology.

Gabriel "Gabe" Brathwaite, A.K.A. Cherub

Flight via thrusters that look like wings, and a sonic/acoustic blast from a tool that is disguised as a hand harp. The kids theorize that this is mobility and demolition tech.

Carmen Maria Cruz, A.K.A. Gimmick

Absorption and manipulation of kinetic energy and the ability to charge objects with that energy through gauntlets/gloves -- charged objects discharge energy through controlled explosions. The kids theorize that this is some sort of excavation technology.

Benjamin "Benny" Thomas, A.K.A. Marvel Guy

Can affect living beings through pheromones via a small handheld tool incorporated into his gloves -- it appears as if it is psychic suggestion, but is closer to a chemically induced empathic suggestion. The kids theorize this tech was primarily used to clear areas of animals or maybe as a perimeter control, as it doesn't cause any lasting changes/harm.

Jason "Jay Jay" Thomas, A.K.A. Daycrawler, A.K.A. Nighty-Nightcrawler

Short-range teleportation of self and/or of other objects via a small teleportation-field generator on his belt controlled by tech in his gloves, which operates a little like folding space or creating a small wormhole. The kids theorize this tech is to aid in sample gathering. (Note: The smoke comes from a small smoke machine that Carmen rigged to go off whenever Jay Jay teleports.)

The Children of the Atom also have headgear that blocks telepathy -- they got them off the mutant paraphernalia black market. Some are pieces of old Magneto helmets that were modified and sold, others are from unknown origins. Carmen modified them and incorporated them into the costumes.

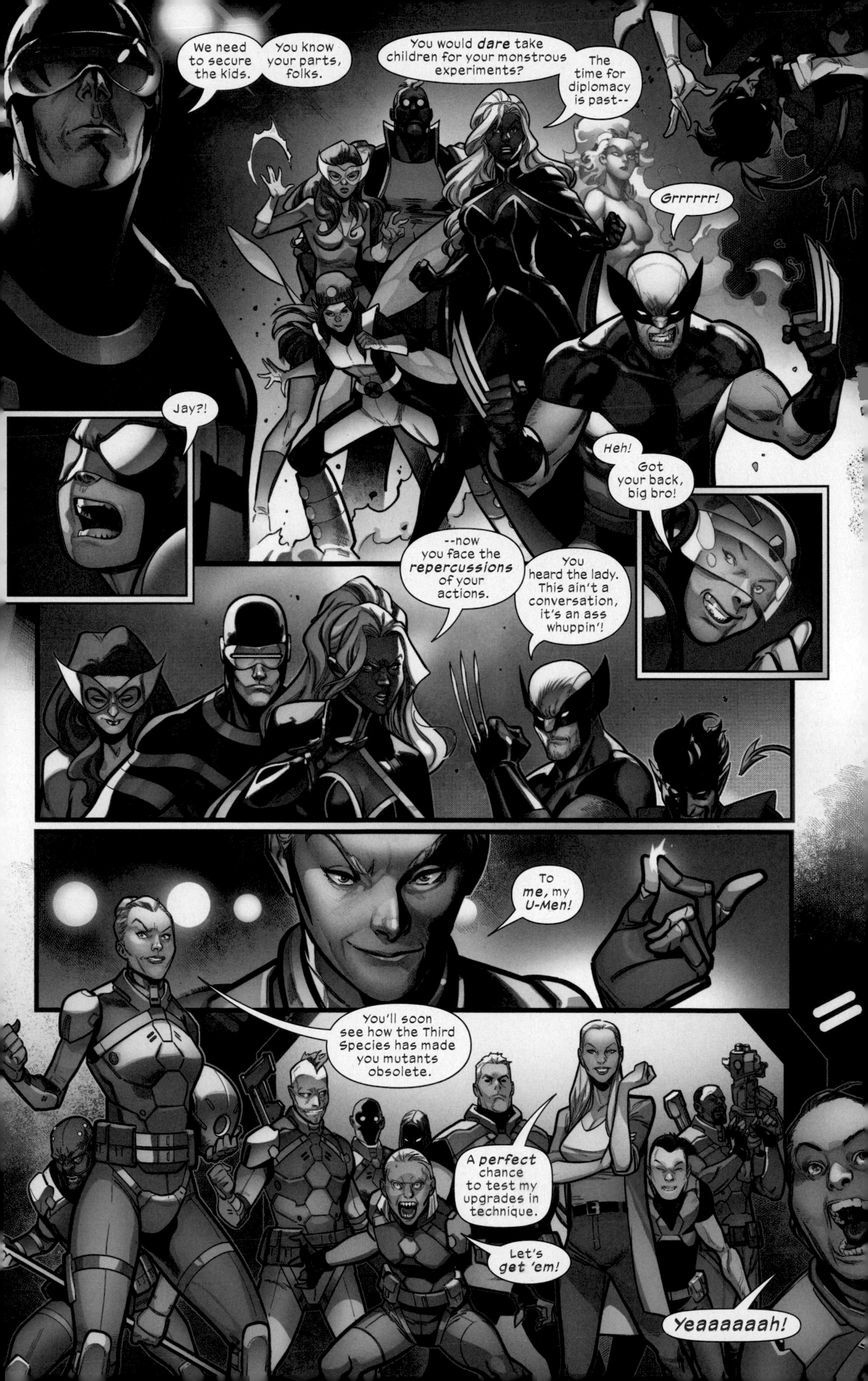
We need to secure the kids.
You know your parts, folks.
You would *dare* take children for your monstrous experiments?
The time for diplomacy is past--
Grrrrrr!
Jay?!
Heh!
Got your back, big bro!
--now you face the *repercussions* of your actions.
You heard the lady. This ain't a conversation, it's an ass whuppin'!
To *me*, my *U-Men!*
You'll soon see how the Third Species has made you mutants obsolete.
A *perfect* chance to test my upgrades in technique.
Let's *get 'em!*
Yeaaaaaah!

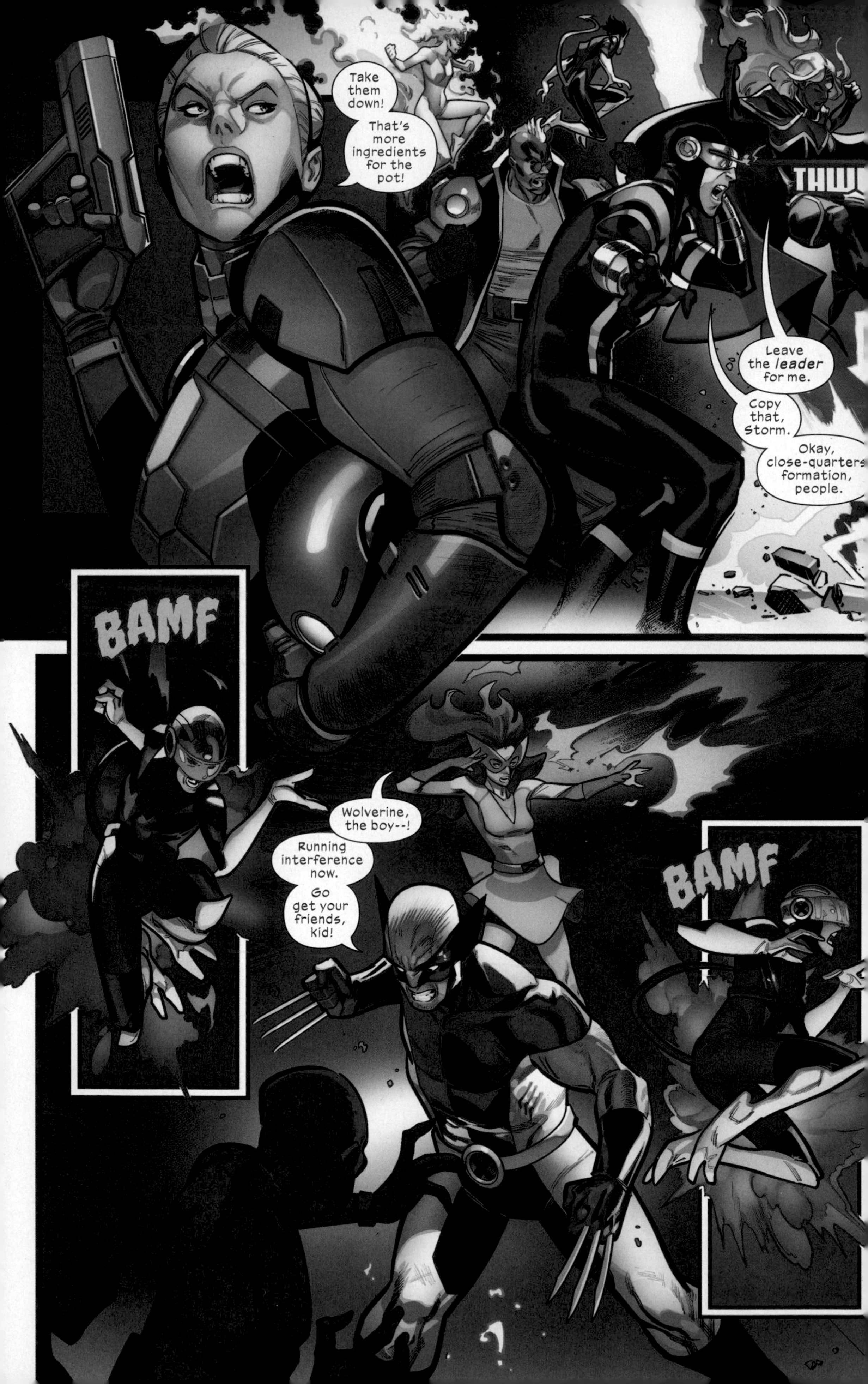
Take them down!
That's more ingredients for the pot!
THWU
Leave the *leader* for me.
Copy that, Storm.
Okay, close-quarters formation, people.
BAMF
Wolverine, the boy--!
Running interference now.
Go get your friends, kid!
BAMF

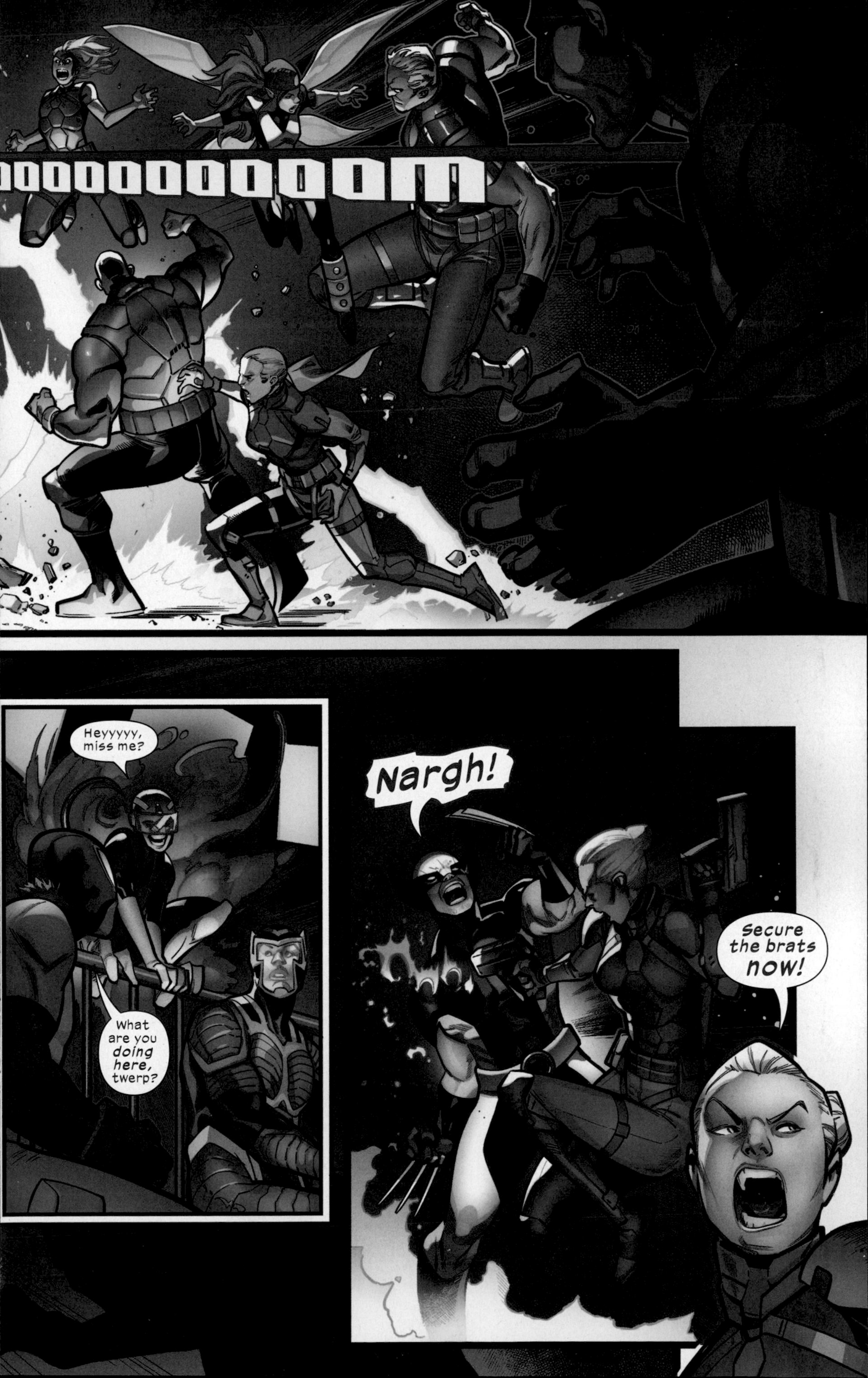

OOOOOOOOOOOOOM
Heyyyyy, miss me?
What are you doing here, twerp?
Nargh!
Secure the brats now!

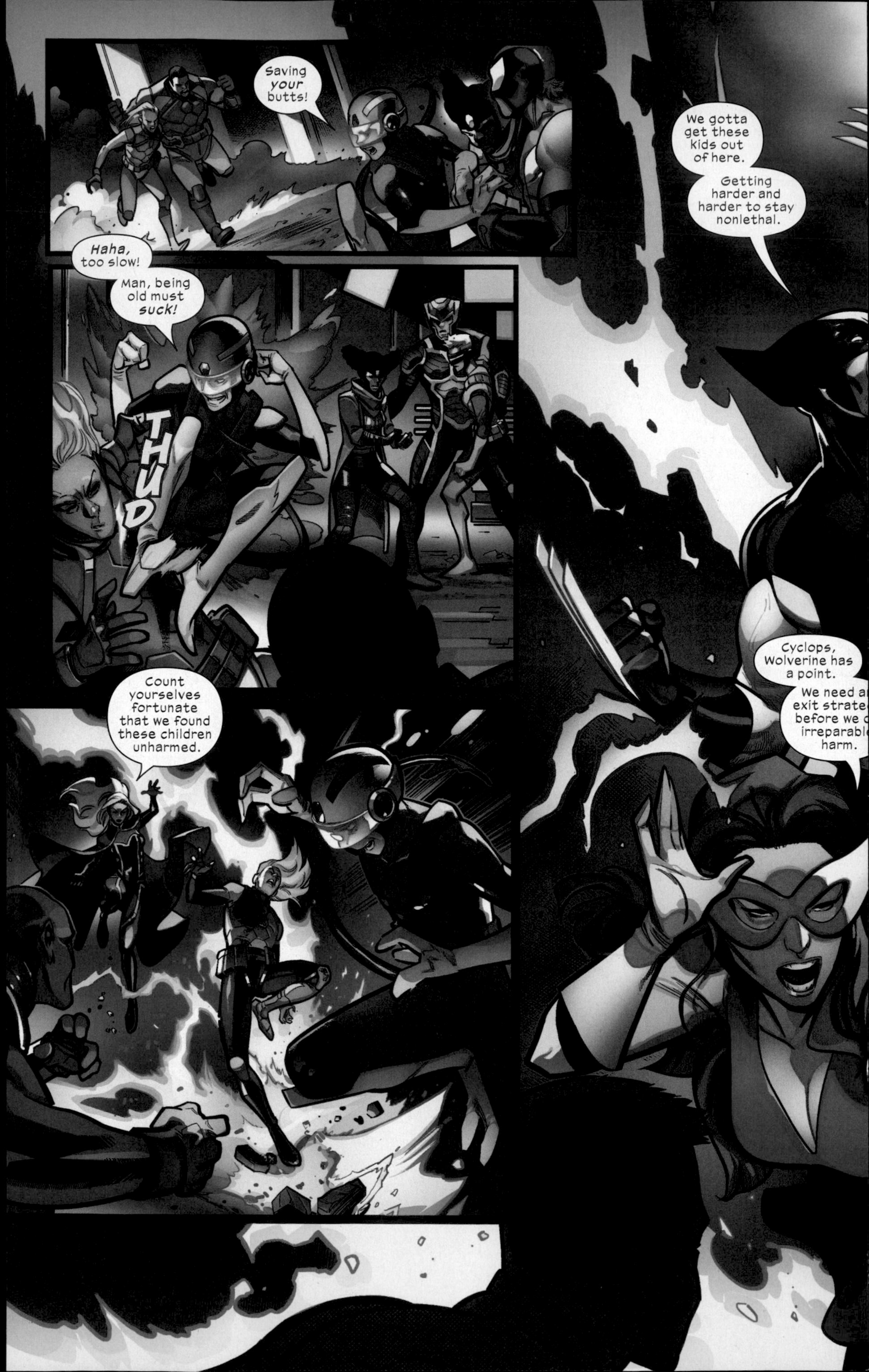

Saving your butts!
We gotta get these kids out of here.
Getting harder and harder to stay nonlethal.
Haha, too slow!
Man, being old must suck!
THUD
Count yourselves fortunate that we found these children unharmed.
Cyclops, Wolverine has a point.

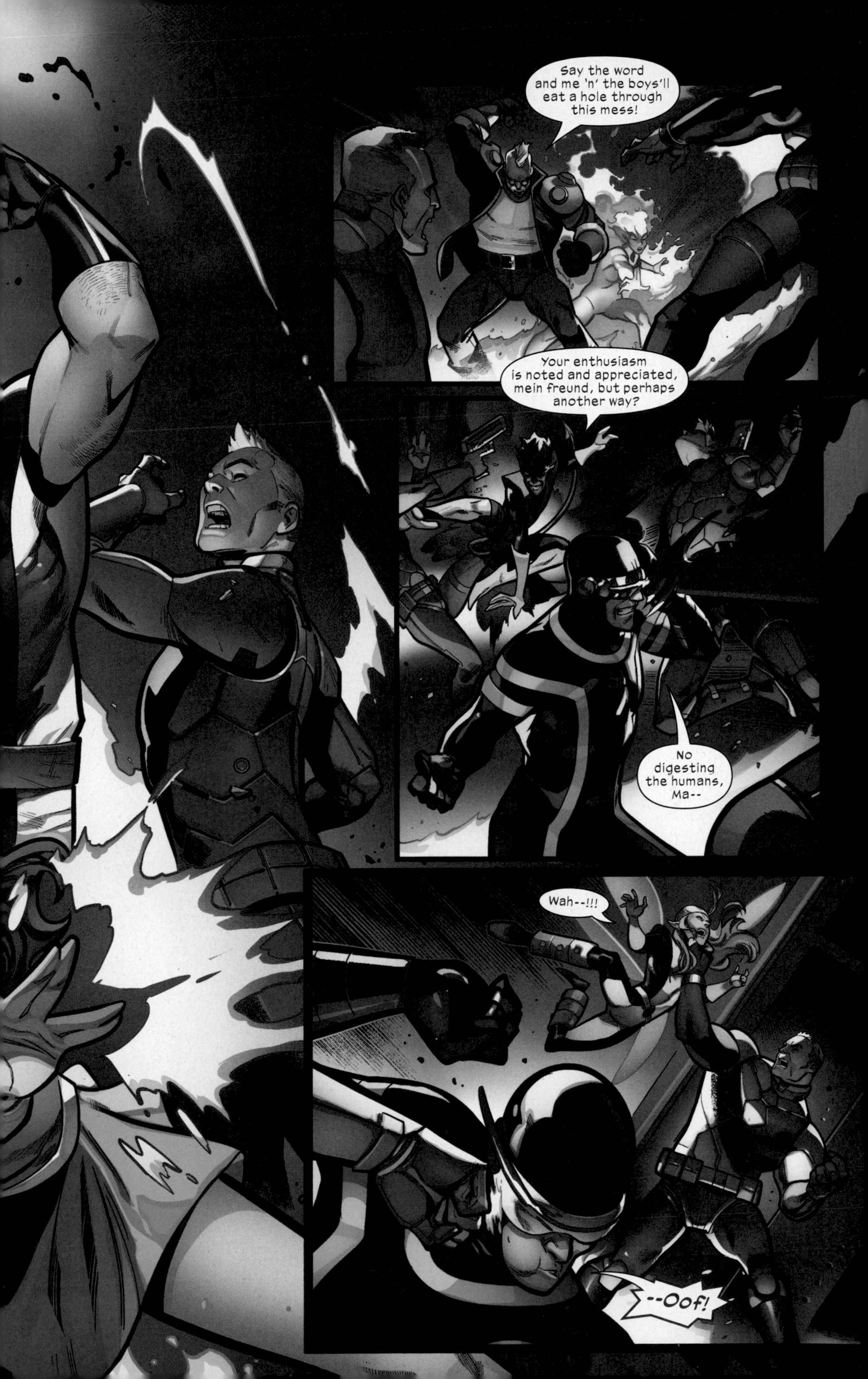

Say the word and me 'n' the boys'll eat a hole through this mess!
Your enthusiasm is noted and appreciated, mein freund, but perhaps another way?
No digesting the humans, Ma--
Wah--!!!
--Oof!

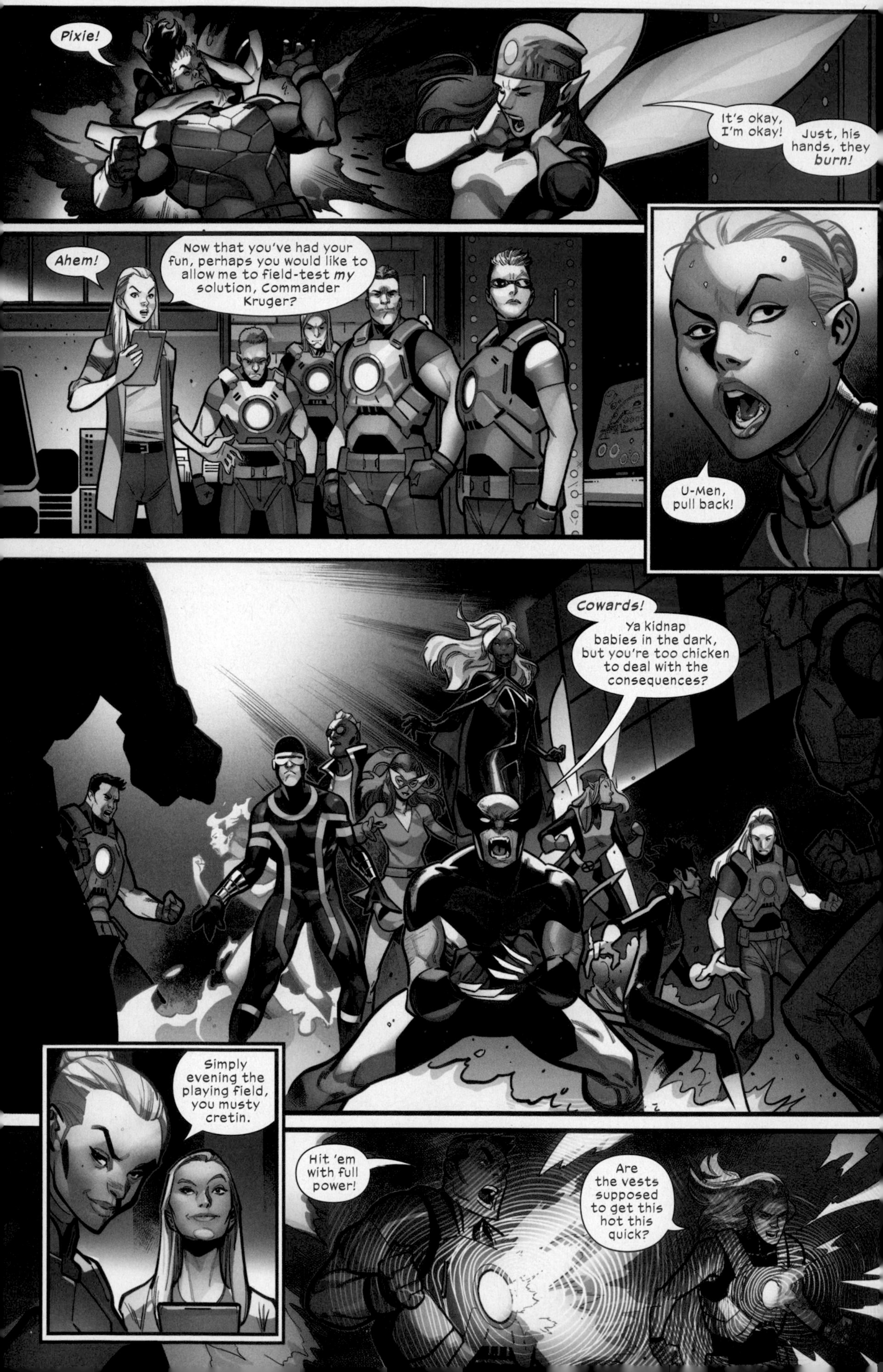
Pixie!
It's okay, I'm okay!
Just, his hands, they *burn!*
Ahem!
Now that you've had your fun, perhaps you would like to allow me to field-test *my* solution, Commander Kruger?
U-Men, pull back!
Cowards!
Ya kidnap babies in the dark, but you're too chicken to deal with the consequences?
Simply evening the playing field, you musty cretin.
Hit 'em with full power!
Are the vests supposed to get this hot this quick?

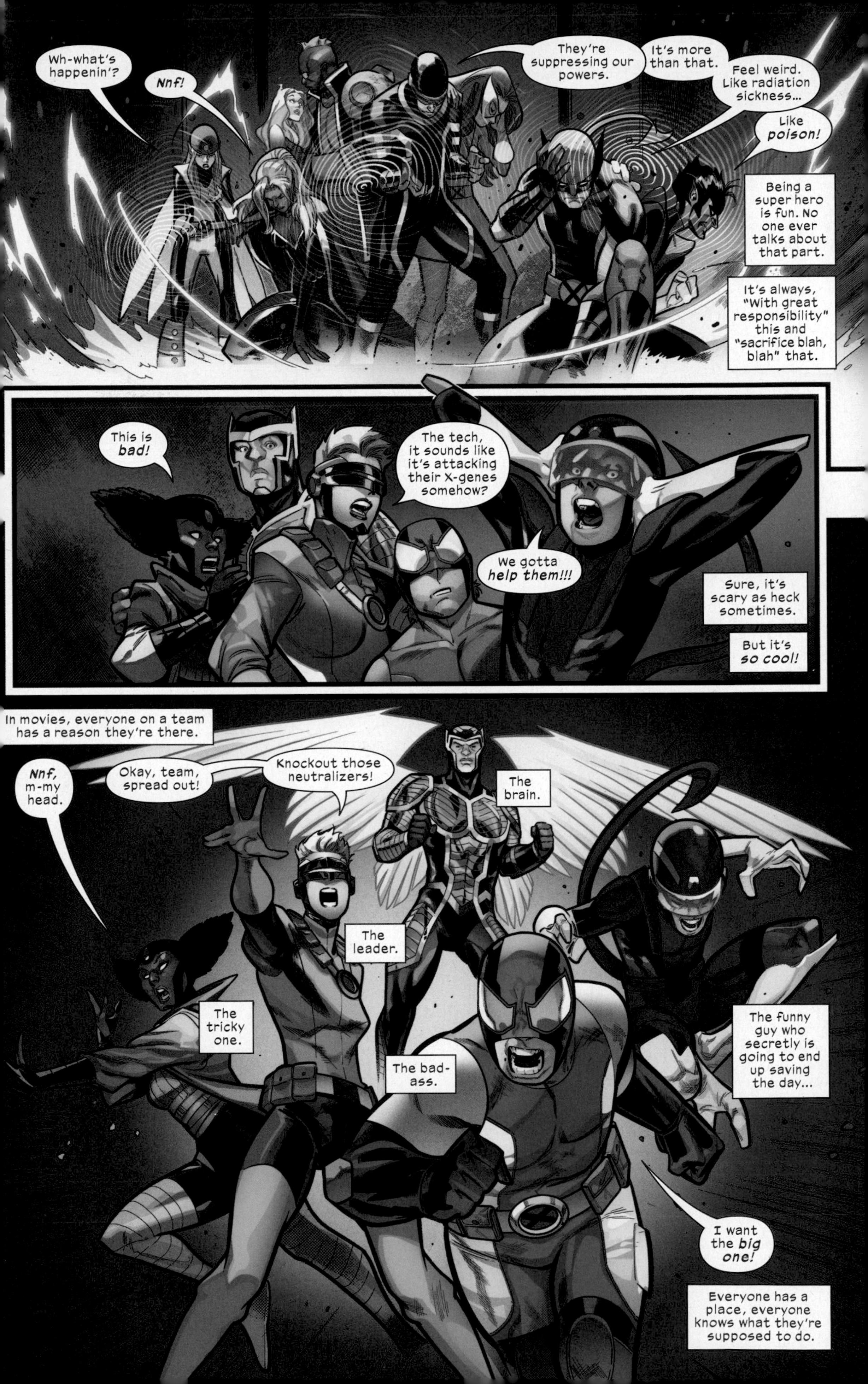

Wh-what's happenin'?
Nnf!
They're suppressing our powers.
It's more than that.
Feel weird. Like radiation sickness...
Like poison!
Being a super hero is fun. No one ever talks about that part.
It's always, "With great responsibility" this and "sacrifice blah, blah" that.
This is bad!
The tech, it sounds like it's attacking their X-genes somehow?
We gotta help them!!!
Sure, it's scary as heck sometimes.
But it's so cool!
In movies, everyone on a team has a reason they're there.
Nnf, m-my head.
Okay, team, spread out!
Knockout those neutralizers!
The brain.
The leader.
The tricky one.
The bad-ass.
The funny guy who secretly is going to end up saving the day...
I want the big one!
Everyone has a place, everyone knows what they're supposed to do.

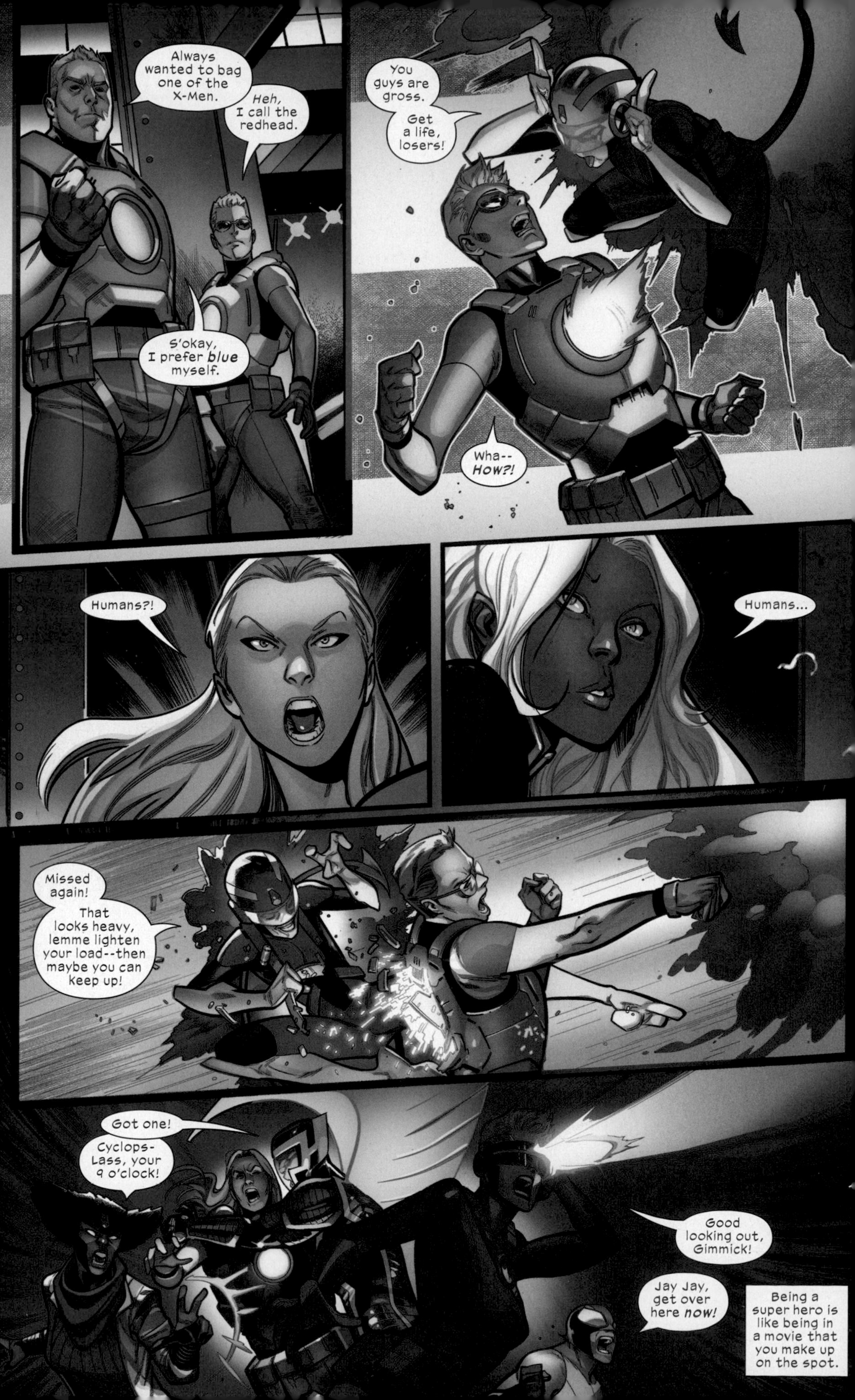
Always wanted to bag one of the X-Men.
Heh, I call the redhead.
S'okay, I prefer *blue* myself.
You guys are gross.
Get a life, losers!
Wha-- *HOW?!*
Humans?!
Humans...
Missed again!
That looks heavy, lemme lighten your load--then maybe you can keep up!
Got one!
Cyclops-Lass, your 9 o'clock!
Good looking out, Gimmick!
Jay Jay, get over here *now!*
Being a super hero is like being in a movie that you make up on the spot.

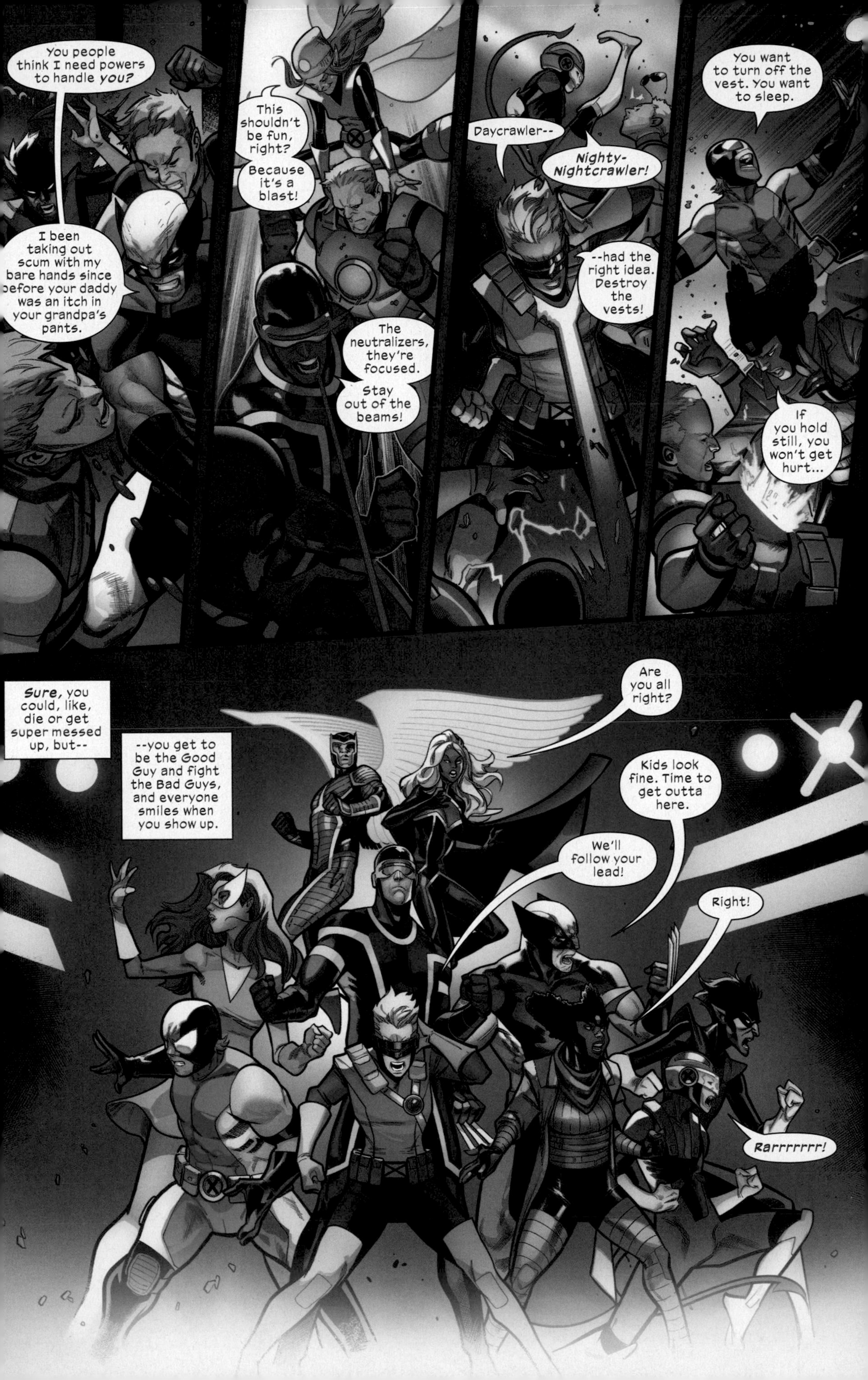
You people think I need powers to handle *you?*
I been taking out scum with my bare hands since before your daddy was an itch in your grandpa's pants.
This shouldn't be fun, right?
Because it's a blast!
The neutralizers, they're focused.
Stay out of the beams!
Daycrawler--
Nighty-Nightcrawler!
--had the right idea. Destroy the vests!
You want to turn off the vest. You want to sleep.
If you hold still, you won't get hurt...
Sure, you could, like, die or get super messed up, but--
--you get to be the Good Guy and fight the Bad Guys, and everyone smiles when you show up.
Are you all right?
Kids look fine. Time to get outta here.
We'll follow your lead!
Right!
Rarrrrrrr!

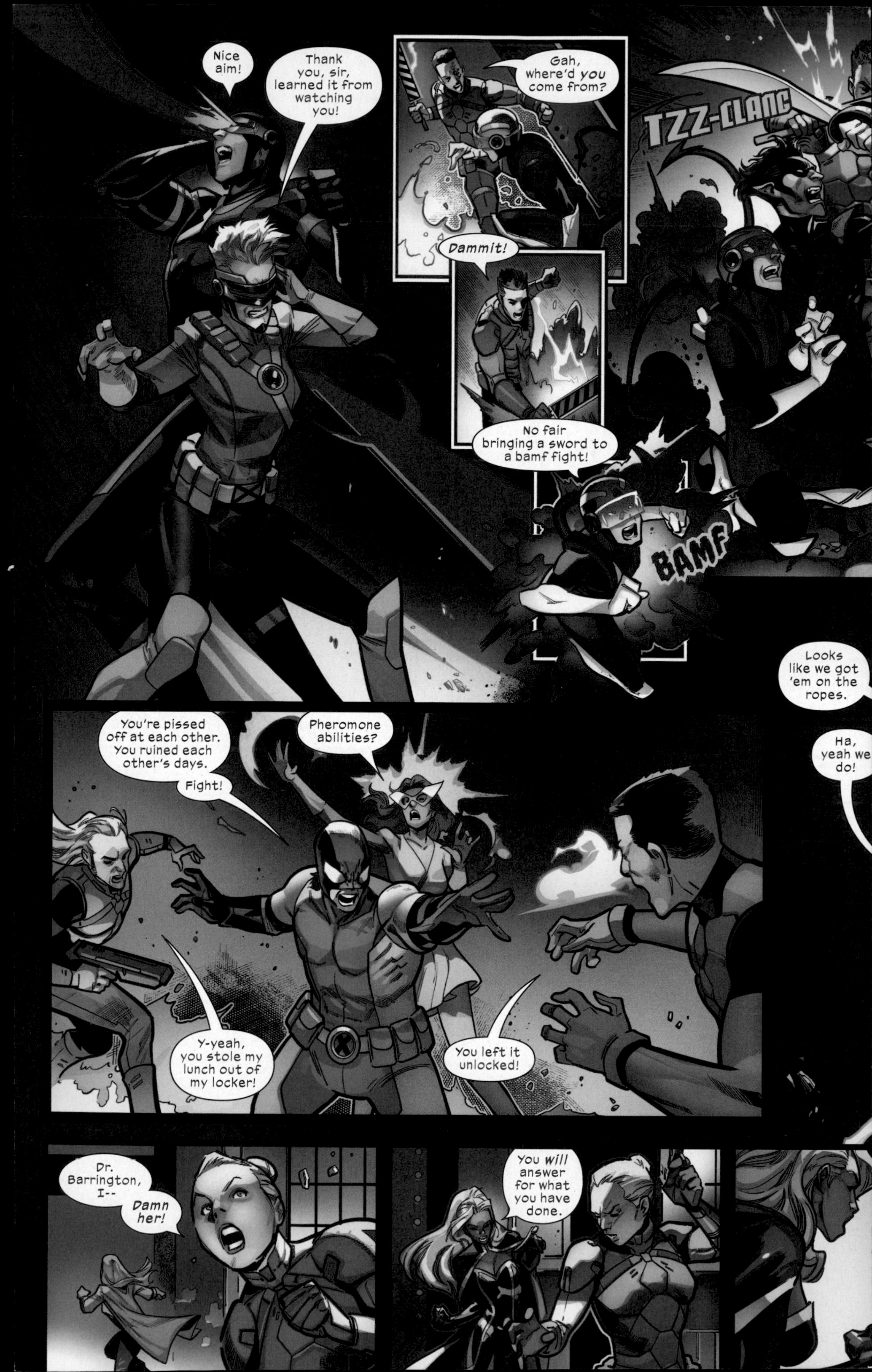

Nice aim!
Thank you, sir, learned it from watching you!
Gah, where'd *you* come from?
TZZ-CLANG
Dammit!
No fair bringing a sword to a bamf fight!
BAMF
Looks like we got 'em on the ropes.
Ha, yeah we do!
You're pissed off at each other. You ruined each other's days.
Fight!
Pheromone abilities?
Y-yeah, you stole my lunch out of my locker!
You left it unlocked!
Dr. Barrington, I--
Damn her!
You *will* answer for what you have done.

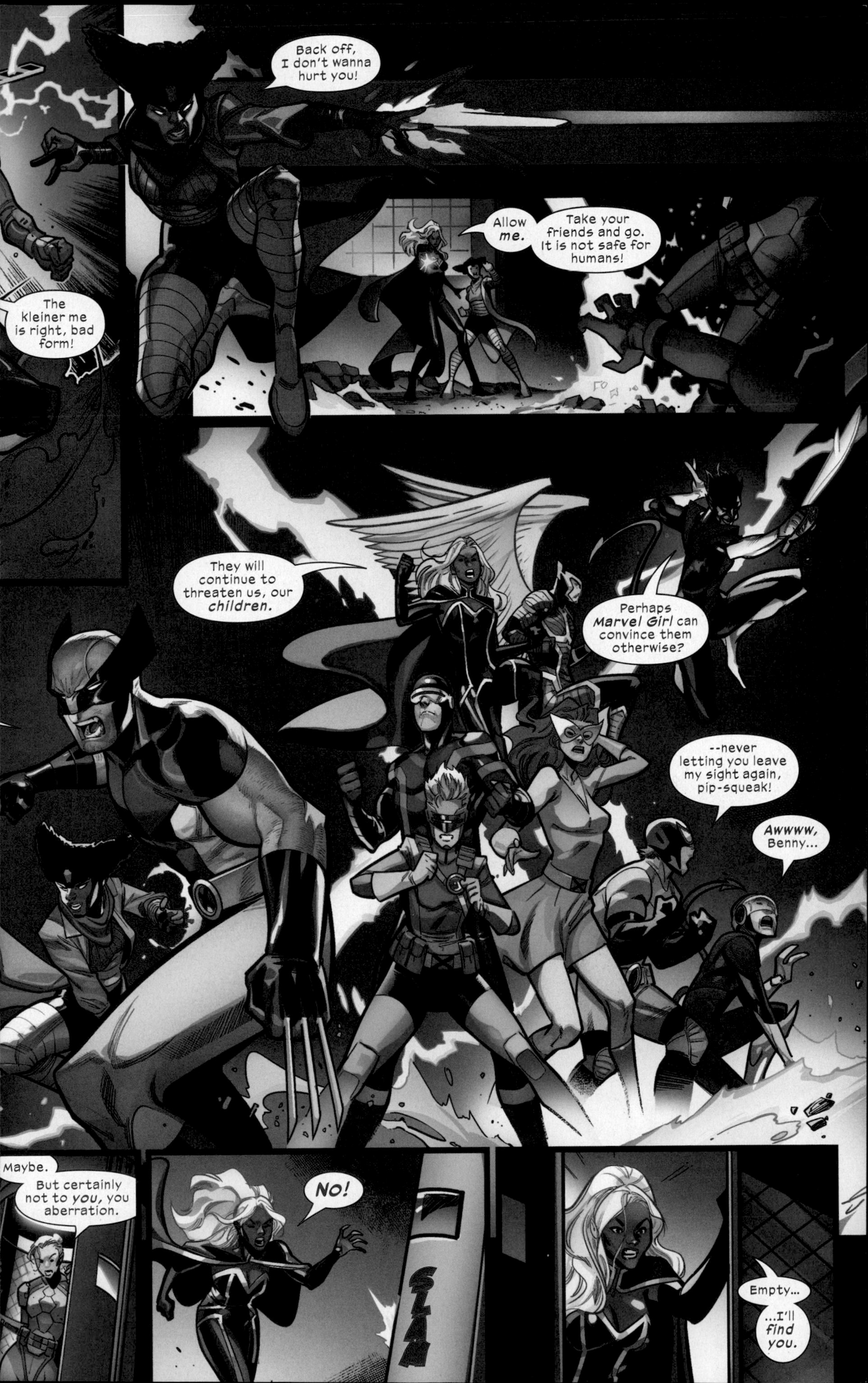
Back off, I don't wanna hurt you!
The kleiner me is right, bad form!
Allow *me.*
Take your friends and go. It is not safe for humans!
They will continue to threaten us, our *children.*
Perhaps *Marvel Girl* can convince them otherwise?
--never letting you leave my sight again, pip-squeak!
Awwww, Benny...
Maybe.
But certainly not to *you,* you aberration.
NO!
Empty...
...I'll *find* you.

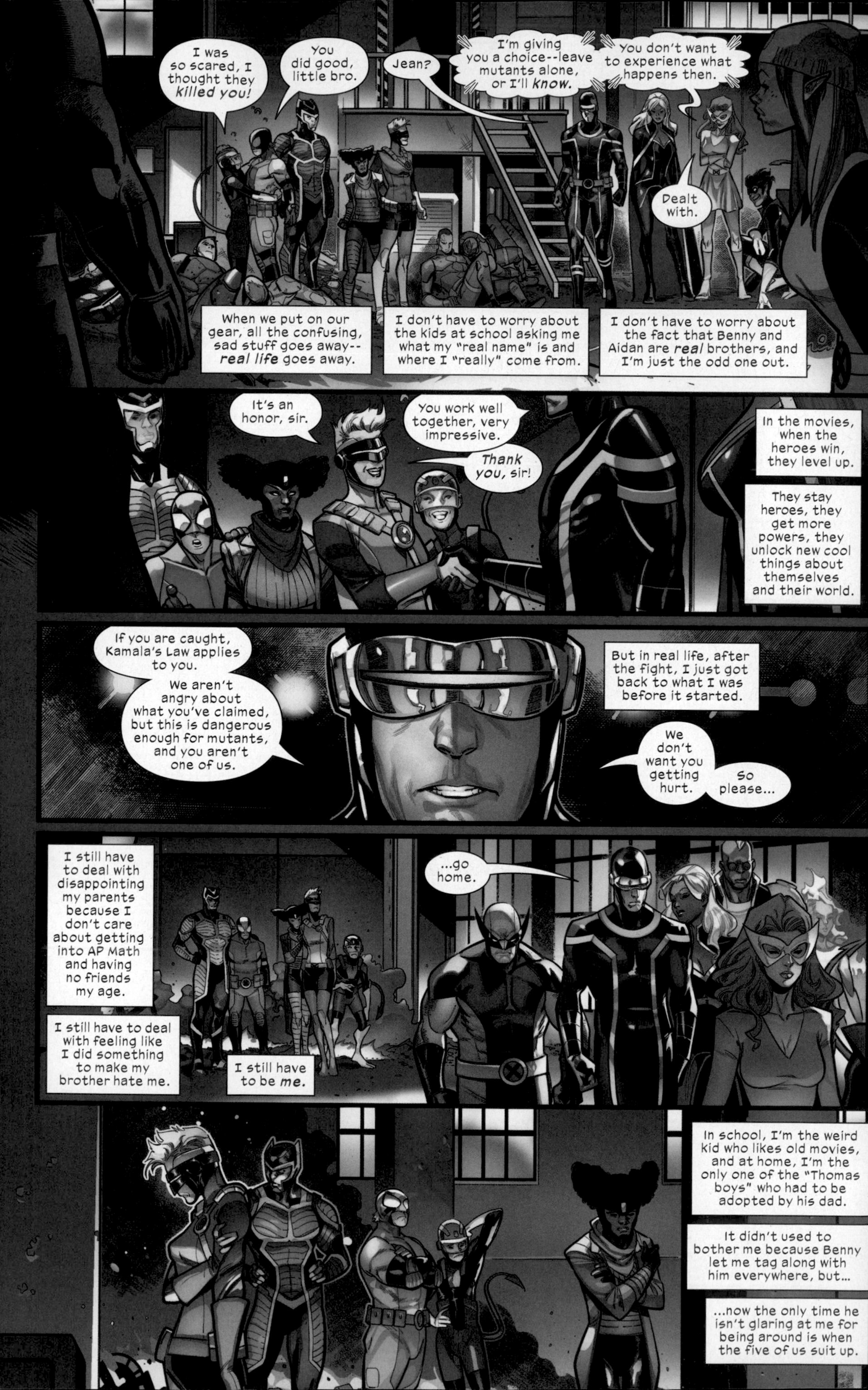

I was so scared, I thought they *killed you!*
You did good, little bro.
Jean?
I'm giving you a choice--leave mutants alone, or I'll *know.*
You don't want to experience what happens then.
Dealt with.
When we put on our gear, all the confusing, sad stuff goes away-- *real life* goes away.
I don't have to worry about the kids at school asking me what my "real name" is and where I "really" come from.
I don't have to worry about the fact that Benny and Aidan are *real* brothers, and I'm just the odd one out.
It's an honor, sir.
You work well together, very impressive.
Thank you, sir!
In the movies, when the heroes win, they level up.
They stay heroes, they get more powers, they unlock new cool things about themselves and their world.
If you are caught, Kamala's Law applies to you.
We aren't angry about what you've claimed, but this is dangerous enough for mutants, and you aren't one of us.
But in real life, after the fight, I just got back to what I was before it started.
We don't want you getting hurt.
So please...
I still have to deal with disappointing my parents because I don't care about getting into AP Math and having no friends my age.
I still have to deal with feeling like I did something to make my brother hate me.
I still have to be *me.*
...go home.
In school, I'm the weird kid who likes old movies, and at home, I'm the only one of the "Thomas boys" who had to be adopted by his dad.
It didn't used to bother me because Benny let me tag along with him everywhere, but...
...now the only time he isn't glaring at me for being around is when the five of us suit up.

 **DAYCRAWLER'S CHATTER FEED**

 # C.R.A.D.L.E._OFFICIAL 1h

The purpose of the UNDERAGE SUPERHUMAN WELFARE ACT, also known as Kamala's Law, is to protect both minors with extra-human abilities and their non-powered peers. In making un-mentored "super hero activity" illegal, we hope to encourage all minors who want to pursue such a noble calling to seek adult guidance and to dissuade those who are not serious about helping others to seek their thrills elsewhere.

Such guidance is available through C.R.A.D.L.E., the Child Hero Reconnaissance and Disruption Law Enforcement organization, as well as many other approved sources.

It has come to the attention of this organization that a group of teenage mutants calling themselves the Children of the Atom have been operating in New York as vigilantes without proper approvals and mentors. They are putting themselves and the city at risk.

If anyone has information about these children, click through the link: HELP C.R.A.D.L.E.

 1,726

Trending: *#YoungXMen, #ChildrenOfTheAtom, #KamalasLaw*

 # KRAKOA_OFFICIAL 3h

Through their actions, the group known as the Children of the Atom have helped Krakoa find and welcome back three lost citizens, as well as locate and disband a violent anti-mutant hate group.

Though they are not in any way a state-sanctioned group, the Children of the Atom, being involved with mutant affairs in New York City, have prevented the incarceration, dismemberment and death of countless mutants, and Krakoa thanks them for their service.

 13,189 6,511

Trending: *#YoungXMen, #ChildrenOfTheAtom, #KamalasLaw*

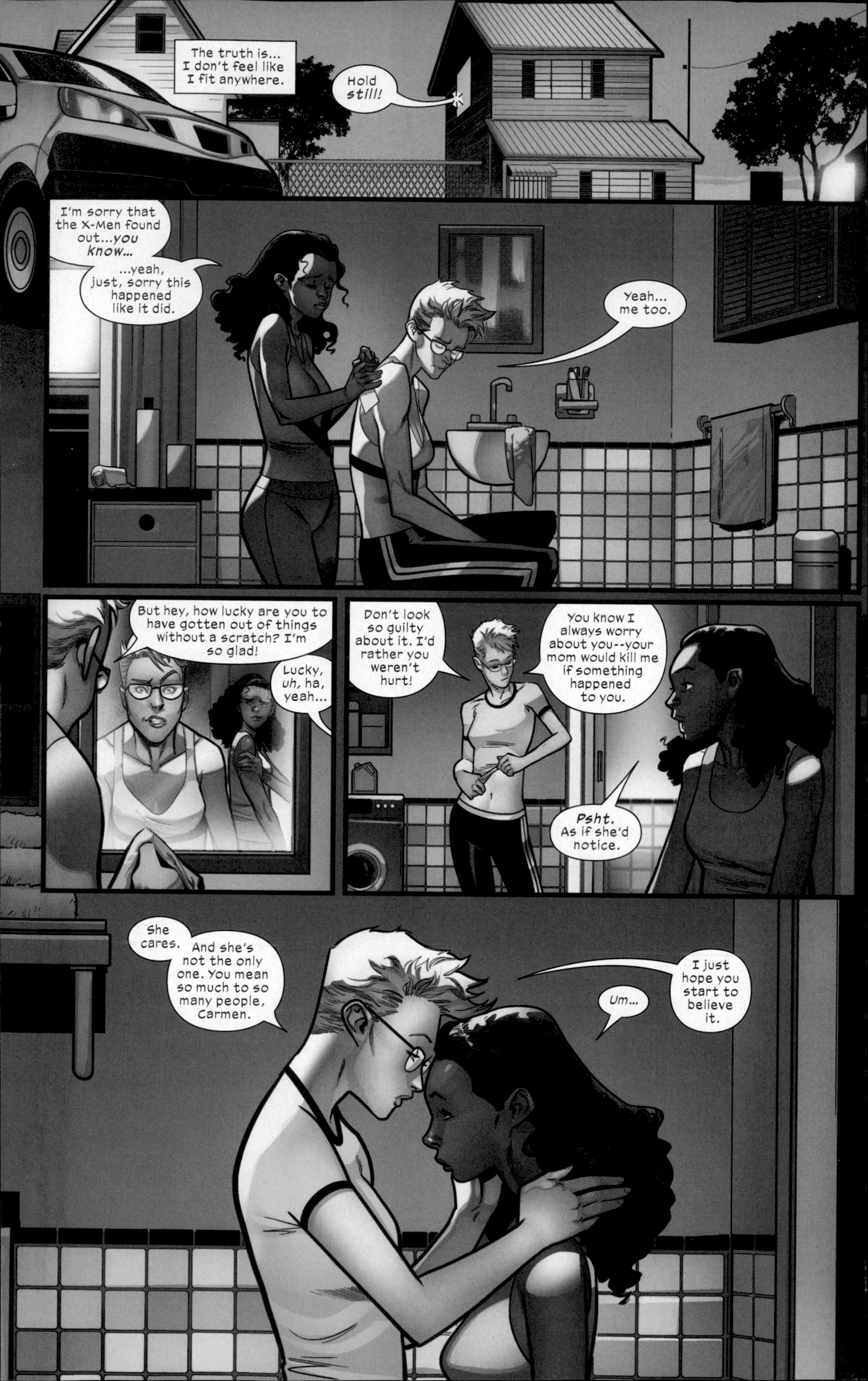
The truth is... I don't feel like I fit anywhere.
Hold *still!*
I'm sorry that the X-Men found out...*you know...*
...yeah, just, sorry this happened like it did.
Yeah... me too.
But hey, how lucky are you to have gotten out of things without a scratch? I'm so glad!
Lucky, *uh,* ha, yeah...
Don't look so guilty about it. I'd rather you weren't hurt!
You know I always worry about you--your mom would kill me if something happened to you.
Psht. As if she'd notice.
She cares.
And she's not the only one. You mean so much to so many people, Carmen.
Um...
I just hope you start to believe it.

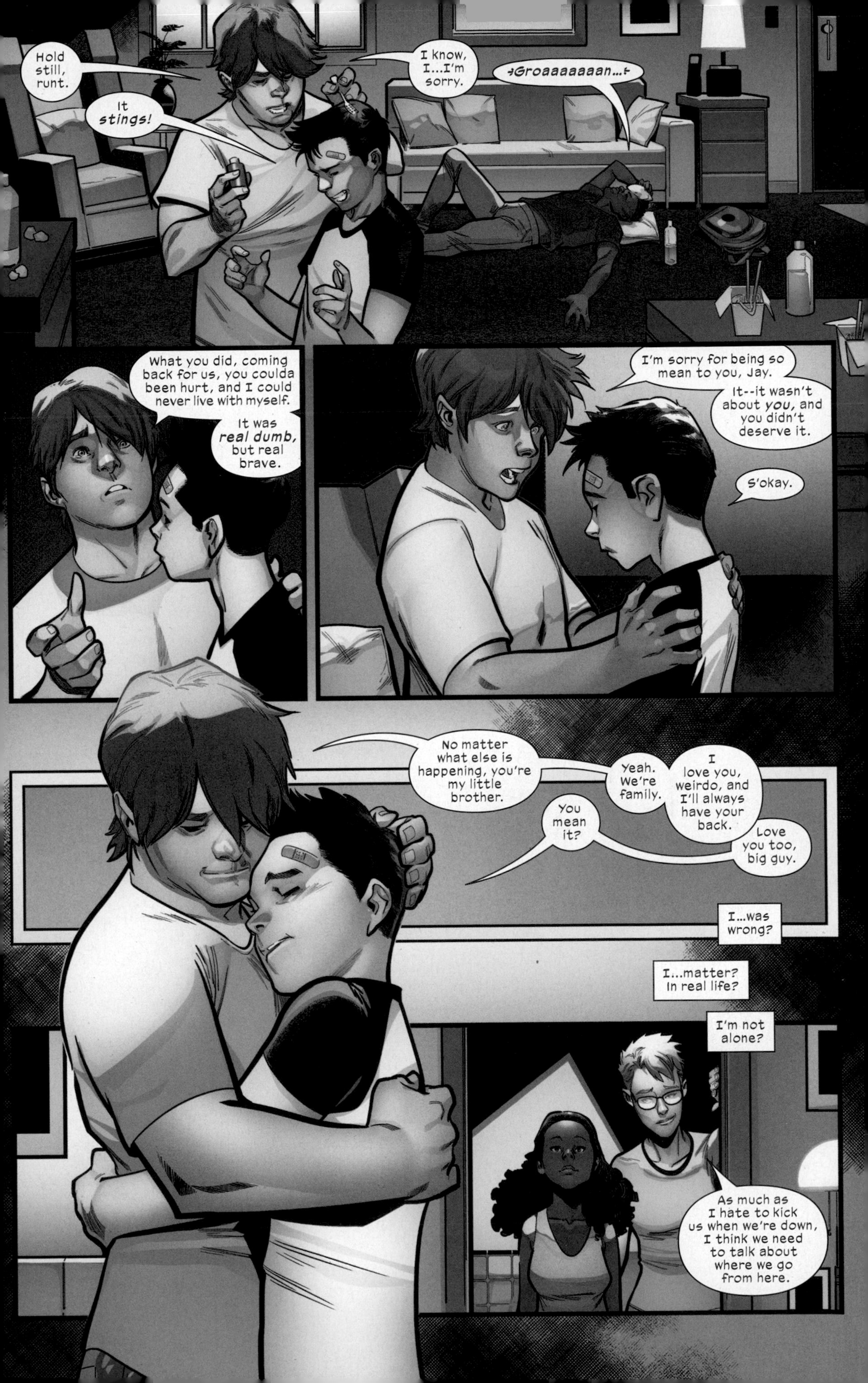
Hold still, runt.
It stings!
I know, I...I'm sorry.
Groaaaaaaan...
What you did, coming back for us, you coulda been hurt, and I could never live with myself.
It was real dumb, but real brave.
I'm sorry for being so mean to you, Jay.
It--it wasn't about you, and you didn't deserve it.
S'okay.
No matter what else is happening, you're my little brother.
You mean it?
Yeah. We're family.
I love you, weirdo, and I'll always have your back.
Love you too, big guy.
I...was wrong?
I...matter? In real life?
I'm not alone?
As much as I hate to kick us when we're down, I think we need to talk about where we go from here.

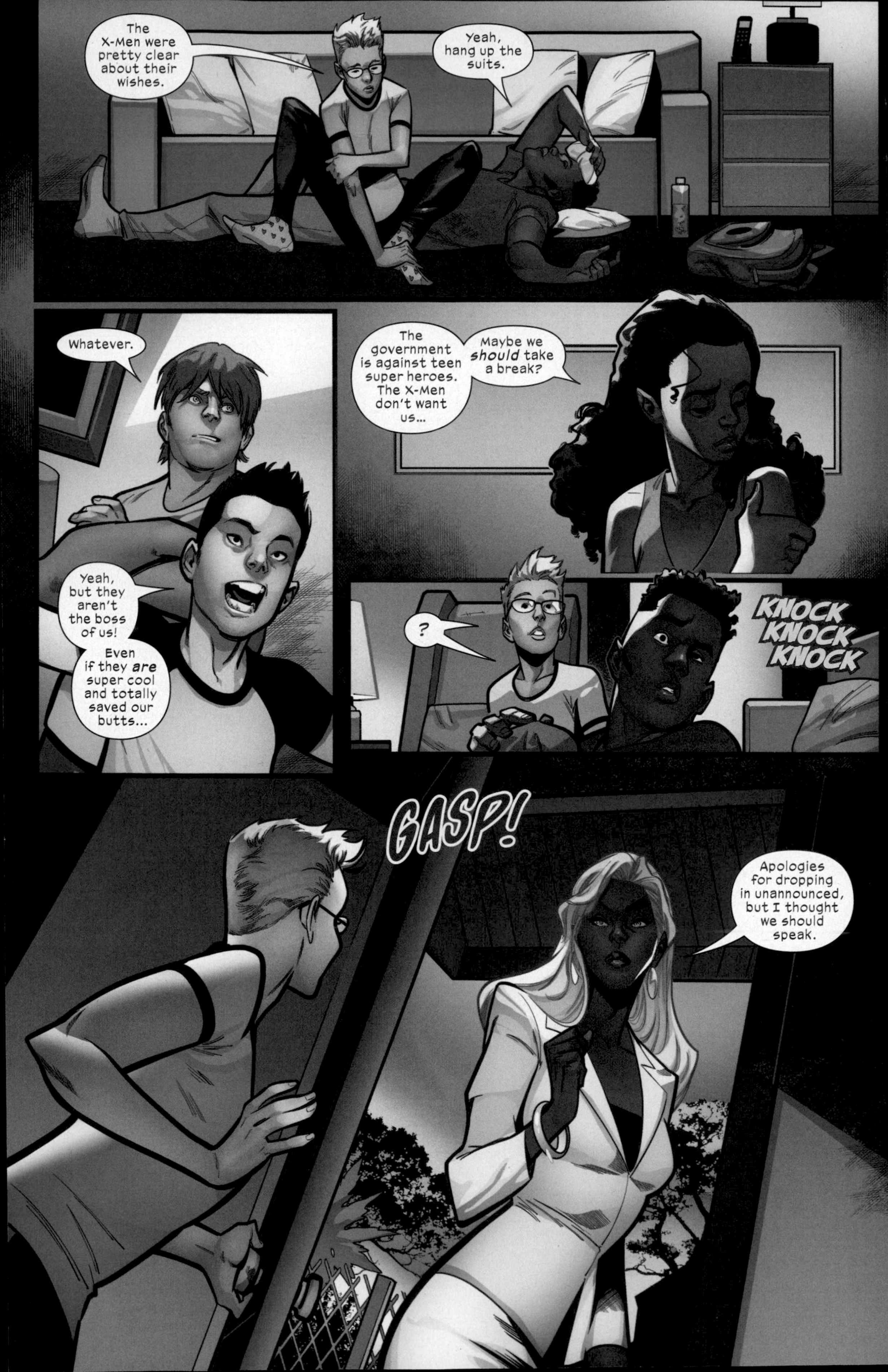

The X-Men were pretty clear about their wishes.
Yeah, hang up the suits.
Whatever.
The government is against teen super heroes. The X-Men don't want us...
Maybe we *should* take a break?
Yeah, but they aren't the boss of us!
Even if they *are* super cool and totally saved our butts...
?
KNOCK KNOCK KNOCK
GASP!
Apologies for dropping in unannounced, but I thought we should speak.

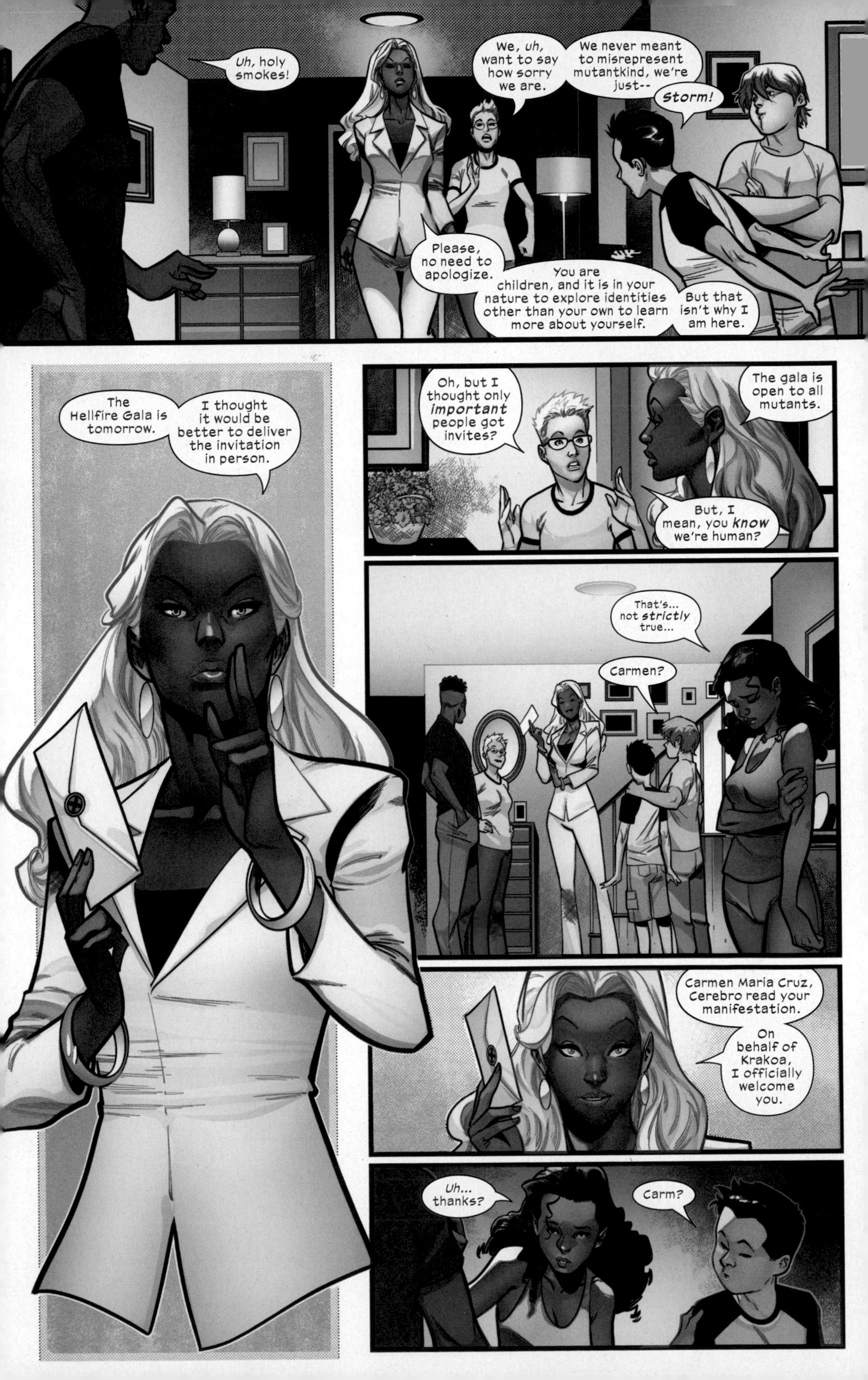

Uh, holy smokes!
We, uh, want to say how sorry we are.
We never meant to misrepresent mutantkind, we're just--
Storm!
Please, no need to apologize.
You are children, and it is in your nature to explore identities other than your own to learn more about yourself.
But that isn't why I am here.
The Hellfire Gala is tomorrow.
I thought it would be better to deliver the invitation in person.
Oh, but I thought only important people got invites?
The gala is open to all mutants.
But, I mean, you know we're human?
That's... not strictly true...
Carmen?
Carmen Maria Cruz, Cerebro read your manifestation.
On behalf of Krakoa, I officially welcome you.
Uh... thanks?
Carm?

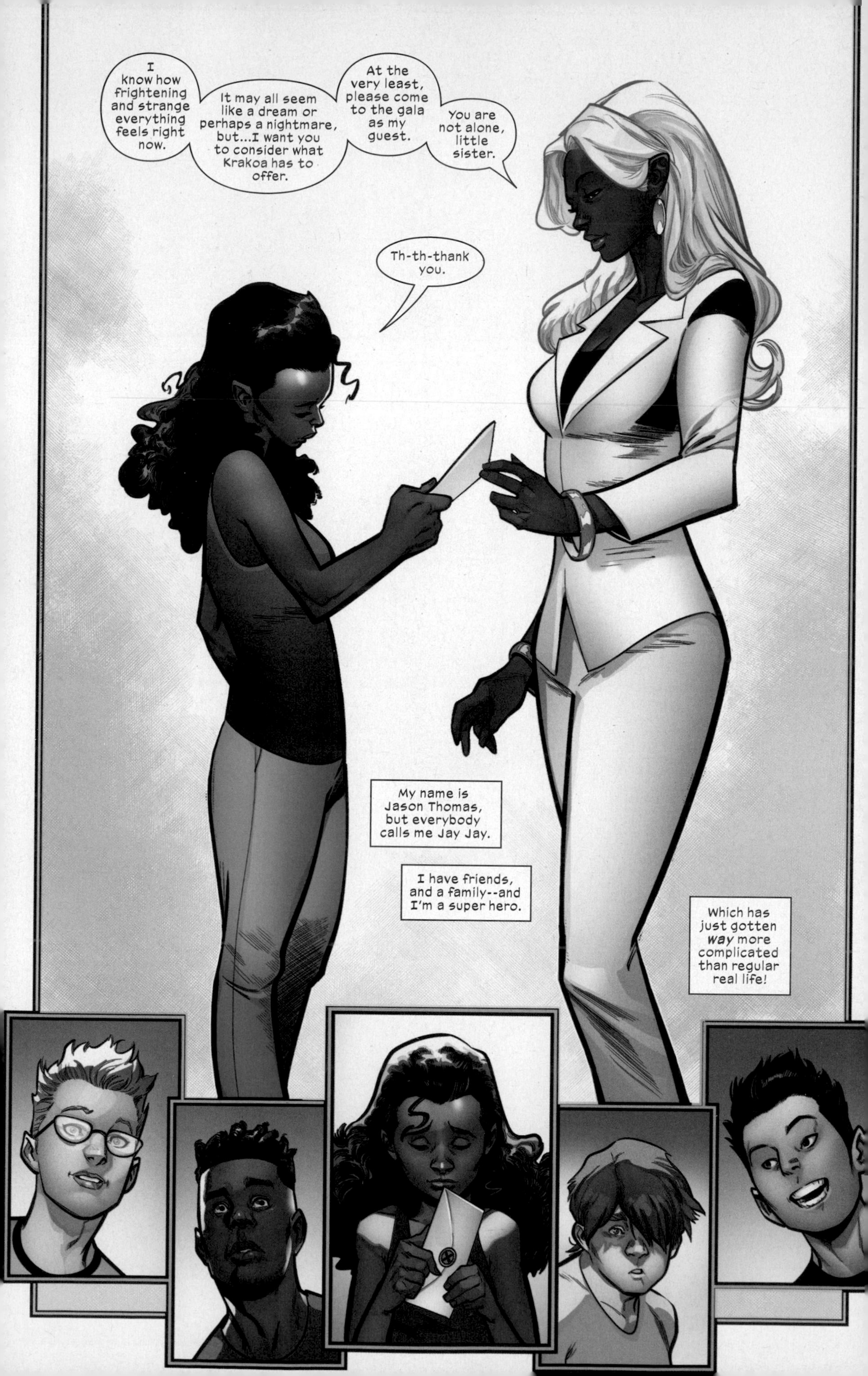
I know how frightening and strange everything feels right now.
It may all seem like a dream or perhaps a nightmare, but...I want you to consider what Krakoa has to offer.
At the very least, please come to the gala as my guest.
You are not alone, little sister.
Th-th-thank you.
My name is Jason Thomas, but everybody calls me Jay Jay.
I have friends, and a family--and I'm a super hero.
Which has just gotten *way* more complicated than regular real life!

[reign_of_x]

[Child[REN]_of]
[____the_A[TOM]

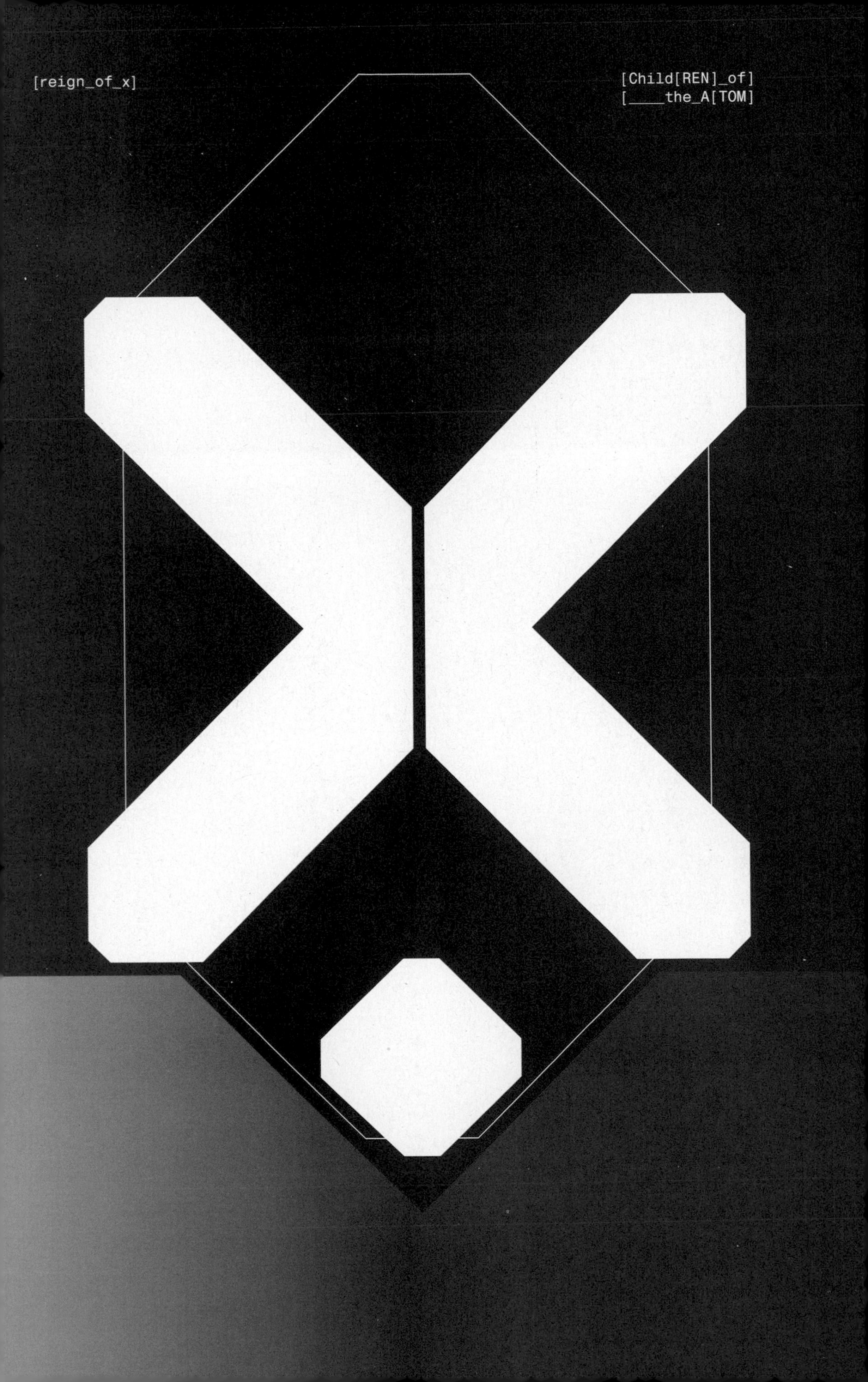

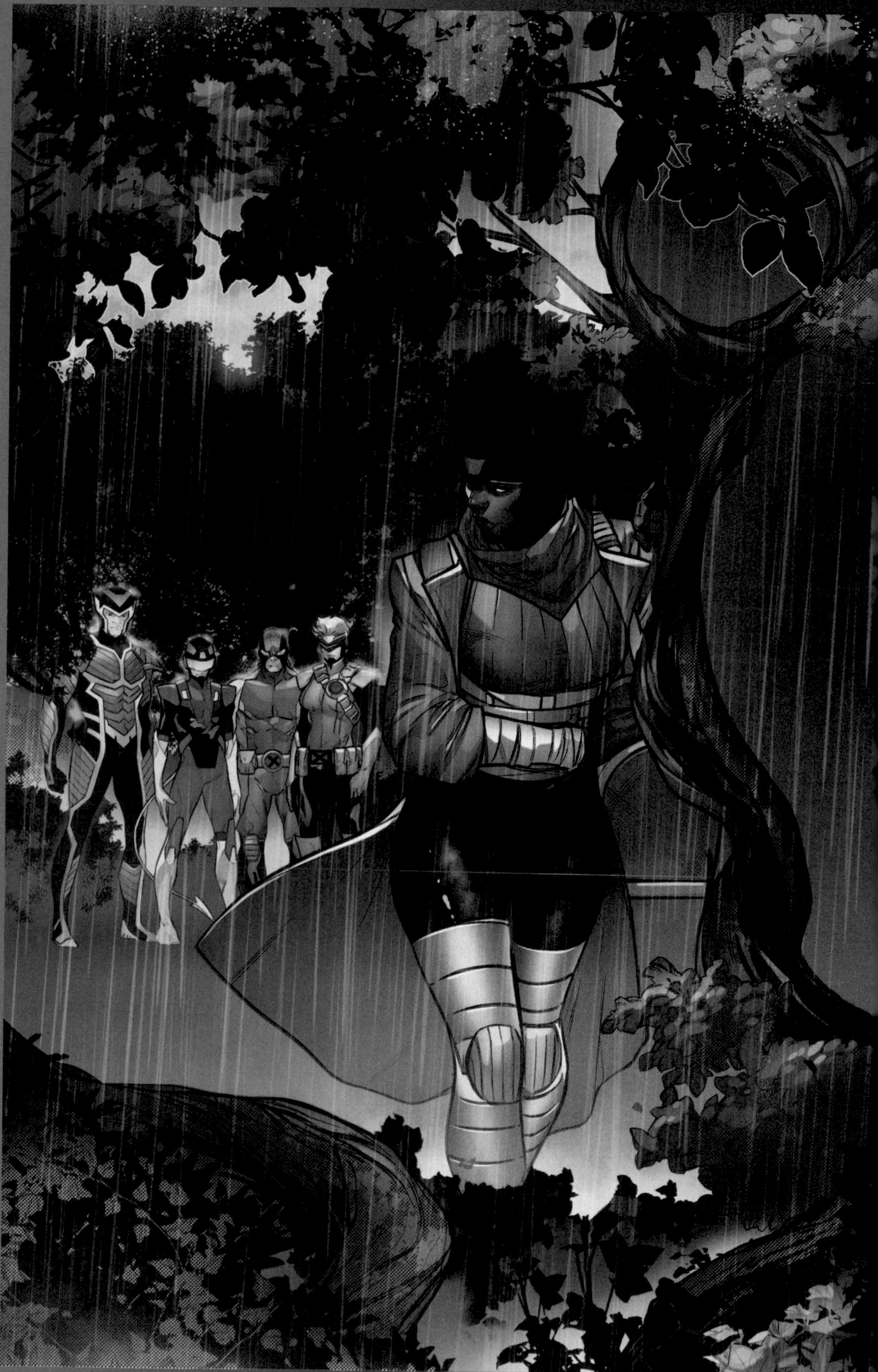

Party of One

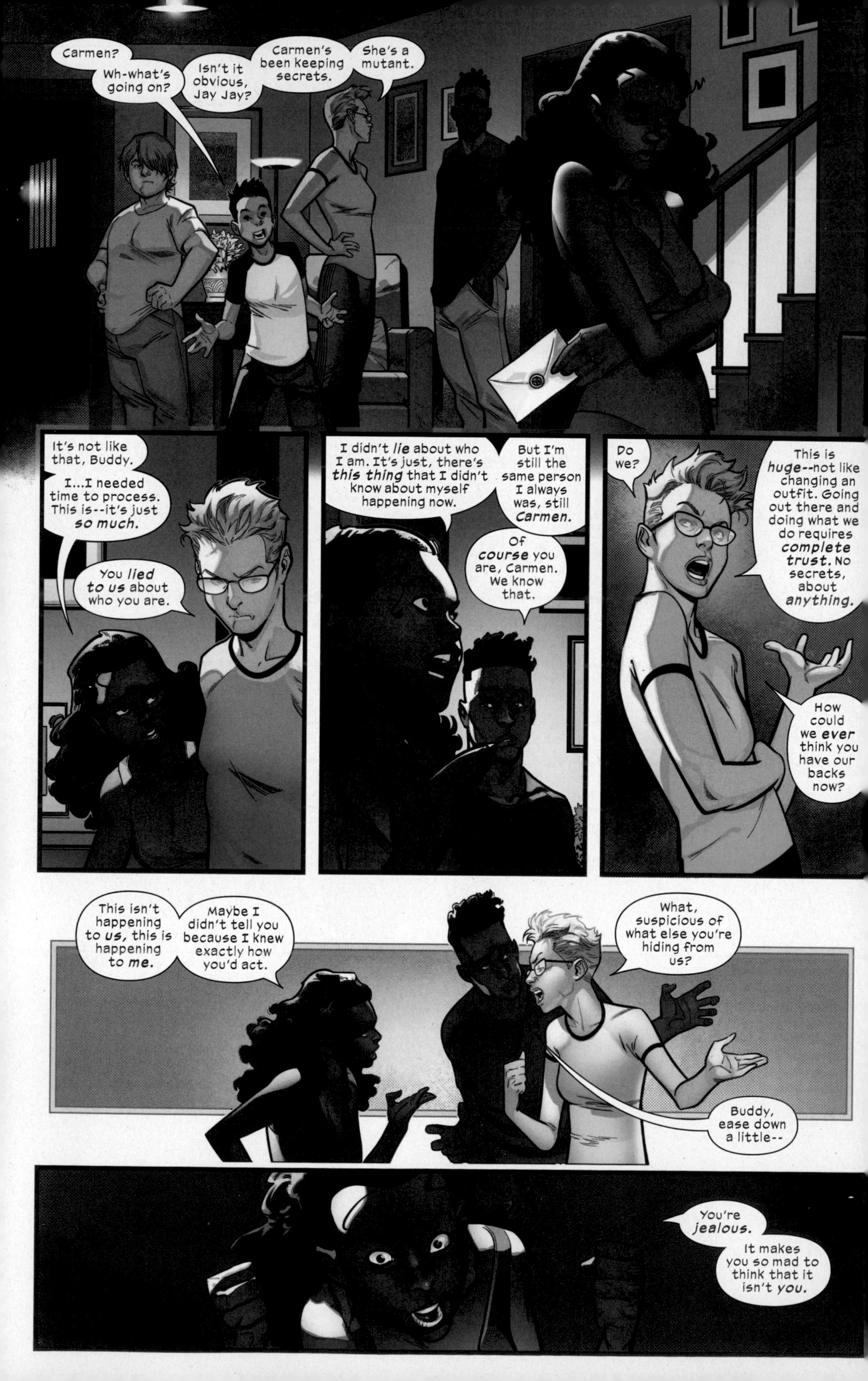
Carmen?
Wh-what's going on?
Isn't it obvious, Jay Jay?
Carmen's been keeping secrets.
She's a mutant.
It's not like that, Buddy.
I...I needed time to process. This is--it's just *so much.*
You *lied to us* about who you are.
I didn't *lie* about who I am. It's just, there's *this thing* that I didn't know about myself happening now.
But I'm still the same person I always was, still *Carmen.*
Of *course* you are, Carmen. We know that.
Do we?
This is *huge*--not like changing an outfit. Going out there and doing what we do requires *complete trust.* No secrets, about *anything.*
How could we *ever* think you have our backs now?
This isn't happening to *us,* this is happening to *me.*
Maybe I didn't tell you because I knew exactly how you'd act.
What, suspicious of what else you're hiding from us?
Buddy, ease down a little--
You're *jealous.*
It makes you so mad to think that it isn't *you.*

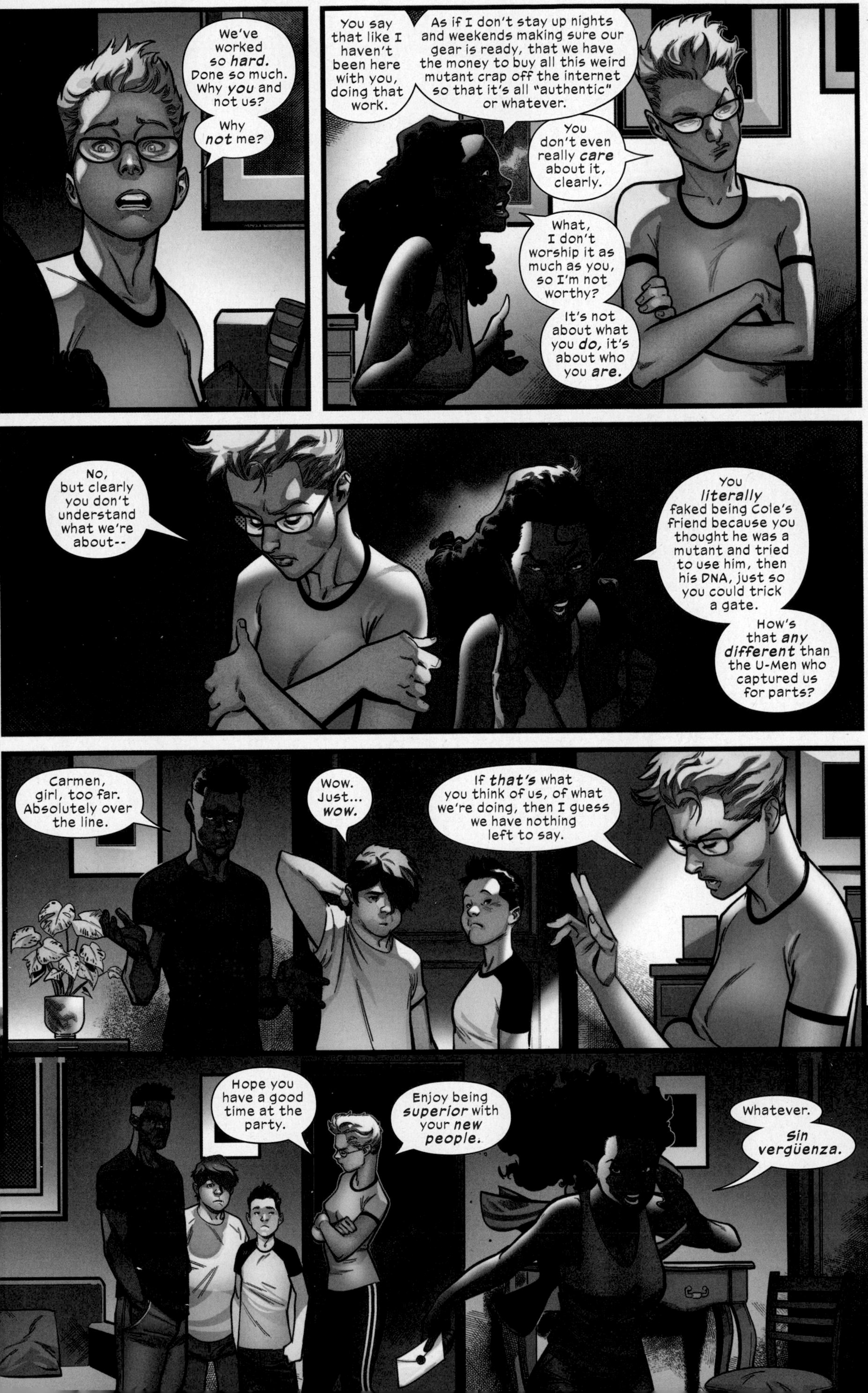
We've worked so hard. Done so much. Why you and not us?
Why not me?
You say that like I haven't been here with you, doing that work.
As if I don't stay up nights and weekends making sure our gear is ready, that we have the money to buy all this weird mutant crap off the internet so that it's all "authentic" or whatever.
You don't even really care about it, clearly.
What, I don't worship it as much as you, so I'm not worthy?
It's not about what you do, it's about who you are.
No, but clearly you don't understand what we're about--
You literally faked being Cole's friend because you thought he was a mutant and tried to use him, then his DNA, just so you could trick a gate.
How's that any different than the U-Men who captured us for parts?
Carmen, girl, too far. Absolutely over the line.
Wow. Just... wow.
If that's what you think of us, of what we're doing, then I guess we have nothing left to say.
Hope you have a good time at the party.
Enjoy being superior with your new people.
Whatever.
Sin vergüenza.

YOU ARE CORDIALLY INVITED TO THE

Hellfire Gala

The Hellfire Trading Company

ON THE EVENING OF THE SUMMER SOLSTICE

Host Emma Frost invites you to celebrate mutant culture and to strengthen Krakoa's friendship with the nations of man.

GATES OPEN 7PM GMT

COCKTAIL

INTRO

CE

CLOS
YEA

F

Ms. Cruz,

You are to be my personal guest to the gala, and I hope to be able to show you around before my duties take me elsewhere.

Krakoa has a lot to offer and teach you about your gifts, and you have a lot to offer us with your new perspective.

It gives me great pleasure to welcome you to our community.

Be well,
Storm

PS: You should begin thinking about your mutant name--it is an important step in claiming your identity (though you can always change it if you outgrow it).

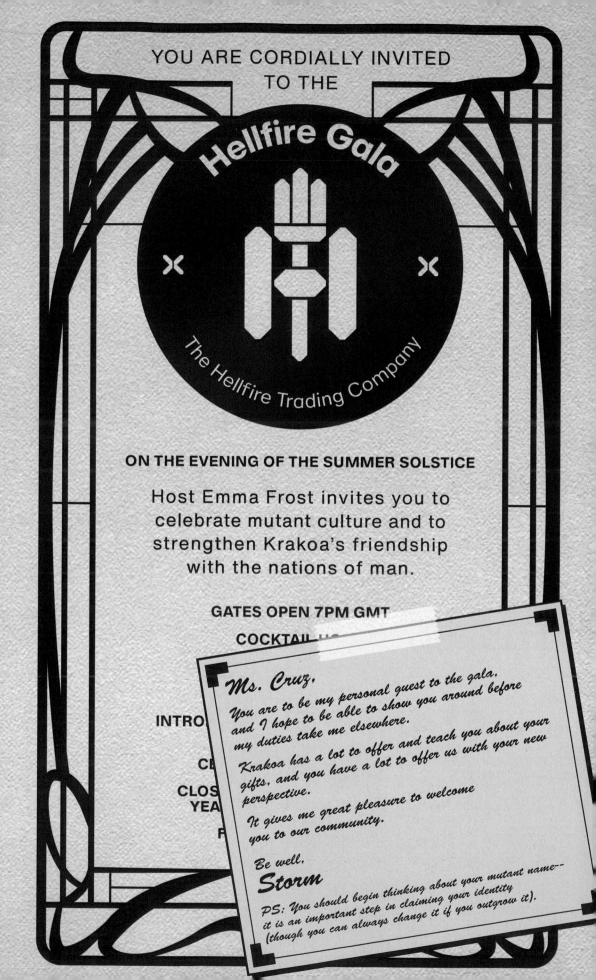

HELLFIRE GALA

Mutants around the world have flocked to the island-nation of Krakoa for safety, security and to be part of the first mutant society. Back in New York City, new teen vigilantes CHILDREN OF THE ATOM dream of becoming mutants and joining their heroes, the X-MEN, on Krakoa.

Recently, the X-Men helped the young heroes escape Dr. Barrington and her army of U-Men. But in the ensuing chaos, the COTA kids' secret was revealed: It is alien technology that gives them their powers, not mutant abilities.

Heartbroken, the kids returned home to treat their wounds and recover their losses. But when Storm arrived with a personal invitation to the Hellfire Gala, the team was shocked by an even bigger secret: Carmen is a mutant!

Hellfire Gala

The Hellfire Trading Company

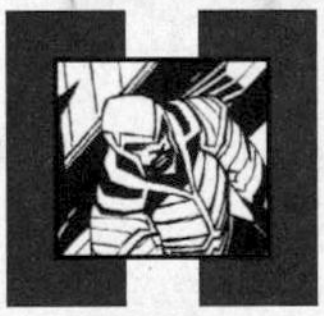

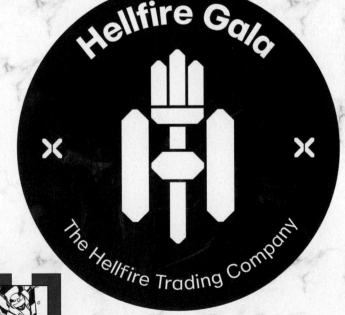

Cherub

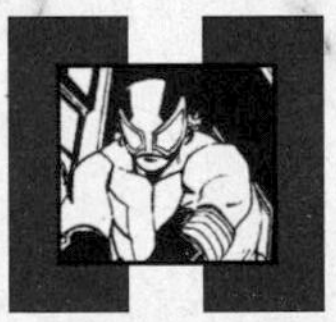

Marvel Guy

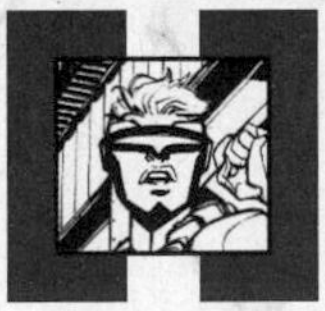

Cyclops-Lass

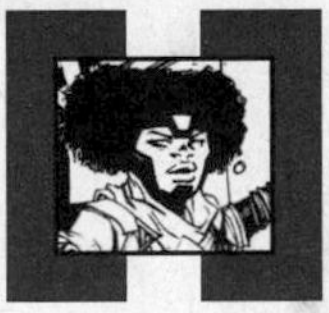

Gimmick

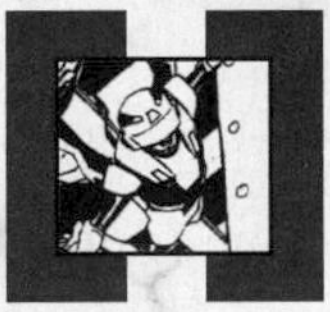

Daycrawler

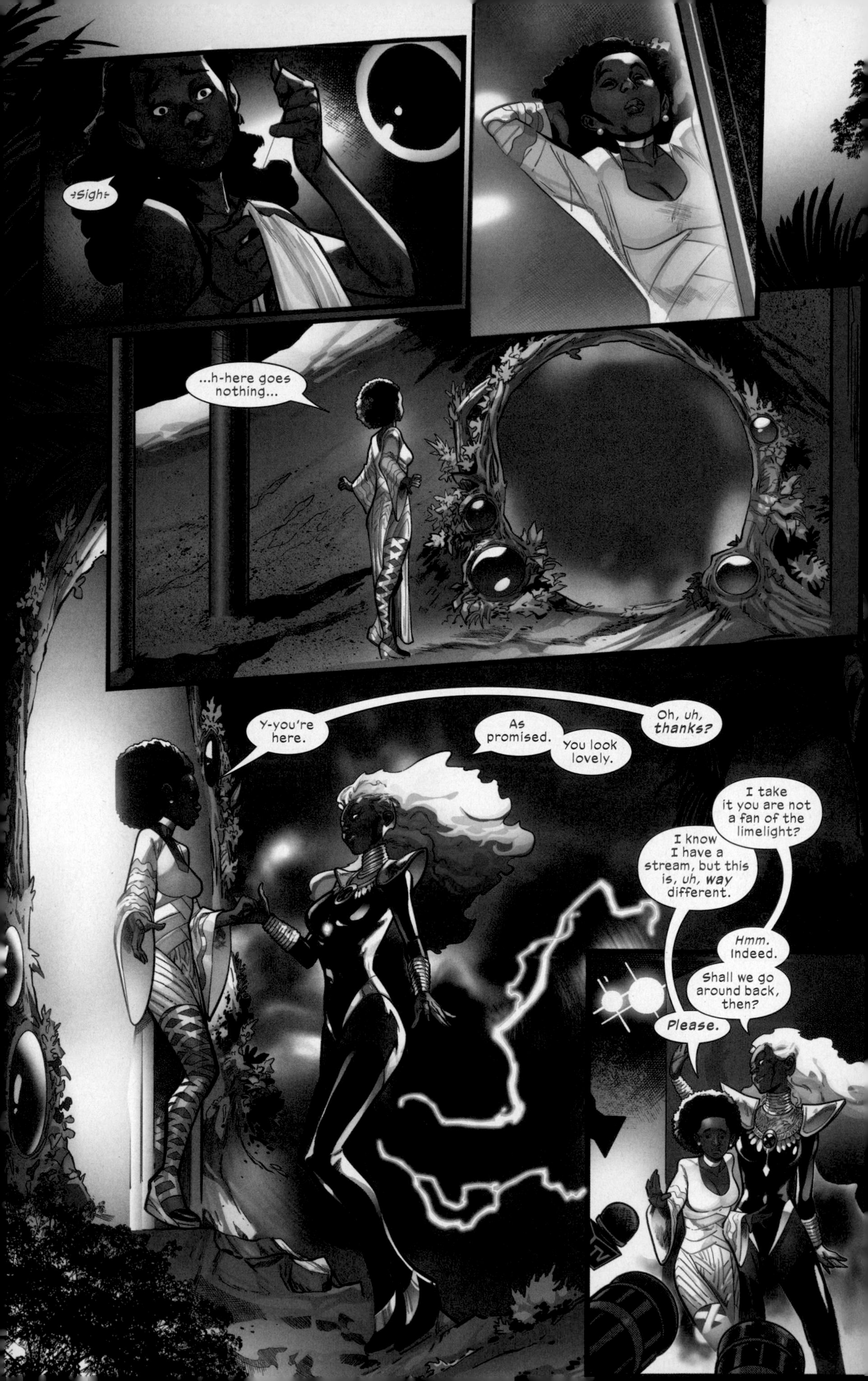
-Sigh-
...h-here goes nothing...
Y-you're here.
As promised.
You look lovely.
Oh, uh, *thanks?*
I take it you are not a fan of the limelight?
I know I have a stream, but this is, *uh, way* different.
Hmm. Indeed.
Shall we go around back, then?
Please.

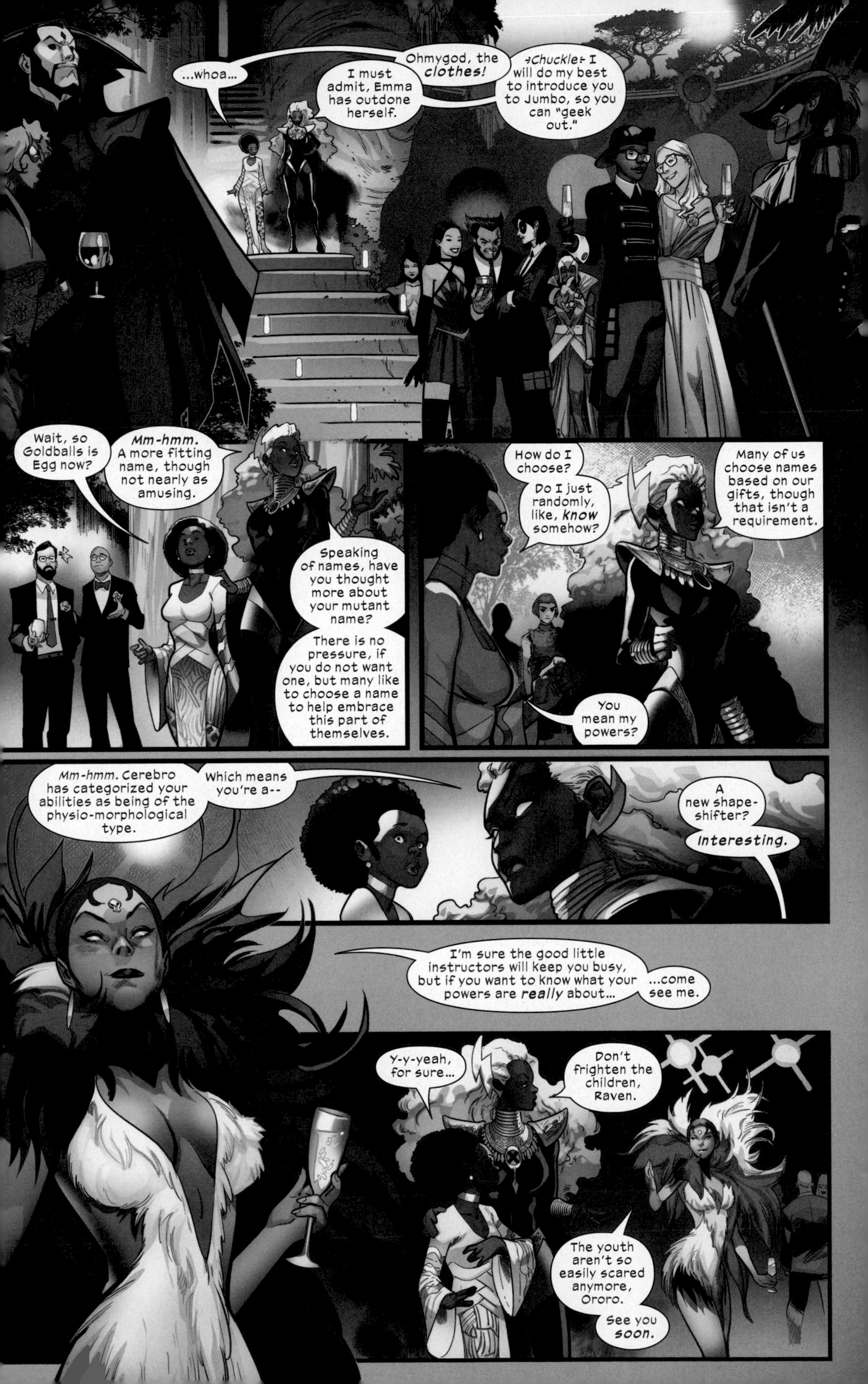

...whoa...
Ohmygod, the *clothes!*
I must admit, Emma has outdone herself.
⩫Chuckle⩪ I will do my best to introduce you to Jumbo, so you can "geek out."
Wait, so Goldballs is Egg now?
Mm-hmm. A more fitting name, though not nearly as amusing.
Speaking of names, have you thought more about your mutant name?
There is no pressure, if you do not want one, but many like to choose a name to help embrace this part of themselves.
How do I choose?
Do I just randomly, like, *know* somehow?
Many of us choose names based on our gifts, though that isn't a requirement.
You mean my powers?
Mm-hmm. Cerebro has categorized your abilities as being of the physio-morphological type.
Which means you're a--
A new shape-shifter?
Interesting.
I'm sure the good little instructors will keep you busy, but if you want to know what your powers are *really* about...
...come see me.
Y-y-yeah, for sure...
Don't frighten the children, Raven.
The youth aren't so easily scared anymore, Ororo.
See you *soon.*

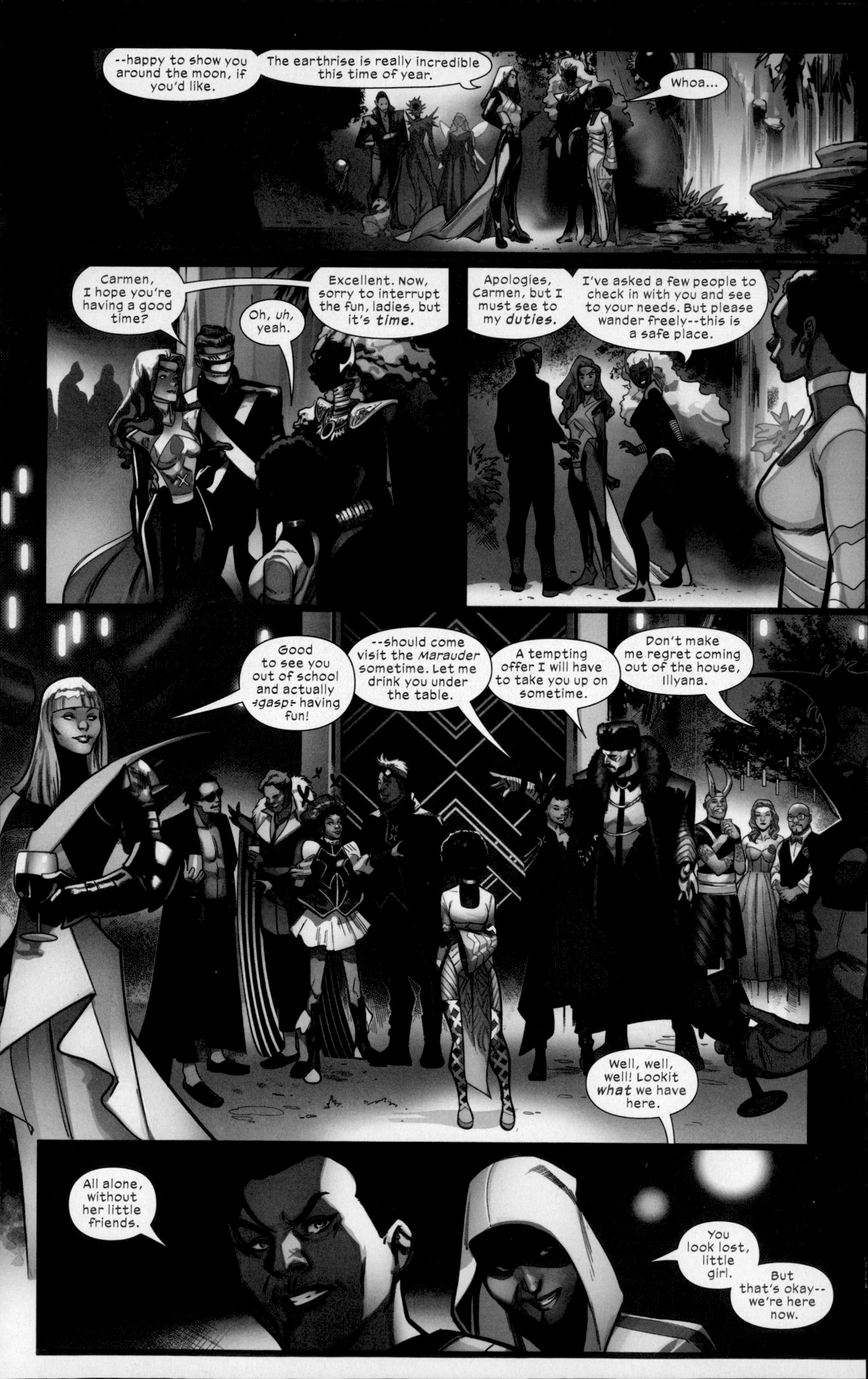
--happy to show you around the moon, if you'd like.
The earthrise is really incredible this time of year.
Whoa...
Carmen, I hope you're having a good time?
Oh, uh, yeah.
Excellent. Now, sorry to interrupt the fun, ladies, but it's time.
Apologies, Carmen, but I must see to my duties.
I've asked a few people to check in with you and see to your needs. But please wander freely--this is a safe place.
Good to see you out of school and actually -gasp- having fun!
--should come visit the Marauder sometime. Let me drink you under the table.
A tempting offer I will have to take you up on sometime.
Don't make me regret coming out of the house, Illyana.
Well, well, well! Lookit what we have here.
All alone, without her little friends.
You look lost, little girl.
But that's okay--we're here now.

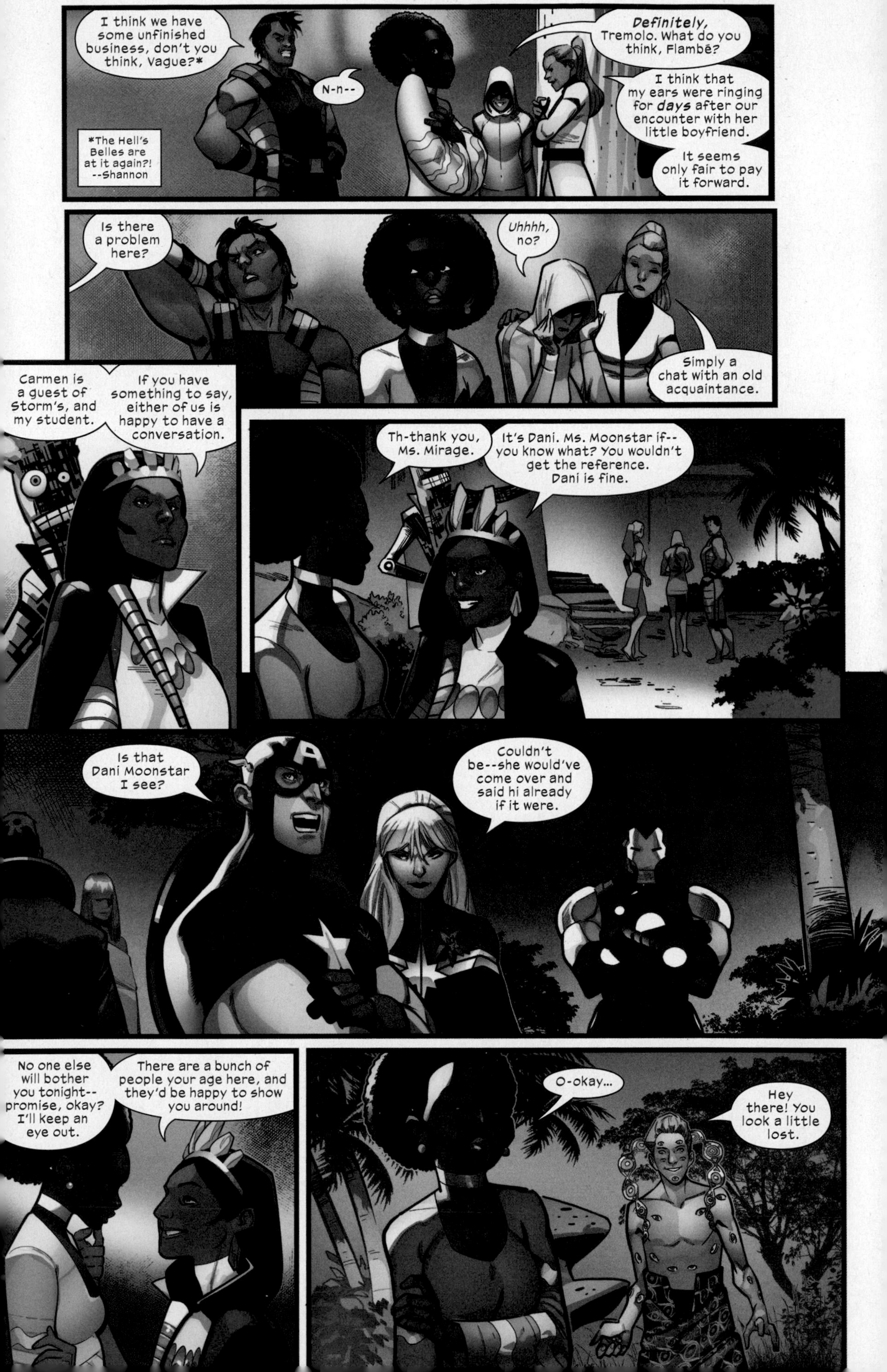
I think we have some unfinished business, don't you think, Vague?*
N-n--
*The Hell's Belles are at it again?! --Shannon
Definitely, Tremolo. What do you think, Flambé?
I think that my ears were ringing for days after our encounter with her little boyfriend.
It seems only fair to pay it forward.
Is there a problem here?
Uhhhh, no?
Simply a chat with an old acquaintance.
Carmen is a guest of Storm's, and my student.
If you have something to say, either of us is happy to have a conversation.
Th-thank you, Ms. Mirage.
It's Dani. Ms. Moonstar if--you know what? You wouldn't get the reference. Dani is fine.
Is that Dani Moonstar I see?
Couldn't be--she would've come over and said hi already if it were.
No one else will bother you tonight--promise, okay? I'll keep an eye out.
There are a bunch of people your age here, and they'd be happy to show you around!
O-okay...
Hey there! You look a little lost.

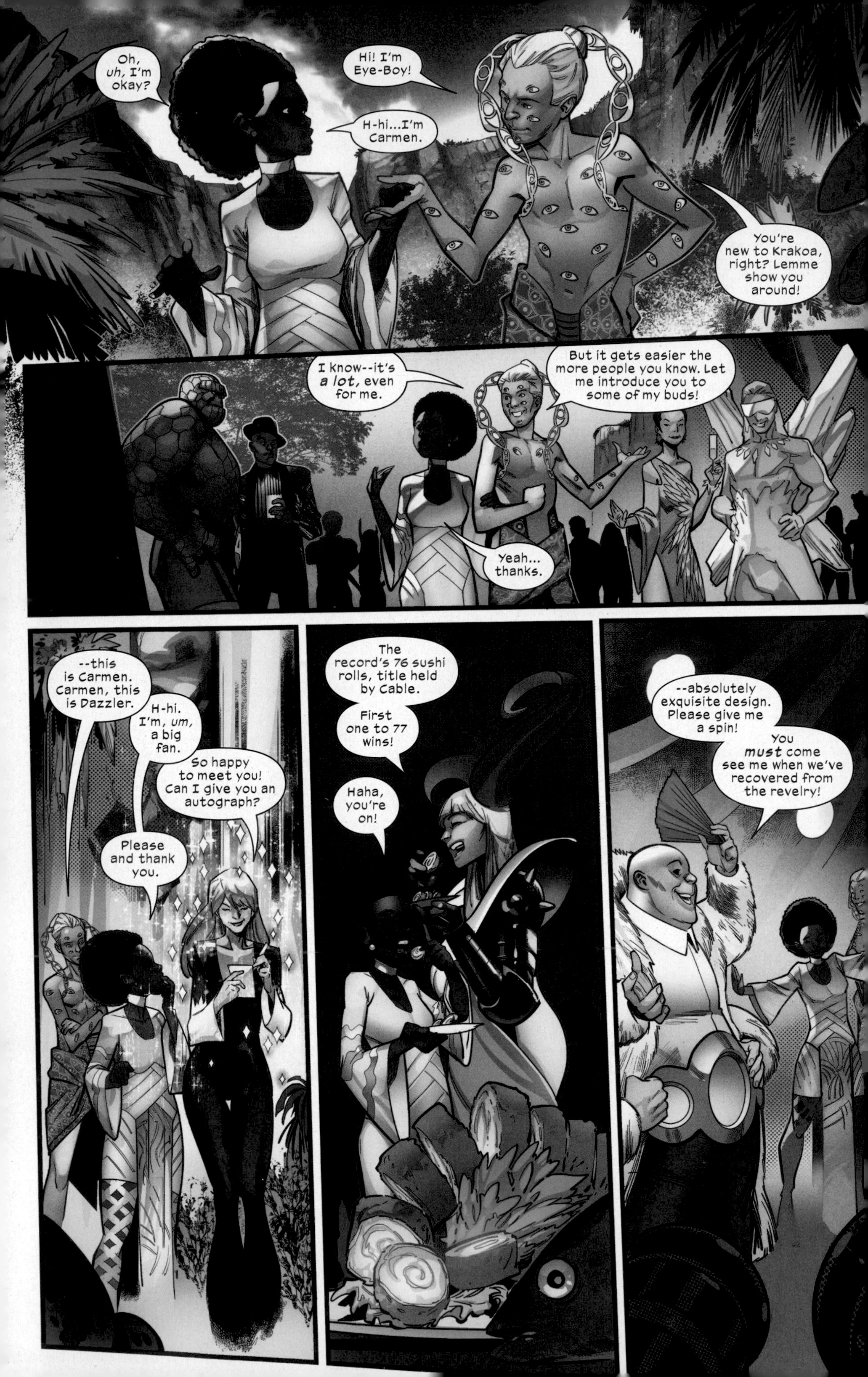
Oh, uh, I'm okay?
Hi! I'm Eye-Boy!
H-hi...I'm Carmen.
You're new to Krakoa, right? Lemme show you around!
I know--it's a lot, even for me.
But it gets easier the more people you know. Let me introduce you to some of my buds!
Yeah... thanks.
--this is Carmen. Carmen, this is Dazzler.
H-hi. I'm, um, a big fan.
So happy to meet you! Can I give you an autograph?
Please and thank you.
The record's 76 sushi rolls, title held by Cable.
First one to 77 wins!
Haha, you're on!
--absolutely exquisite design. Please give me a spin!
You must come see me when we've recovered from the revelry!

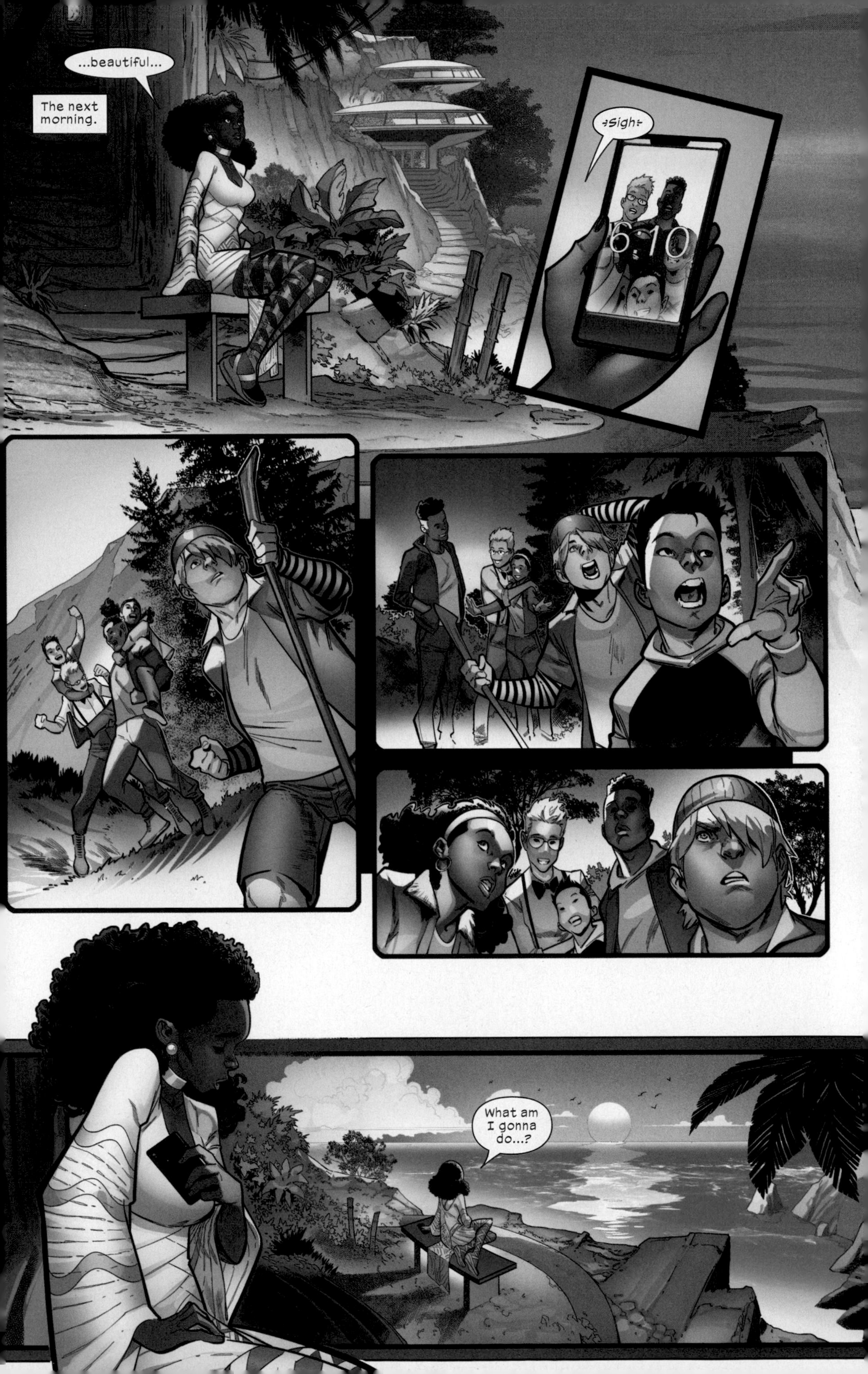

...beautiful...
The next morning.
Sigh
What am I gonna do...?

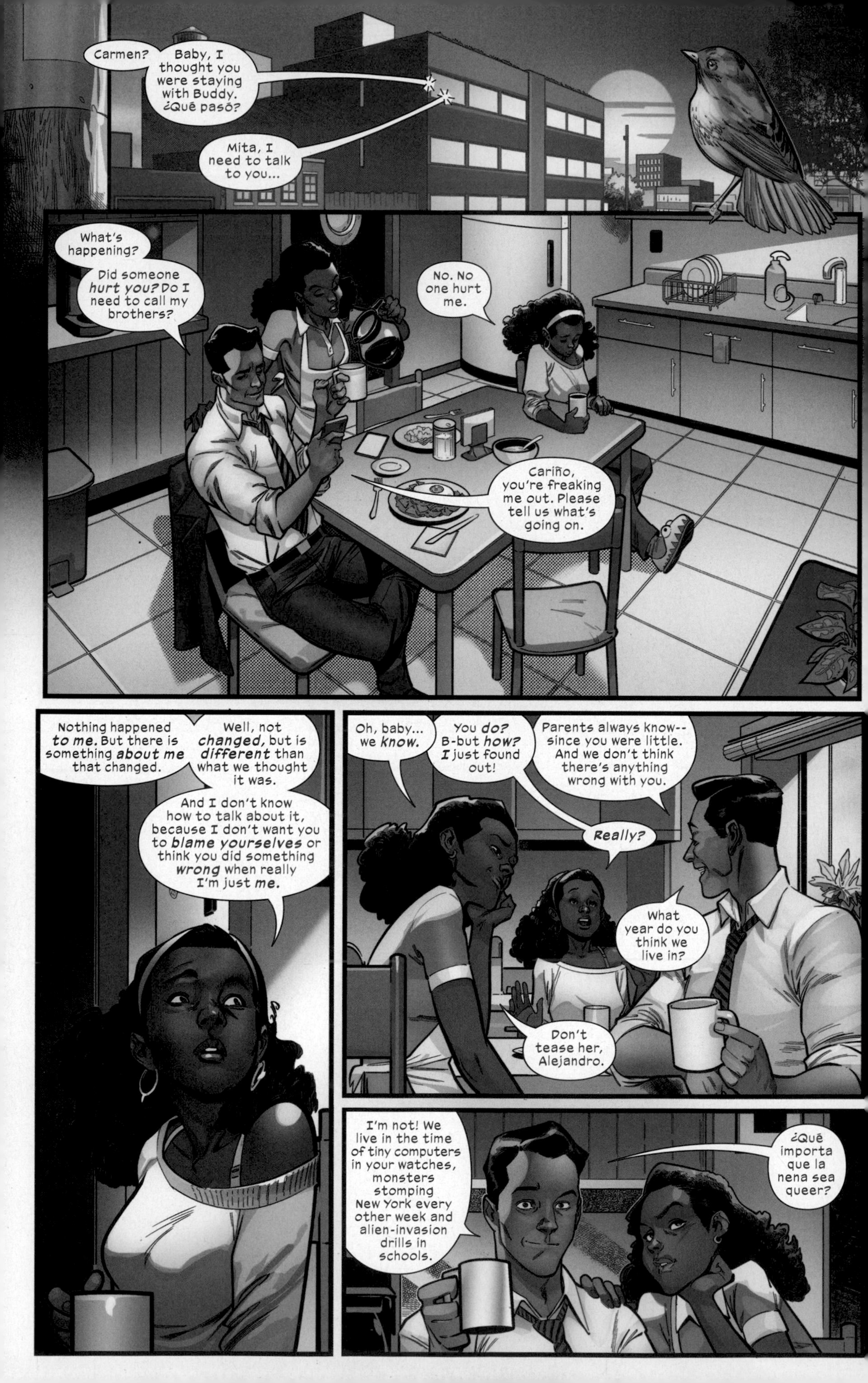
Carmen?
Baby, I thought you were staying with Buddy. ¿Qué pasó?
Mita, I need to talk to you...
What's happening?
Did someone *hurt you?* Do I need to call my brothers?
No. No one hurt me.
Cariño, you're freaking me out. Please tell us what's going on.
Nothing happened *to me.* But there is something *about me* that changed.
Well, not *changed,* but is *different* than what we thought it was.
And I don't know how to talk about it, because I don't want you to *blame yourselves* or think you did something *wrong* when really I'm just *me.*
Oh, baby... we *know.*
You *do?* B-but *how? I* just found out!
Parents always know--since you were little. And we don't think there's anything wrong with you.
Really?
What year do you think we live in?
Don't tease her, Alejandro.
I'm not! We live in the time of tiny computers in your watches, monsters stomping New York every other week and alien-invasion drills in schools.
¿Qué importa que la nena sea queer?

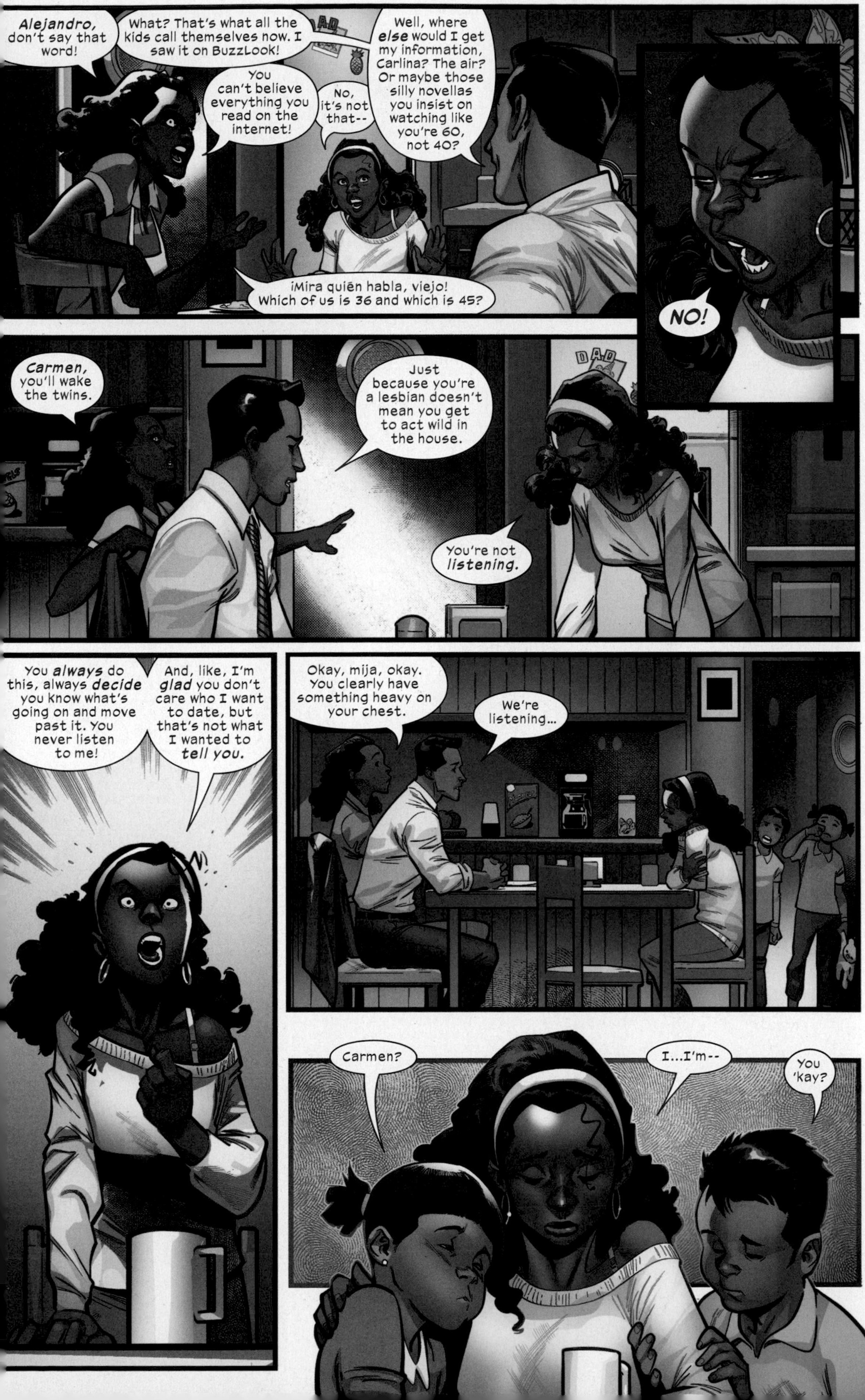

Alejandro, don't say that word!
What? That's what all the kids call themselves now. I saw it on BuzzLook!
You can't believe everything you read on the internet!
No, it's not that--
Well, where else would I get my information, Carlina? The air? Or maybe those silly novellas you insist on watching like you're 60, not 40?
¡Mira quién habla, viejo! Which of us is 36 and which is 45?
NO!
Carmen, you'll wake the twins.
Just because you're a lesbian doesn't mean you get to act wild in the house.
You're not listening.
You always do this, always decide you know what's going on and move past it. You never listen to me!
And, like, I'm glad you don't care who I want to date, but that's not what I wanted to tell you.
Okay, mija, okay. You clearly have something heavy on your chest.
We're listening...
Carmen?
I...I'm--
You 'kay?

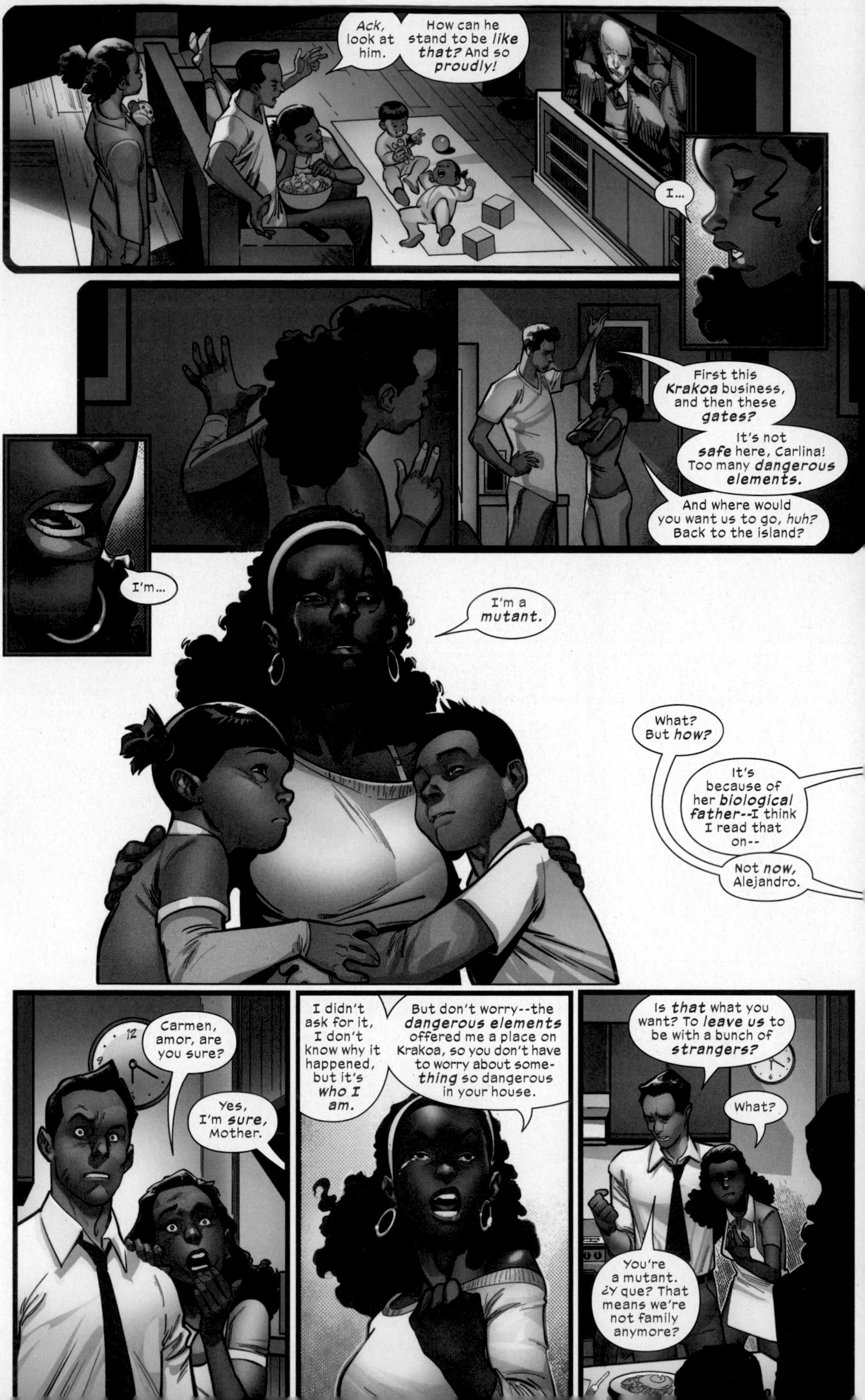
Ack, look at him.
How can he stand to be *like that?* And so *proudly!*
I...
First this *Krakoa* business, and then these *gates?*
It's not *safe* here, Carlina! Too many *dangerous elements.*
And where would you want us to go, *huh?* Back to the island?
I'm...
I'm a *mutant.*
What? But *how?*
It's because of her *biological father*--I think I read that on--
Not *now,* Alejandro.
Carmen, amor, are you sure?
Yes, I'm *sure,* Mother.
I didn't ask for it, I don't know why it happened, but it's *who I am.*
But don't worry--the *dangerous elements* offered me a place on Krakoa, so you don't have to worry about some-*thing* so dangerous in your house.
Is *that* what you want? To *leave us* to be with a bunch of *strangers?*
What?
You're a mutant. ¿Y que? That means we're not family anymore?

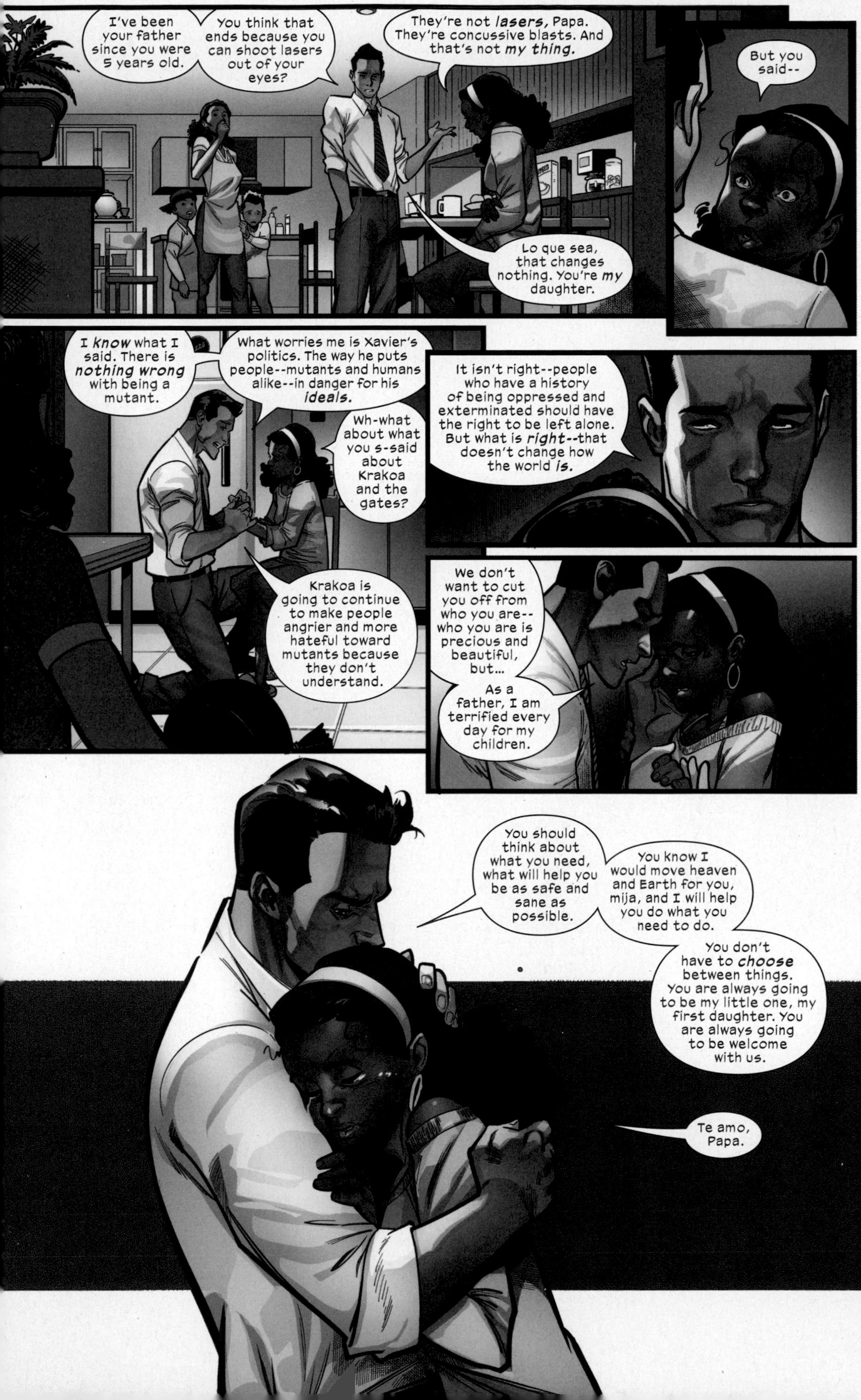
I've been your father since you were 5 years old.
You think that ends because you can shoot lasers out of your eyes?
They're not lasers, Papa. They're concussive blasts. And that's not my thing.
Lo que sea, that changes nothing. You're my daughter.
But you said--
I know what I said. There is nothing wrong with being a mutant.
What worries me is Xavier's politics. The way he puts people--mutants and humans alike--in danger for his ideals.
Wh-what about what you s-said about Krakoa and the gates?
Krakoa is going to continue to make people angrier and more hateful toward mutants because they don't understand.
It isn't right--people who have a history of being oppressed and exterminated should have the right to be left alone. But what is right--that doesn't change how the world is.
We don't want to cut you off from who you are--who you are is precious and beautiful, but...
As a father, I am terrified every day for my children.
You should think about what you need, what will help you be as safe and sane as possible.
You know I would move heaven and Earth for you, mija, and I will help you do what you need to do.
You don't have to choose between things. You are always going to be my little one, my first daughter. You are always going to be welcome with us.
Te amo, Papa.

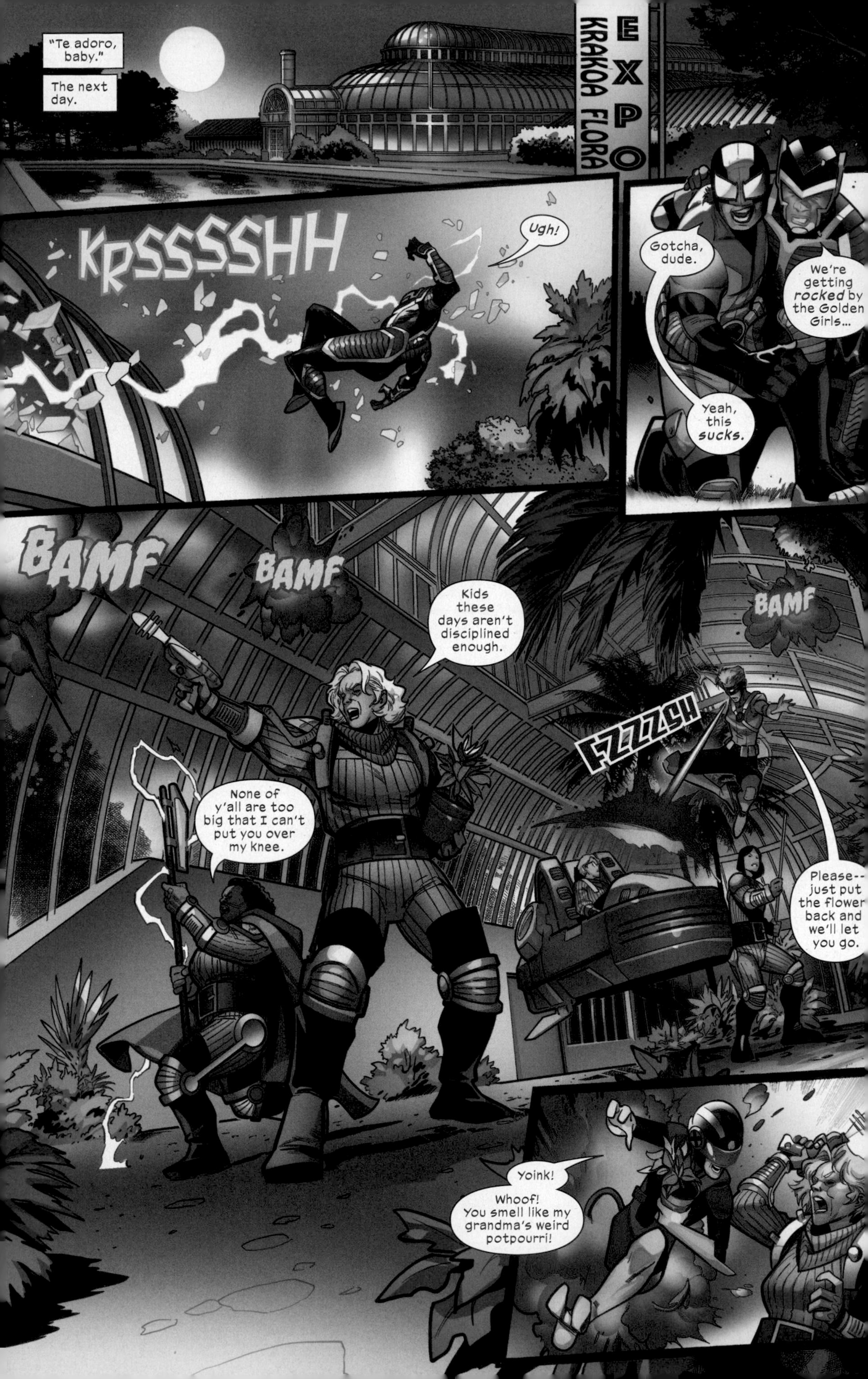
"Te adoro, baby."
The next day.
EXPO
KRAKOA FLORA
KRSSSSHH
Ugh!
Gotcha, dude.
We're getting *rocked* by the Golden Girls...
Yeah, this *sucks*.
BAMF
BAMF
Kids these days aren't disciplined enough.
BAMF
FZZZSH
None of y'all are too big that I can't put you over my knee.
Please--just put the flower back and we'll let you go.
Yoink!
Whoof! You smell like my grandma's weird potpourri!

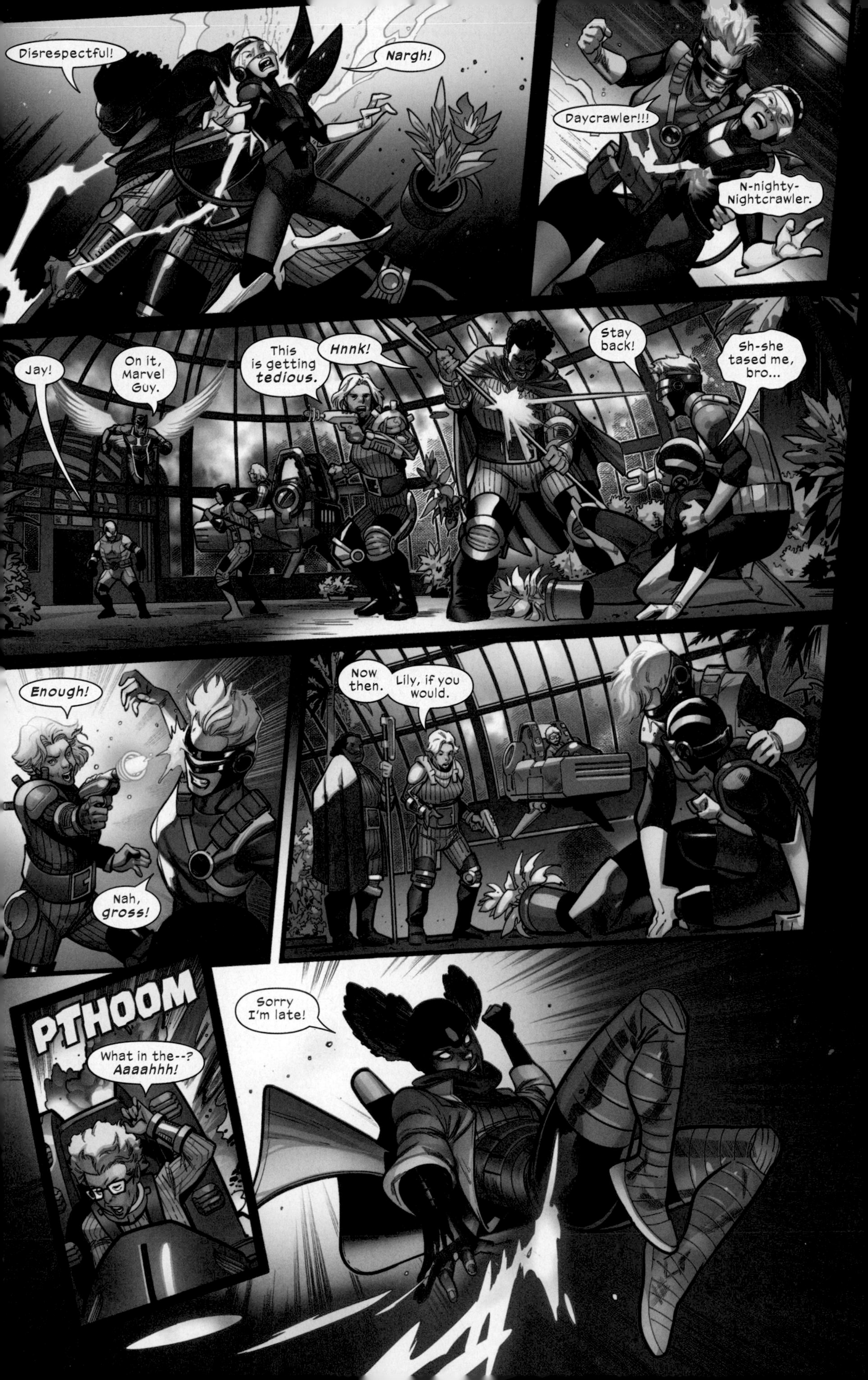

Disrespectful!
Nargh!
Daycrawler!!!
N-nighty-Nightcrawler.
Jay!
On it, Marvel Guy.
This is getting tedious.
Hnnk!
Stay back!
Sh-she tased me, bro...
Enough!
Nah, gross!
Now then.
Lily, if you would.
PTHOOM
What in the--? Aaaahhh!
Sorry I'm late!

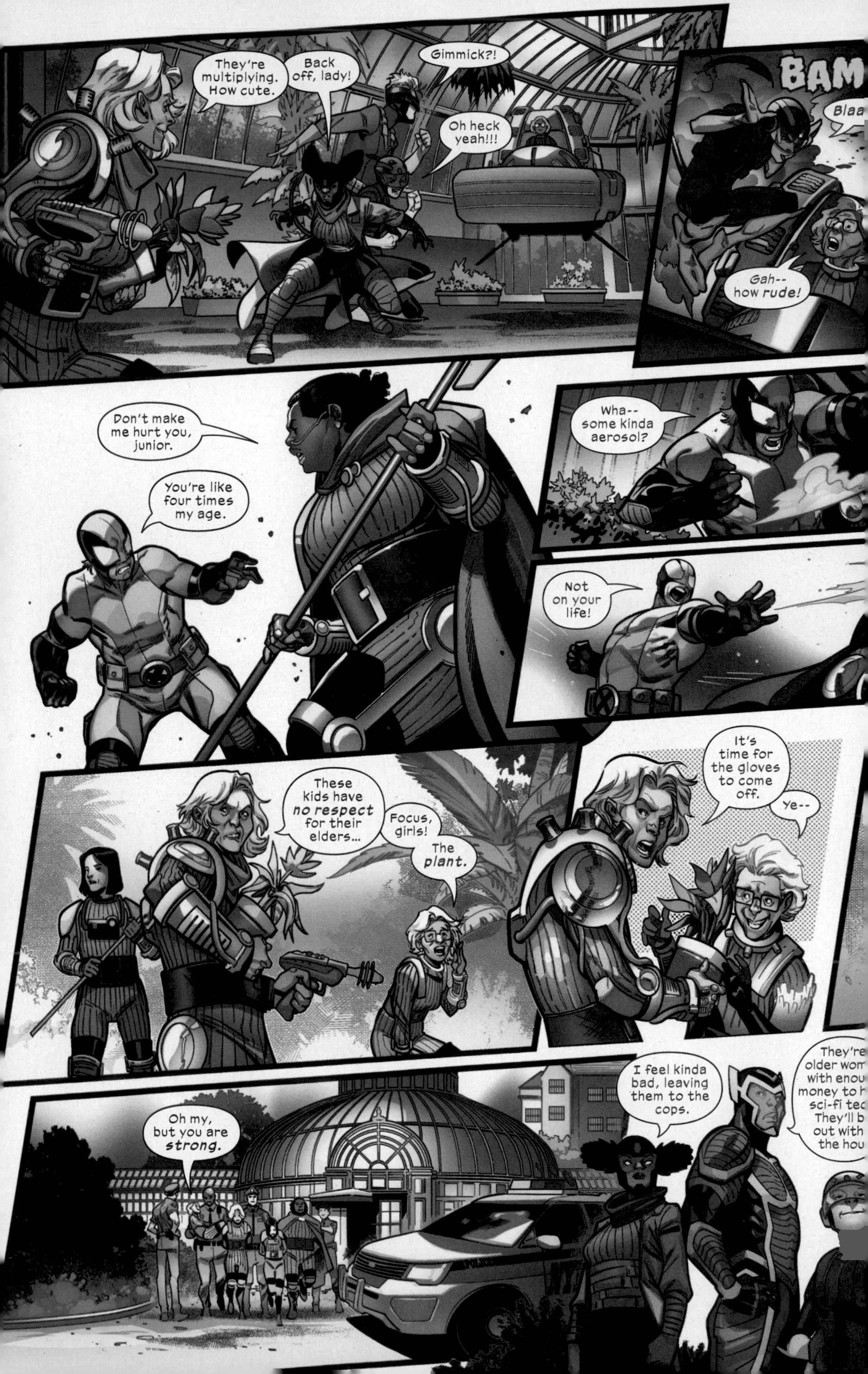

They're multiplying. How cute.
Back off, lady!
Gimmick?!
Oh heck yeah!!!
BAM
Blaa
Gah-- how rude!
Don't make me hurt you, junior.
You're like four times my age.
Wha-- some kinda aerosol?
Not on your life!
These kids have no respect for their elders...
Focus, girls! The plant.
It's time for the gloves to come off.
Ye--
Oh my, but you are strong.
I feel kinda bad, leaving them to the cops.

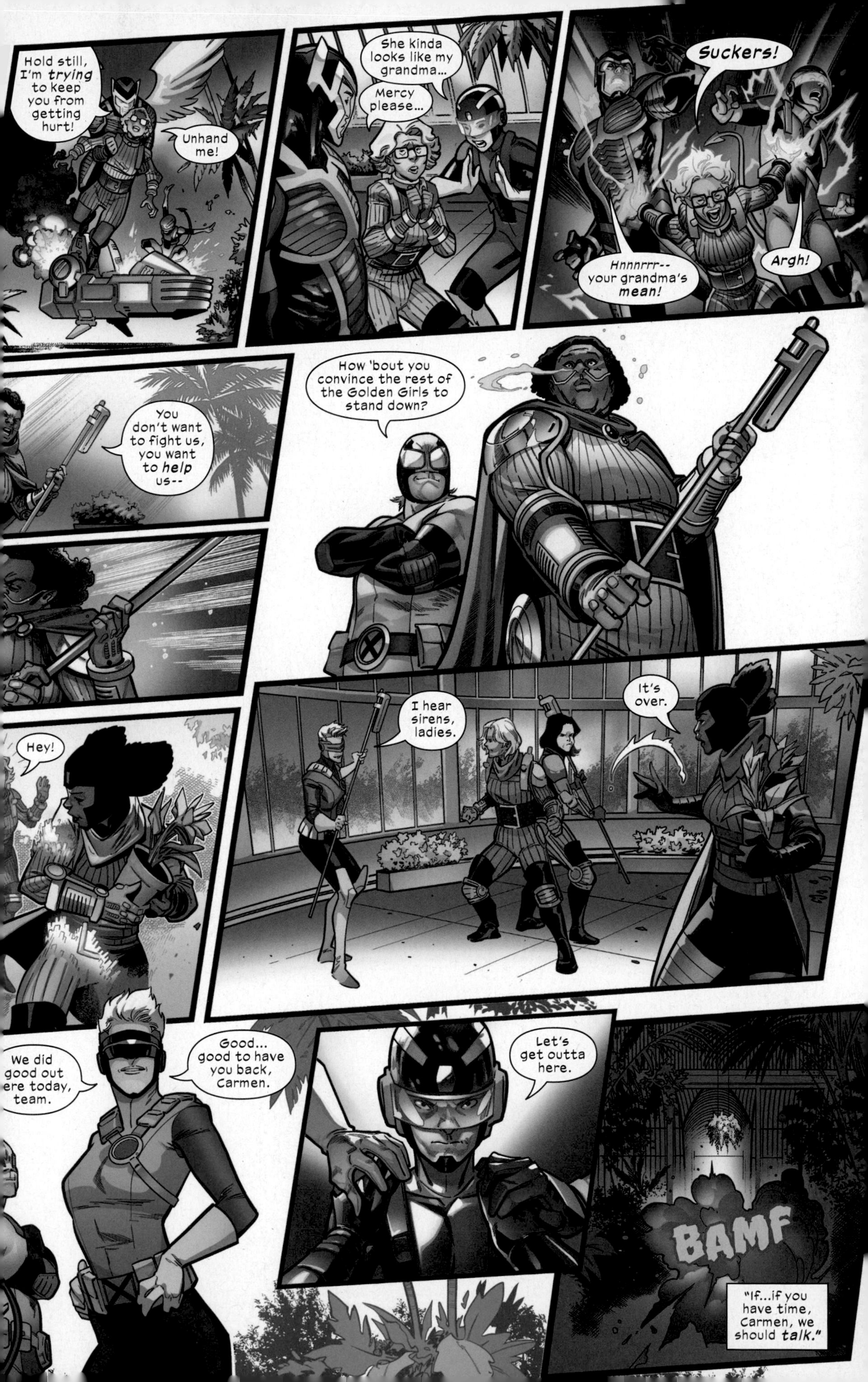
Hold still, I'm *trying* to keep you from getting hurt!
Unhand me!
She kinda looks like my grandma...
Mercy please...
Suckers!
Hnnnrrr-- your grandma's *mean!*
Argh!
You don't want to fight us, you want to *help* us--
How 'bout you convince the rest of the Golden Girls to stand down?
Hey!
I hear sirens, ladies.
It's over.
We did good out ere today, team.
Good... good to have you back, Carmen.
Let's get outta here.
BAMF
"If...if you have time, Carmen, we should *talk*."

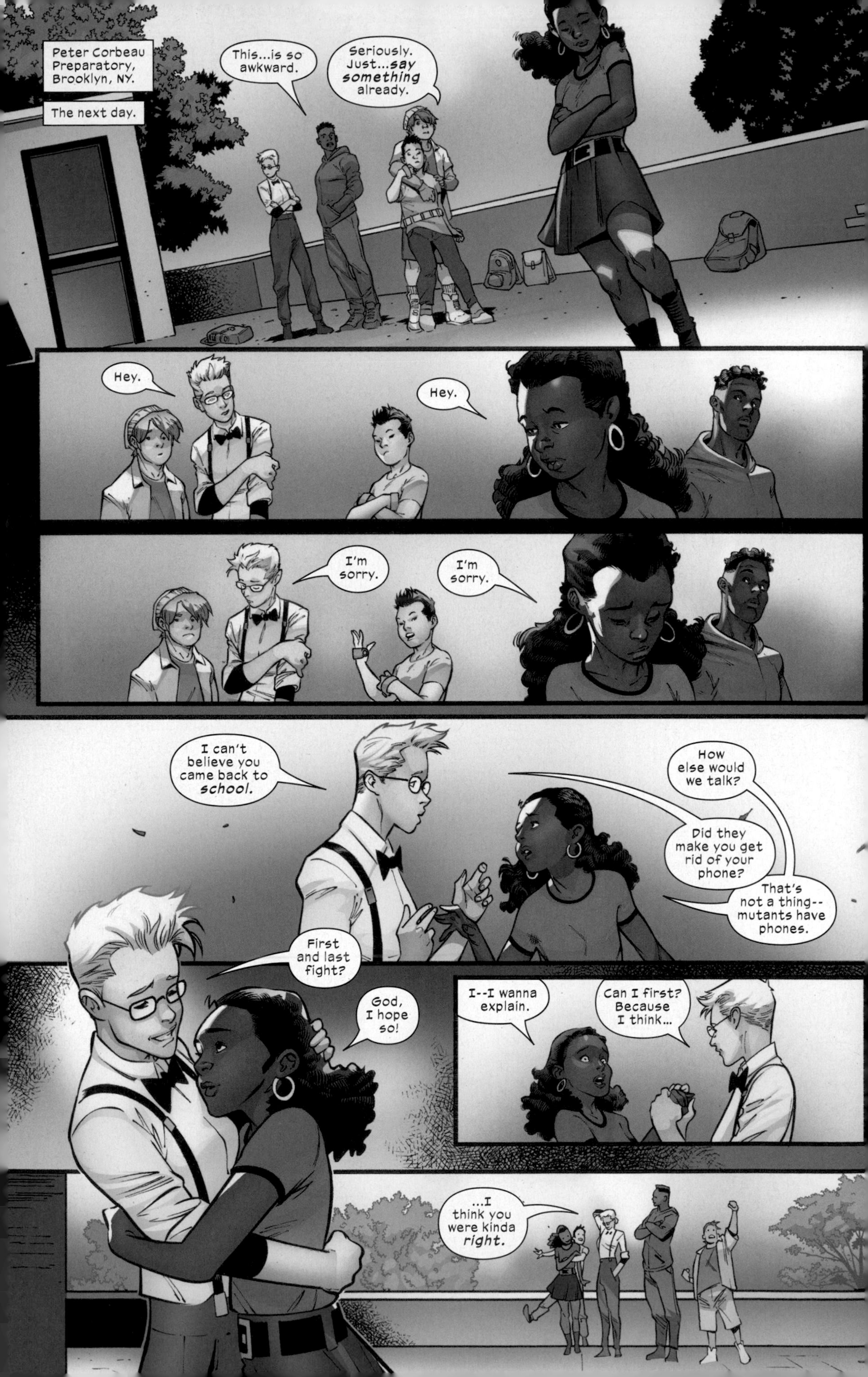
Peter Corbeau Preparatory, Brooklyn, NY.
The next day.
This...is so awkward.
Seriously. Just...say something already.
Hey.
Hey.
I'm sorry.
I'm sorry.
I can't believe you came back to school.
How else would we talk?
Did they make you get rid of your phone?
That's not a thing-- mutants have phones.
First and last fight?
God, I hope so!
I--I wanna explain.
Can I first? Because I think...
...I think you were kinda right.

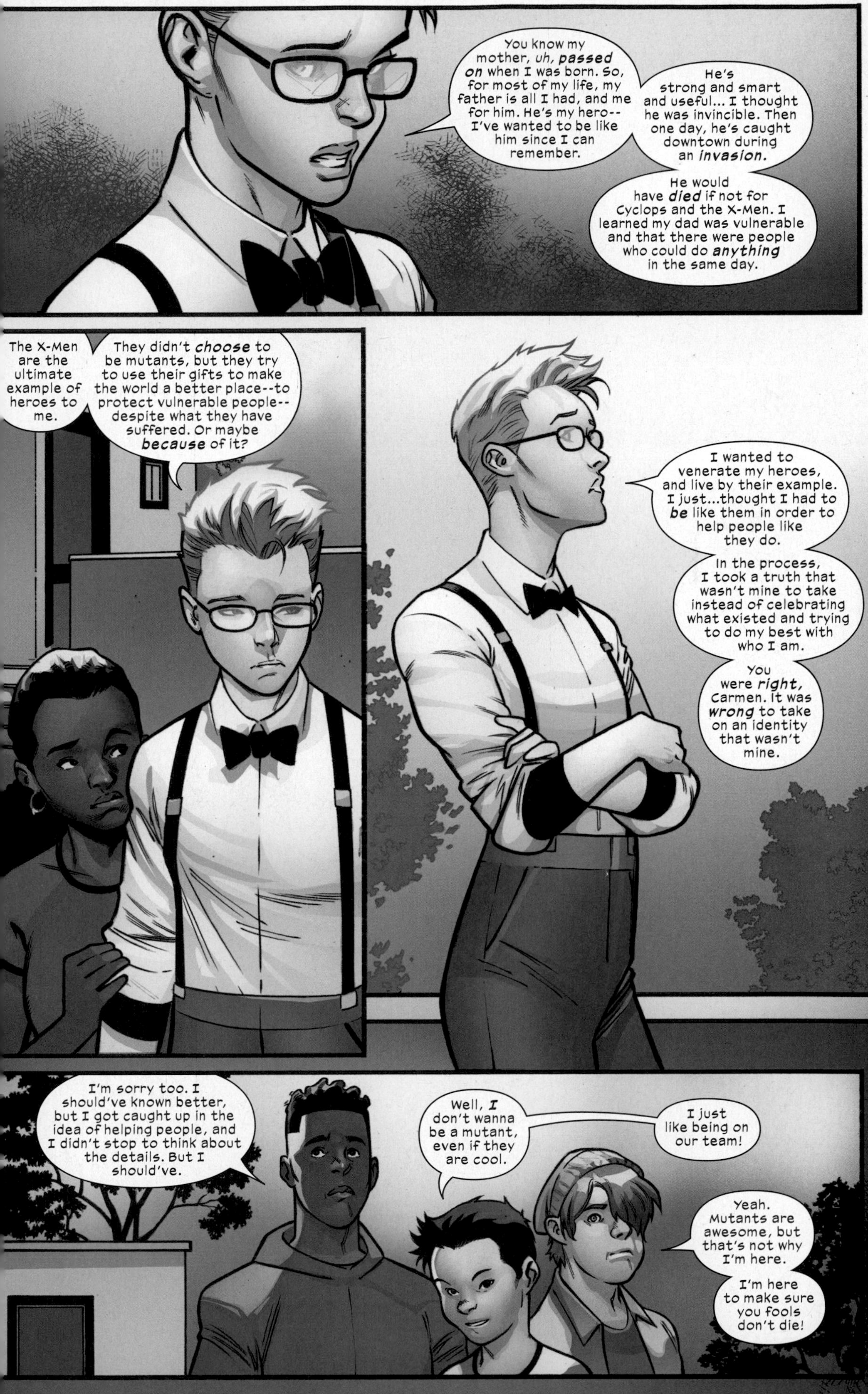

You know my mother, *uh,* ***passed on*** when I was born. So, for most of my life, my father is all I had, and me for him. He's my hero-- I've wanted to be like him since I can remember.
He's strong and smart and useful... I thought he was invincible. Then one day, he's caught downtown during an ***invasion.***
He would have ***died*** if not for Cyclops and the X-Men. I learned my dad was vulnerable and that there were people who could do ***anything*** in the same day.
The X-Men are the ultimate example of heroes to me.
They didn't ***choose*** to be mutants, but they try to use their gifts to make the world a better place--to protect vulnerable people--despite what they have suffered. Or maybe ***because*** of it?
I wanted to venerate my heroes, and live by their example. I just...thought I had to ***be*** like them in order to help people like they do.
In the process, I took a truth that wasn't mine to take instead of celebrating what existed and trying to do my best with who I am.
You were ***right,*** Carmen. It was ***wrong*** to take on an identity that wasn't mine.
I'm sorry too. I should've known better, but I got caught up in the idea of helping people, and I didn't stop to think about the details. But I should've.
Well, ***I*** don't wanna be a mutant, even if they are cool.
I just like being on our team!
Yeah. Mutants are awesome, but that's not why I'm here.
I'm here to make sure you fools don't die!

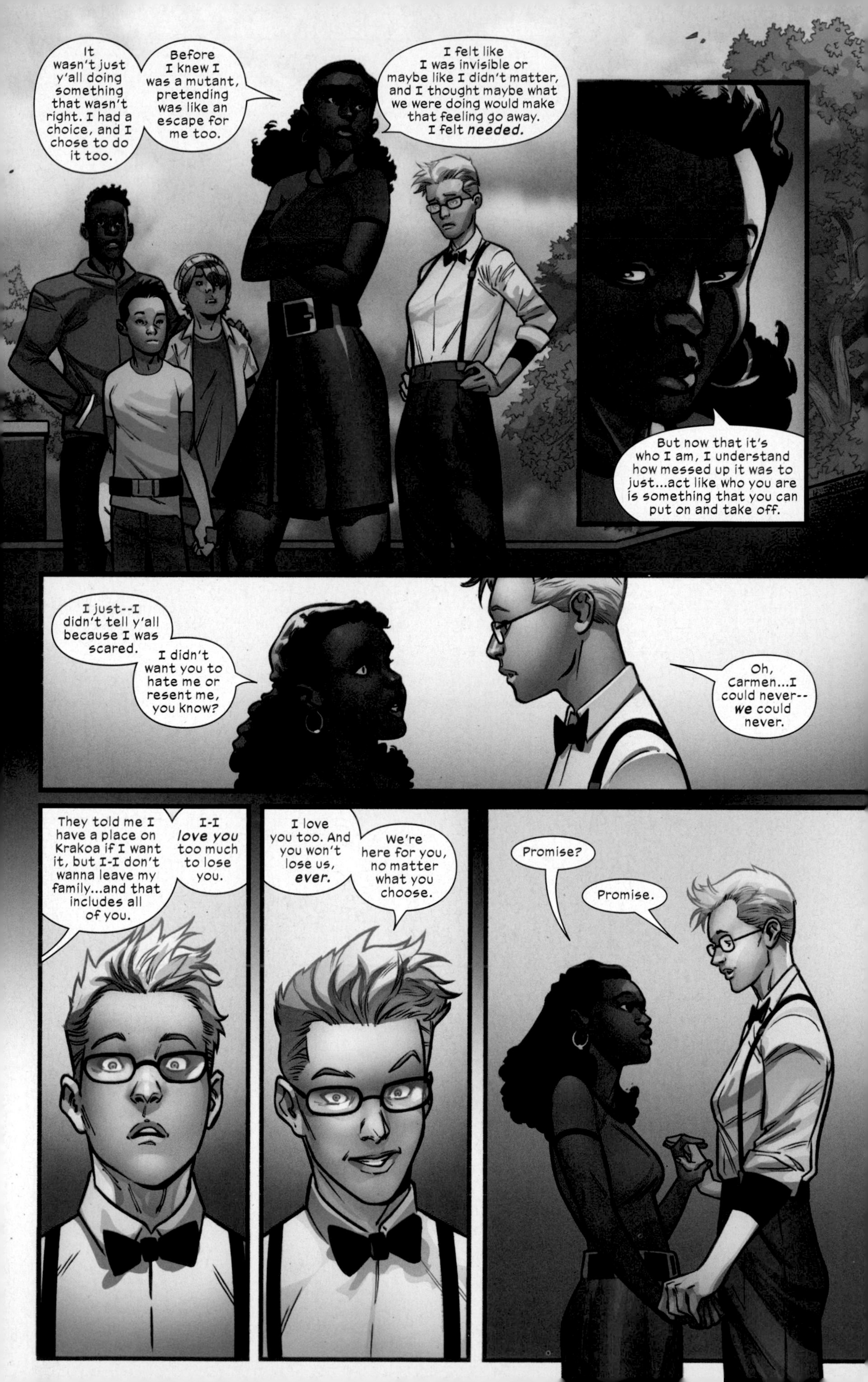
It wasn't just y'all doing something that wasn't right. I had a choice, and I chose to do it too.
Before I knew I was a mutant, pretending was like an escape for me too.
I felt like I was invisible or maybe like I didn't matter, and I thought maybe what we were doing would make that feeling go away. I felt *needed.*
But now that it's who I am, I understand how messed up it was to just...act like who you are is something that you can put on and take off.
I just--I didn't tell y'all because I was scared.
I didn't want you to hate me or resent me, you know?
Oh, Carmen...I could never-- *we* could never.
They told me I have a place on Krakoa if I want it, but I-I don't wanna leave my family...and that includes all of you.
I-I *love you* too much to lose you.
I love you too. And you won't lose us, *ever.*
We're here for you, no matter what you choose.
Promise?
Promise.

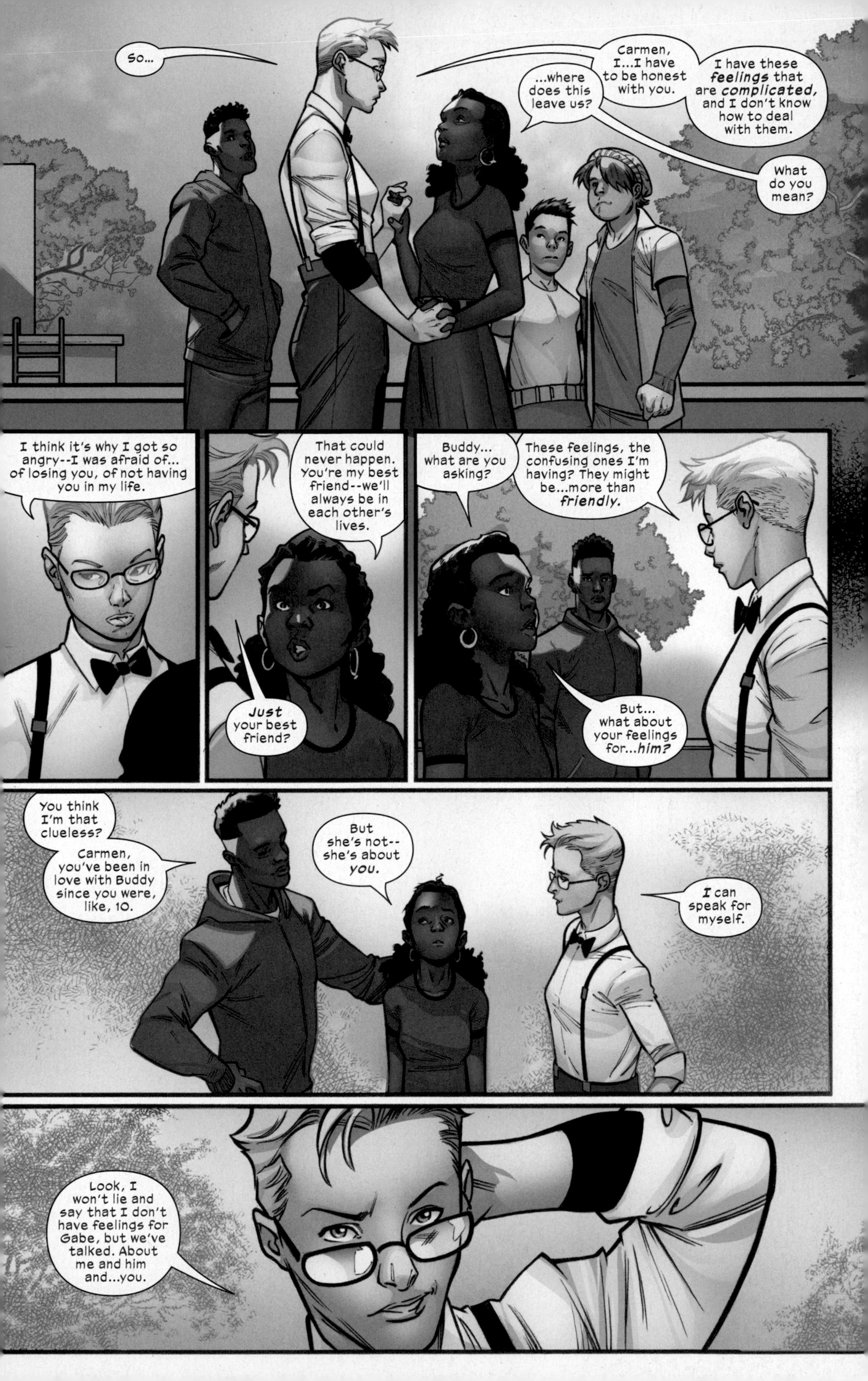
So...
Carmen, I...I have to be honest with you.
I have these *feelings* that are *complicated,* and I don't know how to deal with them.
...where does this leave us?
What do you mean?
I think it's why I got so angry--I was afraid of... of losing you, of not having you in my life.
That could never happen. You're my best friend--we'll always be in each other's lives.
Just your best friend?
Buddy... what are you asking?
These feelings, the confusing ones I'm having? They might be...more than *friendly.*
But... what about your feelings for...*him?*
You think I'm that clueless?
Carmen, you've been in love with Buddy since you were, like, 10.
But she's not-- she's about *you.*
I can speak for myself.
Look, I won't lie and say that I don't have feelings for Gabe, but we've talked. About me and him and...you.

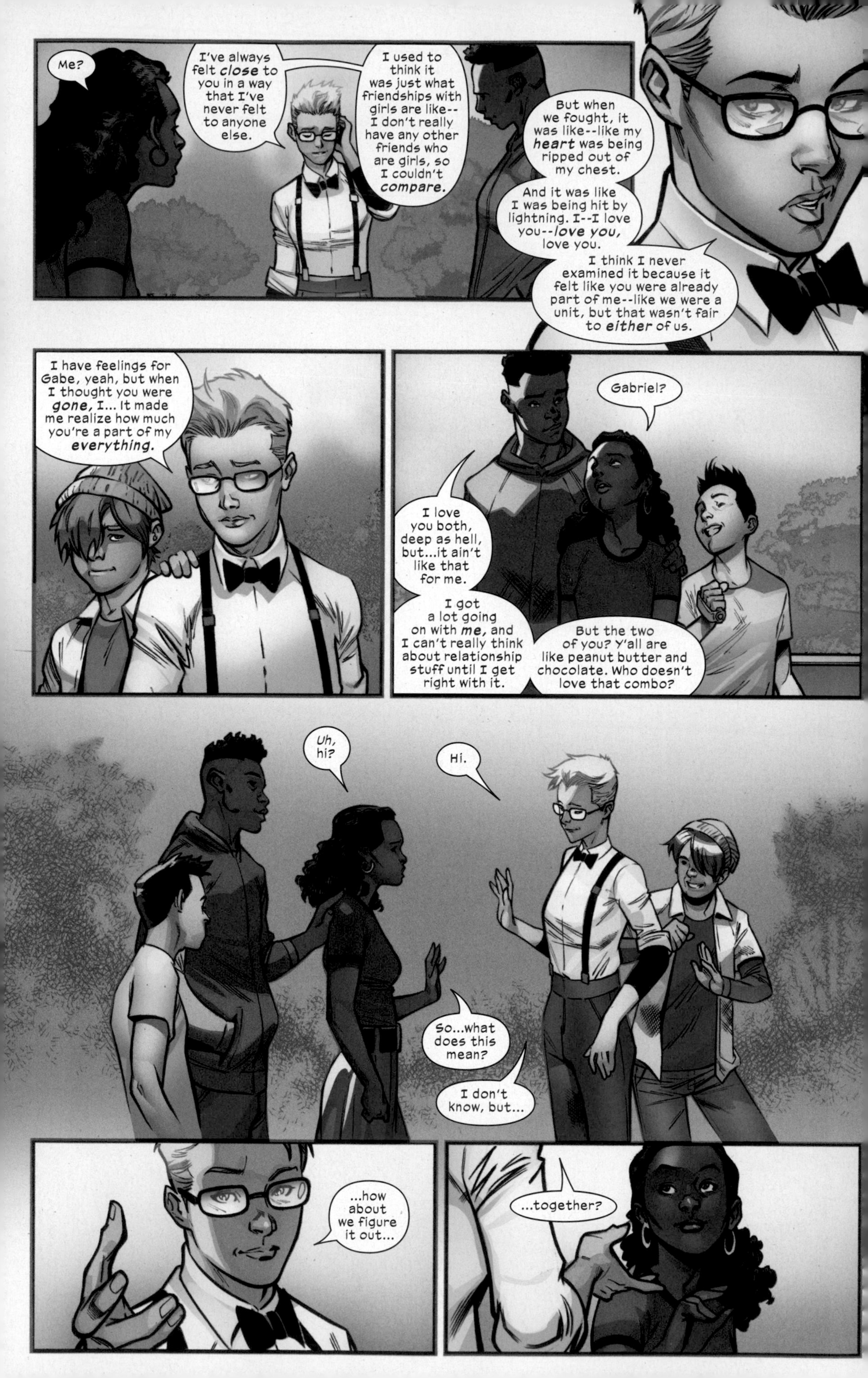
Me?
I've always felt close to you in a way that I've never felt to anyone else.
I used to think it was just what friendships with girls are like-- I don't really have any other friends who are girls, so I couldn't compare.
But when we fought, it was like--like my heart was being ripped out of my chest.
And it was like I was being hit by lightning. I--I love you--love you, love you.
I think I never examined it because it felt like you were already part of me--like we were a unit, but that wasn't fair to either of us.
I have feelings for Gabe, yeah, but when I thought you were gone, I... It made me realize how much you're a part of my everything.
Gabriel?
I love you both, deep as hell, but...it ain't like that for me.
I got a lot going on with me, and I can't really think about relationship stuff until I get right with it.
But the two of you? Y'all are like peanut butter and chocolate. Who doesn't love that combo?
Uh, hi?
Hi.
So...what does this mean?
I don't know, but...
...how about we figure it out...
...together?

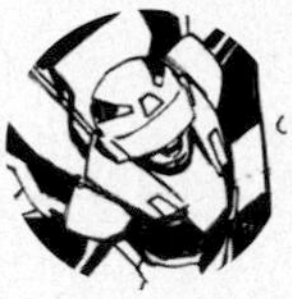

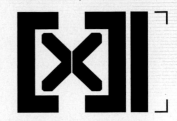

Nighty-Nightcrawler

Children of the Atom

We are the Children of the Atom!
We let rumors get out of control, and it's time to fix that. All you need to know about our team.
This isn't a rebranding--it's a proper introduction!

♫ *"That's My Name" by WeaponXtra*

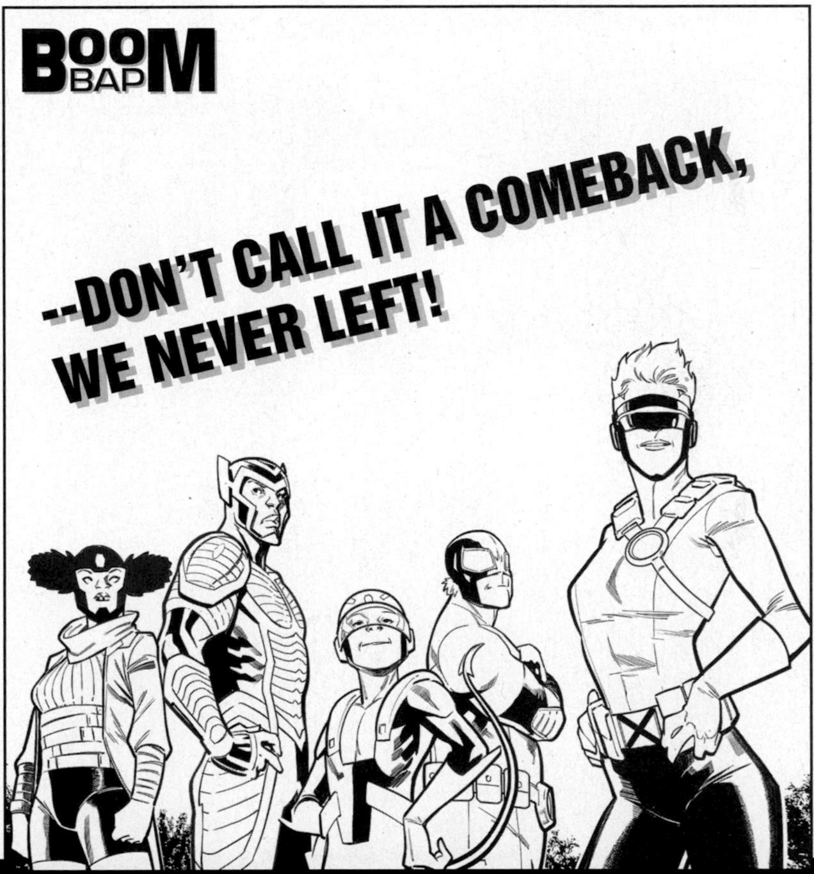
BOOM BAP
--DON'T CALL IT A COMEBACK, WE NEVER LEFT!

M.O.D.O.K.'S LeftToe: Wait, so they're human? What a rip-off!

NightyNightCrawler: One of us is not, if you paid attention to the video. But either way, we technically never said we were. You guys just assumed, and you know what they say about assumptions...

ArchivistX: The mission has not changed. Help people when you can, how you can.

GimmikStan01: We love you, don't listen to haters!

C.R.A.D.L.E.Official: If anyone has any information as to the whereabouts of these children, please follow this link and let us know. There is a small reward offered. We just want to make sure they are safe.

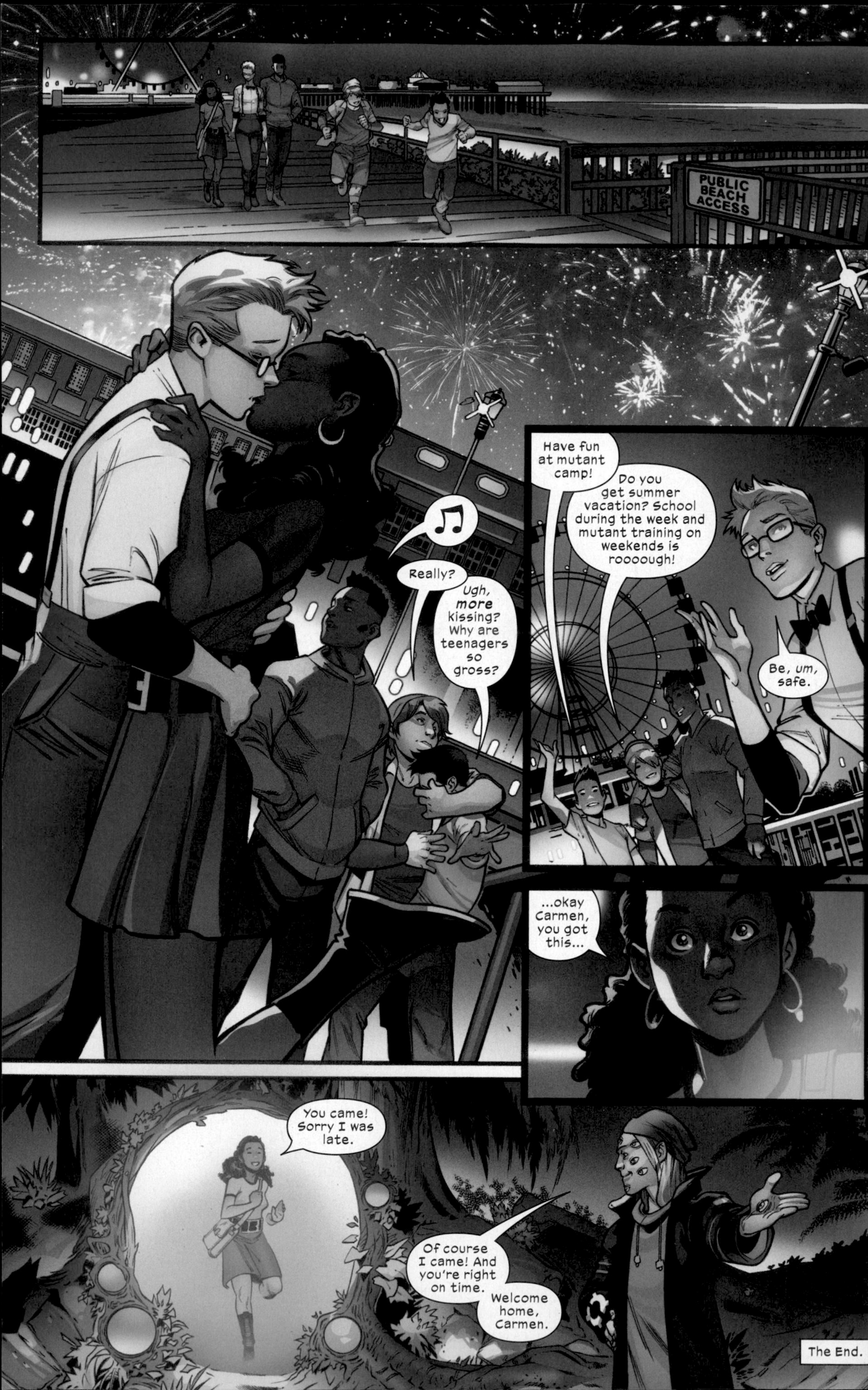
PUBLIC BEACH ACCESS
♫
Really?
Ugh, *more* kissing? Why are teenagers so gross?
Have fun at mutant camp!
Do you get summer vacation? School during the week and mutant training on weekends is roooough!
Be, um, safe.
...okay Carmen, you got this...
You came! Sorry I was late.
Of course I came! And you're right on time.
Welcome home, Carmen.
The End.

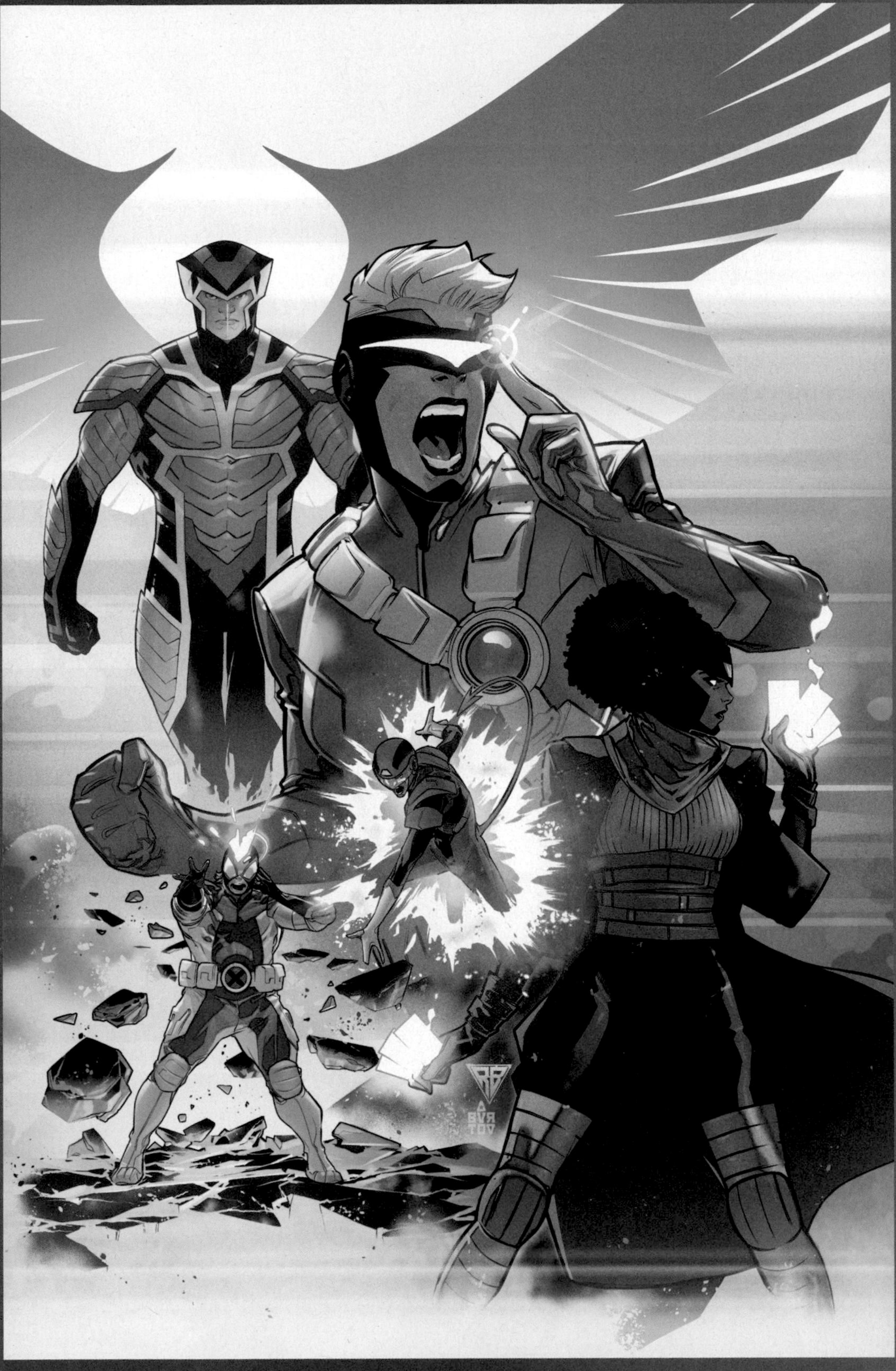

Children of the Atom #1 by R.B. Silva & Jesus Aburtov

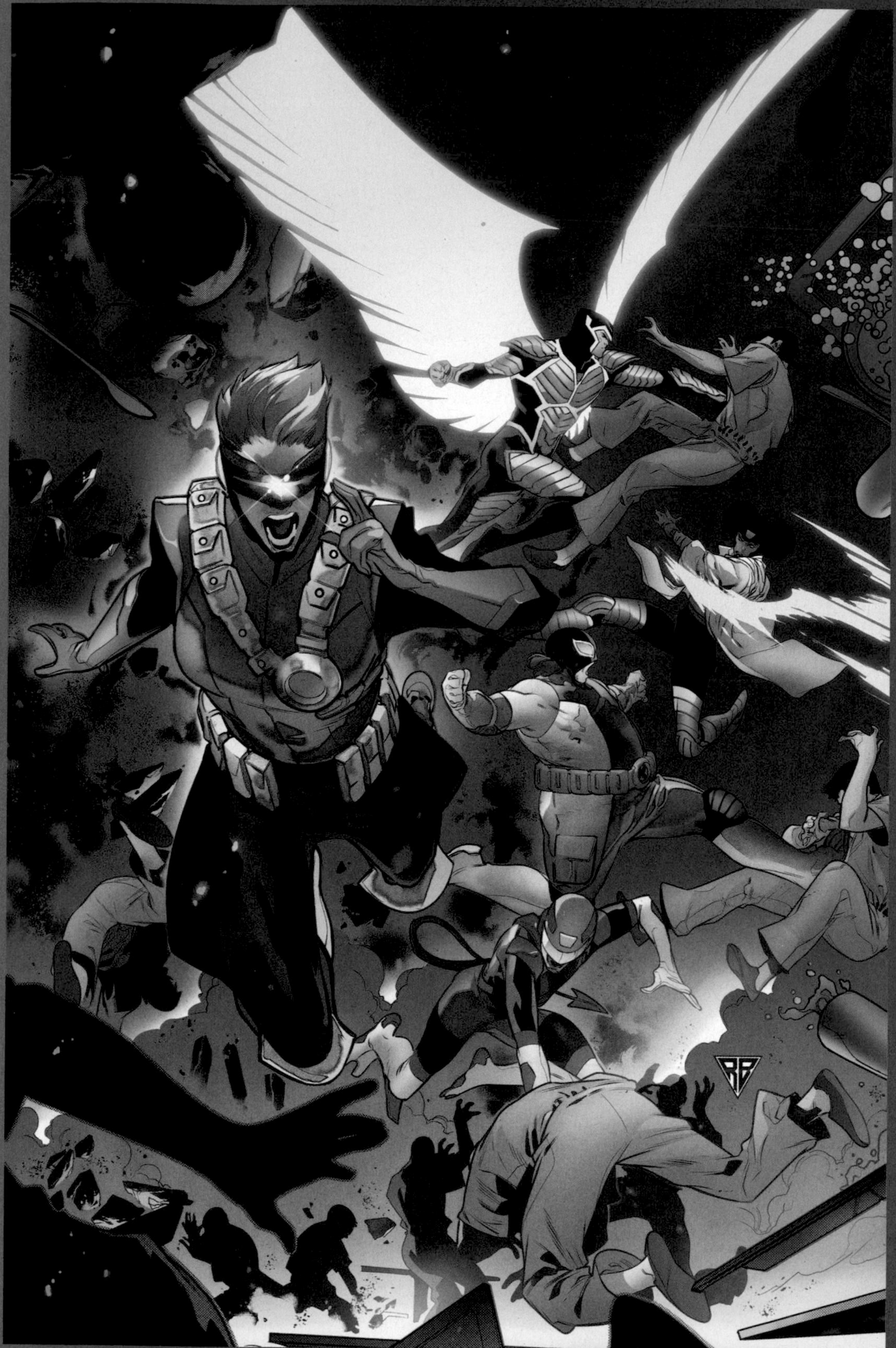
RB

Children of the Atom #2 by R.B. Silva & Erick Arciniega

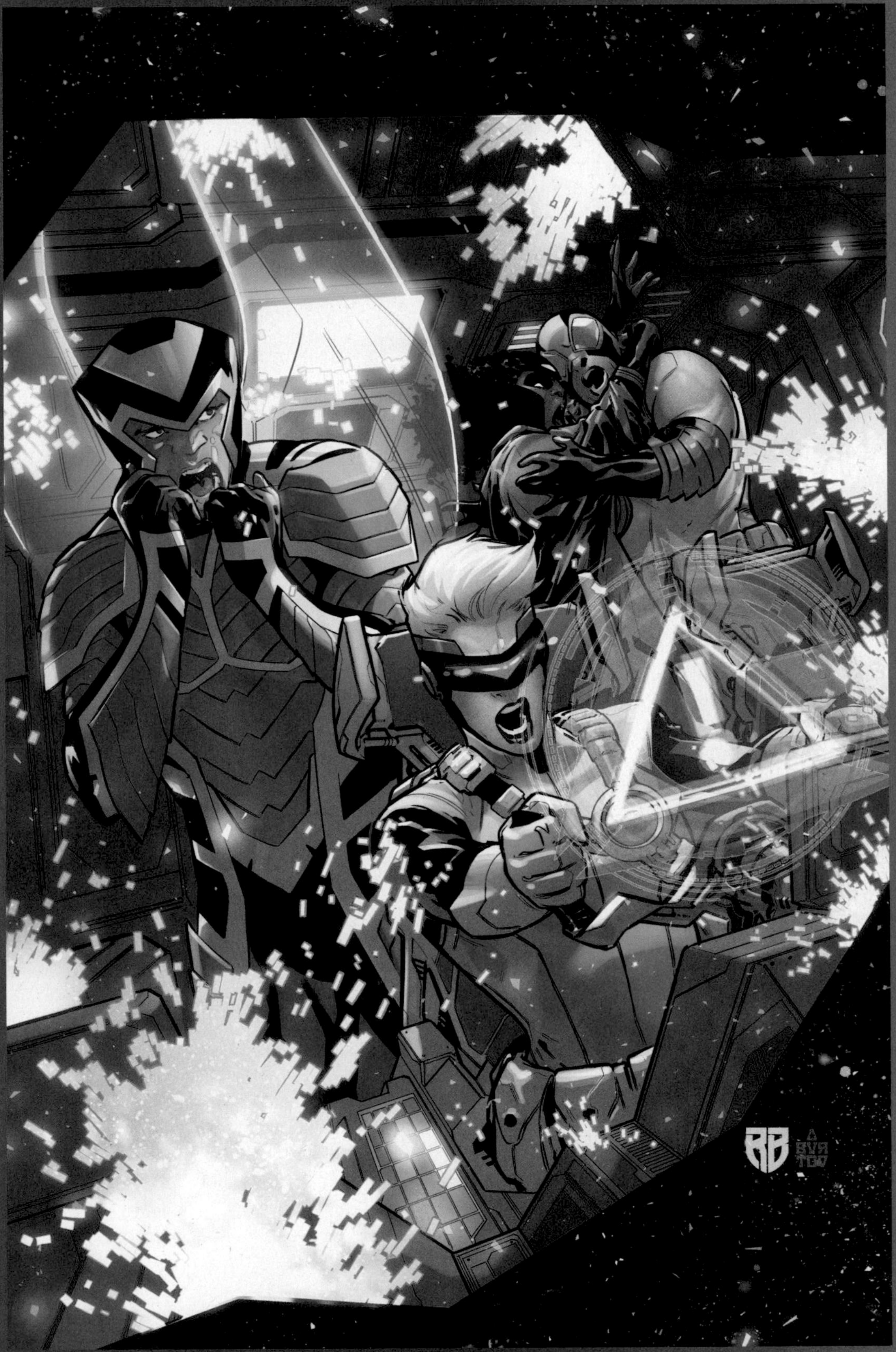

Children of the Atom #3 by R.B. Silva & Jesus Aburtov

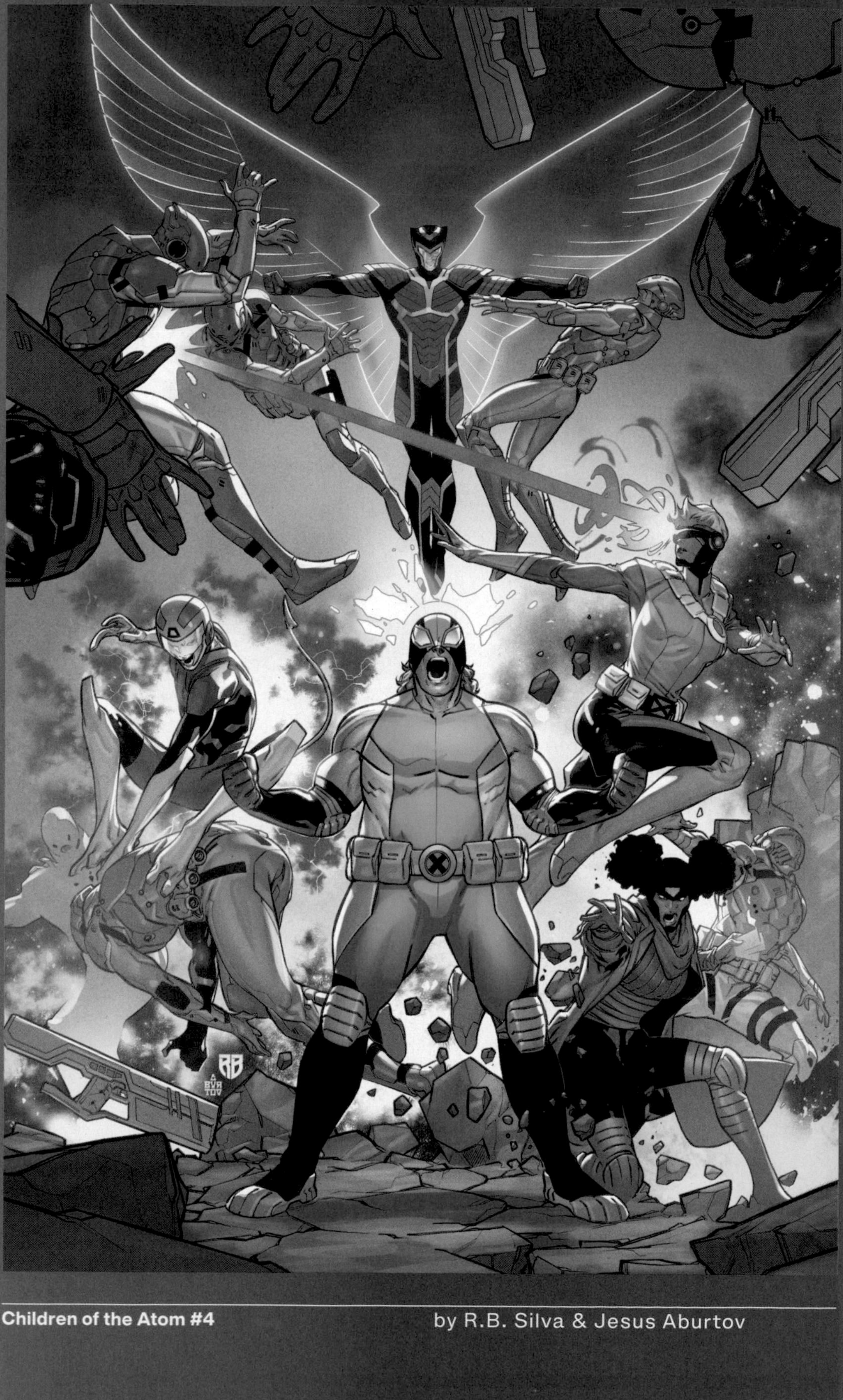

Children of the Atom #4 by R.B. Silva & Jesus Aburtov

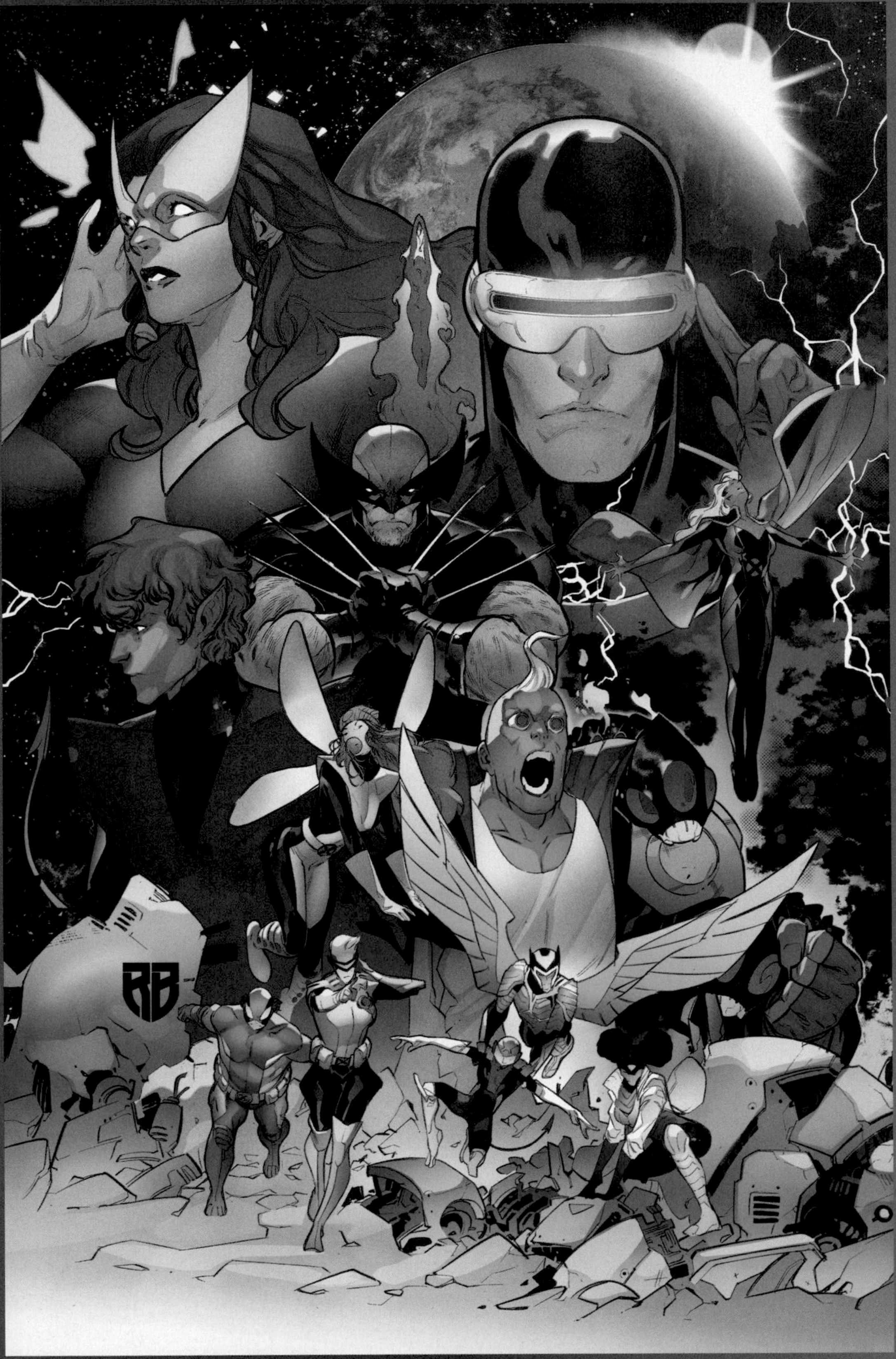
RB

Children of the Atom #5 by R.B. Silva & Erick Arciniega

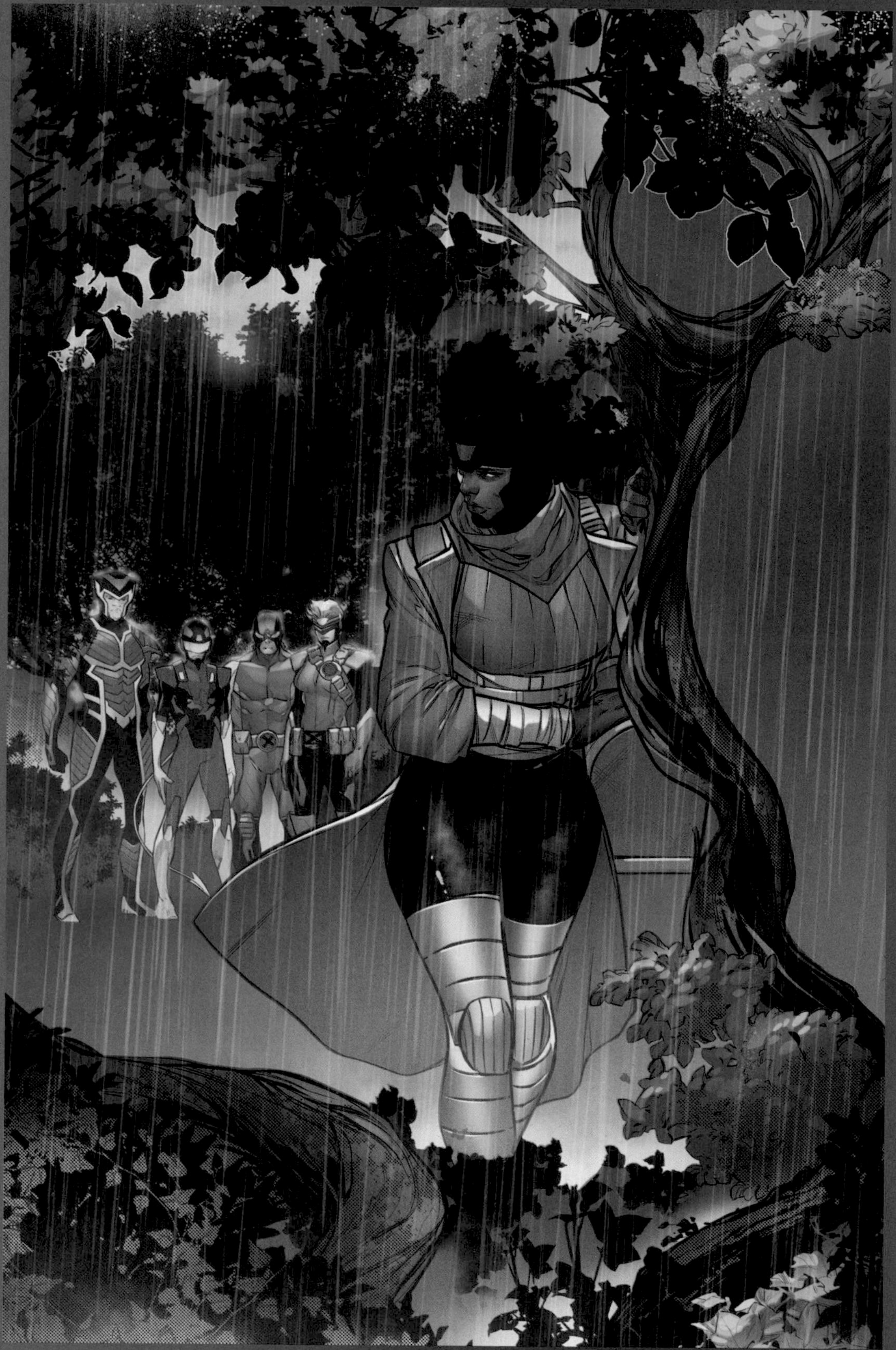

Children of the Atom #6 by R.B. Silva & Erick Arciniega

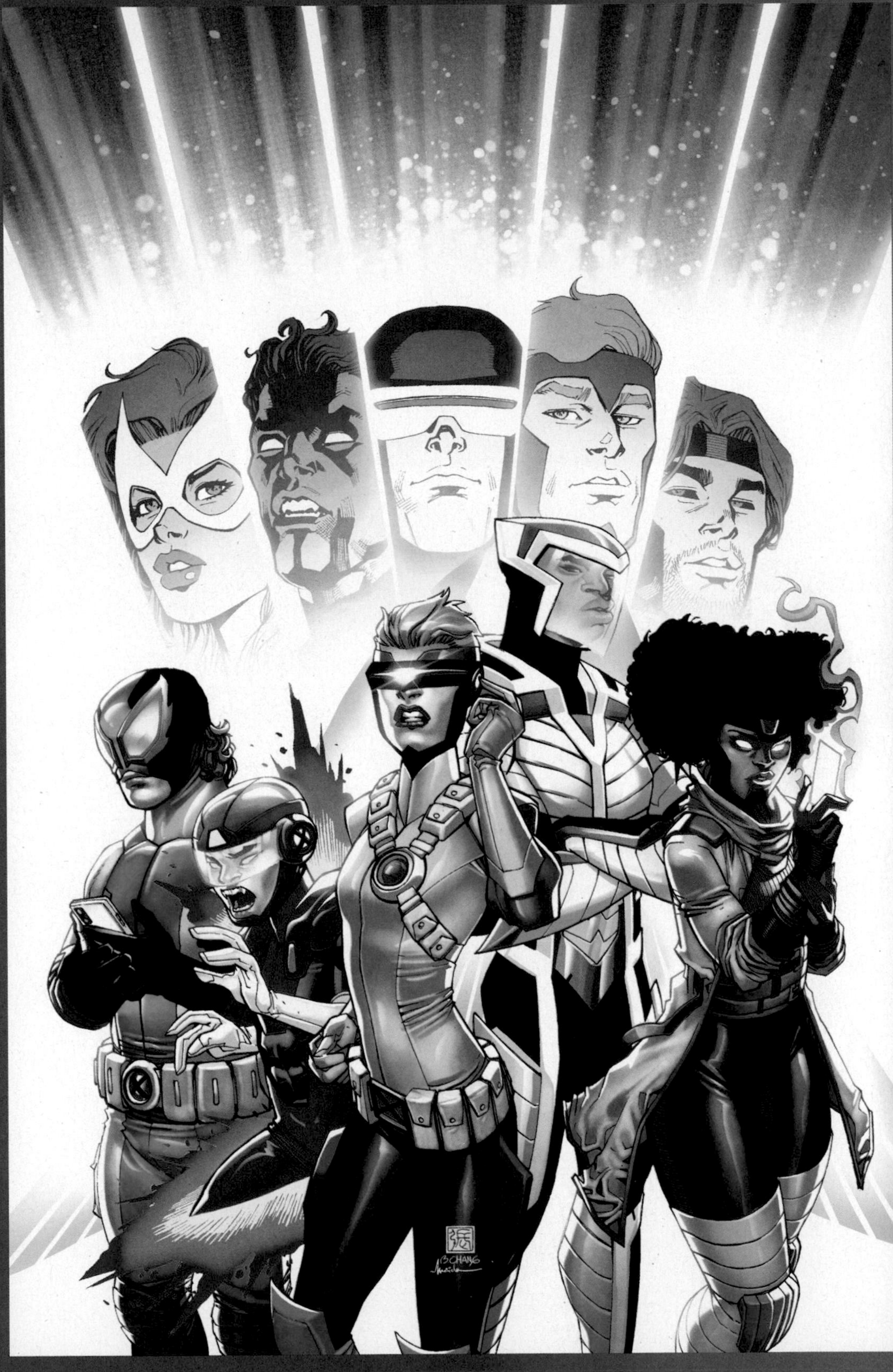

Children of the Atom #1 Variant

by Bernard Chang
& Marcelo Maiolo

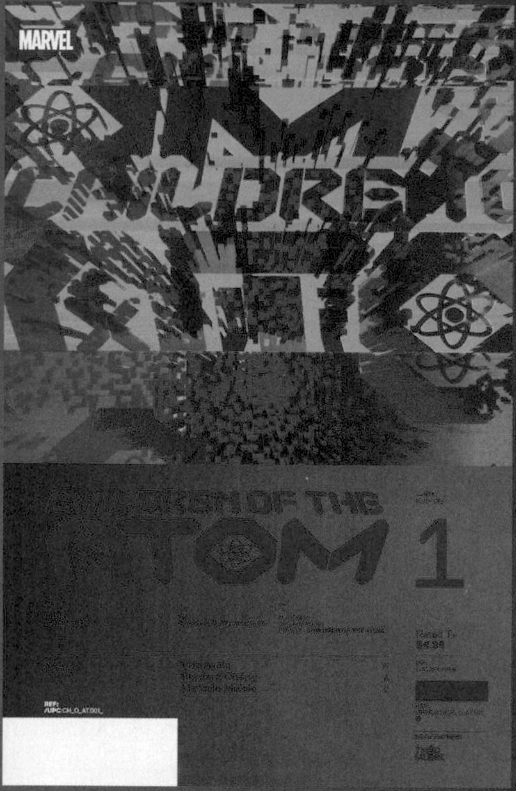
MARVEL
1

Children of the Atom #1 Design Variant
by Tom Muller

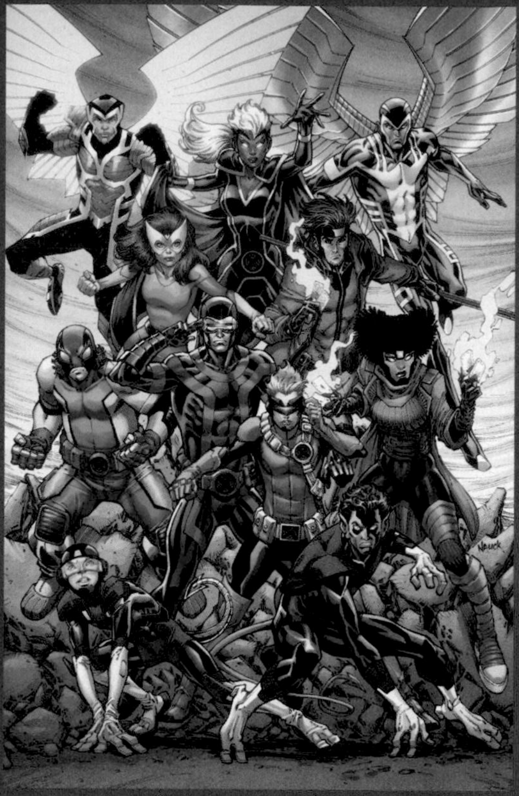
NAUCK

Children of the Atom #1 Variant
by Todd Nauck & Rachelle Rosenberg

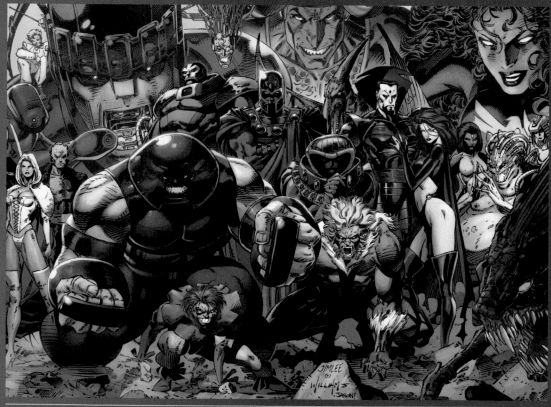

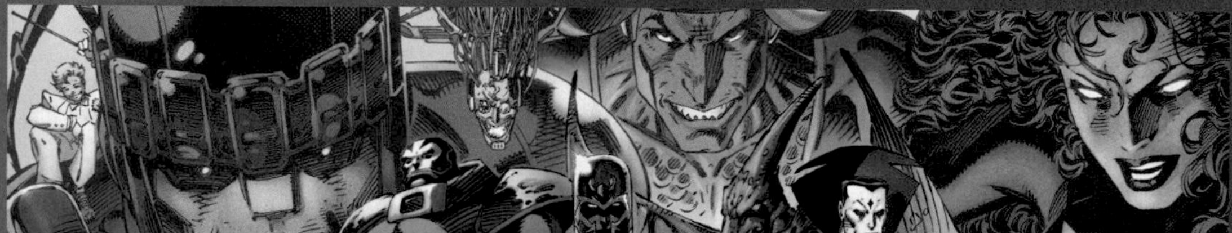
JIM LEE
WILLIAMS
JASON!

Children of the Atom #1 Hidden Gem Variant
by Jim Lee, Scott Williams & Jason Keith

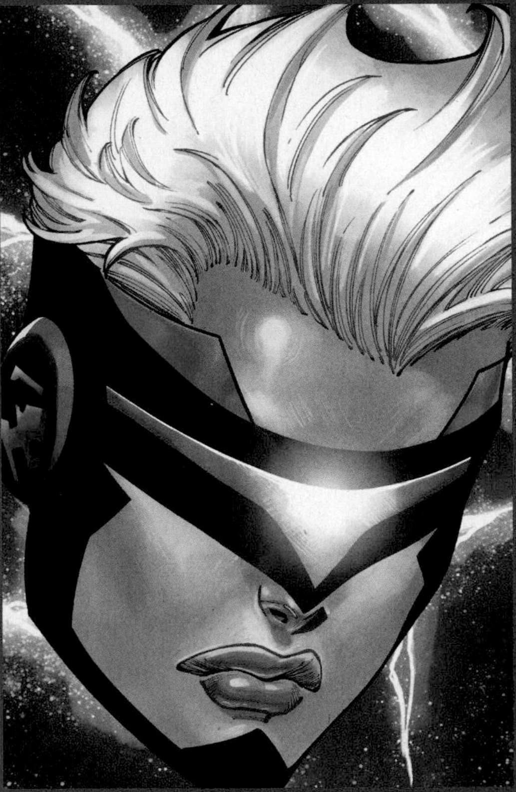

Children of the Atom #2 Headshot Variant
by Todd Nauck & Rachelle Rosenberg

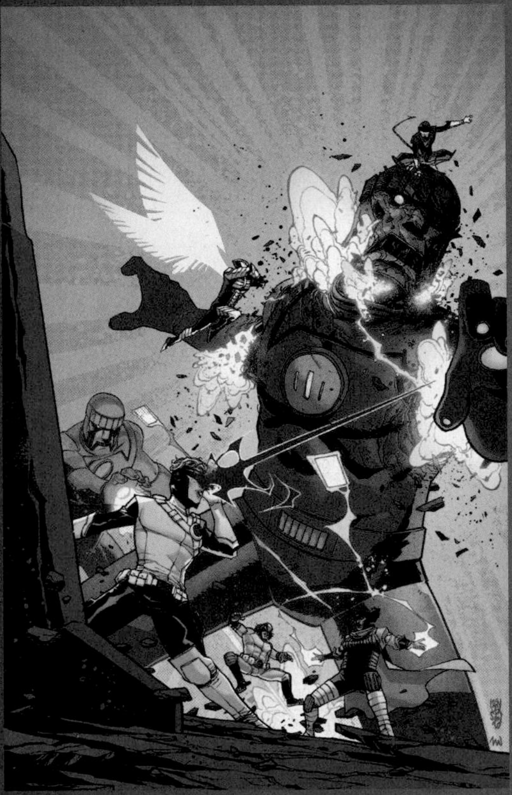

Children of the Atom #2 Variant
by Mike Henderson & Nolan Woodard

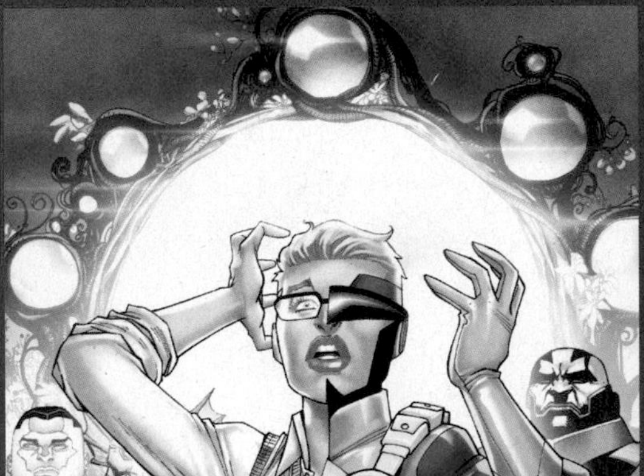

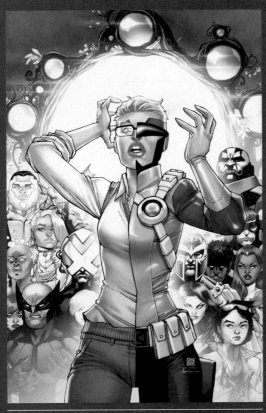

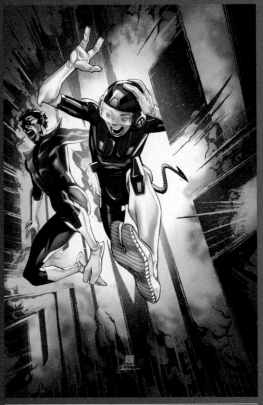

Children of the Atom #3 Variant
by Bernard Chang & Marcelo Maiolo

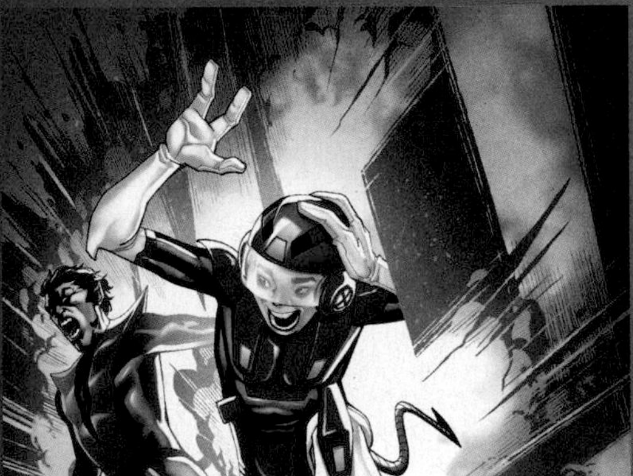

Children of the Atom #4 Variant
by Bernard Chang & Marcelo Maiolo

Children of the Atom #5 Variant

by Bernard Chang
& Marcelo Maiolo

Children of the Atom #6 Variant

by Bernard Chang
& Marcelo Maiolo

Race

B

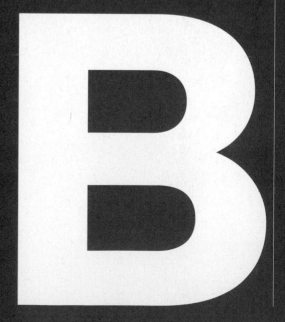

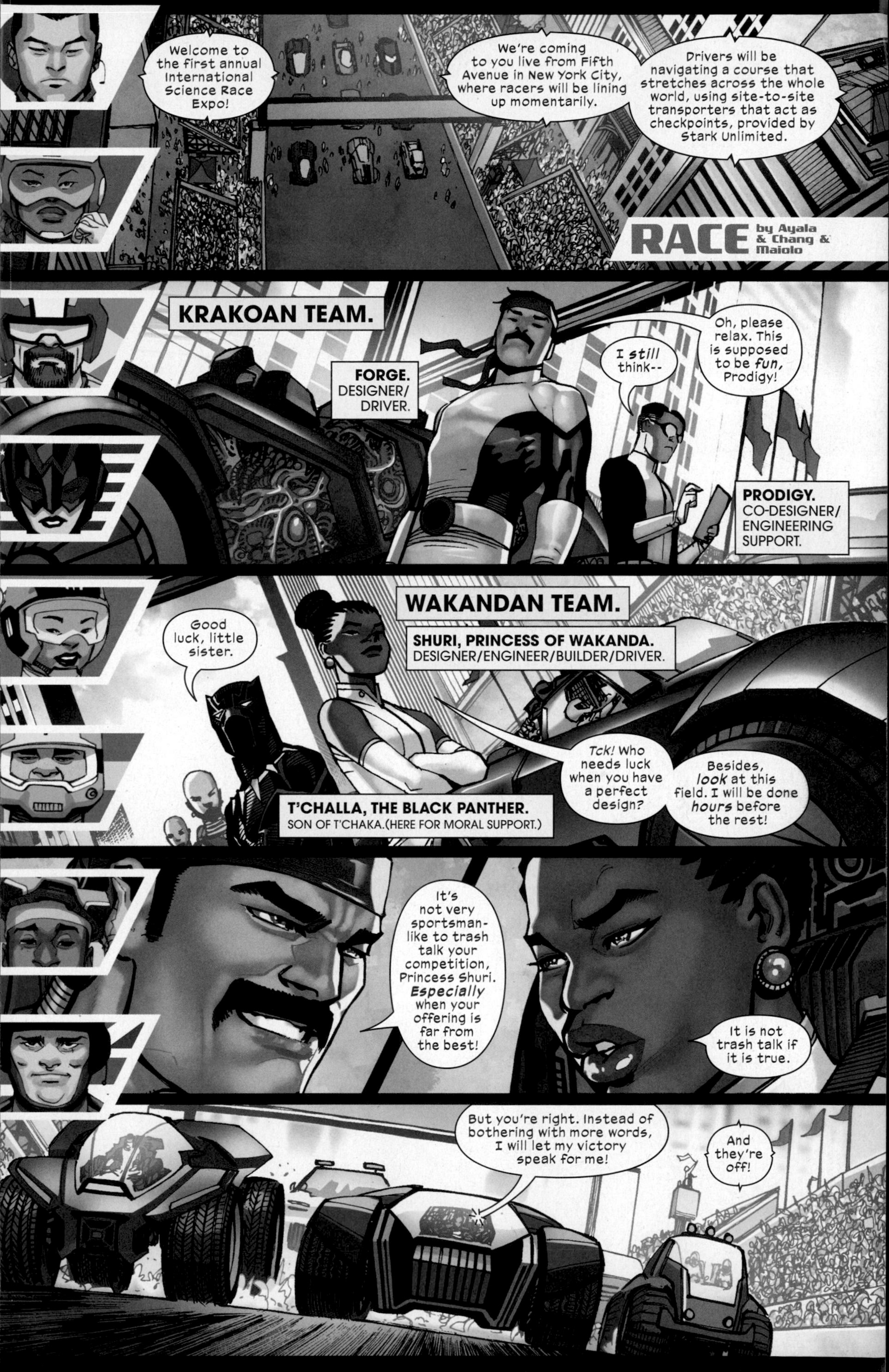
Welcome to the first annual International Science Race Expo!
We're coming to you live from Fifth Avenue in New York City, where racers will be lining up momentarily.
Drivers will be navigating a course that stretches across the whole world, using site-to-site transporters that act as checkpoints, provided by Stark Unlimited.
RACE by Ayala & Chang & Maiolo
KRAKOAN TEAM.
FORGE. DESIGNER/ DRIVER.
I still think--
Oh, please relax. This is supposed to be fun, Prodigy!
PRODIGY. CO-DESIGNER/ ENGINEERING SUPPORT.
WAKANDAN TEAM.
SHURI, PRINCESS OF WAKANDA. DESIGNER/ENGINEER/BUILDER/DRIVER.
Good luck, little sister.
T'CHALLA, THE BLACK PANTHER. SON OF T'CHAKA. (HERE FOR MORAL SUPPORT.)
Tck! Who needs luck when you have a perfect design?
Besides, look at this field. I will be done hours before the rest!
It's not very sportsman-like to trash talk your competition, Princess Shuri. Especially when your offering is far from the best!
It is not trash talk if it is true.
But you're right. Instead of bothering with more words, I will let my victory speak for me!
And they're off!

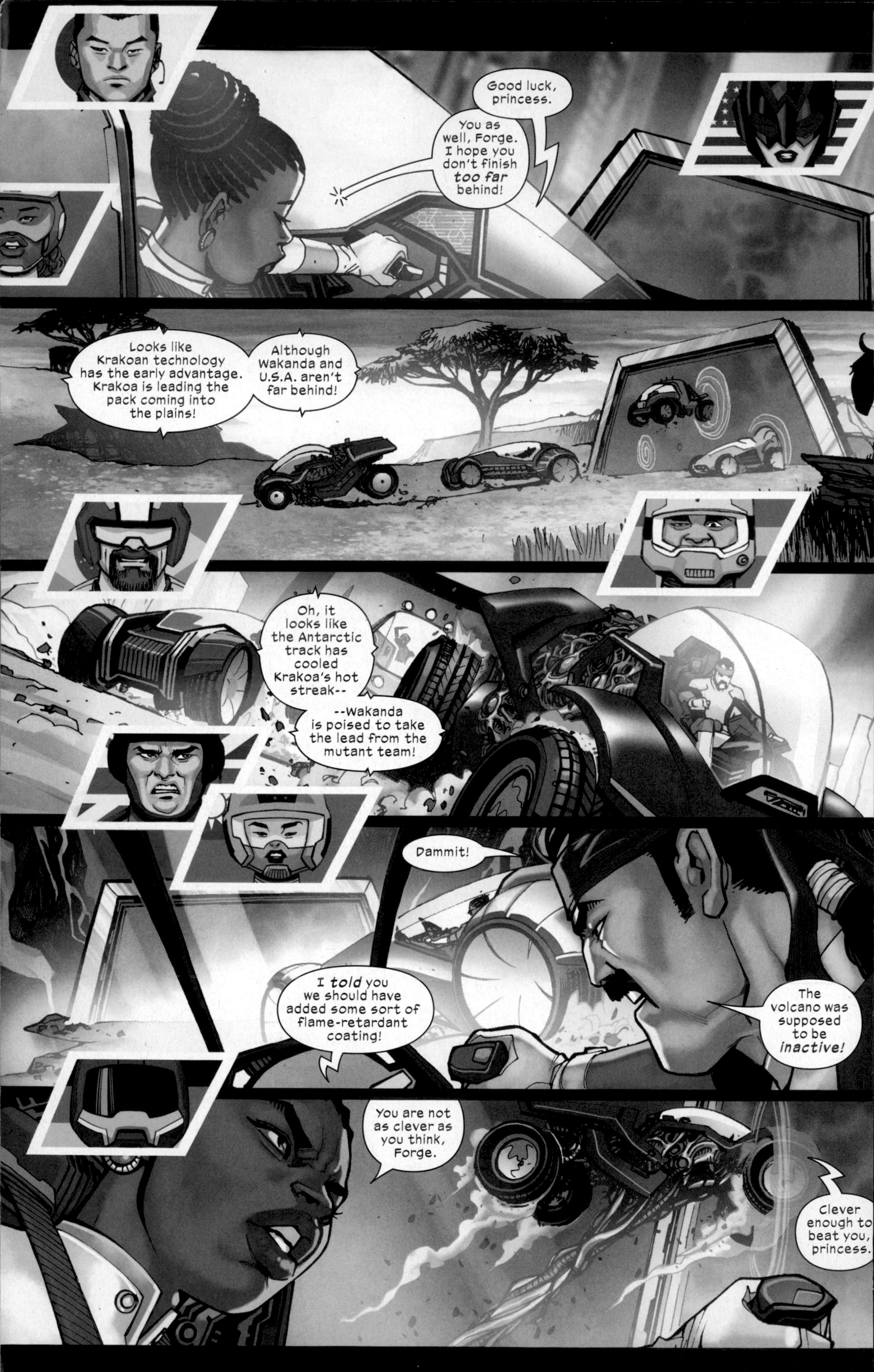
Good luck, princess.
You as well, Forge. I hope you don't finish *too far* behind!
Looks like Krakoan technology has the early advantage. Krakoa is leading the pack coming into the plains!
Although Wakanda and U.S.A. aren't far behind!
Oh, it looks like the Antarctic track has cooled Krakoa's hot streak--
--Wakanda is poised to take the lead from the mutant team!
Dammit!
I *told* you we should have added some sort of flame-retardant coating!
The volcano was supposed to be *inactive!*
You are not as clever as you think, Forge.
Clever enough to beat you, princess.

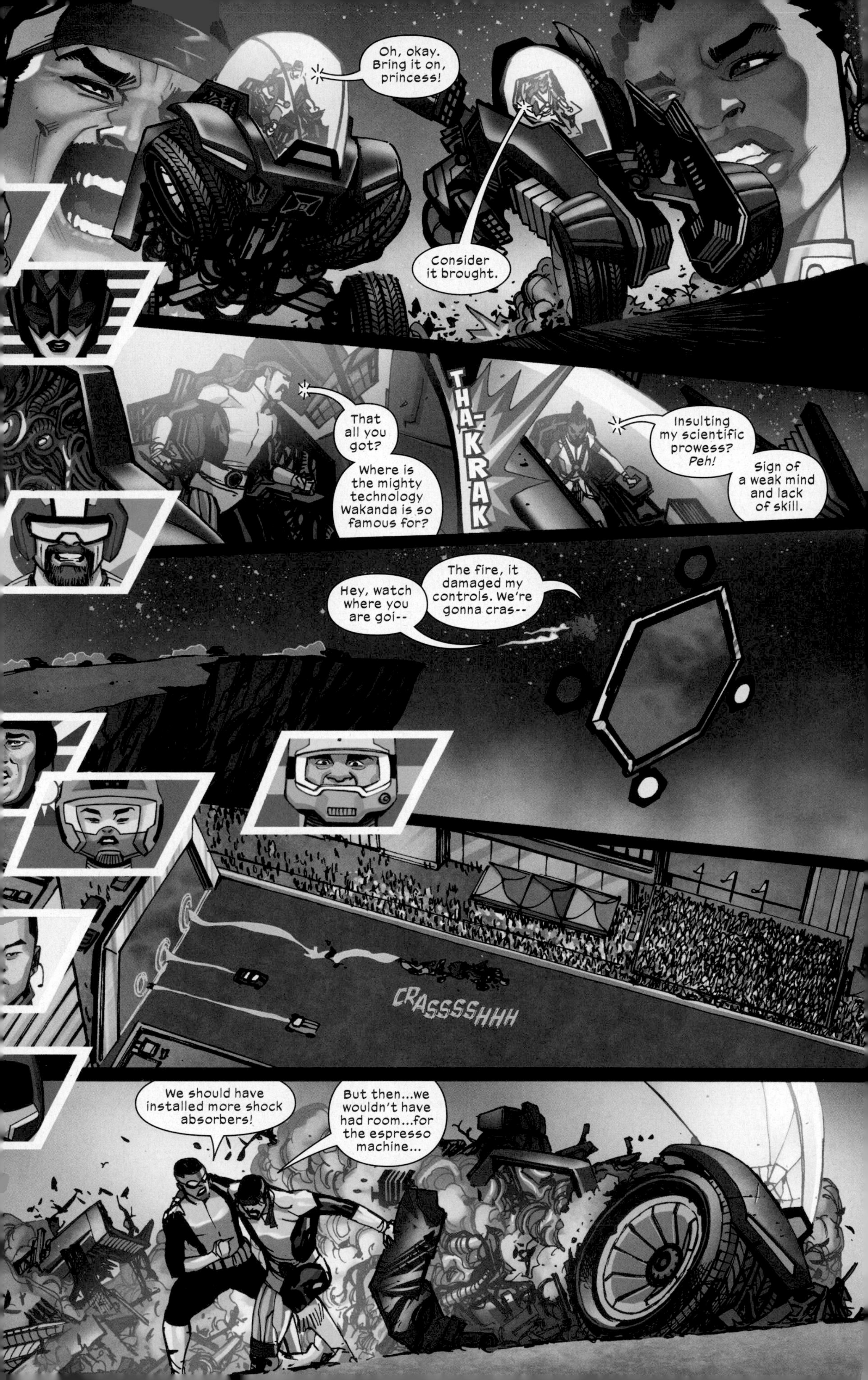
Oh, okay. Bring it on, princess!
Consider it brought.
That all you got?
Where is the mighty technology Wakanda is so famous for?
THA-KRAK
Insulting my scientific prowess? Peh!
Sign of a weak mind and lack of skill.
Hey, watch where you are goi--
The fire, it damaged my controls. We're gonna cras--
CRASSSSHHH
We should have installed more shock absorbers!
But then...we wouldn't have had room...for the espresso machine...

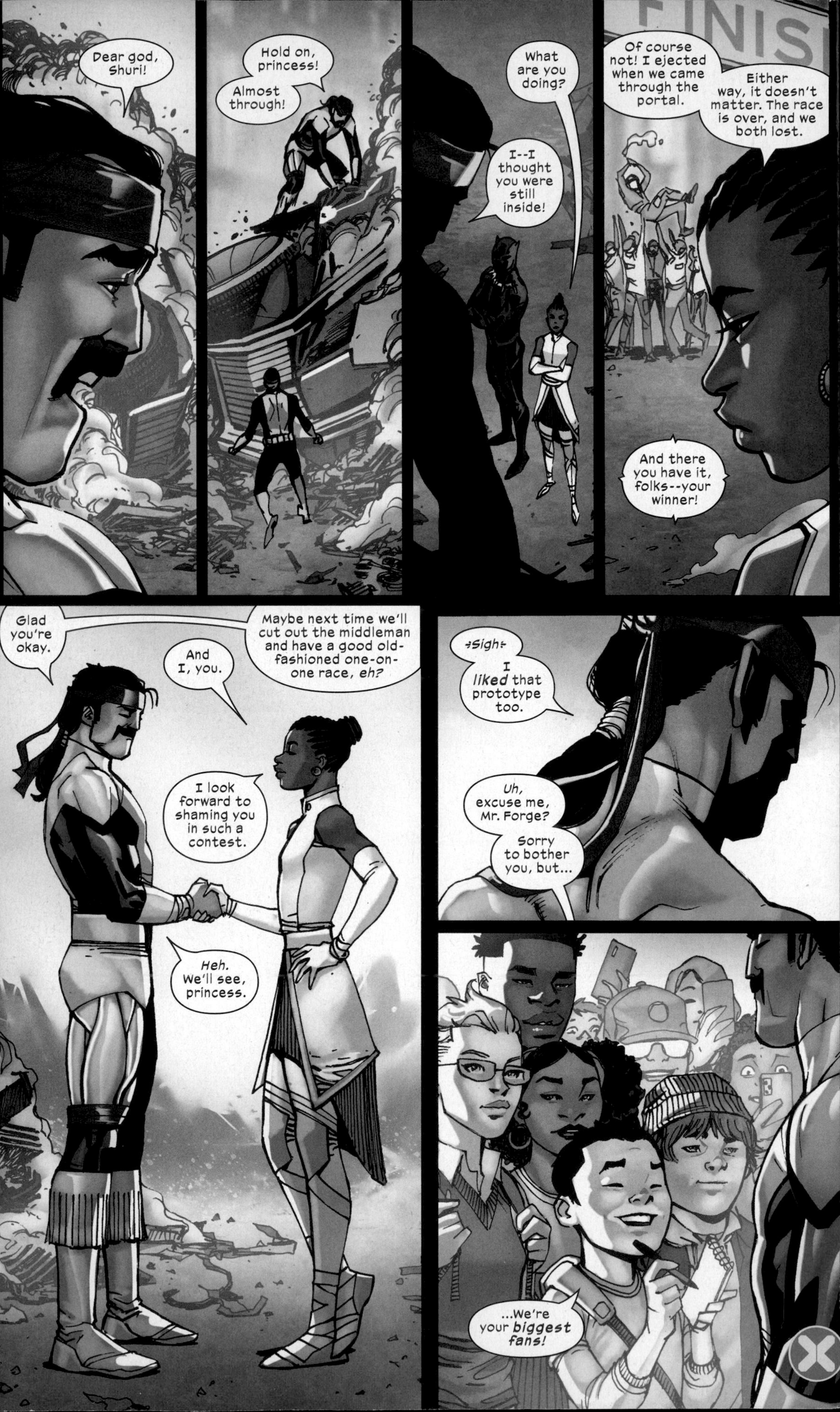
Dear god, Shuri!
Hold on, princess!
Almost through!
What are you doing?
I--I thought you were still inside!
Of course not! I ejected when we came through the portal.
Either way, it doesn't matter. The race is over, and we both lost.
And there you have it, folks--your winner!
Glad you're okay.
And I, you.
Maybe next time we'll cut out the middleman and have a good old-fashioned one-on-one race, *eh?*
I look forward to shaming you in such a contest.
Heh. We'll see, princess.
Sigh
I *liked* that prototype too.
Uh, excuse me, Mr. Forge?
Sorry to bother you, but...
...We're your *biggest fans!*